# Conflictual Democracy and the South African Constitution

I0888179

Human dignity, equality, and freedom are central to the South African Constitution. This book examines these values through a conflictual democratic lens, which views conflict, power, and disagreement as constitutive of democracy.

The book explores the capacity of value-based constitutional interpretation to create openings for democratic dialogue and emancipatory social struggles. Conversely, it also assesses the ability of constitutional interpretation to normalise and depoliticise domination, inequality, and exclusion. The book uses a conflictual frame to shed light on the interplay between the universality of dignity, equality, and freedom and the particularity of the discourses and conventions that mediate their interpretation and enforcement. It argues that such a frame could enable realistic assessments of the ability of the constitutional order to safeguard spaces for emancipatory struggles and respond to radical demands for the reconstitution of society.

Drawing on the text of the Constitution, case law, academic commentary, and constitutional, political, and critical legal theory, this book will be an important read for researchers of constitutional law and critical legal theory, both within South Africa and beyond.

**Henk Botha** is a Professor in the Faculty of Law, Stellenbosch University, South Africa.

# Routledge Contemporary South Africa

**Radio, Public Life and Citizen Deliberation in South Africa**
*Edited by Sarah Chiumbu and Gilbert Motsaathebe*

**Afrikaners and the Boundaries of Faith in Post-Apartheid South Africa**
*Annika Björnsdotter Teppo*

**The Contested Idea of South Africa**
*Edited by Sabelo J. Ndlovu-Gatsheni and Busani Ngcaweni*

**The Short Story in South Africa**
Contemporary Trends and Perspectives
*Edited by Rebecca Fasselt and Corinne Sandwith*

**Generation, Gender and Negotiating Custom in South Africa**
*Edited by Elena Moore*

**Youth Unemployment Scenarios: South Africa in 2040**
*Maximilian Matschke*

**Spectres of Reparation in South Africa**
Re-encountering the Truth and Reconciliation Commission
*Jaco Barnard-Naudé*

**Youth in Post-Apartheid South Africa**
A Sociological Perspective
*Acheampong Yaw Amoateng and Elizabeth Biney*

**Conflictual Democracy and the South African Constitution**
Dignity, Equality, and Freedom
*Henk Botha*

For a full list of available titles please visit:
https://www.routledge.com/Routledge-Contemporary-South-Africa/book-series/RCSOUTHAFRICA

# Conflictual Democracy and the South African Constitution

## Dignity, Equality, and Freedom

**Henk Botha**

Routledge
Taylor & Francis Group
LONDON AND NEW YORK

First published 2025
by Routledge
4 Park Square, Milton Park, Abingdon, Oxon OX14 4RN

and by Routledge
605 Third Avenue, New York, NY 10158

*Routledge is an imprint of the Taylor & Francis Group, an informa business*

© 2025 Henk Botha

The right of Henk Botha to be identified as author of this work has been asserted in accordance with sections 77 and 78 of the Copyright, Designs and Patents Act 1988.

All rights reserved. No part of this book may be reprinted or reproduced or utilised in any form or by any electronic, mechanical, or other means, now known or hereafter invented, including photocopying and recording, or in any information storage or retrieval system, without permission in writing from the publishers.

*Trademark notice*: Product or corporate names may be trademarks or registered trademarks, and are used only for identification and explanation without intent to infringe.

*British Library Cataloguing-in-Publication Data*
A catalogue record for this book is available from the British Library

ISBN: 978-1-032-77321-6 (hbk)
ISBN: 978-1-032-77322-3 (pbk)
ISBN: 978-1-003-48245-1 (ebk)

DOI: 10.4324/9781003482451

Typeset in Times New Roman
by SPi Technologies India Pvt Ltd (Straive)

**For Jolande**

# Contents

# Acknowledgements

In writing this book, I benefitted from conversations with and the support of several people. Bradley Slade and Sandy Liebenberg, my colleagues in the faculty of law at Stellenbosch University, provided invaluable support. Johndré Barnes, Gideon Basson, Jacques de Ville, Louise du Toit, Callixte Kavuro, Ulrike Kistner, Wessel le Roux, Joel Modiri, Richard Shay, Hugo Uys, Karin van Marle, Christiaan van Schalkwyk, and others generously shared literature and ideas.

Christoph Möllers hosted me during a research stay at Humboldt University, Berlin, which was funded by the Alexander von Humboldt Foundation. The National Research Foundation provided financial support.

I am indebted to Gideon Basson for incisive comments on chapter 6 and the anonymous reviewers for valuable suggestions for the improvement of the research proposal and the manuscript.

I am deeply grateful to Jolande, Carma, Theunis, and Johan for their patience, love, and unwavering support and for helping me to stay grounded.

# Introduction

## I.1 Transforming or normalising the status quo?

During the second half of the 1990s and early 2000s, the Constitution of the Republic of South Africa, 1996, was widely hailed as ground-breaking, progressive, and transformative. Several features of the Constitution were cited in support of that reading, including its expressly value-laden nature, commitment to substantive equality, recognition of socio-economic and environmental rights, extension of fundamental rights to the horizontal plane, robust conception of democracy and democratic participation, strong model of judicial review, and creation of independent institutions supporting constitutional democracy. Those features were said to point beyond the stale oppositions that characterised earlier articulations of liberal constitutionalism.[1] The Constitution, on this view, inaugurated a fundamental break with the injustices of the past, and could help facilitate the creation of a democratic, non-racial, non-sexist society that is committed to upholding the human dignity, equality, and freedom of all South Africans.

More than a quarter century after the commencement of the Constitution, it is still regarded as a progressive constitution. However, today, even the most optimistic appraisals of the Constitution's transformative potential must recognise the persistent gap between the constitutional vision and the reality of a society characterised by widespread poverty, inequality, corruption, and failures of democratic accountability and responsiveness.[2] Some commentators go further than simply acknowledging that gap or pointing to the Constitution's untapped potential. For instance, former deputy chief justice Moseneke stated that the revolution inaugurated by the Constitution had failed and that a "reset" was needed. The reset that he proposes demands fundamental reforms to certain democratic institutions and mechanisms – like the electoral system – and a concerted effort to redistribute resources and opportunities.[3] Despite the strong rhetoric, he stops short of blaming the Constitution itself for the revolution's failure – even if some of the reforms he advocates may require constitutional amendments, they appear to be aimed at giving effect to the Constitution's underlying normative vision. On this understanding, the Constitution's transformative vision remains cogent; however, in view of the failures of the past

DOI: 10.4324/9781003482451-1

decades, legislatures, the executive, courts, the legal profession, and civil society need to rekindle their commitment and find new ways of giving effect to the radical promise of that vision.

Some politicians,[4] scholars, and activists take a less sanguine view of the capacity of legal and political processes that are grounded in the Constitution to bring about fundamental change. For example, in the view of scholars who develop and draw on decolonial and abolitionist critiques, the Constitution normalises the enduring effects of colonial dispossession, violence, and epistemicide by signalling that they can no longer be undone,[5] and misconstrues deep-seated structural inequality and violence by rendering them in the language of individual grievances that must be remedied through rights-based, court-centred processes. Rights-based constitutionalism precludes radical change: it aims to include the previously disadvantaged into a society in which personhood, recognition, and autonomy remain premised on conformity to the norms of the oppressors, without addressing the underlying structures of disadvantage.[6] Instead, radical imaginations are needed, which can dismantle the enduring reality of colonial conquest, white supremacy, denigration of black thought, and racial capitalism.[7]

The debates between transformative constitutionalists and decolonial critics not only reveal ruptures within critical legal thought. They are also indicative of a legal and political order that remains suspended between the new and the old; between the constitutional promise of dignity, equality, and freedom for all and the endurance of past patterns of oppression and privilege; and between alternative imaginaries – some of which point beyond the current constitutional dispensation – and pathologies arising from a hegemonic order that combines progressive elements with a neoliberal rationality. Faced with these tensions, legal scholars must come to terms with the possibilities and pitfalls of rights-based strategies. They do not face a stark choice between unbridled constitutional optimism and an outright rejection of the Constitution. Several middle positions are possible, which recognise that constitutional adjudication could sometimes help facilitate democratic and egalitarian struggles, whilst acknowledging that the Constitution is the imperfect product of a contingent set of ideological conflicts, power relations, and local/global dynamics, that law is a limited vehicle for emancipation, and that more radical social imaginaries are needed. In this book, I stake out such a position by focussing on the ability of constitutional interpretation and adjudication to challenge and disrupt extant power relations, on the one hand, and to depoliticise social power and deflect attention away from the systemic nature of domination, inequality, and exclusion, on the other. This stance recognises the need to interrogate the limits of transformative adjudication, analyse the reasons for the persistence of the hierarchies of old, and come to terms with the structural causes of oppression. It does not foreclose the possibility that constitutional interpretation could sometimes help to destabilise entrenched social, economic, and political power; however, it insists that constitutional interpretation is itself immersed in power relations and rejects the idea that the Constitution is the logical and inescapable end point of the struggle for liberation in South Africa.

I use different lenses to explore the capacity of value-based constitutional adjudication to politicise or normalise the status quo. The first is the interconnectedness of democracy and the values of dignity, equality, and freedom. The Constitution treats these values as constitutive of the open and democratic society that it envisages.[8] On this vision, the dignity, equality, and freedom of all South Africans underpin their capacity to participate in public life, make their voices heard, hold the government accountable, and mobilise and organise around political viewpoints or social causes. Conversely, the recognition of dignity, equality, and freedom is only possible in an open and democratic society characterised by inclusive public deliberation and robust contestation. The ideal of democratic self-government, which is based on the equal dignity and freedom of all members of the political community, is a radical aspiration which has never been and probably will never be fully realised.[9] It beckons alternative futures and could serve as a basis for challenges to the aggregation of power in the hands of ruling and managerial elites and the contestation of laws, social practices, knowledges, and distributive patterns that perpetuate domination and inequality.

Secondly, I draw on conflictual understandings of democracy, which insist that conflict, power, and exclusion are constitutive of democracy.[10] Conflictual-democratic theories emphasise the need for an array of discourses, institutions, and practices that enable a variety of conflicting articulations of democratic values. They reject the belief that domination and inequality are vestiges of an exclusionary past that are about to be overcome in the name of democracy and universal human rights. On the one hand, they stress the need to challenge oppression through democratic mobilisation, participation, and contestation. On the other, they insist that there are limits to the capacity of any legal order to accommodate rights claims and democratic demands, and that the emancipatory potential of rights victories tends to be limited through their inscription into the status quo. Democratic citizenship is thus marked by a permanent tension between the constituted legal order and the capacity of democratic struggles to challenge existing power configurations in the name of alternative social imaginaries. A conflictual democratic reading of constitutional values can therefore shed light on constitutional reasoning's emancipatory possibilities as well as its limits, blind spots, and silences.

Thirdly, I am interested in the interplay between the universality of human dignity, equality, and freedom and the particularity of the discourses, conventions, background rules, institutions, and ideological representations that mediate their interpretation and enforcement. Dignity, equality, and freedom are internal to and ground the legal system; they are central to the interpretation of fundamental rights and foundational to the "objective normative value system" created by the Constitution.[11] At the same time, however, dignity, equality, and freedom point beyond positive law towards ethical and political possibilities that are more deeply emancipatory. Drucilla Cornell notes that, as ethical ideals, dignity, equality, and freedom can never be completely incorporated into a legal system; their full realisation is therefore always projected into the future.[12] Elaborations and integrations of these ethical ideals could provide glimpses of alternative futures that lie beyond the domination, exploitation, and inequality arising from structural racism and sexism, capitalism, neoliberal governance, and other mechanisms that institutionalise disadvantage and exclusion.

However, the question remains why oppressive structures are so resilient in the face of attempts to give effect to the Constitution's transformative aspirations. Is it simply because of the tension between the universality of these ideals and the particularity of the legal and social orders into which they are – always imperfectly – incorporated? Or do these universal ideals, with their roots in the European Enlightenment, themselves bear traces of the violence and exclusion of the colonial project? What happens when the meaning of these ideals is filtered through narratives about the past that are necessarily partial, legal concepts and categories that are derived mostly from Europe, and conceptions of personhood, autonomy, and rationality that served historically to justify inequality and exclusion? Does the articulation of the universal within specific contexts raise the danger that hierarchical distinctions between what is considered normal and abnormal, rational and irrational, civilised and uncivilised, or autonomous and dependent will re-emerge within the category of the universal? Does the entrenchment of universal rights, which inhere in all people by virtue of their humanity, blind us into believing that inequality and division are simply temporary obstacles on the road to a just and inclusive future? How must we respond to the tension that arises in the nation state between the supposed universality of these ideals and their mediation through and identification with the status of citizenship? For now, it may be helpful to reduce these questions to a single question, namely whether and how articulations of dignity, equality, and freedom with specific histories, problems, and dynamics could create openings for democratic contestation and emancipatory social struggles or, conversely, result in the normalisation and depoliticisation of inequality and domination.

Two provisos are in order. First, conflictual democracy, in the sense used here, does not mean that those who amass the most power or shout the loudest must prevail, or that antagonism is to be preferred to dialogue or reconciliation. The point is rather to be aware of the structural power and exclusion that are constitutive of the status quo and to be alive to the capacity of social conflict and struggle to disrupt deeply entrenched patterns of privilege and disadvantage. Conflict, power, and disagreement are ineradicable; however, we must continue fighting for more just configurations of power. Second, the interrogation of universal values does not amount to moral relativism. The point is not to hollow out those values or to signal that anything goes. It is, rather, to highlight the extent to which hierarchical distinctions, which are deeply embedded in our colonial, apartheid, and patriarchal past, have seeped into those values, and to be open to new imaginaries, which radicalise the idea that all human beings are entitled to unqualified respect for their dignity, equality, and freedom.

## I.2 Angle

In describing the approach and angle taken in this book, it is helpful to compare it with other studies of the Constitution. In the first place, some studies analyse the reasons behind constitutional decisions or apparent anomalies or contradictions in the constitutional jurisprudence through detailed analyses of institutional considerations like the judiciary's legitimacy, institutional competence, and relationship to state actors or the ruling party. For instance, Theunis Roux explains anomalies in the Constitutional Court's jurisprudence in view of the tension between the Court's commitment to legally principled adjudication and the need to act strategically to secure its institutional legitimacy,[13] while James Fowkes situates the Court's jurisprudence within a broader constitution-building exercise that involves several political actors.[14] These approaches lend themselves to nuanced analyses of the extent to which the options open to judges, their framings of the issues, and their decisions are shaped in part by external factors (e.g., the work done by other branches of government, the struggles of social movements and organisations, and the relationship between courts and other institutions). I accept that judicial decisions are influenced by, and in turn, feed into and become part of a larger configuration of discourses, conflicts, and power relations, and I recognise that analyses of interinstitutional relations could help shed light on the capacity of judicial decisions to reinforce democracy. However, my primary focus in this book is not on those relationships but on the substantive meanings ascribed to constitutional values like democracy, dignity, equality, and freedom. My goal is to examine, through the lens of critical and democratic theory, the capacity of those interpretations to facilitate or close down democratic dialogue and contestation and to normalise or disrupt structural power and disadvantage.[15]

Secondly, the focus on constitutional rights and values distinguishes this project from literature that deals predominantly with the doctrines, institutions, and inter-institutional relationships that structure political competition and democratic government.[16] I would nevertheless caution against overstating the distinction between rights and structural analyses, since rights and democratic structures are best viewed as interdependent, mutually reinforcing, and grounded in the same values.[17] Admittedly, a narrow focus on individual rights could contribute to a failure to address the structural causes of democratic failures; however, there are examples of judicial decisions that are alive to the interconnectedness of democratic rights and structures, and rely on rights to help address structural impediments to the effective functioning of democratic institutions.[18] The book does not focus on day-to-day politics (e.g., what happens during elections or in legislative assemblies, the executive, the state administration, or political parties), but is political to the extent that it enquires into the meaning of a pluralistic democracy and the conditions under which it is possible.[19]

Thirdly, my reliance on critical theory and focus on the capacity of constitutional interpretation both to disrupt and normalise patterns of oppression and privilege distinguish the book from studies that seek to place value-based constitutional interpretation on a principled foundation or develop a post-metaphysical understanding of freedom and selfhood. Unlike Laurie Ackermann's book, which grounds the constitutional right to equality in a Kantian conception of human dignity,[20] the primary lens that I use is a conflictual understanding of democracy. Our projects overlap, since both are interested in the relationship between dignity, equality, and freedom, but differ in their understandings of the universality of human dignity and the politics of adjudication. My project also overlaps with and diverges from Stu Woolman's work on individual selfhood, social change, and constitutional interpretation.[21] Woolman and I agree that social change must be grounded in dialogue, participation, and exposure to difference. However, our starting points differ – his is the self, while mine is democracy. Moreover, his work is grounded above all in a pragmatist commitment to experimental learning and progress, whereas mine is aligned to strands of political theory and critical legal thought that are wary of the idea that a commitment to dialogical, experimental, rights-based processes must result in the progressive overcoming of the barriers to human flourishing. These theories draw attention to the instability and indeterminacy of legal and political commitments and practices, the silences and exclusions that are inherent in our highest ideals and the laws and practices through which we seek to realise them, and "history's power to configure, condition, ghost or constrain our present orders, ordinances, predicaments and possibilities".[22]

This is not a study in comparative constitutional law. At times, I refer to foreign case law to provide further examples of the law's capacity to normalise or disrupt oppression, or to shed light on the nature of constitutional value conflicts or the interplay between universal rights and contingent contexts. However, South Africa remains my primary focus.

## I.3 Outline of chapters

The book consists of six substantial chapters, plus an introduction and conclusion. Chapter 1 considers the turn to value-based interpretation under South Africa's Constitution. It asks what it means to read dignity, equality, and freedom as complementary and mutually supporting values, and how their meaning is synchronised through public processes of interpretation and democratic dialogue. It then examines the capacity of value-based constitutional interpretation to reinforce democracy, and comments on the links between rights and membership in the political community. Finally, the chapter juxtaposes the literature on transformative constitutionalism with decolonial critiques of the Constitution. It suggests a middle position, which is interested in the capacity of constitutional adjudication to interrogate and disrupt the legal underpinnings of social, economic, and political inequality, whilst being alive to the danger that it could divert energy and resources away from other sites of democratic dialogue and contestation and deradicalise democratic struggles.

Chapter 2 critically examines different conceptions of democracy. First, it critiques formal and procedural understandings of democracy for focussing narrowly on the formal link between the electorate and their representatives and failing to attend to socio-economic and structural barriers to democratic accountability and responsiveness. Second, it considers deliberative and participatory conceptions of democracy. It argues that, while they provide a rich account of the need for ongoing engagement between the people and their representatives, they tend to underestimate the extent to which socio-economic inequality is replicated in the political sphere and fail to account for the tendency of deliberative and participatory fora to suppress difference. Third, the chapter considers alternative democratic imaginaries, which foreground indeterminacy, disagreement, conflict, and power. It examines conflictual understandings of democracy as well as decolonial democratic imaginaries, enquires into the resonances and tensions between them, and asks whether and to what extent conflictual understandings of democracy can accommodate radical difference.

Chapter 3 reflects on the capacity of value-based constitutional interpretation to challenge hierarchy, disrupt entrenched power relations, and provide spaces for the articulation of alternative social visions. Conversely, it considers its tendency to induce closure, depoliticise challenges against domination and inequality, and naturalise the status quo. The chapter examines and critiques several attempts to defuse the politics of value-based interpretation. It argues that "neutral" or widely shared principles are an expression of hegemonic beliefs and power relations; that attempts to subsume the particularity of conflict and strife under universal categories are doomed to fail; and that Ronald Dworkin's notion of law as integrity is ill-equipped to resist the pull of inegalitarian and exclusionary assumptions and concepts. The chapter critiques restrictive understandings of the political and argues that the objects and subjects of democratic politics cannot be settled in advance but are themselves subject to democratic contestation. It examines the capacity of articulations of equality and freedom with the demand for unconditional respect for the humanity and uniqueness of every person to assist us in uncovering spaces of contestation, radicalising difference, and guarding against the insertion of hierarchical differences into the definition of the human.

The next three chapters deal with human dignity, equality, and freedom, respectively. Each of the chapters examines the different meanings ascribed to the right/value in question, considers different understandings of its relationship to democracy, critically evaluates its emancipatory potential, and asks whether and to what extent its incorporation into positive law and mediation through received legal categories risk re-inscribing hierarchical distinctions into a supposedly universal right and value. Chapter 4 examines human dignity in view of its perceived ability to mediate between universal human rights and specific contexts. The chapter juxtaposes two broad understandings of dignity, which conceive it as a moral-universal notion that sets limits to democracy, and a legal and political concept that is constitutive of democracy, respectively. It argues that reliance on dignity to justify the outlawing of occupations or religious or cultural practices that are considered to impair the dignity of individuals that willingly partake in them, risks reinserting hierarchies into our understanding of the human. The chapter also explores the relationship between human dignity and citizenship. It considers the danger that dignity's articulation with membership in the political community could re-inscribe status-based distinctions into our understanding of dignity, as well as the possibility that it could politicise and disrupt the boundaries between citizens and non-citizens.

Chapter 5 enquires into the possibilities and limits of a political understanding of equality, which recognises the constitutive role of conflict and power in shaping the meaning of equality and acknowledges the capacity of egalitarian struggles to politicise legal and moral concepts and categories that make deeply unequal social relations appear natural and inevitable. The chapter examines the meaning and implications of a political understanding of equality through the prism of three types of harm, namely misrecognition or status harms, distributive or class injustices, and political misrepresentation. It assesses the capacity of different constructions of these forms of disadvantage – and the intersections between them – to shield social power and privilege from scrutiny or to subject them to democratic contestation. It also explores different constructions of difference through the prism of a political understanding of equality and conflictual conception of democracy.

Chapter 6 notes the precarious state of freedom in view of the erosion of the public-political sphere, hollowing out of citizenship under neoliberalism, and revival of ethnic and nationalist forms of self-identification and belonging. Against that background, it examines the possibilities and limits of relational and political understandings of freedom, which recognise individuals' vulnerability and interdependence and highlight the role played by conflict, power, and disagreement in safeguarding spaces in which freedom can thrive. The chapter explores theories and imaginaries of freedom that enable radical critiques of the unequal distribution of the burdens of vulnerability, stress the responsibility of the political community to create conditions in which everyone can be free, and articulate freedom with equality and respect for radical difference. It also draws on conflictual conceptions of freedom of expression, which highlight the power of speech to disrupt inequality and articulate more humane alternatives, whilst remaining mindful of the ways in which structural discursive violence deprives members of vulnerable groups of the opportunity to participate in public deliberation.

## Notes

1 Cf Klare "Legal Culture and Transformative Constitutionalism" 153 (arguing for a "postliberal" reading of the Constitution). See also Moseneke "Transformative Adjudication"; Langa "Transformative Constitutionalism"; Davis and Klare "Transformative Constitutionalism and the Common and Customary Law".

2 See Terreblanche *A History of Inequality in South Africa 1652–2002* on the failure of the "post-apartheid" political order to redress deep-seated material inequality and poverty.
3 Njilo "Retired Judge Dikgang Moseneke Bewails Failed Revolution, Calls for SA's Reset".
4 In 2022, Lindiwe Sisulu, the Minister of Tourism, criticised the Constitution for failing to redress the economic legacy of the historical dispossession of black people. She called the Constitution neoliberal, argued for "an overhaul of a justice system that does not work for Africa and Africans", and implied that black judges were "mentally colonised". Sisulu "Whose Law Is It Anyway?".
5 Modiri "Conquest and Constitutionalism" 304–305, 307–308; Sibanda "When Do You Call Time on a Compromise?" 390–393.
6 Madlingozi "Social Justice in a Time of Neo-Apartheid Constitutionalism" 125–127.
7 Modiri "Azanian Political Thought and the Undoing of South African Knowledges".
8 Ss 36(1) and 39(1) of the Constitution both refer to "an open and democratic society based on human dignity, equality and freedom". See also ss 1(a), 7(1), 9, 10, 12, 15–19, 21–22.
9 Friedman *Power in Action* 21–27.
10 See Laclau and Mouffe *Hegemony and Socialist Strategy*; Rancière *Disagreement*; Mouffe *The Democratic Paradox*; Balibar *Equaliberty*; Brown *South Africa's Insurgent Citizens*.
11 *Carmichele v Minister of Safety and Security* para 54.
12 Cornell "Bridging the Span Toward Justice" 20, 31. See also Cornell *Law and Revolution in South Africa*.
13 Roux *The Politics of Principle*.
14 Fowkes *Building the Constitution*.
15 Here it is pertinent to refer to Jonathan Klaaren's distinction between "strong transformative constitutionalism" and "democratic constitutionalism". He notes that democratic constitutionalists like James Fowkes, Steven Friedman, Firoz Cachalia, Sanele Sibanda, and Brian Ray go "significantly further [than transformative constitutionalists] in recognising the limited role of the courts in a constitutional democracy" and "in privileging the place of the legislature and the people within a constitutional democracy". Klaaren "Regulatory Politics in South Africa 25 Years after Apartheid" 86. My project resonates with democratic constitutionalism to the extent that it places – conflictual – democracy at the centre of its analysis, situates constitutional adjudication within a broader array of discourses and power relations, and expressly thematises its limits. However, like transformative constitutionalism, it insists that the transformative limits of constitutional adjudication cannot be determined with reference to a pre-existing boundary.
16 Choudhry "He Had a Mandate"; Issacharoff "The Democratic Risk to Democratic Transitions".
17 Klaaren "Structures of Government in the 1996 South African Constitution".
18 See e.g., *My Vote Counts v Minister of Justice*.
19 This distinction overlaps with the distinction made in political theory between politics and the political, where the former refers to political activities that are the subject of empirical research by political scientists and sociologists, while the latter refers to "the constitution of the social space, of the form of society, of the essence of what was once termed the 'city'". Lefort *Democracy and Political Theory* 11. See also Dallmayr "Postmetaphysics and Democracy" 110–111; Van der Walt *Law and Sacrifice* 6–7.
20 Ackermann *Human Dignity*.
21 Woolman *The Selfless Constitution*.
22 Brown "Neoliberalized Knowledge" 116.

## Bibliography


Ackermann L *Human Dignity: Lodestar for Equality in South Africa* (2012) Cape Town: Juta.

Balibar É *Equaliberty* (2014, translation J Ingram) Durham: Duke University Press.

Brown J *South Africa's Insurgent Citizens: On Dissent and the Possibility of Politics* (2015) Auckland Park: Jacana Media.

Brown W "Neoliberalized Knowledge" (2011) 1 *History of the Present* 113.

Choudhry S "'He Had a Mandate': The South African Constitutional Court and the African National Congress in a Dominant Party Democracy" (2009) 2 *Constitutional Court Review* 1.

Cornell D "Bridging the Span Toward Justice: Laurie Ackermann and the Ongoing Architectonic of Dignity Jurisprudence" 2008 *Acta Juridica* 18.

Cornell D *Law and Revolution in South Africa: Ubuntu, Dignity, and the Struggle for Constitutional Transformation* (2014) New York: Fordham University Press.

Dallmayr F "Postmetaphysics and Democracy" (1993) 21 *Political Theory* 101.

Davis D and Klare K "Transformative Constitutionalism and the Common and Customary Law" (2010) 26 *South African Journal on Human Rights* 403.

Fowkes J *Building the Constitution: The Practice of Constitutional Interpretation in Post-Apartheid South Africa* (2016) Cambridge: Cambridge University Press.

Friedman S *Power in Action: Democracy, Citizenship and Social Justice* (2018) Johannesburg: Wits University Press.

Issacharoff S "The Democratic Risk to Democratic Transitions" (2012) 5 *Constitutional Court Review* 1.

Klaaren J "Regulatory Politics in South Africa 25 Years after Apartheid" (2021) 56 *Journal of Asian and African Studies* 79.

Klaaren J "Structures of Government in the 1996 South African Constitution: Putting Democracy Back into Human Rights" (1997) 13 *South African Journal on Human Rights* 3.

Klare K "Legal Culture and Transformative Constitutionalism" (1998) 14 *South African Journal on Human Rights* 146.

Laclau E and Mouffe C *Hegemony and Socialist Strategy: Towards a Radical Democratic Politics* (1985) London: Verso.

Langa P "Transformative Constitutionalism" (2006) 17 *Stellenbosch Law Review* 351.

Lefort C *Democracy and Political Theory* (1988, translation D Macey) Oxford: Polity Press.

Madlingozi T "Social Justice in a Time of Neo-Apartheid Constitutionalism: Critiquing the Anti-Black Economy of Recognition, Incorporation and Distribution" (2017) 28 *Stellenbosch Law Review* 123.

Modiri J "Azanian Political Thought and the Undoing of South African Knowledges" (2021) 68 *Theoria* 42.

Modiri J "Conquest and Constitutionalism: First Thoughts on an Alternative Jurisprudence" (2018) 34 *South African Journal on Human Rights* 300.

Moseneke D "Transformative Adjudication" (2002) 18 *South African Journal on Human Rights* 309.

Mouffe C *The Democratic Paradox* (2000) London: Verso.

Njilo N "Retired Judge Dikgang Moseneke Bewails Failed Revolution, Calls for SA's Reset" *Daily Maverick* (23 Oct 2022). https://www.dailymaverick.co.za/article/2022-10-23-retired-judge-dikgang-moseneke-bewails-failed-revolution-calls-for-sas-reset/

Rancière J *Disagreement: Politics and Philosophy* (1999, translation J Rose) Minneapolis: University of Minnesota Press.

Roux T *The Politics of Principle: The First South African Constitutional Court, 1995-2005* (2013) Cambridge: Cambridge University Press.

Sibanda S "When Do You Call Time on a Compromise? South Africa's Discourse on Transformation and the Future of Transformative Constitutionalism" (2020) 24 *Law Democracy & Development* 384.
Sisulu L "Whose Law Is It Anyway?" *Mail & Guardian* (8 Jan 2022). https://mg.co.za/thought-leader/opinion/2022-01-08-lindiwe-sisulu-whose-law-is-it-anyway/
Terreblanche S *A History of Inequality in South Africa 1652-2002* (2002) Pietermaritzburg: University of Natal Press.
Van der Walt J *Law and Sacrifice: Towards a Post-Apartheid Theory of Law* (2005) London: Birkbeck Law Press.
Woolman S *The Selfless Constitution: Experimentalism and Flourishing as Foundations of South Africa's Basic Law* (2013) Cape Town: Juta.

## Case law

*Carmichele v Minister of Safety and Security* 2001 (4) SA 938 (CC)
*My Vote Counts NPC v Minister of Justice and Correctional Services* 2018 (8) BCLR 893 (CC)

# 1 Democracy and the turn to values

The Constitution of the Republic of South Africa, 1996 ("the Constitution") is said to represent a radical break with the apartheid past, in which the black majority and other vulnerable groups were subjected to routine violations of basic human rights. Under apartheid, black people were denied the rights and freedoms associated with citizenship. They were treated as objects of administrative control, in terms of laws that were premised on the idea that they were incapable of becoming autonomous human beings who were worthy of equal treatment and free to actualise themselves in accordance with their own morality and ideals. The Constitution, by contrast, contains a justiciable Bill of Rights, which enshrines the rights of all people in South Africa. It is, moreover, an expressly value-laden document. Section 1 lists, among the values on which the Republic is founded, "human dignity, the achievement of equality and the advancement of human rights and freedoms". Similar formulations are used in other provisions. Section 7(1) states that the Bill of Rights "affirms the democratic values of human dignity, equality and freedom", while section 39(1) provides that the Bill of Rights must be interpreted to "promote the values that underlie an open and democratic society based on human dignity, equality and freedom". The same values must also guide determinations of the constitutionality of fundamental rights limitations under section 36(1), as well as the interpretation of legislation and the development of the common law and customary law.[1]

Not only do these provisions place human dignity, equality, and freedom at the centre of the Constitution's normative vision, but they also construe them as interconnected and mutually reinforcing values which should, as far as possible, be realised together. But what happens when dignity, equality, and freedom come into conflict? What light, if any, can the grouping together of these values shed on conflicts between equality and freedom (as in the case of private discrimination), or between dignity and freedom (as in the case of racist or offensive speech), or between different interpretations and mutual articulations of these values? In trying to make sense of these questions, the chapter turns to a fourth value or principle, namely democracy, and enquires into its relationship with dignity, equality, and freedom. There are several reasons for this strategy, which will be elaborated more fully in the rest of the chapter. In the first place, democracy is premised on the equal dignity, membership, and

DOI: 10.4324/9781003482451-2

freedom of all citizens. Since dignity, equality, and freedom are constitutive of democracy,[2] judicial elaborations of the meaning of those values can enhance or diminish democracy. Secondly, the meaning of constitutional rights and values, and the relationship between them, are determined through public processes of interpretation, contestation, and dialogue. The institutionalisation in a democracy of competition between different ideologies and political parties provides spaces for the articulation of different constitutional interpretations, which can help facilitate decision-making that takes account of diverse perspectives and keeps contending visions in play. Thirdly, because the realisation of dignity, equality, and freedom is so closely bound up with a democratic society, the meaning ascribed to democracy, which is a contested concept, is likely to have important implications for the interpretation and mutual articulation of these rights and values. Fourthly, there is a close link between the political rights attached to citizenship and full access to and the effective enforcement of constitutional rights. Since citizens enjoy rights of political participation, they tend to be in a better position to enforce civil and social rights than noncitizens, who are traditionally denied political rights.

The chapter neither proposes democracy as a meta-principle or theory that places the adjudication of constitutional value conflicts on a neutral and objective grounding nor uses it as a basis for arguing for a form of avoidance that insists on deciding one case at a time, without the need for theoretical elaboration.[3] It utilises a democratic lens not to try to resolve or circumvent the politics of adjudication but, rather, to foreground it. The chapter accordingly asks what law's political nature reveals about the transformative possibilities and limits of value-based interpretation. It thus paves the way for the consideration in the next chapter of conflictual understandings of democracy, which view indeterminacy, power, conflict, and disagreement as constitutive of democracy.

The chapter starts with a brief elaboration of the turn to value-based legal reasoning and interpretation under a supreme Constitution, with reference to value conflicts and the unity of constitutional values. Next, it considers the relationship between democracy and the values of dignity, equality, and freedom. It distinguishes between different judicial constructions of that relationship; examines the capacity of fundamental rights adjudication to enhance democratic representation and participation; and explores the role of democratic contestation, deliberation, and decision-making in the interpretation, concretisation, and enforcement of fundamental rights and values. Finally, it critically examines the idea that value-based constitutional interpretation can enhance democracy through the lens of debates between transformative readings of the Constitution and decolonial critiques.

## 1.1 From "value-neutral" to value-based adjudication

The turn to values represents a break with the past, in which adherence to parliamentary sovereignty, the influence of legal positivism, and a strict division between the legislative and judicial functions resulted in an aversion to value-based forms of legal reasoning.[4] Before 1994, the dominant approach to statutory interpretation aimed to give effect to the intention of the legislature, as distilled from the plain meaning of the legislative text. This approach sought to minimise the influence of considerations that could introduce an element of subjectivity into judicial decision-making. It narrowly circumscribed the role of contextual factors, which were, as a rule, considered only when the plain meaning of the words was ambiguous, vague, or misleading, or would result in a glaring absurdity.[5] It precluded value-based reasoning. On this view, judicial recourse to values would transgress the boundary between law and morals, blur the line between law making and interpretation, and impinge on Parliament's sovereignty by allowing judges to add to or subtract from the meaning of legislation.

As several commentators have shown, this approach rests on questionable assumptions about language and meaning, the nature of legal norms, and the nature of adjudication. It erroneously assumes that language has a fixed meaning, which can be determined without reference to the surrounding context.[6] It conflates the ordinary meaning of words with the subjective intention of the legislature.[7] It fails to recognise that interpretation invariably has a creative dimension, which arises from the gap between the generality of legislation and the particularity of the contexts in which it finds application.[8] It equates values with subjective beliefs, convictions, and attitudes. It fails to see that judges who profess to interpret legislation in a value-neutral manner by searching for the intention of the legislature or by giving effect to the plain meaning of words cannot avoid having recourse to moral, political, and ideological beliefs. John Dugard and others argued that these formalist creeds, combined with a legal positivist mind-set that strictly separated law from morals, concealed the inarticulate premises that shaped judicial decision-making. According to Dugard, the major inarticulate premise was the loyalty of judges, who were all white, to the apartheid status quo.[9]

Some of the same assumptions and attitudes that were at work in statutory interpretation also played a prominent role in the development of the common law, where reliance was placed on concepts and principles that would ensure law's objectivity and neutrality and give it a "scientific" grounding. This is nowhere more evident than in private law, with its roots in the Roman-Dutch civil law tradition. As André van der Walt demonstrated, the civil law tradition shows a clear preference for abstract, conceptual, and rule-bound forms of reasoning. This enabled it to legitimate inequality, even at the height of apartheid, by upholding a strict division between law and politics, and between the private and public spheres. It divorced private law from a political system that resulted in the dislocation, destitution, and disenfranchisement of black people, and gave it the appearance of a scientific system of law, which is uncontaminated by oppressive laws and policies. It thus concealed the power relations in which legal rules and principles are embedded, masked the value choices behind legal rules and principles, obscured social struggle and dissent, and made the social and economic status quo appear natural and necessary.[10]

The Constitution, by contrast, renounces the idea that legal meaning is fixed, and that statutory interpretation or the development of the common law entails the application of value-neutral maxims and principles. It places values at the centre of constitutional and statutory interpretation and the development of the common law and customary law. The Constitution recognises that legislation may be open to more than one reasonable interpretation. Where that is the case, preference should be given to an interpretation that is consistent with constitutional values. Section 39(2), which requires interpreters to promote the spirit, purport, and objects of the Bill of Rights, is used to avoid invalidating legislative provisions that are prima facie unconstitutional, where they are reasonably capable of a less restrictive interpretation that would bring them within the bounds of what is constitutionally permissible.[11] However, section 39(2)'s application is not restricted to cases in which one interpretation would result in the unconstitutionality of the legislation. It imposes a general obligation on courts to read legislative provisions in view of constitutional values, even where their constitutionality is not in issue.[12] Thus, the Constitutional Court held that "all statutes must be interpreted through the prism of the Bill of Rights", and that statutory interpretation must always take account of the Constitution's commitment to transform society in accordance with constitutional values.[13] The Constitution is "the starting point in interpreting any legislation", and "the interpretation that is placed upon a statute must, where possible, be one that would advance at least an identifiable value enshrined in the Bill of Rights".[14]

The Court further held that the Constitution embodies "an objective, normative value system" which must inform the development of all branches of law, including private law,[15] and that courts are under a general obligation to develop the common law in accordance with constitutional values.[16] There are, accordingly, not two parallel systems, one based on the Constitution and another on the common law. The Court stated in *Pharmaceutical Manufacturers*: "There is only one system of law. It is shaped by the Constitution which is the supreme law, and all law, including the common law, derives its force from the Constitution and is subject to constitutional control".[17] Frank Michelman argues that the idea of the unity of the legal system should not be understood only in formal terms to denote the pervasiveness of the Constitution's norms and its status as the foundation of all law. It also has a substantive dimension, as it depends on value-based forms of reasoning to bring legislation, the common law, and customary law in line with the Constitution. Law's systemic unity is not an absolute value but is directed towards the vindication of values like human dignity, equality, freedom, non-racialism, and non-sexism. For that reason, the rule of law does not simply refer to a formal "rule of rules". It is infused with constitutional values, and encompasses "the rule of justice, as the Final Constitution envisions justice".[18]

The Constitution does not reduce values to the private moral and political beliefs or policy preferences of an individual interpreter. It is concerned with public values, that is, values that are constitutive of the society envisaged in the Constitution,[19] whose concrete meaning is shaped and crystallised through a public dialogue, in which legislatures, the executive, courts, and various layers of civil society participate.[20] The meaning of these values derives not from subjective or idiosyncratic individual beliefs, but from intersubjective processes of debate, engagement, and interpretation.[21] Of course, that does not mean that there is universal agreement about their meaning – there will inevitably be differences in the manner in which different people understand and prioritise values within particular contexts. However, judges or litigants who rely on constitutional values are constrained to explain how they understand them, and how, on that understanding, they relate to the relevant provisions in the constitutional text, the relevant legislation or common law rules, judicial precedent, and the context of the case. Their explication of the meaning of constitutional values must be plausible, even if it does not command universal assent, and must draw these different strands together into a coherent narrative. This understanding of values is far removed from the idea that a value-based jurisprudence will give free rein to judicial whim and arbitrariness and has helped to facilitate a shift in conceptions of judicial impartiality. The Constitutional Court has acknowledged that it "is appropriate for judges to bring their own life experience to the adjudication process", and that "[a]bsolute neutrality on the part of a judicial officer can hardly if ever be achieved".[22] This is consistent with the view that judges must articulate their understanding of constitutional values, and of the social and historical context, as this is more conducive to judicial accountability than tacit reliance on unexamined assumptions.[23]

Constitutional scholars have argued that the turn to values necessitates a fundamental rethink of basic legal and constitutional concepts like state authority and the separation of powers. Etienne Mureinik points out that, in the new constitutional order, authority no longer derives from a chain of command running from a sovereign Parliament to the state bureaucracy, whose decisions demand unquestioning obedience. The old, authoritarian culture characterising apartheid rule made way for

> a culture in which every exercise of power is expected to be justified; in which the leadership given by government rests on the cogency of the case offered in defence of its decisions, not the fear inspired by the force of its command. The new order must be a community built on persuasion, not coercion.[24]

The Constitution places values like human dignity, equality, and freedom at the centre of the democratic culture of justification and reason giving. It thus makes it clear that the state exists for the benefit of individuals, and not vice versa, and that its authority is grounded in dialogic processes aimed at the realisation of democratic values.

## 1.2 Value conflicts and the unity of constitutional values

Different constitutional visions competed for ascendancy during the negotiations and deliberations that produced the 1993 and 1996 constitutions. These visions revealed ideological differences relating, inter alia, to the relationship between equality and freedom, between democracy and individual rights, between the state and civil society, between continuity and change, between property and redistribution, and between traditional values and the rights of women.[25] The tension between these positions is reflected in the constitutional text, which combines features that are typical of liberal democracies (like the protection of individual rights and freedoms and the rule of law) with a concern for substantive equality, social justice, and participatory democracy. To mention but a few examples: the 1996 Constitution guarantees civil and political as well as socio-economic rights, provides for the vertical and horizontal application of fundamental rights, and balances the protection of property against arbitrary deprivation with land reform and restitution.[26] Section 29(2) seeks to reconcile the right to receive education in the official language of one's choice with the need to redress the legacy of racially discriminatory laws, while section 31(2) subjects the rights of cultural, religious, and linguistic communities to other rights in the Bill of Rights, including the right to gender equality.

These provisions could be read to suggest that the tension between equality and freedom is constitutive of South Africa's constitutional democracy. This is confirmed by sections 1(a), 7(1), 36(1), and 39(1), which place equality and freedom, together with human dignity, at the centre of the society envisaged by the Constitution. These provisions treat dignity, equality, and freedom as distinctive values, which are interdependent and mutually supportive. On this reading, the society envisaged by the Constitution would be placed in danger if one of these values were to be collapsed onto the others, or if the connection between them were to be severed. The idea that they are distinctive yet interdependent and should be optimised as far as possible in cases of conflict resonates with the notion of the unity of the Constitution, which entails that constitutional provisions should be interpreted not in isolation, but in view of the Constitution as a whole.[27] The unity of constitutional values is a natural outgrowth of this idea. It requires the mutual articulation of constitutional values through interpretation. Read together, different values modify, transform, and reinforce one another. The unity of values also finds expression in the principle of proportionality, which requires constitutional interpreters to optimise conflicting constitutionally protected rights and interests as far as possible.

The Constitutional Court's jurisprudence confirms that dignity, equality, and freedom are interconnected and mutually reinforcing. The Court has held that dignity and freedom are "inseparably linked",[28] that the prohibition of unfair discrimination gives expression to the equal dignity of all human beings,[29] and that freedom and equality are closely connected.[30] While the idea of a hierarchy of values seems at odds with the Court's pronouncements on the indivisibility and interdependence of human dignity, equality, and freedom,[31] some of its references to the intersectionality of constitutional rights and values appear to privilege dignity over other values.[32] The Court has also stressed the connection between these and other constitutional values, like non-racialism,[33] the rule of law,[34] and democracy.

Once it has been found that a constitutional right has been limited, either in a vertical dispute involving the constitutionality of state conduct or legislation or in a horizontal dispute between private entities under section 8(2) and 8(3), it must be determined whether the limitation is reasonable and justifiable in terms of section 36(1) of the Constitution. According to the Constitutional Court, that involves "the weighing up of competing values, and ultimately an assessment based on proportionality".[35] It does not entail the abstract ranking of conflicting values, but requires their mutual articulation, on a case-by-case basis, with careful attention to the constitutional text and the relevant context(s). The Court has opted for a flexible approach, in terms of which the standard of justification depends on the severity of the limitation. The more substantial the incursion on fundamental rights, the greater the burden of justification to demonstrate that the limitation serves an important purpose, that it could not be achieved through less restrictive means, and that the effects of the limitation are proportionate to the purpose.[36]

Thus, both when elaborating the values underlying fundamental rights and weighing up conflicting rights and interests, courts highlight the interdependence of constitutional values. Sometimes, this is done to emphasise the severity of a fundamental-rights limitation, as a showing that a limitation affects different intersecting constitutional values can be used to argue for a tightening of the burden of justification. For example, in *Khosa* the Constitutional Court stated that the exclusion of permanent residents from social assistance benefits implicated several rights and values (equality, human dignity, life, and access to social assistance) "which reinforce one another at the point of intersection".[37] It held that the limitation was unjustifiable, particularly in view of its severe impact on the dignity of those concerned.[38] At other times, the interdependence of constitutional values underpins arguments in favour of a restrictive interpretation to a fundamental right, or justifying its limitation. For instance, in *NCGLE I* and *Fourie*, the Court made it clear that freedom of religion does not include the right to use the power of the state to deny sexual minorities the opportunity to live their lives in accordance with their chosen ends.[39] The reasoning arguably rests on an articulation of equality and freedom: since all individuals have an equal right to pursue their own ends, no-one is entitled to use his or her freedom to deny the freedom of others.

The unity of values should not be taken to imply that there is, or can ever be, a perfect coherence between them. Étienne Balibar notes that the French Revolution gave us the radical proposition of what he terms "equaliberty", namely the idea that equality and freedom are inextricably linked. The two ideals are not identical; however, they require the same historical conditions to flourish. If freedom is severed from equality, it comes to denote the superiority or privilege of some and the subjection of others, which is inconsistent with the idea that every human being has the right to be free. If, on the other hand, equality is reduced to a sameness that negates the freedom of every person to determine the course of her own life, it loses the ability to resist forms of subjection and mastery, such as political tyranny, that are fundamentally at odds with the idea of equality.[40] Institutionalising the unity of these two political ideals is, however, a different matter – their universality constantly comes up against the historical contingency of the legal and political order, and their realisation is left "to practice, to struggle, to social conflict".[41]

Drucilla Cornell's notion of synchronisation can also shed light on the unity of constitutional values. Synchronisation means that conflicting legal principles are understood through an appeal to a rational whole. In Hegel's thought, the ideal of reciprocal symmetry between the "I" and the "We" provides the basis for such appeals. Cornell acknowledges that, unlike Hegel, we can no longer assume "that there is a dynamic *telos* which inevitably leads to the actualization of dialogic reciprocity in the modern democratic state".[42] She states, with reference to the critical legal studies movement, that conflicts between competing rights and between individual and communal interests "may not be able to yield a 'coherent' whole".[43] And yet, she argues that, despite its limits and inevitable failures, the promise of synchronisation remains vital to law's transformative potential. Because it aims to mediate between conflicting values and principles, rather than eradicate such conflicts, synchronisation facilitates a dialogic process that is open to competing social visions and articulations of constitutional values. Because it is alive to the complexity and plurality characterising modern societies, it recognises the provisional nature of every attempted articulation of and mediation between constitutional rights and values. As a result, existing understandings of a legal community's constitutive commitments are always open to reinterpretation and revision. In fact, the very failure to synchronise rights and interests into a coherent whole can help to uncover transformative possibilities and resist normative closure, by giving rise to new struggles against domination, exclusion and inequality, and new articulations of a legal community's often conflicting commitments.[44]

Seen through that lens, the unity of constitutional values refers not to their logical or conceptual coherence, but to their mutual articulation through public processes of constitutional interpretation and democratic dialogue. It is a unity that needs to be forged, again and again, from the disparate materials constituting the constitutional tradition, as changing circumstances and new struggles challenge the sense of closure to which tradition becomes prone. The interpretive processes through which this unity is forged, are constrained by the demand for reasoned justification, as participants need to weave their proposed interpretations into a narrative that makes sense of the constitutional text, past interpretations of that text, and the gap between the Constitution's emancipatory promise and a reality characterised by inequality and exclusion. At the same time, however, they are characterised by contestation and ongoing revision and re-imagination, as every attempt to order different constitutional values into a coherent whole is necessarily partial.

## 1.3 What is democratic about human dignity, equality, and freedom?

The link made in the constitutional text between dignity, equality, and freedom, on the one hand, and democracy, on the other, is often neglected in case law and academic literature. The references to "democratic values" in section 7(1) and "an open and democratic society" in sections 36(1) and 39(1) are sometimes treated as mere rhetorical flourishes, which shed little if any light on the meaning of "human dignity, equality and freedom". However, there are judgments that recognise that dignity, equality, and freedom qualify and shape our constitutional vision of democracy, or that democratic deliberation, participation, and contestation are vital to the realisation of dignity, equality, and freedom.

Some of the Constitutional Court's early judgments focussed predominantly on the tension between democracy and dignity, equality, and freedom. For instance, in *Makwanyane* the Court insisted, in response to the contention that the majority of South Africans were in favour of the retention of the death penalty, that public opinion cannot be decisive of questions of constitutionality. To decide constitutional issues based on public opinion would effectively amount to a return to parliamentary sovereignty. It would signal the acceptance of a crude majoritarianism, which is at odds with the very reason for accepting a supreme Constitution, namely "to protect the rights of minorities and others who cannot protect their rights adequately through the democratic process".[45] Chaskalson P quoted approvingly from a judgment of the United States Supreme Court, in which Jackson J famously stated:

> The very purpose of a Bill of Rights was to withdraw certain subjects from the vicissitudes of political controversy, to place them beyond the reach of majorities and officials and to establish them as legal principles to be applied by the courts. One's right to life, liberty, and property, to free speech, a free press, freedom of worship and assembly, and other fundamental rights may not be submitted to vote; they depend on the outcome of no elections.[46]

Although the Court highlights the tension between fundamental rights and majoritarian conceptions of democracy, it does not necessarily imply that democracy and individual rights are diametrically opposed. It could rather be read to suggest that, under South Africa's supreme Constitution, the meaning of democracy is qualified by the recognition of the rights of marginalised minorities and vulnerable individuals whose interests tend to be overlooked by legislative majorities. This reading is confirmed by the concurring judgment of O'Regan J, who quotes approvingly from a Canadian judgment, which states that "[i]t is the dignity and importance of the individual which is the essence and the cornerstone of democratic government".[47] However, while the Court recognises that respect for life and human dignity is constitutive of the Constitution's vision of an open and democratic society, it shows little appreciation for the role of democratic processes of deliberation and contestation in the conceptualisation and protection of these rights.

The *Ferreira* case similarly pits individual rights against Parliament's regulatory power. In his minority judgment, Ackermann J gave an extensive interpretation to the right to freedom and security of the person in terms of section 11(1) of the interim Constitution. On this interpretation, section 11(1) confers a general constitutional right to freedoms that are not expressly mentioned in the Constitution. He grounded this right both in freedom's intrinsic value and in its close relationship to human dignity.[48] The majority of the Court, by contrast, gave section 11(1) a far more restrictive interpretation, and held that it is primarily concerned with the protection of every person's physical integrity.[49] Chaskalson P referred in his majority judgment to the interim Constitution's requirement that limitations of this right must be necessary, in addition to being reasonable. Giving the right an extensive interpretation would impose a burden on the state to show that any regulatory law that limits the general right to freedom is necessary in an open and democratic society. This may lead to serious judicial intrusions into the functions of the legislature,[50] and entrench an understanding of freedom that is out of sync with the realities of an industrial society.[51] The judges' disagreement about the interpretation of section 11(1) thus rehearses themes associated with debates about the counter-majoritarian dilemma. It pits individualistic values against the power of legislative majorities to regulate the economy and redistribute wealth; and opposes generous interpretations of individual rights against the need to avoid a Lochnerian type of overreach that would impair the legitimacy of the judiciary and thwart the state in its exercise of regulatory powers.

Some later judgments place less emphasis on the tension between democracy and rights and highlight their complementary relationship. On the one hand, there are judgments in which courts, when interpreting constitutional provisions relating to the right to vote, or the procedures to be followed by legislatures, emphasise the inclusive, deliberative, and participatory dimensions of democracy. Some of these judgments draw not only on democratic values like openness, accountability, and responsiveness, but also on human dignity and equality. They recognise that human dignity and equality are constitutive of the democratic society inaugurated by the Constitution, and that the right to participate in democratic processes and to hold the government accountable is an expression of the equal dignity to which all members of the political community are entitled. For example, in *August* the Constitutional Court called universal adult suffrage "a badge of dignity and of personhood", which signals that all South African citizens, regardless of their socio-economic status, have full membership in the political community.[52] In *Doctors for Life* the Court stressed that democratic participation enhances the civic dignity of participants, and that it has an important role to play in promoting political equality.[53]

On the other hand, some judgments use ideas of democratic citizenship to shed light on the meaning of rights like equality and human dignity. For instance, the Court declared in *Hugo* that it is inconsistent with the right to equality to treat some people as "second-class citizens".[54] It stated in *National Coalition I* that the criminalisation of same-sex sodomy not only impairs individuals' freedom to shape their private lives, but also deprives gay men of "full moral citizenship" and equal public recognition.[55] Even though the judgments in question acknowledge the need to protect dignity, equality, and freedom against legislative incursions, they do not define these rights and values in contradistinction to democracy. Instead, they link (without necessarily equating) membership in the moral community of free and equal persons to citizenship, with its connotations of democratic participation and full membership in the political community.

The next two sections consider the relationship between democracy and dignity, equality, and freedom through the lens of two claims: that fundamental rights adjudication can enhance democracy, and that democratic decision-making can enhance the protection of fundamental rights.

## 1.4 Enhancing democracy through fundamental rights adjudication

The idea that judicial review of decisions of legislative bodies and the executive can enhance democracy is eloquently expressed in the work of political process theorists. These theorists argue that judicial review can provide a corrective to distortions of the democratic process and the under-representation of certain voices and interests. John Hart Ely famously argued, with reference to the *Carolene Products* footnote,[56] that the political process malfunctions when representatives use their power to restrict democratic representation or participation, or when the political majority systematically disadvantages certain minority groups. In these instances, the judiciary must prevent powerful interests from blocking the democratic process or from making it difficult for minorities to be heard.[57]

Political process theory developed in the United States against the background of concerns about the legitimacy of judicial review. Theorists like Ely insisted that, rather than basing their decisions on substantive values, and thus imposing their subjective beliefs on the democratic process, judges should concern themselves with the integrity and inclusivity of the democratic process. Their enquiry should be limited to "whether the opportunity to participate either in the political process by which values are appropriately identified and accommodated, or in the accommodation those processes have reached, has been unduly constricted".[58] In his view, this approach not only sits well with what courts are best equipped to do, namely, to ensure the fairness of decision-making processes, but is consistent with the American system of representative democracy, which leaves substantive value choices to the representatives elected by the people.[59] Political process theory's distinction between process and substantive values is, however, unstable, and the attempted flight from substance is illusory. As Laurence Tribe points out, the political community values process not for its own sake, but as an expression of substantive values,[60] and judges who decide whether a law unduly burdens a particular group must make a substantive evaluation of the interests at stake.[61] Ronald Dworkin similarly argues that, to determine the process to be followed in any given case, the judge must first decide "what rights people have or do not have".[62] He criticises Ely's contention that, while racially discriminatory laws are impermissible on the ground that they systematically disadvantage racial minorities, judgments that strike down laws prohibiting contraceptives and abortion impermissibly intrude on the legislature's powers. The distinction between these two scenarios cannot be justified simply by appealing to "democracy" or the "democratic process". Democracy is a contested idea, and a judge who strikes down a law on the ground that it impedes the democratic process must explain the conception of democracy that informs her judgment. In doing so, she cannot avoid making substantive decisions based on political morality.[63]

Ely's insistence that judges should focus on process, rather than substantive values, raises questions about political process theory's relevance in the South African context, given the Constitution's extensive catalogue of rights, its express commitment to value-based interpretation, and the Constitutional Court's insistence that all exercises of public power are justiciable.[64] However, in recent years, comparative studies of political process theory have infused it with examples from constitutional systems that are expressly value-laden and take a more robust view of the judiciary's role in overseeing the legislature and executive. For example, these studies have taken a keen interest in judgments in which South Africa's Constitutional Court invalidated parliamentary rules and procedures in cases dealing with parliamentary oversight of the executive.[65] Some of these studies suggest that political process theorists must move beyond the dichotomy between process and substantive value and broaden their understanding of the types of laws and decisions that can result in the distortion of the democratic process or the under-representation of certain voices and interests.[66] Some authors further acknowledge that representation-reinforcing review cannot and should not be limited to the enforcement of rights (like political rights, access to information, and freedom of expression, association, and assembly) that have a direct bearing on citizens' participation in democratic processes of opinion- and will-formation, or the ban on discrimination on a restricted number of grounds. In their view, the violation of a wider range of fundamental rights could, potentially, diminish a person's equal democratic citizenship.[67] These developments could open the door for enquiries into the role played by an array of civil rights, like dignity, equality, privacy, and freedom and security of the person, in guaranteeing individuals' status as full members of society who are shielded from deprivations of "private" rights and freedoms that may undermine their ability to participate in political life. The same goes for socio-economic rights, like education and access to housing and social security, which can promote citizens' participatory rights and capacity to make informed choices.[68]

There are, however, limits to political process theory's capacity to account for the complex interplay between civil and socio-economic rights, on the one hand, and rights of political participation, on the other. In the first place, analyses of the impact of anti-poor policies or laws that discriminate against members of the LGBTQI+ community on the capacity of those groups to participate in the political process seem far removed from political process theory's core concerns. Even if traditional understandings of what constitutes failures of the political process are expanded, careful, contextual analyses of laws and policies' substantive implications for the citizenship and participatory rights of marginalised groups remain largely outside the tradition's concern with process and structure.[69]

Secondly, political process theory rests on assumptions about the nature of politics and the functioning of political institutions that are not conducive to rigorous scrutiny of the interplay between politics, on the one hand, and material disadvantage and structural inequality, on the other. According to Richard Parker, political process theorists in the United States rely on two tenets: that the political process "normally functions well enough", and that it is subject only to "occasional, systemic malfunctions".[70] He argues that their standard for assessing the functioning of the process is surprisingly low. They are largely unconcerned with the fact that a considerable percentage of citizens do not vote, do not make their voice heard on issues that may affect them, and are politically uninformed. They also seem to regard the disproportionate political power of certain minorities as compatible with representative democracy. Moreover, their discussion of the malfunctioning of the democratic process is confined to two narrow categories: restrictions on the right of the people to use their voice and vote; and systematic discrimination against minorities. This blinds them to the possibility that the majority may effectively be cut off from meaningful participation in the political process, not because they are officially disenfranchised or silenced, but because of massive inequalities of power, wealth, status, and education.[71]

The tendency to treat the functioning of political institutions as unrelated to skewed distributions of resources, structural power relations, and the disproportionate power wielded by minorities is linked to the idea, expressed by Ely, that judicial intervention is justified to the extent that it corrects "the political market" when it "is systematically malfunctioning".[72] The conceptualisation of politics in market terms can explain the need for judicial intervention in cases where the ordinary mechanisms of democratic accountability are blocked or the political participation or voice of discrete minorities is clearly eroded. However, it struggles to account for threats to democracy that are more closely entwined with societal structures or emanate from the extension of market inequalities into the social and political spheres. The market analogy is further unable to come to terms with democracy's dialogical, intersubjective, and conflictual dimensions.

The idea that constitutional interpretation and adjudication can reinforce democracy thus needs to be recast in substantive terms, with emphasis on values like political equality and democratic citizenship. Such an approach could help draw attention to the capacity of seemingly neutral laws to strengthen social stigma and prejudice, entrench the disproportionate power of minorities, and duplicate the effects of social hierarchies within the political sphere. It should be better equipped to detect and respond to blockages in the political process and the under-representation of certain voices and interests and to help open up spaces for the articulation of democratic visions that are more radically egalitarian and participatory.[73]

## 1.5 Enhancing fundamental rights through citizenship, dialogue, and contestation

The mutual interdependence of democracy and rights does not only refer to the idea that fundamental rights adjudication can enhance democracy. It also entails that democratic contestation, deliberation, and decision-making play a vital role in the interpretation, concretisation, and enforcement of the rights that give expression to the values of dignity, equality, and freedom.

Conflicts between constitutional interpretations and visions are mediated through a variety of legislative, administrative, and judicial processes, and through debates within the public sphere of civil society. It is thus in the public realm that different interpretations of constitutional rights and values are articulated and compete for ascendancy. The capacity of those processes and discourses to unmask and challenge the denial of basic rights and freedoms and to secure their effective protection depends to a significant extent on the openness and inclusivity of the public-political sphere, and the ability of the individuals and communities concerned to voice their concerns. According to Jürgen Habermas, individuals' private autonomy and their public autonomy as citizens are internally connected, as the ability to defend private rights and freedoms goes hand in hand with the capacity to participate in public law-making processes.[74] He states, with reference to struggles for gender equality, that the individual rights that are invoked to safeguard women's autonomy within the private sphere "cannot even be appropriately formulated unless those affected articulate and justify in public discussion what is relevant to equal or unequal treatment".[75] The struggles of women and other vulnerable groups to carve out spaces in which they can shape their own lives, free from coercion, is intimately connected to their struggles for equal recognition within the public sphere.

A person's legal, political, and social status has an important bearing on her capacity to challenge rights violations. The link between personal autonomy and rights of membership and participation is most evident when looked at from the perspective of individuals who are not part of a political community that is willing and able to guarantee their rights. Hannah Arendt noted that the loss of a political home has devastating consequences for the rights of refugees and stateless persons and reveals the impotency of human rights when they are detached from rights of political participation and membership.[76] When people are deprived of "a place in the world which makes opinions significant and actions effective",[77] their supposedly universal human rights come to naught. However, it would be a mistake to think that it is only a lack of access to the formal legal status of citizenship that makes it difficult or impossible for some people to vindicate their rights. Other factors, like race, religion, gender, and poverty also play a role. The different treatment extended in Europe to refugees from Syria and from Ukraine provides a powerful example of the intersection of immigration status with other grounds of disadvantage.[78] Moreover, basic rights are routinely denied to classes of citizens that are perceived as different, abnormal, or deviant. The formal legal status of citizenship does not shield them from internal borders, which have a profound impact on their membership of the political community.[79] The existence of grey areas, in which exclusion based on "anthropological differences" occurs alongside universal citizenship,[80] complicates Arendt's account and suggests that the ability to participate in public life and challenge rights violations hinges on a constellation of power relations, which is not reducible to the distinction between citizens and non-citizens. While citizenship is an important part of the picture, it needs to be reconceived to take account of the complex and structural nature of the power relations at work, and to provide the basis for a nuanced analysis of the capacity of rights challenges to disrupt the hegemony of certain interests, knowledge forms, and ways of being in the world.

When the public and private spheres are viewed in dichotomous terms, difference tends to be relegated to the private sphere. The public sphere, by contrast, is shielded from the distorting effects of "private" differences. Citizens entering the public realm need to adopt a universal perspective to prevent them from imposing their private preferences and prejudices on others. However, this dichotomy ignores the close affinity between democracy and difference. It is often stated, with reference to Arendt, that plurality is the enabling condition of democratic politics.[81] For Arendt, political action is only possible in an agonistic public sphere in which unique individuals insert themselves into the human world through speech and action. Plurality presupposes the equality of citizens; at the same time, it is predicated on the singularity of every citizen, as revealed through speech and action.[82] Iris Marion Young interprets this to mean that citizens should not be required, upon entering the public sphere, to leave their particularity behind and to adopt a universal perspective. The public sphere is characterised precisely by the multiplicity of participants' experiences and perspectives. Attempts to reduce this plurality of outlooks to an impartial perspective risk destroying the heterogeneity that defines the idea of the public.[83]

The legal recognition of different lifestyles, cultural and religious practices, family formations, and sexual identities and orientations is therefore not simply a matter of private freedom but is closely connected to the ideal of an open and pluralistic public sphere characterised by robust engagement between opposing viewpoints. On the one hand, the plurality of beliefs, perspectives, and backgrounds that is vital to democratic politics derives, in part, from the rich diversity of experiences and relationships developed within the private and intimate sphere. On the other hand, laws, decisions, and discourses generated in the public sphere play an important role in expanding or circumscribing the range of beliefs, practices, and ways of being in the world that are considered legitimate and opening up or closing down spaces in which alternative social imaginations and subjectivities can flourish.

The above reflections on the importance of democratic contestation and dialogue to the protection of fundamental rights suggest that we need to radicalize our understanding of democracy, citizenship, and difference. We must come to terms with the ways in which the reproduction of "private" inequality within the public sphere introduces gradations within the notion of citizenship, which, in turn, inhibit the ability of those cast as second-class citizens to challenge their exclusion. We need to be open to more radically egalitarian and participatory understandings of democratic citizenship, which conceive it not as a pre-existing status but as a capacity that needs to be seized by subaltern groups to challenge their marginalisation.[84] We need to commit ourselves to the ideal of a truly heterogeneous public sphere which does not premise membership in the political community on the adoption of a "universal" perspective. This is a tall order, and it is by no means certain whether and to what extent constitutional interpretation and adjudication can help facilitate the enactment of radical reimaginations of democracy and citizenship. The next sections try to shed light on these questions through an examination of different assessments of constitutional adjudication's transformative potential.

## 1.6 Disrupting entrenched power: transformative value-based interpretation

The previous sections suggest that legal and constitutional interpretation is inevitably value-based and cannot consist in the neutral application of bright line boundaries separating law from politics, public power from private rights, process- from substance-based values, or legitimate state intervention in individuals' lives from impermissible rights infringements. Law and politics are closely enmeshed; public and private power and public and private freedom intersect in complex ways; and attempts to extricate process from substance end up obscuring the normative biases inherent in legal rules and institutions and the power relations underlying them. Instead of pretending that their judgments transcend politics, legal interpreters must recognise that they play a creative role in synchronising different norms and values and that their attempts to do so are necessarily partial and provisional. They must use their powers of legal interpretation and enforcement to help secure an open and democratic society in which different normative visions, beliefs, ideologies, and identities can coexist peacefully, and where normative closure and undue concentrations of power are actively resisted. On this view, legal interpretation is political. Interpreters do not simply enforce pre-existing boundaries but are active participants in the processes through which a community constructs, redefines, and mutually articulates the norms and values that are constitutive of the legal and political order.

This assessment resonates with the literature on transformative constitutionalism. In a celebrated article, Karl Klare uses the term "transformative constitutionalism" to denote the idea of "a long-term project of constitutional enactment, interpretation, and enforcement committed … to transforming a country's political and social institutions and power relationships in a democratic, participatory, and egalitarian direction".[85] He refers to several features that distinguish the Constitution from constitutions that stabilise the status quo or prioritise continuity with the past. Klare points out that, in contrast to "classical liberal" constitutions, it guarantees socio-economic rights, promises substantive equality, imposes affirmative duties on the state, provides for the horizontal application of fundamental rights, infuses representative democracy with participatory elements, and envisages ongoing processes of transformation and reinvention.[86] On that reading, the interpretation and enforcement of the Constitution cannot and should not consist in policing pre-existing boundaries between democracy and rights or privileging stability over change. The Constitution views democracy and rights, collective and individual self-determination, and political and social democracy as inextricably linked.[87] Its vision of active and engaged citizens who have the capacity to participate fully in social, economic, and political life requires careful attention to the multiple, intersecting causes of systemic inequality and disadvantage and invites interpreters to make sense of the interconnectedness of civil, political, and socio-economic rights. It thus enables contending articulations of constitutional values and encourages interpretations that politicise laws and practices that enable and normalise continued poverty, inequality, and dehumanisation.

Transformative constitutionalism requires a critical awareness on the part of lawyers and judges of their methodological presuppositions and conceptions of the judicial role, and a willingness to adopt alternative approaches to legal analysis and reasoning that are conducive to the transformation of social relations in line with the Constitution's normative vision.[88] At this point, a tension arises between transformative constitutionalism and the conservatism of South African legal culture. Klare notes that lawyers and judges' capacity for critical self-reflection is inhibited by the persistence of traditional understandings of legal reasoning and the judicial function, which view judicial reliance on personal beliefs and political values as inconsistent with the rule of law.[89] He sees the traditional conception of rule-bound reasoning and interpretive fidelity as hopelessly inadequate. In the first place, it assumes that legal texts generate their own meaning when, in fact, they are full of gaps, conflicts, and ambiguities. The application of legal materials to a particular case is not simply a function of the materials' inherent properties but arises from the interaction between the text and the work done by the judge interpreting it.[90] Judges' training and understanding of their function inevitably play a role, as do the choices they make, which bear the mark of their moral and political values.

Secondly, the dominant understanding takes a too restrictive view of the politics of adjudication. It assumes that judges act politically when they reconsider their initial reading of the legal materials in view of their intuition that a different interpretation would be more just. However, it fails to see that a judge "who is so steeped in traditional values and assumptions that she does not perceive gaps, conflicts and ambiguities that would appear under more searching analysis", similarly "enacts a politics external to the materials".[91] According to Klare, that is because this type of reliance on external values that privilege the status quo is so conventional that it often goes undetected. When we conflate the politics of adjudication with reliance on a judge's personal beliefs, we miss the point that judges can also act politically when they fall back on assumptions, practices, and reflexes that are interpersonal in nature, in the sense that they are widely shared within the professional community of judges, legal academics, and legal practitioners. These assumptions, practices, and reflexes may be so deeply ingrained in professional legal attitudes that they are often invisible. They operate mostly in the background, as a filtering mechanism that allows us to distinguish between the legally relevant and irrelevant, between legitimate and illegitimate discursive moves, and between permissible and impermissible exercises of the judicial function. It is precisely because they are so deeply embedded within professional practices and discourses that they appear to be natural and inevitable, rather than the contingent products of a particular legal culture and history. Klare refers in this regard to the conservatism of South African legal culture, i.e., the "reluctance to press legal materials towards the limits of their pliability, a tendency to underestimate the plasticity of the legal materials, and an exaggerated concern to give the appearance of conforming to traditional canons of interpretive fidelity".[92] These reflexes and habits, which are shared even by progressive lawyers and judges, threaten to undermine the Constitution's transformative potential.

On Klare's view, the politics of adjudication is inescapable and pervasive. It arises not because judges stray from the path of interpretive fidelity, but because legal materials are full of gaps, conflicts, and ambiguities. When interpreting them, judges need to make interpretive choices. The politics of adjudication is not only at work when judges are aware of the choices they make, or consciously draw on moral beliefs, political convictions, or ideological commitments. It also comes into play when they fail to see that there are other interpretive possibilities or are unaware of the value choices underpinning their judgments. His analysis suggests that the politics of adjudication is particularly powerful when it goes unnoticed. In such cases, judges draw on background assumptions and rhetorical strategies that are so deeply embedded within legal-professional discourse that they appear natural and necessary. When judges believe that their findings unavoidably follow from the legal materials, they feel unconstrained to explain the intermediate judgments and choices that link their findings to the relevant legal materials. In Klare's view, the only remedy to this is open acknowledgement of the politics of adjudication. Judges need to develop a substantive and self-conscious style of legal reasoning, which allows them, as far as possible, to acknowledge and explain the presuppositions and value choices informing their judgments.[93]

The danger is not only that judges will hide their value choices behind supposedly neutral and determinate legal rules, standards, or concepts. There is also a danger that they will use values in a non-transformative way. That happens when they interpret constitutional values in isolation from each other, uncritically reduce their meanings to those ascribed to them at common law, pretend that their meaning and mutual articulation are uncontested, fail to situate their interpretation within a social and historical context of domination, inequality and exclusion, neglect to explain the reasoning behind their interpretive choices, or fail to set out the intermediate reasons that link together their readings of constitutional values, other legal and constitutional norms, and the relevant facts and surrounding contexts. A value-based jurisprudence cannot disrupt the conservatism of legal culture if it itself falls back into the formalistic habits of old.

## 1.7 Normalising oppression: decolonial and racial critiques

Scholars who draw on critical race theory and decolonial theory take issue with portrayals of the Constitution as a radically transformative document. They argue that the tenacity of the gap between the Constitution's promise and the degradation and poverty that characterise the lives of millions of black South Africans after three decades of constitutionalism is not simply the result of a failure on the part of legal interpreters to exploit the Constitution's full transformative potential. In their view, it also points to problems inherent in the Constitution itself. Rather than confronting those problems, the literature on transformative constitutionalism obfuscates them by pretending that the Constitution can reverse the effects of centuries of institutionalised disadvantage and precludes radical alternative visions from taking hold.[94]

Some scholars are critical of the constitution-making process, with its secret deals, compromises among political elites, and reliance on legal expertise. In their view, the two-stage process, which bound the Constitutional Assembly to the Constitutional Principles agreed upon at the Multiparty Negotiating Forum and required the text of the final Constitution to be certified by the Constitutional Court, unduly limited the range of options available to the Constitutional Assembly and precluded it from redressing the injustices of the past. It guaranteed the survival of key aspects of the colonial and apartheid legal order, turned the constitution-making process into the preserve of lawyers, judges, and technocrats, effectively reduced the constituent power of the people to constituted power, and entrenched the interests of elites, rather than opening a path to real emancipation for millions of poor and dispossessed people.[95]

Decolonial critics further argue that the centrality of the Constitution to legal, moral, and political discourse has restricted the space for democratic contestation. Joel Modiri links what he calls "constitutional worship" to "colonial unknowing", which refers to "the disavowal, dissociation and normalisation of the history and horror of colonialism, land dispossession, white domination and racism".[96] For him, the Constitution signals that it is no longer possible to reverse the effects of colonial injustices. It effectively rules out any alternative politics that detaches itself from the historical narratives and normative assumptions underpinning the Constitution, and that is committed to remedying colonial wrongs.[97] Sanele Sibanda similarly suggests that the notion of transformative constitutionalism perpetuates the idea that it is not possible to undo the effects of colonialism. He argues that the term "transformation" denotes a commitment to change but does not specify the ideological or philosophical nature of the change required. The substance and extent of the transformation therefore hinge on compromises between rival interests and ideologies.[98] In a country characterised by enormous and deeply entrenched racial and class inequality, any such compromises can be expected to fall well short of undoing historical injustices.

These theorists argue that the Constitution, with its preoccupation with fundamental rights as a remedy for the injustices of the past and fixation on court-centred processes, blinds participants in constitutional discourse to the underlying causes of the disadvantage suffered by poor black people. Mogobe Ramose identifies those causes as the subjugation of indigenous peoples through colonial conquest, the destruction of their sovereignty, and the denigration of their knowledge and experience.[99] Modiri similarly states that the Constitution leaves fundamental aspects of colonialism and apartheid untouched. These include genocide, the dispossession of black people's land, racial capitalism, psychological degradation, and the obliteration of indigenous knowledge.[100] Tshepo Madlingozi argues that the failure of the "post-apartheid" constitutional order to make a fundamental break with the past has relegated large parts of the population to the status of colonial subjects, who live outside the linear time of the constitutional transition.[101] According to these theorists, the Constitution's aim is not to dismantle the colonial conqueror's world, but to include black people in it. However, inclusion is conditional on conformity to certain standards of "civilisation" or modes of being in the world.[102] Only certain elites gain entrance – the vast majority of black people continue to have a marginal existence that is, for the most part, beyond the protective reach of fundamental rights.

Decolonial critics argue that rights-based strategies to address the enduring legacy of past injustices are too limited to have true emancipatory potential. The language of fundamental rights fails to come to terms with the systemic nature of historical injustice. It does not do nearly enough to unsettle current distributions of wealth, power, and recognition, as it creates a framework in which individual rights claims must be accommodated within a status quo that has its roots in the subjugation of black people through conquest and dispossession. Any attempt to undo the injustices of the past must therefore fail due to the need to balance the rights of poor and dispossessed people against vested rights and interests.[103] The role of courts as the ultimate interpreters and enforcers of the Constitution compounds these problems. Madlingozi argues that, even though rights-based litigation strategies can help social movements to achieve strategic victories, they cannot undo the structural violence that is at the root of black people's oppression or effect a "radical redistribution of economic and political power".[104]

Critics further argue that a rights-based paradigm has ideological effects that are detrimental to anti-racist and anti-poverty struggles. This critique consists of several strands. The first is that rights-based constitutionalism deflects attention away from the systemic nature of racial and class prejudice, and thereby depoliticises the oppression of poor black people and renders it invisible. Modiri writes, with reference to Wendy Brown, that rights discourse, with its focus on individuals as abstract bearers of rights, fails to "address the social powers and historical inequalities that stratify and subjugate our concrete selves".[105] He claims that its emphasis on individual cases of deprivation and inequality masks the systemic nature of racism, patriarchy and poverty, and leads us to believe that we can overcome disadvantage by providing individual relief for fundamental rights violations.[106] The language of rights appears to include disadvantaged others into a legal order based on universal citizenship and human rights, but in doing so, draws attention away from the structural features of the economic, social, and cultural order that condemn poor black people to a life characterised by systemic violence and neglect. Because it assumes that poverty can be alleviated through the progressive realisation of socio-economic rights, human rights discourse precludes more radical challenges to the structural underpinnings of racial capitalism, neoliberalism, and neo-apartheid.[107]

A second strand of this critique is that the rights-based paradigm premises social and political inclusion on adherence to Western values and conformity to white, middle-class standards. According to decolonial theorists, this is a consequence of the Constitution's failure to undo the oppression and epistemicide that characterised colonialism. The Constitution allows a growing black middle class to enjoy the rights enshrined in it but fails to overthrow a hierarchical social order in which those who do not or cannot conform to Western standards of civilisation are condemned to a life at the margins of the legal order. They also link it to the historical exclusion of black people from human rights, and the construction in modern legal and political thought of the humanity and autonomy of the rights-bearing subject in contradistinction to the inhumanity, irrationality, and dependence of non-Western others.[108]

A third criticism relates to the role of lawyers and NGOs in human rights advocacy and litigation. Madlingozi notes that the constitutional transition coincided with the marginalisation of township-based civic organisations and the leading role played by predominantly white-led social justice organisations that specialise in legal advocacy and the representation of poor and vulnerable clients. This shift has an adverse impact on the power of poor black communities to define the terms of their own struggles, as "an overwhelmingly white epistemic community theorises social justice, calibrates its agenda, selects 'test cases' and engages in 'strategic litigation' on behalf of 'poor communities'".[109] He argues that this reinforces notions of white supremacy, juridifies emancipatory struggles, and de-radicalizes them by focussing primarily on the enforcement of state duties, rather than the need to challenge and overcome systemic anti-black racism.

Fourthly, drawing on Foucauldian analyses of the link between rights and disciplinary power, Modiri argues that rights discourse defines poor people in terms of their need, vulnerability, and dependence, and subjects them to "numerous techniques of juridical disciplinary domination in the form of registration, statistical monitoring, econometric calculation, data gathering and surveillance".[110] It empowers welfare institutions to define the needs of impoverished people and to condition their continued access to rights on the observance of certain rules. The recognition of the rights of poor and vulnerable individuals therefore goes hand in hand with the exercise of bureaucratic control. This produces subjects who are defined as lacking autonomy, and who face stigmatisation because of their apparent inability to take control of their own lives.

A fifth criticism relates to neoliberal policies that reduce human beings to economic units or disposable commodities and ascribe poverty to individuals' failure to develop their own human capital.[111] Decolonial critics suggest that there are limits to the capacity of rights-based strategies to challenge the tendency of those policies to deepen patterns of inequality and disadvantage. Given the pervasiveness of neoliberalism as a governing rationality and its ability to be dressed up in the language of individual rights and freedoms, rights discourse could be used to legitimate neoliberal policies and to normalise a world in which the worth of individuals is measured in economic terms.[112]

The focus on colonialism and conquest allows these critics to draw attention to the continuities between South Africa's colonial and apartheid past and the "post-apartheid" present – and to present those continuities not as temporary obstacles to the realisation of the Constitution's vision, but as structural features of the legal and social order. For them, this raises questions not only about the capacity of rights-based constitutionalism to undo the injustices of the past, but also about its role in legitimating the status quo and precluding alternative visions. It also provides an opportunity to imagine radical understandings of ideals like human dignity, equality, freedom, and democracy, which may be better able to rectify the injustices of the past and to place economic and political power in the hands of the people. Decolonial theorists draw on a variety of sources that contain traces of such alternative visions, including political traditions like Black Consciousness and Pan-Africanism,[113] historical examples of grassroots mobilisation and participatory democracy during anti-colonial and anti-apartheid struggles,[114] and contemporary social movements.[115]

## 1.8 Rethinking the possibilities and limits of value-based interpretation

Transformative constitutionalists and decolonial critics agree that the politics of law inheres in law's propensity to insulate current distributions of wealth, status, and power from contestation and critique. Their focus is different, though, and they have divergent views on the capacity of value-based constitutional interpretation to help safeguard spaces in which different visions of dignity, equality, and freedom and radical reimaginations of democracy and citizenship can flourish. Drawing on both those perspectives, this section offers tentative observations that can provide the outlines of a middle position that avoids both an outright rejection of and boundless confidence in the transformative potential of value-based constitutional reasoning. The observations are informed by my belief that questions about the transformative potential of value-based constitutional interpretation cannot be answered in the abstract or through recourse to a bright line boundary between law and politics but must be considered in view of the relevant contexts and power dynamics.[116]

In the first place, decolonial theorists are right to point out that the material, spatial, psychological, and political legacy of colonialism and apartheid is still very much alive. Despite the Constitution's message of dignity, equality, and freedom for all, full membership in the moral and political community continues to hinge on conformity to the image of the idealised citizen, who displays attributes traditionally associated with white, heterosexual, able-bodied, middle-class men. We have not been liberated from the yoke of the past; and further exercises of constituent power are needed to reconstitute society. That raises the question whether and to what extent the Constitution, which can only be amended through special procedures and special majorities,[117] places obstacles in the way of the reconstitution of the social. Firoz Cachalia argues, correctly in my view, that the Constitution does not provide a blueprint for citizenship, recognition, or redistribution in the postcolonial state, but establishes a framework for democratic politics. Although that framework contains certain pre-commitments, it is "replete with gaps, silences and abeyances",[118] and leaves it to democratic politics to interpret, complete, and revise those commitments. The Constitution, on this view, does not cement the political, social, and economic orthodoxy that developed after the end of the Cold War and the demise of the apartheid state. Rather than erasing the constituent power of the people by conflating it with what is already instituted, it enables ongoing processes of contestation and revision, which are made possible by the tension between general constitutional norms and ideals, which forever remain incomplete, and the contingency of shifting contexts, power relations, and social struggles.[119] The constitutional vision of an open and democratic society based on human dignity, equality, and freedom is arguably compatible with – and even requires – certain radical changes to social relations and the political economy. Cachalia claims, for example, that the Constitution does not lock a capitalist system into place, and that it could accommodate "the sort of deep structural economic changes that have historically been associated with Socialism".[120]

I agree that we should not be too quick to dismiss the idea that the Constitution can accommodate social visions and struggles that demand radical change and that we should be open to the capacity of value-based constitutional interpretation to exploit the gaps and contradictions in legal texts to transformative ends. At the same time, we should be realistic about the challenges. In trying to come to terms with the Constitution's capacity to respond to and create spaces for anti-racist, anti-sexist, and anti-capitalist struggles, on the one hand, and the afterlife of colonialism and apartheid, on the other, it may be helpful to distinguish between different impediments to the reconstitution of society. Some problems may derive from features of the Constitution itself, like the constitutional property clause in section 25, which, while attempting to find a balance between ownership and redistribution, has been criticised for favouring property rights acquired through conquest and white domination.[121] These features remind us that the Constitution is the contingent product of ideological conflicts, power relations, and compromises and that it provides an imperfect vehicle for the transformation of social relations. Other impediments arise when social hierarchies that are deeply embedded in South Africa's exclusionary past seep into official understandings of seemingly inclusive and egalitarian laws and constitutional provisions. These barriers draw attention to the profound difficulties inherent in attempts to undo South Africa's past, as the meaning of emancipatory ideals – like human dignity, equality, freedom, democracy, and ubuntu – is infiltrated and qualified by the social rankings of old. There is no easy fix for these problems. They call for challenges – in several fora, including the streets, shopfloors, legislative assemblies, and courtrooms – to the dehumanisation, silencing, inequality, and unfreedom experienced by marginalised populations, as well as the development of more deeply democratic and egalitarian social imaginaries. Invariably, these struggles, discourses, and imaginaries will position themselves differently in relation to the Constitution. These positions may range from relying directly on the Constitution to disavowing it. Moreover, even when the Constitution is invoked, the challenges and social visions that are articulated in its name may at the same time gesture towards possibilities that point beyond it.

Secondly, it is a legitimate concern that a rights-based, courts-centred approach could deflect attention away from the systemic nature of poverty and disadvantage. It is also true that courts lack the constitutional power, institutional capacity, and democratic legitimacy to institute large-scale programmes aimed at redressing the legacy of the injustices of colonialism and apartheid, or to bring about a radical redistribution of opportunities and resources. While courts should be cognisant of the impact of institutionalised racism, sexism, and poverty on people's rights, their orders cannot bring down the whole edifice of structural inequality and oppression. However, that does not mean that rights-based strategies are powerless in the face of systemic racism, sexism, and poverty, or simply a means of sugar coating them. Apart from providing relief to individuals and communities affected by laws and policies that deepen inequality and domination or deny them a voice, courts can develop standards that go beyond the facts of individual disputes, which can go some way towards responding to structural impediments to the realisation of basic rights.[122] They can also make orders that disrupt existing power relations and dominant mind-sets. This echoes Roberto Unger's idea of destabilisation rights, which "protect the citizen's interest in breaking open the large-scale organizations or the extended areas of social practice that remain closed to the destabilizing effects of ordinary conflict and thereby sustain insulated hierarchies of power and advantage".[123] Put differently, rights-based challenges can sometimes help to open up reified social categories, practices, and hierarchies to democratic contestation and social critique.[124]

Thirdly, critical legal theorists are right that rights-based strategies can have undesirable ideological effects. These include the depoliticisation of challenges against domination and dispossession by recasting them in the language of morality, legal neutrality, or bureaucratic expertise.[125] They further show that celebratory discourses that describe the Constitution as the best or the most progressive constitution in the world and romanticise the constitutional transition, the Truth and Reconciliation Commission, and the Constitutional Court rest on a sanitised rendering of history which normalises the enduring legacy of colonialism and apartheid. These discourses portray deprivation, inequality, and unfreedom as temporary obstacles to the imminent realisation of the Constitution's normative vision. They thus circumscribe the space for critical thinking and rule out the need for alternative imaginaries and the possibility of radical, anti-hegemonic struggles that do not fit within the dominant liberal, rights-based frame.[126] However, a commitment to transformative value-based interpretation and adjudication does not necessarily rest on such an ahistorical and apolitical account. Transformative constitutionalists' claims about the Constitution's transformative reach and depth tend to be held in balance by an awareness of the contingency of legal and political constructs and the pervasiveness of institutionalised domination and inequality. They are, accordingly, distrustful of sweeping narratives about the constitutional transition that erase certain injustices from the historical record and overlook the overlaps between different forms of disadvantage. They believe that the vindication of the dignity, equality, and freedom of marginalised people depends on interpretive commitment and political contestation, rather than following inexorably from the intrinsic logic of human rights or the application of an objective interpretive method. This is an important point, but it does not refute the charge that value-based adjudication can depoliticise challenges against poverty, inequality, and exclusion. After all, avowedly political practices of interpretation also have blind spots and rest on assumptions that seldom if ever rise to the level of conscious examination.

While rights-based strategies can have depoliticising effects, the converse is also true. Sometimes they can help secure spaces in which communities and movements can challenge social hierarchies and mobilise around alternative social visions. They can also help to politicise legal rules and concepts that play an important role in the legitimation of domination and inequality. As Dennis Davis and Karl Klare remind us, legal rules and principles dispose distributive and ideological stakes. Private law rules relating to contracts, delicts, property, and succession do not only determine access to economic resources and opportunities,[127] but can also make the harsh distributive consequences of decisions taken by businesses and industries appear like natural and inevitable consequences of a legal system that is committed to the protection of private property and free economic enterprise. Legal rules play an important part in normalising, outlawing, or subverting inequality and oppression, and recognising or delegitimising certain people, lifestyles, and subjectivities.[128] Such laws have a profound impact on people's agency and bargaining power – whether in the workplace, the family, commercial relations, or vis-à-vis the state or administrative agencies.[129] Ostensibly neutral legal rules have a powerful hold on legal consciousness and the popular imagination, as they operate mostly in the background to reflect and reinforce a set of assumptions about property, consent, and desert that have profound distributive consequences.[130] Declining to use constitutional rights and values to challenge such rules risks missing an important opportunity to politicise the ideological assumptions on which they rest and distributive patterns to which they give rise.

Finally, it is true that litigation could divert energy and resources away from other sites of democratic dialogue and contestation and that the attendant shifts – e.g., from the politics of the street to the politics of the courtroom and from the language of need to the stylised language of the law – could deradicalise democratic struggles and diminish the voice and agency of ordinary people. However, as argued above, judicial decisions could also open up spaces of contestation and disrupt the balance of power between powerful and marginalised social actors. Jackie Dugard refers, for example, to the judgment in *Baleni*,[131] in which the High Court held that the Minister of Mineral Resources lacked the authority to grant mining rights without the consent of the community living on the land. The point is not only that the decision could alter the balance of power between the state, mining companies, and the affected communities. It is also that the litigation empowered the community, which claimed that the proposed mining activities would threaten their way of life, to articulate and advance "a socio-ecological alternative to mega-project development in which community members live in partnership off the land, invoking collective decision-making in the interests of community cohesion and sustainable development".[132] The case provides a striking illustration of a point made by Julian Brown, namely that the formal equality afforded to litigants sometimes enables vulnerable groups and communities to counterpose their lived experiences and knowledge to the expertise wielded by the state and powerful economic actors.[133]

None of this suggests that the Constitution provides a blueprint for emancipation or that constitutional adjudication could ever be a substitute for political contestation, mobilisation, and organisation. A critical awareness of the limits and pitfalls of the Constitution and constitutional reasoning is imperative, but so is an understanding of their capacity to help safeguard spaces for disagreement and struggle.

In view of the elaboration in this chapter of the relationship between human dignity, equality, and freedom, on the one hand, and democratic citizenship, contestation, and dialogue, on the other, the next chapter turns to consider different constitutional conceptions of democracy. It is particularly interested in conflictual understandings of democracy, which view conflict, power, and indeterminacy as constitutive of the political, and which could provide the basis for a realistic assessment of the emancipatory possibilities and limits of value-based constitutional adjudication.

## Notes

1 S 39(2) states: "When interpreting any legislation, and when developing the common law or customary law, every court, tribunal or forum must promote the spirit, purport and objects of the Bill of Rights".

2 The limitation and interpretation provisions referred to above lend textual support to the proposition that dignity, equality, and freedom are intimately linked to an open and democratic society.

3 Cf. the debate between Currie "Judicious Avoidance" (relying on Cass Sunstein's work to argue for a strategy of "judicious avoidance" or "decisional minimalism" which avoids deep theoretical engagement and comprehensive judgments); and Roederer "Judicious Engagement" 492 (arguing, with reference to Ronald Dworkin, that judicious avoidance is only possible where judges "judiciously engage theory at the level of judgement").

4 See generally Dugard "The Judicial Process, Positivism and Civil Liberty".

5 This is the so-called golden rule of interpretation, as first formulated in *Venter v R* 914 and confirmed in a long line of cases.

6 Schreiner JA put forward an alternative approach to the role of context in statutory interpretation in his dissenting judgment in *Jaga v Dönges* 662G-664H. He noted that language is seldom "so clear that the possibility of differences of meaning is wholly excluded", and preferred an approach that considers context from the onset, together with the language of the provision. His judgment is often cited with approval by courts in post-apartheid South Africa. See, e.g., *Natal Joint Municipal Pension Fund v Endumeni Municipality* para 19.

7 See Du Plessis *Re-interpretation of Statutes* 101–111.

8 7–11, 225–239.

9 Dugard "The Judicial Process, Positivism and Civil Liberty" 190. The political nature of adjudication became particularly evident in the 1980s, when the government used its draconian powers under security legislation and the imposition of a protracted state of emergency to quell dissent. The Appellate Division in a series of judgments vindicated the state's actions and declined to make use of the interpretive techniques that it had relied on in the past to uphold individual freedom. Some judgments (e.g., *Minister of Law and Order v Hurley*) nevertheless showed that courts could employ the maxims of statutory interpretation to protect individual rights, even in the face of provisions that appeared to oust their jurisdiction. The contrast between these judgments, and between the executive-mindedness of the Appellate Division under Chief Justice Rabie and the greater willingness to protect fundamental rights under his successor, Chief Justice Corbett, made it

difficult to deny the influence of politics on adjudication and drew attention to the inadequacy of intention-based approaches to statutory interpretation. See Ellmann *In a Time of Trouble*.

10 Van der Walt "Tradition on Trial". See also Corder and Davis "Law and Social Practice" 2.

11 See, e.g., *De Lange v Smuts* para 85.

12 *Fraser v Absa Bank* para 47; *Makate v Vodacom* paras 87–89.

13 *Investigating Directorate v Hyundai Motor Distributors* para 21.

14 *Bato Star Fishing v Minister of Environmental Affairs* para 72.

15 *Carmichele v Minister of Safety and Security* para 54.

16 Para 39.

17 *Pharmaceutical Manufacturers Association* para 44.

18 Michelman "The Rule of Law, Legality and the Supremacy of the Constitution" 11–38.

19 *S v Jordan* para 104.

20 *S v Mhlungu* para 129.

21 Woolman and Botha "Limitations" 163–168.

22 *President v South African Rugby Football Union* para 42.

23 As Froneman J stated in *Ngxuza v Permanent Secretary* 1327I–1328A, "the outcome of this case is not dictated by precedent or deductive reasoning alone: my interpretation of section 38 of the Constitution is inevitably also influenced by my own views of the context in which it is to be interpreted and applied".

24 Mureinik "A Bridge to Where?" 32.

25 See Du Plessis and Corder *Understanding South Africa's Transitional Bill of Rights* 22–35 on the tension between "libertarians", who sought to protect individual rights and freedoms from state interference, and "liberationists", who did not want a constitution to stand in the way of redistributing wealth and resources and redressing the wrongs of the past.

26 See Klug *Constituting Democracy* 124–136 for an analysis of the – local and global – influences, tensions, processes, and struggles that framed the drafting of section 25, the constitutional property clause.

27 In *Matatiele Municipality v President* para 36, the Constitutional Court stated that the Constitution "has an inner unity, and the meaning of any one part is linked to that of other provisions".

28 *Ferreira v Levin* para 49.

29 *President v Hugo* para 41. See also *Prinsloo v Van der Linde* paras 31–33; *Harksen v Lane* paras 46, 50, 51, 53, 91–92.

30 *MEC for Education v Pillay* paras 62–68.

31 E.g., in *Government v Grootboom* para 83 the Court held: "The proposition that rights are interrelated and are all equally important is not merely a theoretical postulate. The concept has immense human and practical significance in a society founded on human dignity, equality and freedom". See also *Makana People's Centre v Minister of Health* para 69.

32 See, e.g., *S v Makwanyane* para 144 (dignity and the right to life are "the most important of all human rights, and the source of all other personal rights" in the Bill of Rights), *Dawood v Minister of Home Affairs* para 35 (dignity "informs the interpretation of many, possibly all, other rights").

33 *South African Revenue Service v Commission for Conciliation* paras 5, 55.

34 *S v Makwanyane* paras 156, 163, 166; *Dawood v Minister of Home Affairs* paras 37, 47, 57–58.

35 *S v Makwanyane* para 104. Sachs J stated in *Prince v President of the Law Society* para 155 that s 36 requires "the maximum harmonisation of all the competing considerations, on a principled yet nuanced and flexible case-by-case basis".

36 *S v Bhulwana* para 18; *S v Manamela* para 32.

37 *Khosa v Minister of Social Development* para 41.
38 Para 80. See also paras 41–42.
39 *National Coalition v Minister of Justice* paras 37, 38; *Minister of Home Affairs v Fourie* paras 94, 98.
40 Balibar *Equaliberty* 46–49.
41 50.
42 Cornell "Institutionalization of Meaning" 1222.
43 1211.
44 1210–1211.
45 *S v Makwanyane* para 88.
46 *S v Makwanyane* para 89, citing *West Virginia State Board of Education v Barnette* 638.
47 *S v Makwanyane* para 330, citing *Kindler v Canada* 237.
48 *Ferreira v Levin* para 49.
49 Para 170.
50 Para 174.
51 Para 182.
52 *August v Electoral Commission* para 17.
53 *Doctors for Life v Speaker* para 115.
54 *President v Hugo* para 41, quoting from the judgment of L'Heureux-Dubé J in *Egan v Canada* 104–105.
55 *National Coalition v Minister of Justice* paras 23–25, 127.
56 In *United States v Carolene Products Co* 152–153 n 4, Stone J mooted the possibility that a stricter standard of review (than a mere rationality standard) may apply in the case of "legislation which restricts those political processes which can ordinarily be expected to bring about the repeal of undesirable legislation", or which, since they rest on "prejudice against discrete and insular minorities", tend to "curtail the operation of those political processes ordinarily to be relied upon to protect minorities".
57 Ely *Democracy and Distrust* 75–76.
58 77.
59 101–102.
60 Tribe "The Puzzling Persistence of Process-Based Constitutional Theories" 1072.
61 1076.
62 Dworkin *A Matter of Principle* 66.
63 64.
64 See Fowkes "A Hole where Ely Could Be".
65 Gardbaum "Pushing the Boundaries"; Gardbaum "Comparative Political Process Theory" 1435–1437. See also Cachalia "Precautionary Constitutionalism".
66 Gardbaum "Comparative Political Process Theory" 1449, 1434–1448.
67 Schacter "Ely at the Altar" 1407–1410.
68 See Van der Walt "A South African Reading of Frank Michelman's Theory of Social Justice" 189–193; Cachalia "Separation of Powers" 310.
69 Gardbaum "Comparative Political Process Theory" 1449 states that comparative political process theory remains "wholly situated within the space occupied" by the first function of democratic constitutions, namely that of "establish[ing] the institutional structures and political processes within which democratic politics operates", as opposed to the second function, which concerns "establish[ing] the sphere and boundaries of democratic politics".
70 Parker "The Past of Constitutional Theory" 240 (emphasis omitted).
71 249–252.
72 Ely *Democracy and Distrust* 103.
73 Gargarella "From 'Democracy and Distrust' to a Contextually Situated Dialogic Theory".

74 Habermas "Struggles for Recognition" 113–114.
75 116.
76 Arendt *The Origins of Totalitarianism* 267–302.
77 296.
78 Freedman, Sahraoui and Tyszler "Asylum, Racism, and the Structural Production of Sexual Violence".
79 Balibar *Citizenship* 63–65, 69–70.
80 79–81.
81 Arendt *The Human Condition* 7.
82 8, 176.
83 Young *Inclusion and Democracy* 111.
84 Balibar *Citizenship* 66 (emphasis omitted) contends that the act of seizing "the active ability to assert rights in a public space" can amount to an exercise of constituent power, through which marginalised groups resist their exclusion.
85 Klare "Legal Culture and Transformative Constitutionalism" 150. See also Moseneke "Transformative Adjudication"; Langa "Transformative Constitutionalism"; Davis and Klare "Transformative Constitutionalism and the Common and Customary Law".
86 Klare "Legal Culture and Transformative Constitutionalism" 153–156.
87 Klare "Self-Realisation, Human Rights, and Separation of Powers" 465–468.
88 Klare "Legal Culture and Transformative Constitutionalism" 156.
89 168–172.
90 159–160.
91 162.
92 171.
93 164–165.
94 See, e.g., Madlingozi "Social Justice in a Time of Neo-Apartheid Constitutionalism"; Modiri "Towards a Post-Apartheid Critical Race Jurisprudence"; Modiri "Conquest and Constitutionalism"; S Sibanda "Not Purpose-Made!"; Sibanda "When Do You Call Time on a Compromise?".
95 Mutua "Hope and Despair for a New South Africa" 81. See also Botha "Instituting Public Freedom or Extinguishing Constituent Power?".
96 Modiri "Conquest and Constitutionalism" 308.
97 304–305, 307–308.
98 Sibanda "When Do You Call Time on a Compromise?" 390–393.
99 Ramose "In Memoriam".
100 Modiri "Conquest and Constitutionalism" 315.
101 Madlingozi "Social Justice in a Time of Neo-Apartheid Constitutionalism" 125–127.
102 The literature echoes Biko's warning that integration into a world dominated by white values "is an integration in which black will compete with black, using each other as rungs up a step ladder leading them to white values. It is an integration in which the black man will have to prove himself in terms of these values before meriting acceptance and ultimate assimilation, and in which the poor will grow poorer and the rich richer in a country where the poor have always been black". Biko *I Write What I Like* 101.
103 Modiri "Conquest and Constitutionalism" 321–322; Sibanda "When Do You Call Time on a Compromise?" 397, 401.
104 Madlingozi "Post-Apartheid Social Movements and Legal Mobilisation" 123.
105 Modiri "Law's Poverty" 249 (emphasis in original omitted).
106 247–248.
107 253.

108 Stewart "Rights Discourse and Practices, Everyday Violence and Social Protests" 17; Madlingozi "Social Justice in a Time of Neo-Apartheid Constitutionalism" 136.
109 144.
110 Modiri "Law's Poverty" 257.
111 See Gibson "Upright and Free" 697–703; Olivier "Decolonisation, Identity, Neo-Colonialism and Power" 9–15 on the resonance between decolonisation and resistance to the hegemony of neoliberal economic policies and ideas.
112 Madlingozi "Post-Apartheid Social Movements and Legal Mobilisation" 123.
113 Madlingozi "Social Justice in a Time of Neo-Apartheid Constitutionalism" 132–135; Modiri "Azanian Political Thought and the Undoing of South African Knowledges".
114 See the discussion of the role played by the United Democratic Front during the 1980s in Brooks, Ngwane and Runciman "Decolonising and Re-theorising the Meaning of Democracy" 25–28; Saul "On Taming a Revolution" 219–223.
115 See the discussion of Abahlali baseMjondolo in Gibson "Upright and Free" 704–707; Madlingozi *Mayibuye iAfrika?* 161–197.
116 See Santos "Beyond Neoliberal Governance" 54–56.
117 S 74.
118 Cachalia "Democratic Constitutionalism in the Time of the Postcolony" 380.
119 380–381. See also Botha "Fundamental Rights and Democratic Contestation".
120 Cachalia "Democratic Constitutionalism in the Time of the Postcolony" 397.
121 Sibanda and Raboshakga "A Question of Underlying Interests"; Jeewa "Yes, There is a Right to Property – Just Not for Everybody".
122 See Liebenberg "Engaging the Paradoxes of the Universal and Particular in Human Rights Adjudication"; Brand "The South African Constitutional Court and Livelihood Rights" on the tension between doing justice to individual litigants and addressing the structural impediments to the realisation of socio-economic rights.
123 Unger *False Necessity* 530.
124 E.g., where a court strikes down a law or practice that is complicit in the subordination of certain groups or grants an order that requires extensive stakeholder participation. See Woolman *The Selfless Constitution*; Liebenberg and Young "Adjudicating Social and Economic Rights".
125 See Brand "The 'Politics of Need Interpretation' and the Adjudication of Socio-Economic Rights Claims in South Africa" 17; Thomas "Racial Justice" 84.
126 Van Marle "Lives of Action, Thinking and Revolt"; Barnard-Naudé "She Reigns and He Does Not Govern" 274–278; Modiri "Conquest and Constitutionalism" 308.
127 Davis and Klare "Transformative Constitutionalism and the Common and Customary Law" 445–448; *King v De Jager* paras 198, 202.
128 Davis and Klare "Transformative Constitutionalism and the Common and Customary Law" 448.
129 See Kennedy "The Stakes of Law, or Hale and Foucault!" 344–345 (a rule excluding marital rape from the definition of rape or evidentiary rules that place a heavy burden on the state to prove the absence of consent in rape cases can severely curtail women's decisional freedom and ability to negotiate a more favourable distribution of work within the household).
130 See Davis "Developing the Common Law of Contract in the Light of Poverty and Illiteracy" 848–850, 862; Williams "The Legal Construction of Poverty" 468–470.
131 *Baleni v Minister of Mineral Resources*.
132 Dugard "Evaluating Transformative Constitutionalism in South Africa" 386.
133 Brown *South Africa's Insurgent Citizens* 137–146.

**Bibliography**

Arendt H *The Human Condition* (1958) Chicago: University of Chicago Press.
Arendt H *The Origins of Totalitarianism* (1968) San Diego: Harcourt.
Balibar É *Citizenship* (2015, translation T Scott-Railton) Cambridge: Polity Press.
Balibar É *Equaliberty* (2014, translation J Ingram) Durham: Duke University Press.
Barnard-Naudé J "'She Reigns and He Does Not Govern': The Discourse of the Anxious Hysteric in Post-apartheid South Africa" (2017) 28 *Law & Critique* 267.
Biko S *I Write What I Like* (2004) Johannesburg: Picador Africa.
Botha H "Fundamental Rights and Democratic Contestation: Reflections on Freedom of Assembly in an Unequal Society" (2017) 21 *Law, Democracy & Development* 221.
Botha H "Instituting Public Freedom or Extinguishing Constituent Power? Reflections on South Africa's Constitution-Making Experiment" (2010) 26 *South African Journal on Human Rights* 66.
Brand D "The 'Politics of Need Interpretation' and the Adjudication of Socio-Economic Rights Claims in South Africa" in AJ van der Walt (ed) *Theories of Economic and Social Justice* (2005) 17 Stellenbosch: Sun Press.
Brand D "The South African Constitutional Court and Livelihood Rights" in O Vilhena, U Baxi & F Viljoen (eds) *Transformative Constitutionalism: Comparing the Apex Courts of Brazil, India and South Africa* (2013) 414 Pretoria: Pretoria University Law Press.
Brooks H, Ngwane T and Runciman C "Decolonising and Re-theorising the Meaning of Democracy: A South African Perspective" (2020) 68 *Sociological Review* 17.
Brown J *South Africa's Insurgent Citizens: On Dissent and the Possibility of Politics* (2015) Auckland Park: Jacana Media.
Cachalia F "Precautionary Constitutionalism, Representative Democracy and Political Corruption" (2019) 9 *Constitutional Court Review* 45.
Cachalia F "Separation of Powers, Active Liberty and the Allocation of Public Resources: The E-Tolling Case" (2015) 132 *South African Law Journal* 285.
Cachalia F "Democratic Constitutionalism in the Time of the Postcolony: Beyond Triumph and Betrayal" (2018) 34 *South African Journal on Human Rights* 375.
Corder H and Davis D "Law and Social Practice: An Introduction" in H Corder (ed) *Essays on Law and Social Practice in South Africa* (1988) 1 Cape Town: Juta.
Cornell D "Institutionalization of Meaning, Recollective Imagination and the Potential for Transformative Legal Interpretation" (1988) 136 *University of Pennsylvania Law Review* 1135.
Currie I "Judicious Avoidance" (1999) 15 *South African Journal on Human Rights* 138.
Davis D "Developing the Common Law of Contract in the Light of Poverty and Illiteracy: The Challenge of the Constitution" (2011) 22 *Stellenbosch Law Review* 845.
Davis D and Klare K "Transformative Constitutionalism and the Common and Customary Law" (2010) 26 *South African Journal on Human Rights* 403.
Du Plessis L and Corder H *Understanding South Africa's Transitional Bill of Rights* (1995) Kenwyn: Juta.
Du Plessis L *Re-interpretation of Statutes* (2002) Durban: LexisNexis Butterworths.
Dugard J "Evaluating Transformative Constitutionalism in South Africa: A View from the Mineral Rights Adjudication Looking Glass" (2021) 39 *Nordic Journal of Human Rights* 373.
Dugard J "The Judicial Process, Positivism and Civil Liberty" (1971) 88 *South African Law Journal* 181.
Dworkin R *A Matter of Principle* (1985) Oxford: Clarendon Press.

Ellmann S *In a Time of Trouble: Law and Liberty in South Africa's State of Emergency* (1992) Oxford: Clarendon Press.
Ely JH *Democracy and Distrust: A Theory of Judicial Review* (1980) Cambridge, Massachusetts: Harvard University Press.
Fowkes J "A Hole where Ely Could Be: Democracy and Trust in South Africa" (2021) 19 *International Journal of Constitutional Law* 476.
Freedman J, Sahraoui N and Tyszler E "Asylum, Racism, and the Structural Production of Sexual Violence against Racialised Women in Exile in Paris" (2022) 11 *Social Sciences* 426.
Gardbaum S "Comparative Political Process Theory" (2020) 18 *International Journal of Constitutional Law* 1429.
Gardbaum S "Pushing the Boundaries: Judicial Review of Legislative Procedures in South Africa" (2019) 9 *Constitutional Court Review* 1.
Gargarella R "From 'Democracy and Distrust' to a Contextually Situated Dialogic Theory" (2020) 18 *International Journal of Constitutional Law* 1466.
Gibson NC "Upright and Free: Fanon in South Africa, from Biko to the Shackdwellers' Movement (Abahlali baseMjondolo)" (2008) 14 *Social Identities* 683.
Habermas J "Struggles for Recognition in the Democratic Constitutional State" in C Taylor (ed) *Multiculturalism: Examining the Politics of Recognition* (1994) 107 Princeton: Princeton University Press.
Jeewa T "Yes, There is a Right to Property – Just Not for Everybody: An Audit of the Legitimacy of the South African Property System Thirty Years Down the Line" (2024) 8 *Journal of Law, Property, and Society* 49.
Kennedy D "The Stakes of Law, or Hale and Foucault!" (1991) 15 *Legal Studies Forum* 327.
Klare K "Self-Realisation, Human Rights, and Separation of Powers: A Democracy-Seeking Approach" (2015) 26 *Stellenbosch Law Review* 445.
Klare K "Legal Culture and Transformative Constitutionalism" (1998) 14 *South African Journal on Human Rights* 146.
Klug H *Constituting Democracy: Law, Globalism and South Africa's Political Reconstruction* (2000) Cambridge: Cambridge University Press.
Langa P "Transformative Constitutionalism" (2006) 17 *Stellenbosch Law Review* 351.
Liebenberg S "Engaging the Paradoxes of the Universal and Particular in Human Rights Adjudication: The Possibilities and Pitfalls of 'Meaningful Engagement'" (2012) 12 *African Human Rights Law Journal* 1.
Liebenberg S and Young K "Adjudicating Social and Economic Rights: Can Democratic Experimentalism Help?" in H Aliviar García, K Klare and L Williams (eds) *Social and Economic Rights in Theory and Practice: A Critical Assessment* (2014) 237 Oxon: Routledge.
Madlingozi T *Mayibuye iAfrika? Disjunctive Inclusions and Black Strivings for Constitution and Belonging in "South Africa"*, unpublished thesis, Birkbeck, University of London (2018).
Madlingozi T "Post-Apartheid Social Movements and Legal Mobilisation" in M Langford, B Cousins, J Dugard and T Madlingozi (eds) *Socio-economic Rights in South Africa: Symbols or Substance?* (2014) 92 Cambridge: Cambridge University Press.
Madlingozi T "Social Justice in a Time of Neo-Apartheid Constitutionalism: Critiquing the Anti-Black Economy of Recognition, Incorporation and Distribution" (2017) 28 *Stellenbosch Law Review* 123.
Michelman F "The Rule of Law, Legality and the Supremacy of the Constitution" in S Woolman, M Bishop & J Brickhill (eds) *Constitutional Law of South Africa* 2 ed (2005) chapter 11 Cape Town: Juta.
Modiri J "Azanian Political Thought and the Undoing of South African Knowledges" (2021) 68 *Theoria* 42.

Modiri J "Conquest and Constitutionalism: First Thoughts on an Alternative Jurisprudence" (2018) 34 *South African Journal on Human Rights* 300.

Modiri J. "Law's Poverty" (2015) 18 *Potchefstroom Electronic Law Journal* 223.

Modiri J "Towards a Post-Apartheid Critical Race Jurisprudence: Divining our Racial Themes" (2012) 27 *SA Public Law* 231.

Moseneke D "Transformative Adjudication" (2002) 18 *South African Journal on Human Rights* 309.

Mureinik E "A Bridge to Where? Introducing the Interim Bill of Rights" (1994) 10 *South African Journal on Human Rights* 31.

Mutua M "Hope and Despair for a New South Africa: The Limits of Rights Discourse" (1997) 10 *Harvard Human Rights Journal* 63.

Olivier B "Decolonisation, Identity, Neo-Colonialism and Power" (2019) 20 *Phronimon* 1.

Parker R "The Past of Constitutional Theory – And Its Future" (1981) 42 *Ohio State Law Journal* 223.

Ramose MB "In Memoriam: Sovereignty and the 'New' South Africa" (2007) 16 *Griffith Law Review* 310.

Roederer C "Judicious Engagement: Theory, Attitude and Community" (1999) 15 *South African Journal on Human Rights* 486.

Santos B "Beyond Neoliberal Governance: The World Social Forum as Subaltern Cosmopolitan Politics and Legality" in B Santos and C Rodríguez-Garavito (eds) *Law and Globalization from Below: Towards a Cosmopolitan Legality* (2005) 29 Cambridge: Cambridge University Press.

Saul J "On Taming a Revolution" (2013) 49 *Socialist Register* 212.

Schacter J "Ely at the Altar: Political Process Theory through the Lens of the Marriage Debate" (2011) 109 *Michigan Law Review* 1363.

Sibanda S "Not Purpose-Made! Transformative Constitutionalism, Post-Independence Constitutionalism and the Struggle to Eradicate Poverty" (2011) 22 *Stellenbosch Law Review* 482.

Sibanda S "When Do You Call Time on a Compromise? South Africa's Discourse on Transformation and the Future of Transformative Constitutionalism" (2020) 24 *Law Democracy & Development* 384.

Sibanda S and Raboshakga N "A Queston of Underlying Interests: Economic Justice, Constitutional History and the Capture of the South African State by White Economic Interests" (2023) 27 *Law Democracy & Development* 539.

Stewart L "Rights Discourse and Practices, Everyday Violence and Social Protests: Who Counts as Subject and Whose Lives are Real in the Neo-Colonial South African Nation State?" (2014) 18 *Law Democracy & Development* 1.

Thomas K "Racial Justice" in A Sarat, B Garth and R Kagan (eds) *Looking Back at Law's Century* (2002) 78 Ithaca: Cornell University Press.

Tribe L "The Puzzling Persistence of Process-Based Constitutional Theories" (1980) 89 *Yale Law Journal* 1063.

Unger R *False Necessity: Anti-Necessitarian Social Theory in the Service of Radical Democracy* (1987) Cambridge: Cambridge University Press.

Van der Walt A "A South African Reading of Frank Michelman's Theory of Social Justice" in H Botha, A van der Walt and J van der Walt (eds) *Rights and Democracy in a Transformative Constitution* (2003) 163 Stellenbosch: SUN Press.

Van der Walt A "Tradition on Trial: A Critical Analysis of the Civil-Law Tradition in South African Property Law" (1995) 11 *South African Journal on Human Rights* 169.

Van Marle K "Lives of Action, Thinking and Revolt – A Feminist Call for Politics and Becoming in Post-Apartheid South Africa" (2004) 19 *SA Public Law* 605.

Williams L "The Legal Construction of Poverty: Gender, 'Work' and the 'Social Contract'" (2011) 22 *Stellenbosch Law Review* 463.

Woolman S and Botha H "Limitations: Shared Constitutional Interpretation, an Appropriate Normative Framework & Hard Choices" in S Woolman and M Bishop (eds) *Constitutional Conversations* (2008) 149 Pretoria: Pretoria University Law Press.
Woolman S *The Selfless Constitution: Experimentalism and Flourishing as Foundations of South Africa's Basic Law* (2013) Cape Town: Juta.
Young I *Inclusion and Democracy* (2000) Oxford: Oxford University Press.

## Case law

### *Canada*

*Egan v Canada* (1995) 29 CRR (2d) 79 SC
*Kindler v Canada* (1992) 6 CRR (2nd) 193 SC

### *South Africa*

*August v Electoral Commission* 1999 (3) SA 1 (CC)
*Baleni v Minister of Mineral Resources* 2019 (2) SA 453 (GP)
*Bato Star Fishing (Pty) Ltd v Minister of Environmental Affairs and Tourism* 2004 (4) SA 490 (CC)
*Carmichele v Minister of Safety and Security* 2001 (4) SA 938 (CC)
*Dawood; Shalabi; Thomas v Minister of Home Affairs* 2000 (3) SA 936 (CC)
*De Lange v Smuts NO* 1998 (3) SA 785 (CC)
*Doctors for Life International v Speaker of the National Assembly* 2006 (6) SA 416 (CC)
*Ferreira v Levin NO and Vryenhoek v Powell NO* 1996 (1) SA 984 (CC)
*Fraser v Absa Bank Ltd* 2007 (3) BCLR 219 (CC)
*Government of the Republic of South Africa v Grootboom* 2001 (1) SA 46 (CC)
*Harksen v Lane NO* 1998 (1) SA 300 (CC)
*Investigating Directorate: Serious Economic Offences v Hyundai Motor Distributors (Pty) Ltd* 2001 (1) SA 545 (CC)
*Jaga v Dönges* 1950 (4) SA 653 (A)
*Khosa v Minister of Social Development; Mahlaule v Minister of Social Development* 2004 (6) SA 505 (CC)
*King NO v De Jager* 2021 (5) BCLR 449 (CC)
*Makana People's Centre v Minister of Health* 2023 (5) SA 1 (CC)
*Makate v Vodacom (Pty) Ltd* 2016 (6) BCLR 709 (CC)
*Matatiele Municipality v President of the Republic of South Africa* 2007 (1) BCLR 47 (CC)
*MEC for Education: KwaZulu-Natal v Pillay* 2008 (1) SA 474 (CC)
*Minister of Home Affairs v Fourie; Lesbian and Gay Equality Project v Minister of Home Affairs* 2006 (1) SA 524 (CC)
*Minister of Law and Order v Hurley* 1986 (3) SA 549 (A)
*Natal Joint Municipal Pension Fund v Endumeni Municipality* 2012 (4) SA 593 (SCA)
*National Coalition for Gay and Lesbian Equality v Minister of Justice* 1999 (1) SA 6 (CC)
*Ngxuza v Permanent Secretary, Department of Welfare, Eastern Cape* 2000 (12) BCLR 1322 (E)
*Pharmaceutical Manufacturers Association of SA in re: the Ex Parte Application of the President of the RSA* 2000 (2) SA 674 (CC)

*President of the Republic of South Africa v South African Rugby Football Union* 1999 (4) SA 147 (CC)
*President RSA v Hugo* 1997 (6) BCLR 708 (CC)
*Prince v President of the Law Society of the Cape of Good Hope* 2002 (2) SA 794 (CC)
*Prinsloo v Van der Linde* 1997 (6) BCLR 759 (CC)
*S v Bhulwana; S v Gwadiso* 1996 (1) SA 388 (CC)
*S v Jordan* 2002 (6) SA 642 (CC)
*S v Makwanyane* 1995 (3) SA 391 (CC)
*S v Manamela (Director-General of Justice Intervening)* 2000 (3) SA 1 (CC)
*S v Mhlungu* 1995 (3) SA 867 (CC)
*South African Revenue Service v Commission for Conciliation, Mediation and Arbitration* 2017 (1) SA 549 (CC)
*Venter v R* 1907 TS 910

**United States**

*United States v Carolene Products Co* 304 US 144 (1938)
*West Virginia State Board of Education v Barnette* 319 US 624 (1943)

# 2 Reimagining democracy

Different constitutional judgments highlight different dimensions of democracy. As indicated in the previous chapter, some judgments accentuate democracy's formal dimensions, such as the principles of democratic representation and majoritarian decision-making, and the extent to which they are qualified and limited by a supreme Constitution containing a justiciable Bill of Rights. Other judgments stress the interrelatedness of democracy and rights and place more emphasis on the importance of an inclusive and active citizenship, which enables all layers of society, including the marginalised, to participate in the social, economic, and political life of the nation.[1] These dimensions track the distinction between formal and procedural conceptions and deliberative and participatory understandings of democracy. These terms, as used here, do not refer to fully worked out theoretical positions that inform the Court's jurisprudence. They refer, rather, to broad orientations, influential sets of assumptions and intuitions, or lenses or frames through which democracy is viewed. The metaphor of a lens or frame suggests that the same constitutional interpreter may rely on or prioritise different conceptions of democracy at different times, depending on the context. However, it is also consistent with the idea that an individual interpreter may generally be more inclined to rely on one specific conception or frame of democracy than others.

The term "formal and procedural conceptions of democracy" is used to refer broadly to understandings that emphasise the representative nature of democratic institutions and the role of regular elections in legitimating public power. They foreground the formal link between the electorate and their representatives and the procedures through which that link is established.[2] They are less interested in substantive questions such as the material conditions under which the people can be said to be self-governing, and whether citizens truly have an opportunity to participate in the processes through which laws and policies are adopted. They also pay relatively little attention to the capacity of structural features of the representative system, such as the role of political parties, and socio-economic realities, like poverty, to distort the outcomes of the democratic process. These understandings are sometimes criticized for collapsing the meaning of democracy onto the formal existence of electoral processes and democratic institutions. In the view of critics, their failure to give

DOI: 10.4324/9781003482451-3

substantive content to the values of democratic accountability, responsiveness, and openness results in an overly formal and ritualistic understanding of the link between the electorate and their representatives.[3]

The term "deliberative and participatory conceptions of democracy" is used to refer to a broad range of ideas that resist the notion that law is legitimate simply because it is enacted by bodies or officials that are popularly elected or can be held to account in terms of democratic procedures.[4] Proponents of participatory democracy worry about the distance between the electorate and their representatives, and the impact of deeply entrenched inequalities on individuals' capacity for meaningful participation in political, economic, and social life. They accordingly argue for the extension of participatory rights beyond elections as a powerful way of countering inequality. Their proposals include the democratisation of the state by making Parliament, the state administration, and political parties more open and accountable, and the democratisation of society by extending rights of self-government to local communities and the workplace.[5] Proponents of deliberative democracy maintain that law's legitimacy stems from the quality of the deliberations that produce it. Deliberation must be characterised by a willingness to learn more about the issues, to take account of others' views, to reconsider one's own views in the light of the available information and the diversity of perspectives, and to justify one's views with reference to public reasons, rather than private preferences. These forms of deliberation must take place not only in state institutions, but also in different spheres of civil society.[6]

The chapter also finds traces in some constitutional judgments of a third conception of democracy which could be labelled "conflictual" or "agonistic". On this understanding, conflict and power are constitutive of democratic interaction. Instead of trying to eliminate conflict from political life, democracy should channel its regenerative power while preventing conflict from erupting into forms of antagonism that threaten the existence of the democratic community. Conflictual understandings of democracy are radical – they resist the conflation of democracy with any given set of institutions and practices, insist that domination, inequality, and exclusion are features of all democracies, and are interested in the capacity of democratic and emancipatory struggles to challenge oppression. They are also pluralistic, as they insist that democracy requires the existence of different understandings and articulations of democratic values like freedom and equality.[7]

The chapter draws on case law and academic literature to examine different meanings assigned to democracy and different articulations of democracy with other values, and to evaluate and critique the impact of those interpretations on the adjudication of disputes. It critically evaluates each conception's understanding of the link between the people and their representatives, their views on the nature and limits of democratic inclusion and representation, their implications for the construction and mutual articulation of dignity, equality, and freedom, and their capacity to shed light on the question whether and to what extent the interpretation of these values can be democracy enhancing.

Finally, the chapter reconsiders the meaning of democracy in view of decolonial critiques of dominant political and epistemological traditions. It enquires into the resonances and tensions between decolonial imaginaries and conflictual understandings of democracy and asks whether the latter could help safeguard spaces for developing and enacting decolonial imaginaries and practices, which point beyond (post)colonial constructions of law, politics, economy, and society towards more emancipatory possibilities.

## 2.1 Formal and procedural democracy

The judgments of the Constitutional Court in cases like *NNP* and *UDM* tend to be associated with formal or procedural conceptions of democracy, which emphasise the link that is established, through elections, between voters and their representatives. *NNP* dealt with the constitutionality of provisions in electoral legislation that required voters to have either a bar-coded identity document or a temporary identification certificate. Surveys showed that a significant part of the population did not have the required identification and that the Department of Home Affairs was unlikely to be able to issue all the documents in time for the forthcoming election. However, the Court held that the requirement did not limit the right to vote and served a legitimate government purpose, namely that of ensuring the integrity of the electoral process.

Two aspects of the judgment proved to be particularly controversial. The first relates to the deferential nature of the standard of review that was used. The court insisted that the reasonableness of the electoral scheme was not at issue. The question was, rather, whether there was a rational connection between the legislation and a legitimate government purpose.[8] In the majority's view, a rationality test is less intrusive, and recognises that it lies within the province of Parliament, and not the courts, to determine how voters must identify themselves.[9] As O'Regan J noted in her dissenting judgment, this approach effectively requires voters to show that they have acted reasonably, while exonerating Parliament from having to demonstrate the reasonableness of the measures it adopted.[10] Secondly, the majority's framing of the rationality enquiry precluded it from considering important contextual factors. It held that the constitutionality of the legislation had to be assessed at the time of its enactment, not at the time that its validity was challenged.[11] Moreover, it stated that concerns over the capacity of the Department of Home Affairs to issue the required documents within a short period of time pertained to the implementation of the Act, and had no direct bearing on its constitutionality.[12] Even more importantly, the majority failed to take account of socio-economic and systemic barriers to the meaningful political participation of poor and vulnerable sections of the population. As O'Regan J pointed out, the majority ignored the diversity of South Africa's population, and uncritically assumed that the same standard could be used to determine what is reasonable to expect from educated and affluent urban voters, on the one hand, and poor and illiterate rural voters, on the other.[13]

In *UDM* the Court held that legislation and constitutional amendments that allowed legislators to cross the floor to another political party without losing their seats, violated neither the basic structure of the Constitution nor the constitutional value of multiparty democracy. This is surprising in view of an earlier judgment in which the Court recognised that there is a close link between voters and political parties under a list system of proportional representation, and that an anti-defection clause could play an important role in ensuring that "the will of the electorate is honoured".[14] The Court in *UDM* did little to explain this about-turn, apart from relativising the differences between systems of representation by stating that many of the concerns raised about floor crossing under a list system of proportional representation also apply in the context of a constituency system.[15] The Court also rejected the contention that bigger parties would benefit from the 10% threshold requirement for defections. It stated that "[t]he fact that a particular system operates to the disadvantage of particular parties does not mean that it is unconstitutional".[16] The Court similarly rejected the argument that the legislation violated the right to vote in terms of section 19(3) of the Constitution. It held that between elections, "voters have no control over the conduct of their representatives".[17] If voters are unhappy with the conduct of elected representatives, their remedy lies in not voting for them during the next election.[18] Not surprisingly, the judgment has been criticised for failing to give meaningful content to multiparty democracy, neglecting to situate the relevant laws within the context of the electoral dominance of the ruling party, and conflating representative democracy with elections every five years.[19]

In sum, these judgments are characterised by a shallow understanding of representative and multiparty democracy and the right to vote, a significant degree of deference to the legislature, and a failure to come to terms with socio-economic and structural impediments to full citizenship and equal political rights. In *NNP* the Court failed to appreciate the capacity of seemingly neutral electoral rules to reproduce social inequality and marginalisation within the political sphere. In *UDM* it divorced the right to vote from institutional questions relating to the representative system and role of opposition parties and failed to recognise that background rules can distort the outcome of elections and undermine democratic accountability, even if they do not prevent people from voting.

## 2.2 Deliberative and participatory democracy

Some later judgments have infused representative and multiparty democracy with a deliberative understanding of democracy. For instance, Sachs J's concurring judgment in *Masondo* is informed by a keen awareness of different dimensions of democracy and the difficult task of holding them in balance. He stated:

> The Constitution does not envisage a mathematical form of democracy, where the winner-takes-all until the next vote-counting exercise occurs. Rather, it contemplates a pluralistic democracy where continuous respect

> is given to the right of all to be heard and have their views considered... The open and deliberative nature of the process goes further than providing a dignified and meaningful role for all participants. It is calculated to produce better outcomes through subjecting laws and governmental action to the test of critical debate, rather than basing them on unilateral decision-making.[20]

On this view, law's legitimacy does not hinge solely on its enactment by representative institutions adhering to the relevant pre-established procedures. In addition to that, laws and decisions must derive from open and inclusive processes that facilitate informed discussion. Such discussion must be characterised by participants' willingness to listen to each other and to advance defensible reasons for public actions. At the same time, however, the judgment acknowledges the limits of democratic deliberation. Sachs J recognised that democracy cannot be characterised by endless dialogue, and that an appropriate balance must be struck between deliberation and the need to take binding decisions, between the fair representation of minority views and interests and majority rule, and between inclusivity and effective service delivery.[21]

In the following years, other judgments appeared to embrace a similar vision of democracy.[22] These include judgments that interpret constitutional provisions dealing with legislative procedures in view of deliberative democratic ideals. For instance, in *Oriani-Ambrosini*, the Court invalidated rules of the National Assembly that required the National Assembly's permission before a member could introduce a Bill in terms of s 73(2) of the Constitution. Mogoeng CJ interpreted the relevant constitutional provisions through the lens of representative and participatory democracy, multiparty democracy, pluralism, democratic deliberation, responsiveness, accountability, and openness.[23] Given the National Assembly's deliberative nature, and the right of all members, including those from minority parties, to have their voices heard and their views considered,[24] he held that the power of individual members to initiate, prepare, or introduce legislation should not be placed at the mercy of the legislative majority.[25] Moreover, In Mazibuko, the Court held that it is inconsistent with s 102(2) of the Constitution to leave the decision whether to schedule a motion of no confidence to the whim of the majority of the members of the relevant parliamentary committee.[26]

Deliberative democratic ideals also play a role in the adjudication of claims based on fundamental rights. The Constitutional Court held in *PE Municipality* that the Constitution requires the state to treat people whose eviction is sought as "individual bearer[s] of rights entitled to respect for [their] dignity", and not as "faceless and anonymous squatters automatically to be expelled as obnoxious social nuisances".[27] It noted that mediation can play an important role in this regard. Requiring the parties to an eviction to search for solutions through "respectful face-to-face engagement or mediation" is more respectful of occupiers' dignity and moral agency, more conducive to creating relations of mutual trust, and more likely to yield outcomes that are mutually beneficial.[28] In line with this approach, the Court held in subsequent cases that the state has a duty to engage meaningfully with occupiers before evicting them from their homes.[29] In *Olivia Road*, the Court stressed the need for "structured, consistent and careful engagement" where many people stand to be affected by evictions.[30] In *Joe Slovo*, Sachs J criticised the "top-down approach" adopted by the government, in terms of which the authorities informed the community of decisions rather than treating them "as partners in the process of decision-making".[31] The Court conceives engagement as a partnership that is based on the deliberative principles of mutual respect, a willingness to listen to each other's viewpoints, and ongoing consultation. The aim is not simply to placate residents but to find solutions that are mutually acceptable. The jurisprudence on meaningful engagement nevertheless recognises that the parties are not required to reach agreement on all issues, and that the final decision-making authority remains vested in the government.[32]

The Court has extended the requirement of meaningful engagement to other contexts, like disputes between school governing bodies and the Department of Education.[33] It has also stressed the importance of consultation in accommodating religious and cultural difference. Parties to a dispute must engage in dialogical processes aimed at the "reasonable accommodation of interests". Religious and cultural minorities must be given the opportunity to participate in decision-making processes, and public authorities must endeavour to accommodate minority viewpoints and practices.[34]

A second set of judgments has infused democratic representation with elements of participatory democracy. These judgments draw on constitutional provisions that refer to participatory democracy,[35] provide for public participation in legislative and policy-making processes,[36] recognise the importance of the involvement of communities and community organisations in local government matters,[37] and guarantee the right of citizens to participate in the activities of a political party.[38] It could be argued that the sections that refer to participatory democracy and the facilitation of public involvement are aspirational, rather than legally enforceable. In *Doctors for Life*, the Constitutional Court emphatically rejected that interpretation. It held that the Constitution imposes an enforceable obligation on legislative bodies to facilitate public involvement in the legislative process. Non-compliance with that obligation must result in the invalidation of the legislation. In his majority judgment, Ngcobo J found that Parliament must take proactive measures to ensure that citizens have an effective opportunity to participate in the legislative process, e.g., through public education, providing information, and initiatives aimed at bringing democracy closer to the people.[39] Although the legislature must be afforded a broad discretion in deciding how to enable participation, the question whether the public has been given a reasonable opportunity to participate in the legislative process is justiciable. What is reasonable depends inter alia on the nature of the legislation, its importance, its impact on the public, its urgency, and Parliament's own views on what would be appropriate.[40]

The dissenting judgment of Yacoob J is underpinned by a different understanding of democracy, which effectively reduces the will of the people to the decisions of elected representatives. He held that the Constitution does not unequivocally impose an enforceable obligation on Parliament to facilitate public participation. The existence of such an obligation is not borne out by the historical record either, since the struggle for democracy in South Africa was first and foremost a struggle for universal adult suffrage, not for public participation in law making. In Yacoob J's view, the judicial creation of a right to political participation would diminish "the value of the right to vote acquired through bitter struggle",[41] "undermine the political will of the people", and "negate their choice at free and fair elections".[42] The judgment is clearly premised on the idea of the unity or identity of the people and their representatives, which is secured through the expression of the will of the people during elections. While accepting that constitutional mechanisms aimed at promoting democratic accountability, responsiveness, and openness can strengthen the bond between the people and their representatives, he insists that the judicial imposition of participatory requirements that are not grounded directly and unambiguously in the Constitution would demean the value of the right to vote by disturbing the "uninterrupted chain of legitimacy" that passes from the people to their representatives.[43]

By contrast, Ngcobo J stated in his majority judgment that the people had not bestowed absolute power on Parliament, but "reserved for themselves part of the sovereign legislative authority that they otherwise delegated to the representative bodies they created".[44] On his view, the power of the people exceeds that of their representatives. There is always a remainder of their original – constituent – power that precludes representatives from making totalising claims in their name. Since elections do not forge the identity of the people with representative bodies, the vote needs to be supplemented through other forms of political participation and the legitimacy of representative institutions must be strengthened through an ongoing dialogue with the electorate. In Ngcobo J's view, public participation is particularly important in a country in which economic and social inequality continues to relegate poor black people to a position of voicelessness and marginality. He stated that public participation, "because of its open and public character acts as a counterweight to secret lobbying and influence peddling",[45] and could help integrate poor and marginalised people into the political community.[46]

These themes were echoed in the *Matatiele* case. The case concerned the constitutionality of legislation and a constitutional amendment that removed the Matatiele Municipality from the province of KwaZulu-Natal and incorporated it into the Eastern Cape. The provincial legislature of KwaZulu-Natal approved the constitutional amendment, as required, but did not facilitate public involvement. In his majority judgment, Ngcobo J dismissed the government's submission that the provincial legislature spoke on behalf of the people of the province and therefore did not need to consult them. He held that the democracy inaugurated by the Constitution includes both representative and participatory elements and envisages "a dialogue between the elected representatives of the people and the people themselves".[47] His finding that the legislature did not act reasonably in failing to hold public hearings was based inter alia on the right of the people of Matatiele to live in the province of their choice, the practical implications of the move for service delivery, and the need to facilitate involvement where legislation affects "a discrete and identifiable section of the population".[48]

In the *Land Access Movement* case, which concerned the constitutionality of the Restitution of Land Rights Amendment Act 15 of 2014, the Court emphasised the impact of land dispossession on the dignity of individuals and communities who were subjected to forced removals and the loss of property under colonialism and apartheid.[49] It also stressed the importance of the restitution of land rights to the restoration of their dignity,[50] and the link between public participation in the legislative process and the dignity of members of groups that were historically silenced.[51] Given the importance of the Act, its potential impact on those disadvantaged in the past, the unduly short timeline adopted for the facilitation of public participation, and the inadequacy of the notices given by some of the provincial legislatures, the Court held that the public participation process was unreasonable and that the Act was constitutionally invalid. More recently, in *Mogale*, the Court invalidated the Traditional and Khoi-San Leadership Act 3 of 2019 – a highly controversial piece of legislation, which was criticised inter alia for reinforcing the power of traditional leaders and undermining the equal citizenship of black people living in rural areas – based on irregularities in the public participation process. The irregularities included inadequate notice, which left the public too little time to prepare for the hearings, a failure to provide accurate and accessible information, a tendency to give traditional leaders the chance to speak, while preventing ordinary members of the community from doing so, and inadequate reporting of the views expressed at the hearings.[52]

These judgments promise to reinforce the democratic representation and participation of poor and vulnerable groups. They emphasise the agency and voice of people who were historically excluded from participatory rights and require the creation of conditions in which all citizens can participate in decision-making processes. They further rest upon a conception of political equality that resists the reduction of the public interest to the interests of elites and subjects the power and influence of the rich and well-connected to the demand for democratic openness and accountability.

### 2.3 Rethinking democratic accountability, responsiveness, and openness

The turn towards deliberative and participatory notions of democracy has given rise to a richer understanding of the democratic values of accountability, responsiveness, and openness, and a greater willingness on the part of the judiciary to intervene in cases where those values are under threat. This has stood the Constitutional Court in good stead in cases involving the ruling party's disregard for constitutional norms of accountability during Jacob Zuma's Presidency.[53]

The Court intervened in several cases in which the ruling party attempted to block efforts to hold the government accountable. For instance, in *EFF I*, the Constitutional Court held that the President's failure to comply with the remedial action taken against him by the Public Protector in relation to the upgrades to his unofficial residence in Nkandla constituted a breach of his obligation to uphold, defend, and respect the Constitution.[54] It further ruled that the National Assembly, by seeking to absolve the President from compliance with the Public Protector's remedial action, acted in breach of its constitutional obligation to scrutinise and oversee executive action.[55] In *EFF II*, the majority of the Court held, rather controversially, that the National Assembly's failure to make rules for determining whether grounds exist for the President's impeachment, prior to taking the vote, amounted to a failure to hold the President to account.[56]

There are several reasons why deliberative and participatory conceptions of democracy resonate with a rich understanding of the democratic norms of accountability, openness, and responsiveness. First, these notions of democracy resist the idea that the will of democratic representatives is identical to the will of the people. Instead, they subject the legitimacy of laws and government decisions to certain conditions, such as that they must emanate from participatory processes that are characterised by inclusivity, mutual recognition, open and informed discussion, and the giving of reasons. These obligations arise, first, from the idea that representatives derive their power from the people, and secondly, from the fact that the people are subject to the laws and decisions made by their representatives. Democracy, on this view, means more than simply the registration of the electorate's preferences every five years. It also refers to what happens between elections to ensure that those elected to positions of power are held accountable and remain responsive to the needs of the people.

Secondly, on deliberative and participatory understandings, the values of human dignity, equality, and freedom do not simply impose external limits to what democratically elected legislatures may do. Rather, these values are partly constitutive of democracy. They must guide legislatures in relation to their own internal processes, the facilitation of public participation, and the substance of their decisions. Democratic processes must be designed to respect the dignity of those subject to the laws emanating from them. Participation in these processes can and should play an important role in restoring the dignity of those who were silenced in the past. It can also help to counter the effects of social and economic inequality. Moreover, the diversity of perspectives and viewpoints that is the lifeblood of democracy, and that demands respect for the participatory and other rights of minorities, is intimately connected to these values.[57]

Thirdly, when judges rely on deliberative and participatory understandings of democracy, they tend to be more sensitive to the contexts in which electoral and parliamentary rules operate.[58] That is because they are interested in the conditions under which the decisions of elected representatives would amount to legitimate expressions of the people's will. Those conditions have to do with the inclusivity of the process and the capacity of participants, including legislative minorities and poor and vulnerable individuals and communities, to participate freely and to have their views considered. They are arguably absent in cases where the democratic process is distorted through the exclusion of minority parties or members of certain groups from meaningful participation in the political process, or through attempts by the ruling party to use its parliamentary majority to thwart mechanisms designed to hold the executive accountable. The same goes for cases involving the manipulation of the internal processes of a political party,[59] the subjection of the public interest to the private interests of corrupt politicians and businesspeople, and the withholding of information that is important for an informed exercise of the right to participate in political life. For this reason, deliberative and participatory conceptions of democracy appear more perceptive to the capacity of seemingly neutral electoral and parliamentary rules to perpetuate the political marginalisation of minorities and vulnerable populations, distort the outcome of the vote, or diminish democratic accountability, responsiveness, and openness.

*UDM II* provides a good example of the link between context-sensitive modes of interpretation and analysis and reliance on nuanced conceptions of democracy and accountability. The case concerned a challenge to the refusal of the Speaker of the National Assembly to allow a motion of no confidence to be decided by secret ballot. The Court situated its interpretation of section 102 of the Constitution, which provides for motions of no confidence, within a broader consideration of the surrounding context and purpose of the provision and the values underlying it.[60] It referred to constitutional provisions dealing with the collective and individual accountability of members of the cabinet to Parliament, and with Parliament's role in scrutinising and overseeing executive action. It also highlighted the role played by motions of no confidence in ensuring that the existing mechanisms aimed at promoting executive accountability between elections, remain effective.[61] The Court noted that the Constitution leaves the procedure for motions of no confidence open, and that the rules of the National Assembly allow for both open and secret ballots. The Speaker therefore has a choice. In exercising that choice, she must consider different factors. On the one hand, members must be allowed to vote without the fear of reprisal from party leaders. This is a pressing concern under a list system of proportional representation where voters vote for political parties, and where members' political future hinges on their position on the party list. In these circumstances, democratic accountability will sometimes be served best by a secret ballot, which will make it easier for members of the ruling party to vote according to their conscience, and thus to remain faithful to their oath to uphold the Constitution and laws of the Republic. Another factor that may favour a secret ballot is the likelihood that corruption will distort the outcome of the vote.[62] On the other hand, the Court acknowledged that "the electorate is at times entitled to know how their representatives carry out even some of their most sensitive obligations",[63] and that the Speaker must take account of the need for openness and transparency in the functioning of the National Assembly. The decision to conduct the vote via an open or secret ballot is thus situation-specific and must be based on a careful weighing of different contextual factors. In the final analysis, it must be guided by the constitutional imperative to ensure that Parliament's accountability mechanisms function effectively.[64] The Speaker must exercise the discretion in a manner that affirms and strengthens the ties between those in government and the people on whose behalf they govern and to whom, ultimately, all state power belongs.[65]

The judgment in *My Vote Counts* is similarly informed by a rich understanding of democracy, and a sensitivity to the surrounding context. The Constitutional Court held that the effective exercise of the right to make political choices requires access to information on the private funding of political parties and independent candidates. It declared the Promotion of Access to Information Act 2 of 2000 invalid to the extent that it fails to provide for the recording, preservation, and disclosure of such funding. The judgment is noteworthy for its insistence that any information that could shed light on what a political party or independent candidate stands for, or by whom they are likely to be influenced, is essential for "an informed exercise of the right to vote".[66] It is also significant for its attention to the capacity of alliances between public representatives and private donors to twist and distort the former's obligation to serve the public interest and to subvert the will of the electorate, and for its articulation of the right to vote with transparency, accountability, and the fight against corruption.[67]

## 2.4 The limits of deliberative and participatory conceptions of democracy

The turn to deliberative and participatory conceptions of democracy promises legislative and decision-making processes that are inclusive, respectful of citizens' dignity, responsive to the needs of those affected, and able to resist the distorting effects of private wealth and power on public decision-making. While that is an attractive vision, there are limits to the transformative potential of this vision of democracy. These limits derive from a range of factors, including the close affinity between deliberative and participatory democracy and representative government, the nature of South Africa's representative system, the reproduction of unequal power relations within deliberative and participatory spaces, the terms of discussion within deliberative and participatory spaces, the types of argument that are considered appropriate in them, and the tendency to conceive those processes in terms of a rational consensus.

In the first place, despite important differences, there is a significant degree of overlap between deliberative and participatory conceptions of democracy and more conventional understandings of representative democracy. While deliberative and participatory democrats seek to raise the bar for the legitimacy of exercises of public power, their proposals stay true to the basic representative framework of government. They complement and reinvigorate the idea of representative democracy by seeking to strengthen the lines of communication and ties of accountability between the people and their representatives; and tend to assume that existing institutions can be made more inclusive, representative, and accommodating of a diversity of needs and viewpoints. This helps to explain the capacity of deliberative and participatory ideals to take root in representative systems. However, it also accounts for the limited effectivity of attempts to bolster democratic accountability and responsiveness through the infusion of deliberative and participatory elements. For instance, in a number of cases, the Constitutional Court dismissed challenges to constitutional amendments that affected the boundaries of specific provinces, which were directly at odds with the public's views, as expressed during the public hearings facilitated by the relevant provincial legislatures.[68] These judgments confirm that, while legislatures are under a constitutional obligation to facilitate public participation, they are not bound by the views expressed by participants.[69] My point is neither that these views should be binding nor that modern societies should jettison representative government in favour of a form of direct democracy.[70] It is simply that there are limits to the capacity of public participation in the legislative process to institute a meaningful dialogue between the public and their representatives, particularly in circumstances where the governing party is so dominant that it can ignore the public's views without fearing that it will lose its majority in the next election.[71]

Secondly, deliberative and participatory forms of democracy are premised on the idea that democratic decision-making should not simply mirror extant power relations. They should rather emanate from open and inclusive processes that are characterised by informed discussion and the willingness of participants to listen to a diversity of viewpoints and to give publicly defensible reasons for their actions. These processes are meant to counter the distorting effects of private wealth and power on representative institutions. However, their capacity to do so is impaired by the tendency of these effects to be reproduced within official participatory spaces. Members of poor and marginalised groups, like women, children, the elderly, and people with disabilities are at a disadvantage in participatory spaces. They lack the power to determine the agenda and terms of engagement and their voices tend to be eclipsed by those of wealthy and organised elites, politicians, bureaucrats, and powerful members of their own communities.[72]

Thirdly, proponents of deliberative democracy often state that participants in deliberative processes must adopt an impersonal or impartial mode of reasoning. They should not appeal simply to their own identity or self-interest but should explain and defend their viewpoints with reference to reasons that transcend their own narrow interests. This is in line with the idea that the legitimacy of democratic institutions is based on reason and persuasion rather than tradition or strategic concerns. However, critics point out that the notion of impartial reasoning can have the opposite effect. James Tully argues that requiring participants to adopt a single mode of reasoning is likely to end up privileging the discursive practices of dominant groups. Portraying certain discursive practices as "universal" and "impartial" hides the extent to which they were shaped by cultural and historical conditions and affirm the views and life experience of particular groups. It also removes those practices and conventions from democratic contestation. As a result, discursive styles and practices that deviate from the "norm" are identified with partiality, particularity, irrationality, or weakness. This has a negative impact on the capacity of members of vulnerable groups to make their voices and viewpoints heard.[73]

Iris Marion Young is similarly critical of the idea that citizens should adopt a universal and impartial point of view when participating in public processes of deliberation. She claims that this idea rests on a public/private dichotomy, which seeks to confine the particularity of bodily needs, desires, and feelings to the private sphere. Once individuals enter the public sphere, they are expected to leave behind the "situational particularities" that are constitutive of who they are.[74] Instead, they must reason from a general point of view and apply universal principles. According to Young, the ideal of impartiality rests on a logic of identity rather than difference, as it seeks to reduce the multiplicity of different experiences and perspectives to the unity of a single "transcendental moral subjectivity".[75] Deliberative democratic theories that embrace an impartial and universal standpoint, which abstracts from the particularity of concrete participants, are therefore contradictory at heart. On the one hand, they commit themselves to open communication and the recognition of plurality, while on the other, their emphasis on impartiality threatens to reduce deliberation to the monological perspective of the "generalized other".[76] In Young's view, the ideal of impartiality privileges bureaucratic modes of decision-making over participatory alternatives, suppresses difference, and entrenches inequality and oppression "by hypostatizing the point of view of privileged groups into a universal position".[77] She argues instead for a heterogeneous public sphere, which allows participants to draw on their particular experiences and does not categorically exclude certain issues or persons from the public sphere.

Fourthly, it is sometimes argued that theories of deliberative democracy obscure ethical and political disagreement, due to their emphasis on the ideals of impartiality, universality, rationality, and consensus. Chantal Mouffe points out that the conception of politics in terms of the search for a rational consensus is predicated on the idea that substantive disagreement can be bracketed from public dialogue and decision-making. However, she argues that value conflicts are constitutive of politics and cannot be excluded from it. The creation of a vibrant, pluralistic public sphere should be grounded not in the proceduralisation of politics or the relegation of disagreement to the private sphere but in attempts to "constitute forms of power more compatible with democratic values".[78]

Finally, even though the infusion of democracy with dignity, equality, and freedom can enrich democratic discourse and help to resist closure, it can also divert attention away from failures of democratic accountability and the reproduction of material and structural inequality within the political sphere. That typically happens when dignity, equality, and freedom are construed in overly individualistic terms, or employed in the service of narratives that foreground the symbolic importance of the shift towards an inclusive South African citizenship.

I have argued elsewhere that the Constitutional Court's dignity-based construction of the right to vote accounts for some of the blind spots and anomalies in its voting rights jurisprudence.[79] Taking its cue from Sachs J's description in *August* of the right to vote as "a badge of dignity and of personhood",[80] the Court has subjected laws that disenfranchise discrete classes of voters to rigorous scrutiny, while showing considerably more restraint where restrictions that do not make it impossible or unduly difficult to vote are imposed under laws governing the mandate of representatives or regulating exercises of the vote.[81] When constitutional interpreters focus predominantly on the dignity of the affected classes of citizens, other relevant considerations, like the obligation on the state to take positive steps to facilitate its exercise, or the capacity of material and other forms of disadvantage to distort the equal representation of all citizens, may be lost from view. A richer, more deeply egalitarian construction of the right to vote is arguably needed, which views it as a mechanism for integrating citizens into the political community, a safeguard against social and political inequality, and a site of contestation and struggle.

The limits of an overly individualistic understanding of political rights are also evident from the *New Nation Movement* case, in which the Constitutional Court held that Parliament's failure to allow individual candidates who are not affiliated to a political party to contest national and provincial elections, violated sections 19(3)(b) (right to stand for public office and, if elected, to hold office) and 18 of the Constitution (freedom of association). The crux of Madlanga J's majority judgment is that freedom of association includes the right not to be forced to associate with others, that section 19(3)(b) must be read as far as possible in harmony with section 18, and that, based on that reading, the Electoral Act unjustifiably limits section 19(3)(b) by compelling individuals who wish to contest national or provincial elections to form or join a political party.[82] Jafta J's judgment, which was also concurred in by the majority, reaches the same conclusion by focussing on the ordinary meaning of the words used in section 19(3)(b).[83] Both judgments place the individual choices of potential electoral candidates at the centre of the enquiry, and give their rights a broad interpretation which is detached from questions about the electoral framework and accountability.[84] While the introduction of independent candidates could help foster greater electoral competition and accountability, the narrow focus on the rights of individual candidates and failure to situate those rights within the larger context of a representative system that is grounded in multiple, and at times, conflicting values,[85] limits the decision's transformative potential. Those features of the judgment have enabled Parliament to remedy the finding of unconstitutionality by means of a legislative amendment that allows independent candidates to contest elections, without addressing the root causes of political inequality and lack of democratic accountability.[86]

In sum, the reconceptualization of democracy along deliberative and participatory lines is not necessarily a remedy for all the ills associated with traditional understandings of representative democracy. On the one hand, deliberative and participatory spaces are not insulated from social, economic, political, and ideological power. Unequal power relations tend to be reproduced within deliberative and participatory settings and are partly constitutive of the discourse and interactions within these settings. On the other hand, deliberative and participatory understandings of democracy may at times mask those power relations through their emphasis on inclusive processes of democratic engagement that are geared towards reaching a rational consensus. Ironically, these ideals may have an exclusionary effect, to the extent that they privilege certain forms of engagement and discourse over others and under-emphasise conflict and disagreement. None of this detracts from the importance of democratic dialogue and participation; however, it suggests the need to stop side-stepping the power relations and suppression of difference that are at play in deliberative and participatory forums and to structure democratic spaces and processes to harness the capacity of conflict and difference to challenge and disrupt existing power relations.[87]

## 2.5 The gap at the heart of democracy

Democracy is a contested concept, which constantly wavers between different meanings, dimensions, and registers. As Giorgio Agamben points out, "democracy designates both the form through which power is legitimated and the manner in which it is exercised". It can therefore mean either "a way of constituting the body politic (in which case we are talking about public law) or a technique of governing (in which case our horizon is that of administrative practice)".[88] References to democracy thus fluctuate between the language of popular sovereignty and that of day-to-day government, between normative ideals like collective and individual self-government and descriptions of governance in societies nominally known as "democratic", and between the political and politics.[89]

Wendy Brown notes that the idea that the people rule themselves, which is central to democracy, is indeterminate. She states:

> Democracy is an unfinished principle – it specifies neither *what* powers must be shared among us for the people's rule to be practiced, *how* this rule is to be organised, nor by *which* institutions or supplemental conditions it is enabled or secured.[90]

It is because democracy refers to an unfinished principle that people from very different ideological persuasions and backgrounds can profess a shared commitment to it. They can ground it in different understandings of the relationship between the people and government, cast it in different institutional – and extra-institutional – moulds, and fill it with different content. For some, democracy requires a radical strengthening of the power of the people; for others, the thinnest veneer of popular consent as expressed through elections is sufficient to qualify a system as democratic. For some, democracy requires a radical redistribution of wealth and resources; for others, it is consistent with the prioritisation of market efficiency and profitability over all else. For some, globalisation requires a fundamental rethink of the basis of membership in the democratic community; for others, it demands the fortification of the boundaries that separate citizens from non-citizens. And so on and so on.

Disagreement over the objects of democratic decision-making, the identity of the people, the organisation of popular self-rule and the institutions through which it is to be secured hardly seems a solid grounding for a concept that is so central to the legitimacy of modern political orders. However, the indeterminacy of the concept of democracy does not come as a surprise. As Claude Lefort indicates,

> Democracy is instituted and sustained by the dissolution of the markers of certainty. It inaugurates a history in which people experience a fundamental indeterminacy as to the basis of power, law and knowledge, and as to the basis of relations between self and other.[91]

Democracy, on this view, marks a fundamental break with medieval society, in which the prince was the embodiment of power. The unity of the realm makes way for political division, social dissent, and uncertainty. The seat of power becomes "an empty place" that "cannot be occupied – it is such that no individual and no group can be consubstantial with it".[92] In Lefort's view, democracy is marked not only by the absence of organic unity but also by the lack of an Archimedean point that stands outside the plurality and conflict that constitute our social world.[93]

## 2.6 Conflictual democracy

Attempts to define and measure democracy in terms of compliance with formal and procedural requirements cannot come to terms with key features of modern democracy, such as the institutionalisation of conflict and indeterminacy.[94] These features also cast doubt on the ability of deliberative and participatory understandings of democracy to account for what is truly distinctive about democratic self-rule. It therefore seems helpful to introduce a third broad conception of democracy, which may be labelled "agonistic" or "conflictual" democracy. This understanding stresses the irreducible role of power, conflict, and antagonism in political life. It views power as constitutive of democratic interaction, whether it takes place in legislative assemblies, other deliberative forums, or on the street. As Mouffe points out, the institutions and practices that facilitate democratic interaction express a particular hegemony, and the identities of participants are constructed discursively and shaped by power relations.[95] In her view, the challenge is not to eliminate power from politics, but to allow a wide range of discourses, institutions, and practices through which conflicting articulations of freedom, equality, and democracy can be developed. It is only thus that democrats can hope to preclude any consensus from hardening into a totalising understanding of social relations.

Democratic decision-making is not only shaped by power relations but is also a determinant of social power. Advocates of a conflictual understanding of democracy recognise that every democratic decision produces an inside and outside. It includes certain people, social visions, and ways of being in the world into the legal and political order, while excluding others. It is therefore illusory to think that democracy can ever become fully inclusive. Democracy's outside is not a temporary obstacle on the way to a rational legal order based on universal inclusion but is constitutive of democracy. Exclusion, like power, is ineradicable. This does not preclude democratic challenges to the boundaries that separate the inside from the outside. However, even where these challenges give rise to the redrawing of the relevant boundaries, the result is a reconfiguration of the line between inclusion and exclusion, and not its erasure.[96] Conflictual democrats do not assume that struggles against inequality and domination will give rise to a perfect symmetry of power among citizens. On the one hand, there may be certain claims or demands that cannot be accommodated within a given legal order. On the other hand, the impact of victories attained through democratic struggles is often limited though their re-inscription into configurations of power that can accommodate the formal extension of rights to members of previously excluded groups, but resist fundamental challenges to current distributions of power, status, and resources.

Proponents of a conflictual conception of democracy are critical of the idea that democracy is or can be grounded in the search for a broad social consensus. In their view, consensus-based understandings of democracy ignore the central role played by power, conflict, and antagonism in democratic life. Conflictual democrats conceive democracy in terms of disagreement. According to Mouffe, the challenge is to convert antagonistic struggles between enemies into agonistic struggles between adversaries. Even though a basic consensus on certain fundamental values is indispensable, "such a consensus is bound to be a 'conflictual consensus'"[97] that invokes competing conceptions of democratic citizenship. Étienne Balibar notes a similar tension. He states that the rights of citizenship are established through conflicts between the "constitution" of citizenship and "the 'insurrectional' power of universalist political movements that aim to conquer rights that do not yet exist, or to widen the scope of existing rights".[98] Democratic citizenship is thus marked by a permanent tension between constituted and constituent power.[99] If it were to be reduced solely to the former, that is, if it were seen wholly in terms of the preservation of democracy, it would lose its power to interrupt, reinvent, and transform the status quo through new democratic struggles. Democracy and citizenship would become anti-political concepts that are stripped from their association with the self-renewal of the body politic.

The idea that conflict and disagreement are at the heart of democracy is closely connected to the insight that the identity of "the people" is essentially contested and incomplete. It is forever suspended between past moments of self-founding and future acts through which those assertions of collective identity are either negated or affirmed retroactively.[100] Or, to use Balibar's terminology, "the people" constantly wavers between the constitutional and insurrectional dimensions of citizenship. Jacques Rancière expresses the link between democracy and the instability of the line dividing "the people" from its constitutive outside quite provocatively. According to him, democracy generates spaces of appearance in which those who have no business to be heard in terms of current configurations of power are afforded the opportunity to declare a dispute.[101]

Conflictual understandings thus provide a nuanced account of the emancipatory possibilities and limits of democratic struggles. Because they stress the irreducible role of conflict, power, and division in politics, they reject the idea that the rules and processes that structure political life are neutral or reflect widespread agreement on the meaning of political ideals like equality, freedom, or citizenship. They also rebuff the belief that domination and inequality are vestiges of an exclusionary past that are about to be overcome in the name of democracy and universal human rights. Domination and inequality cannot be eradicated through the progressive unfolding of the inner logic of a democratic polity based on equality and freedom, but need to be resisted through democratic mobilisation, participation, contestation, and the development of alternative discourses and practices.[102] On this view, democratic values and institutions can only prosper in a polity characterised by rigorous contestation over the meaning and implications of its constitutive commitments.

Theorists of conflictual democracy are not only critical of accounts that ignore the role of conflict and power in the construction of "the people", but also tend to reject the notion that emancipatory struggles can be captured in terms of a meta-narrative that underscores a single form of oppression (e.g., class oppression) or privileges a single agent (e.g., the proletariat or "women"). They alert us instead to the wide range of relations of subordination. According to Mouffe, the challenge is to "establish a chain of equivalence among the different democratic struggles so as to create an equivalent articulation between the demands of women, blacks, workers, gays and others".[103]

Conflictual understandings of democracy provide a helpful frame for the analysis of important features of representative democracies, such as the institutionalisation of the idea of a parliamentary opposition and the existence of different centres of power.[104] The right to vote is also linked to the constitutive role of power and conflict. In her dissenting judgment in *NNP*, O'Regan J clearly articulates the link between the right to vote and political power. She states: "The right to vote is more than a symbol of our common citizenship, it is also an instrument for determining who should exercise political power in our society."[105] Denials of the right to vote cement the position of dominant groups and annihilate the rights of vulnerable groups and individuals, as the history of apartheid shows.[106]

Traces of conflictual democracy can also be found within participatory understandings of democracy. I have referred above to Ngcobo J's statement in *Doctors for Life* that the people "reserved for themselves part of the sovereign legislative authority that they otherwise delegated to the representative bodies they created".[107] In a democracy, all legitimate authority is grounded in the will of the people; however, who the people are and what they stand for is forever in contention. Because "the people" is incomplete, and because articulations of its will are subject to contestation, additional layers of participation need to be built into the democratic process to counter the disproportionate power of elites and to allow a plurality of voices to be heard and a wide range of viewpoints to be expressed.

This reasoning is not limited to public participation in invited spaces, where public authorities afford members of the public the opportunity to comment on, or to participate in public hearings on proposed laws or policies. It applies with equal force to collective forms of public action that take place outside those spaces.[108] Given the high incidence and intensity of protests in South Africa and the absence of a strong parliamentary opposition, it is not surprising that the right to assemble, to demonstrate, to picket, and to present petitions in terms of section 17 of the Constitution has been read through a conflictual-democratic lens.[109] In *Garvas*, the Constitutional Court stated that the right to freedom of assembly

> exists primarily to give a voice to the powerless. This includes groups that do not have political or economic power, and other vulnerable persons. It provides an outlet for their frustrations. This right will, in many cases, be the only mechanism available to them to express their legitimate concerns. Indeed, it is one of the principal means by which ordinary people can meaningfully contribute to the constitutional objective of advancing human rights and freedoms.[110]

The statement acknowledges that there are individuals and groups who, by virtue of their lack of economic and political power, effectively find themselves outside the bounds of representation. On this understanding, the formal status of citizenship alone does not guarantee meaningful political rights. Citizens' effective representation is also connected to economic, social, and political power. Moreover, the Court appreciates the need for forms of public action that occur outside the spaces that are officially designated for that purpose.[111] It recognises that protests and demonstrations may be the only way in which members of certain marginal and vulnerable groups can air their frustrations and make their voices heard. The fact that they are often confrontational supports an agonistic or conflictual democratic reading of the above statement.

The actual decision in *Garvas* can nevertheless be criticised from the perspective of a conflictual understanding of democracy. The case centred on the constitutionality of section 11(2) of the Regulation of Gatherings Act 205 of 1993, which concerns the civil liability of the organisers of a gathering for riot damage. To escape such liability, the organisers must prove that they could not reasonably have foreseen the damage and that they took all reasonable steps within their power to prevent it. The Court conceded that the section "significantly increases the costs of organising protest action" and may inhibit "poorly resourced organisations that wish to organise protest action about controversial causes that are nonetheless vital to society".[112] Despite that, it found that the limitation was justifiable in view of the importance of protecting individuals from riot damage, and the fact that the organisers of a gathering can track down and recover their loss from the actual perpetrators. The judgment has a potentially chilling effect on protests and constrains the ability of civil society organisations to create spaces in which disaffected citizens can make their views known.[113] However, its framing of the right as a mechanism through which marginalised individuals and groups can reclaim their agency and voice has paved the way for the judgments in *Mlungwana* and *Right to Know*, which invalidated incursions on protests.

In *Mlungwana*, the Court invalidated section 12(1)(a) of the Regulation of Gatherings Act, which criminalised a convenor's failure to give notice of a gathering. The Court relied on the reference in *Garvas* to the costs imposed by and deterrent effects of the legislation on the right to protest and held that the imposition of criminal liability inhibits exercises of the right rather than simply regulating them.[114] It concluded that the limitation was unjustifiable in view of the importance of freedom of assembly, the state's failure to show that the limitation served an important purpose (the Court stated inter alia that the state could not rely on a lack of resources to justify the limitation),[115] the sweeping nature of the provision, its impact on vulnerable groups, including children,[116] and the availability of less restrictive means. In *Right to Know*, the Gauteng High Court held that the City of Johannesburg's policy of levying fees for the holding of gatherings amounted to an unjustified infringement of section 17 and fell afoul of the constitutional requirements of legality and rationality. The judgment shows a keen awareness of the structural disadvantage faced by citizens who lack economic and political power and the susceptibility of protests to state repression. The Court noted the disproportionate impact of the policy on the poorest and most disenfranchised members of society who, ironically, "are precisely those who most rely on exercising the section 17 rights to make their voices heard",[117] and insisted that the state is constitutionally obliged to protect the safety of protestors – an obligation that is not subject to the payment of a fee.[118] The judgment is notable for its express rejection of the tendency to regard protests simply as a matter of security,[119] or to view the regulation of protests as the provision of a service that is subject to a neoliberal logic that reduces citizens to paying consumers.[120]

Despite the transformative potential of these judgments, marginalised individuals and communities who wish to participate in protests still face several obstacles, which derive inter alia from shortcomings in the Regulation of Gatherings Act and the policies, practices, and mindsets of municipalities and the police. Jane Duncan shows that municipalities use the notification procedure to impose onerous conditions and administrative burdens, discourage protests that are deemed radical, or are likely to highlight systemic government failures, and keep protestors under surveillance.[121] The problem is not only that local government and the state's security cluster cling to an outdated law-and-order approach to protests. The courts themselves tend to move back and forth between public order and democratic framings of the issues. *Garvas* offers the most obvious example; however, even the *Mlungwana* judgment could have done more to problematise the notification requirement, which in some cases serves little purpose and is often used by the state for improper ends.[122]

Judicial failures to provide rigorous protection to protests also derive from narratives about the constitutional transition, which emphasise the break between the apartheid legal order and the democratic legal order brought about by the Constitution. In *Hotz*, which involved an appeal against the granting of an interdict against students, the Supreme Court of Appeal juxtaposed the #FeesMustFall protests of 2016 to historical instances of civil disobedience (e.g., the refusal of Rosa Parks to sit on a bus seat reserved for black people or, in the South African context, the burning of passes). It claimed that those historical instances of civil disobedience involved "a challenge to an unjust or oppressive political and legal system, which is not present in our constitutional dispensation".[123] On this view, acts of civil disobedience engaged in today fall in a different category from resistance against apartheid before 1994. That is because, under a constitution which institutes democratic government and universal citizenship, the will of the people is the foundation of state authority and is no longer opposed to it. These narratives make sense if we view the constitutional transition through the lens of formal legal processes and institutions. However, when we widen our gaze to include the persistence of inequality, domination and exclusion, and the number and frequency of protests, the narratives appear overly legalistic, incapable of making sense of the continuity between the old and the new, and naïve in their presentation of constitutionalism as a linear progression towards a just and inclusive society. They validate the binary distinction made by state actors and the media between "authentic" citizens who participate in political spaces created by the state and "inauthentic" political actors pursuing their agendas outside those formal spaces.[124] This binary oversimplifies the struggles of community-based groups in poor and marginalised communities, which "move back and forth" between participation in formal (or invited) spaces and informal (or invented) spaces of resistance,[125] and furthers exclusion by casting those participating outside formal structures as prone to extremism and violence. Finally, the narratives in question underestimate the capacity of extra-institutional politics to disrupt the status quo and to help secure the democratic community's vitality and self-renewal.

Some of the judgments referred to above suggest that judicial review can assist in keeping multiple democratic spaces, discourses, and imaginaries in play. To that extent, it can help prevent the hegemony of a particular set of interests and ideological positions from congealing into something fixed and permanent. The converse is also true: judicial decisions can legitimise attempts to restrain alternative spaces and discourses. Judges are not untouched by the hegemony of certain interests or ideologies – as members of a legal-interpretive and professional community, their interpretations of legal materials are necessarily constrained by legal-interpretive conventions and the light that the "hegemonic ideology" casts upon them.[126] Even so, and despite the law's yearning for closure, the interplay between law and real-life conflicts and antagonisms produces a zone of indeterminacy and undecidability, in which judges must come to terms with the law's contingency and "inescapable violence".[127] Their decisions cannot resolve those conflicts once and for all, but they have a bearing on how "law shapes a given antagonism in its collective dimension",[128] and on the capacity of counter-hegemonic struggles to problematise and disrupt the status quo. Rafal Mańko states, with reference to Mouffe, that

> individual judicial decisions in conflicts between representatives of the antagonistic groups can be viewed as steps, more or less significant, more or less decisive, in their on-going struggle, as "temporary respites in an ongoing confrontation".[129]

Courts are not insulated from the effects of systemic inequality and disadvantage. Poverty, illiteracy, language barriers, administrative inefficiency, high legal fees, and insufficient access to legal representation impede the ability of impoverished individuals and communities to obtain judicial redress for violations of their rights.[130] Similar to other formal participatory spaces, courts have a disciplining effect on participants, who must not only acquiesce to the courts' authority, but must formulate their claims in technical legal language that abstracts away from their concrete everyday experience and only partially captures their struggles and demands. Participants in judicial and other formal participatory spaces thus risk diluting the disruptive nature of their politics.[131] And yet, court proceedings can sometimes destabilise existing power relations and help to open up spaces of contestation, reimagination, and critique. Julian Brown argues that litigation can expose the ways in which ostensibly neutral laws and policies favour the interests of wealthy and powerful elites. Moreover, he states, with reference to Rancière's conceptualisation of the relationship between politics and equality, that the formal equality afforded to parties to judicial proceedings sometimes empowers litigants to counterpose the lived experiences and knowledge of vulnerable groups and communities to the expertise wielded by the state and capital. That enables them to disrupt administrative and economic power by invoking "a radical understanding of political and intellectual equality", which resists the subjugation of local knowledge to technical and bureaucratic expertise.[132]

## 2.7 Decolonial imaginaries

Decolonial theorists call for a radical interrogation of norms, belief systems, and power relations that, having enabled and legitimated colonial domination, remain embedded in social structures and are reproduced through new discourses and strategies.[133] Their emphasis on the hegemonic quality of certain institutions, practices, and discourses in the postcolony and the need for counter-hegemonic movements and discourses resonates with conflictual understandings of democracy. However, the relationship between decolonial critiques and conflictual theories of democracy is complicated, as I will show towards the end of this section.

Some decolonial theorists argue that coloniality is constitutive of and pervades modernity. They point out that modernity is based on local European histories and concepts, which have come to be viewed as global designs. Laws, concepts, practices, and ways of being in the world that do not conform to these designs are labelled as pre-modern, and as instantiations of merely local histories that fall short of modernity's claims to universality. Modernity thus makes certain ideals, institutions, subjectivities, and knowledge systems appear incontestable and universally valid, while delegitimising others.[134] A radical questioning of key features of modernity is therefore required to liberate the law and society from the enduring effects of colonial power. These features include, but are not limited to, capitalism, liberalism, and the state.

Decolonial theorists note that capitalism and the state have acquired an air of inevitability, which obscures the specific social and historical settings in which they originated, and the various transformations that characterised their development. Liberalism has similarly dissociated itself from its historical and cultural roots, and has come to be seen as "an unsurpassable political horizon".[135] The hegemonic quality of these institutions and ideologies makes it difficult to acknowledge the failure of the state, capitalism, and civil society to shed their racial and class-based character, to confront the continued relegation of poor black people to a time and space outside modernity, and to perceive alternative ethical ideals and political and social visions. It masks the complicity of these institutions in global domination and inequality, as free market economies and Western understandings of democracy are imposed on countries across the globe, and as new forms of objectification and exclusion render populations unfree and disposable.[136] For these reasons, decolonial scholars believe that true emancipation from the strictures of modernity and coloniality requires radical critiques of the ways in which concepts and institutions like capitalism and the state enable and legitimate inequality and domination, and preclude alternative imaginations. On this view, it is important not only to be alert to the structural contradictions inherent in capitalism and the state, and their impact on the lives of vulnerable people, but also to decentre these concepts and institutions by drawing on alternative practices and forms of knowledge – including ones that are incommensurable with the epistemology of the state and the market.[137]

The continued exclusion of poor black people from true membership in society and meaningful participation in its economic and political spheres appears to be linked to the global context at the time of the constitutional transition, which favoured neoliberal globalisation, and the policies adopted by the government, which promoted financialization, liberalisation, and privatisation.[138] According to Boaventura de Sousa Santos, neoliberal governance developed as a mechanism to make law and government "resistant to two dangerous plagues: on one side, bottom-up, potentially chaotic pressures; on the other side, unpredictable changes in the rules of the game of capital accumulation brought about by state or inter-state regulation".[139] Neoliberal governance is designed to insulate capital from growing popular demands for redistribution and to weaken the capacity of the democratic process to bring about redistribution. It seeks to achieve these ends both by narrowing the scope of democratic politics, and by redrawing the boundaries of who is included in and excluded from participation in decision-making processes. On the one hand, it withdraws important matters from political decision-making. Its emphasis on self-regulation, problem-solving, coordination, and partnerships deflects attention away from social conflict, the broader public interest, and the need for social transformation, and goes hand in hand with the resolution of issues that were previously the subject of political disagreement and mobilisation through legal and technocratic expertise.[140] On the other hand, it favours participation by selected stakeholders over popular participation. The selection of liberal civil society organisations that do not challenge the neoliberal project, rather than counter-hegemonic movements that advocate alternative economic models or promote grassroots forms of democracy, narrows the range of participants, and excludes interests and ideological positions that can be expected to challenge the status quo.[141]

These developments have profound implications for the state and civil society. The state's sovereignty is compromised by the power and mobility of global capital, and by neoliberalism's preference for market-based outcomes and technical solutions. Moreover, the fixation on profit and the stability of markets and investments has devastating consequences for the citizenship and security of a rapidly growing underclass. The weakening of the state, the privatisation of social services, and the erosion of their social and political rights reduce members of this class to a constant state of anxiety and produce a highly stratified civil society, which is split between those who "enjoy high levels of social inclusion", those who are "utterly excluded", and those who "have mixed life experiences of social inclusion and of social exclusion".[142] The resulting patterns of "hyperinclusion and hyperexclusion"[143] undercut the idea of universal citizenship, and provide further justification for decolonial theorists' calls for the decentring of concepts like capitalism and the state.

Decolonial theory challenges us to escape from the strictures of modernist thought, with its focus on universal knowledge, technical mastery over nature, and centralised legal and political control. It dares us to "delink" from the available options, and to imagine alternative understandings of law, nature, personhood, distribution, social and political organisation, and the relationship between local, national, and global law.[144] It draws on subaltern difference to unsettle and disrupt the modern project. Decolonial scholars use the term "subaltern" to refer to identities, practices, and forms of knowledge that have been rendered exterior to modernity. They do not claim that these differences have been untouched by modernity – after all, their position "outside" modernity has been constructed through hegemonic discourses[145] – or that it is possible to return to them in their "pure" state. However, they raise the possibility that these exteriorities could challenge the system in the name of an ethical encounter with the Other and provide sites for the exploration of alternatives to the modern project.[146]

The emphasis on traditions, practices, and knowledge that have been sidelined by modernity is meant to occasion several shifts. The first is from the idea, rooted in the Enlightenment, of truth as unified and universal, to the recognition of a "pluriversality" of "cosmologies, epistemologies, and ways of life across and beyond what now constitutes the modern/colonial divide".[147] Once modern knowledge loses its monopoly on truth and Western worldviews forfeit their claim to universality, the project of social and political emancipation can be recast to recognise multiple discourses on justice and power, and a diversity of languages of human dignity and respect. Conflicting demands relying on different cultural traditions are no longer to be measured in accordance with a single metric of justice but can be situated within processes of cross-cultural dialogue and translation.[148]

A second shift concerns the importance given to local histories and practices, and specific social struggles. Decolonial thought takes issue with the close identification of law with the nation-state. It broadens its vision to include not only the national and global, but also the local scale. It is interested in the capacity of local histories and struggles to shed light on the tension between law's regulatory and emancipatory dimensions, to draw our attention to alternative understandings of legality and justice, and to give rise to alternative articulations of democratic struggles in the local, national, and global scales.[149]

Thirdly, the focus on marginalised and forgotten histories, discourses, and practices enables a reconsideration of the organisation of power within a democracy. In drawing on local histories and struggles and the experiences of counter-hegemonic social movements, decolonial scholars invoke the possibility of "democracy from below". For instance, contemporary counter-hegemonic social movements like Abahlali baseMjondolo are cited as examples of a model of organisation that is bottom-up, non-hierarchical, and based on respect for difference.[150] The civic movement during the 1980s, with its rootedness in local communities, commitment to bottom-up accountability and control, and participatory decision-making, is also juxtaposed to the top-down command structure of the African National Congress in exile, and held up as a valuable resource in reimagining democracy along participatory lines, and establishing direct forms of democratic accountability.[151]

Decolonial and conflictual understandings of democracy overlap in several respects. Both are critical of neoliberal modes of governance that depoliticise social issues and intensify exclusion and highlight the need for a multiplication of counter-hegemonic discourses, practices, and struggles. Their relationship is nevertheless complex. One possible criticism of conflictual accounts of democracy is that their emphasis on the ubiquity and intractability of conflict and power could make them lose sight of important historical and contextual differences. For example, the insight that power is constitutive of all democratic systems could divert attention away from the extent to which domination and inequality remain entrenched in post-apartheid South Africa. It could be used to normalise the persistence of those injustices by presenting them as simply another example of the pervasiveness of conflict and power. However, there is no reason why conflictual theories of democracy cannot engage critically with the historical particularity, nature, scope, and intensity of concrete forms and manifestations of power.

Secondly, and more fundamentally, conflictual understandings of democracy have strong roots in Western political modernity. It is therefore not surprising that some theories of conflictual democracy have been criticised for framing democratic ideals in ways that privilege dominant Western values, knowledge forms, and constructions of individuality and sociality. For example, Jakeet Singh claims that Mouffe's theory of agonistic democracy remains inscribed within Western notions of modernity. Mouffe's later work engages directly with decolonial themes and authors and is critical of attempts to impose Western conceptions of liberal democracy across the globe. However, Singh argues that, while her work "gestures towards difference" by recognising non-Western forms of modernity that are compatible with a radical understanding of democracy, it only accommodates difference as a "variation on an original European ideal type".[152] He further criticises Mouffe for largely ignoring the centrality of land to decolonial struggles in the Western settler colonies that she discusses, and for suggesting that liberal democracies cannot accommodate "claims made by Indigenous peoples – whether regarding shared relationship to the land, or issues of law, jurisdiction, governance, and/or authority – that are based in Indigenous frameworks or, in any case, are not couched in liberal-democratic terms".[153]

These criticisms raise important questions. Are conflictual conceptions of democracy equipped to come to terms with the different dimensions and layers of power – including the epistemic and ontological foundations of law – that enable and constrain challenges to inequality and exclusion? How far does their commitment to plurality go? Is their focus on indeterminacy, plurality, and conflict so intricately linked to Western notions of political modernity that they are incapable of accommodating understandings of personhood and forms of human association that appear, from that vantage point, as premodern? Can they come to terms with claims that are difficult or impossible to express in liberal-democratic language?

These are difficult questions, and for now, two observations must suffice. In the first place, there are limits to the capacity of any legal order to respond to certain challenges. Political communities are necessarily bounded – even if they are committed to values like pluralism and open and robust political contestation. Conflictual understandings of democracy draw attention to those limits and to the impossibility of a legal and political order that is fully inclusive and representative. They insist that every legal and political order has a remainder, which cannot be accommodated within the range of distributions of rights, roles, and spaces that it enables. Mouffe argues that agonistic theories that focus one-sidedly on the need to prevent closure fail to appreciate that a certain degree of closure is constitutive of the political and that a liberal democratic order needs to exclude demands that are irreconcilable with the conflictual consensus on which it is based.[154] While it is true that there are limits to pluralism, it could be asked whether Mouffe does not overemphasise the threats posed to liberal democratic institutions by individuals and groups who refuse to frame their demands in liberal-democratic terms. It has been suggested that that has something to do with her framing of agonistic politics with reference to Carl Schmitt's friend/enemy distinction. Mouffe argues that, in an agonistic democracy, the antagonistic relationship between friend and enemy must be transformed into an agonistic relationship between adversaries who recognise each other's right to advance their respective political positions. Even though her position differs fundamentally from that of Schmitt, the conservativism of his framing nevertheless shines through in her emphasis on the need to protect liberal democratic institutions from threats to their existence.[155] Other conflictual theorists recognise that there are forms of violence and cruelty that make politics impossible, but are careful not to rule out the possibility that encounters with what at first appear like anti-democratic demands may end up strengthening democracy and citizenship.[156] Balibar goes even further. He recognises that allowing dissidence sometimes risks anarchy or the destruction of the political community but insists that that is a risk we must be prepared to take, as the alternative – succumbing to the appropriation of all power by the dominant class or classes – spells the death of democracy.[157]

Secondly, conflictual theories of democracy could be deepened through engagement with decolonial and third-world critiques of dominant (Western) understandings of democracy and constitutionalism. Those critiques draw attention to remnants of colonial oppression that are rooted not only in conquest and dispossession, but also in knowledge structures and constructions of personhood, autonomy, and society that served historically to justify the subjugation of black people and other marginalised groups and continue to brand certain people, modes of knowledge, and forms of association as inferior. The point is not to construct a perfect synergy between conflictual understandings of democracy and decolonial and third-world critiques, but to use them with and against each other in thinking through the constitutive role of conflict and power, and the capacity of protests, struggles, and critique to draw attention to oppression and to politicise dominant constructions of the people and the objects of democratic decision-making.

## Notes

1 See Section 1.3 ("What is democratic about human dignity, equality, and freedom?").
2 These formal and procedural attributes include, in the words of section 1(d) of the Constitution, "universal adult suffrage, a national common voters roll, regular elections and a multiparty system of democratic government".
3 These assumptions and intuitions resonate with a variety of theoretical models of democracy, including what Held *Models of Democracy* 56–79, 125–157 refers to as the "protective model of democracy" developed by liberal thinkers like Jeremy

Bentham and James Mill and the "competitive elitist model" of Max Weber and Joseph Schumpeter. These theories see democracy in instrumental terms as a means to protect the private sphere from undue state interference, or in terms of a bargaining process between competing elites.

4 Even though "participatory democracy" and "deliberative democracy" refer to distinct traditions in constitutional and democratic thought, I will often use the terms together, as they overlap in important respects. See Bishop "Vampire or Prince" 321–323 on the relationship between the two terms.

5 The idea of participatory democracy was developed from the late 1960s by thinkers of the New Left like Carole Pateman, CB Macperson, and Nicos Poulantzas. See Macpherson *The Life and Times of Liberal Democracy* 103–105, 108–114; Pateman *Participation and Democratic Theory*; Held *Models* 209–216.

6 These ideas developed in the late twentieth century in reaction to the superficiality of dominant understandings of democracy. It was feared that those understandings reduce democracy to the registration of the majority's private preferences and fail to provide a basis for critical engagement with the role of political elites in shaping those preferences, the poverty of democratic debate, and decreasing levels of popular interest in the political process. See Habermas *Between Facts and Norms*; Benhabib "Toward a Deliberative Model of Democratic Legitimacy"; Held *Models of Democracy* 231–255.

7 See Laclau and Mouffe *Hegemony and Socialist Strategy*; Mouffe *The Democratic Paradox*; Balibar *Equaliberty*.

8 *New National Party v Government* para 24.

9 Para 19.

10 Para 126.

11 Paras 21–23.

12 Paras 37–47.

13 Para 126. See Roux *The Politics of Principle* 341–350 for a critique, and Fowkes *Building the Constitution* 50–74 for a positive appraisal of the majority judgment.

14 *Ex parte Chairperson of the Constitutional Assembly* para 186.

15 *United Democratic Movement v President* para 34.

16 Para 47.

17 Para 49.

18 Para 50.

19 See Roux *The Politics of Principle* 351–362; Choudhry "He Had a Mandate" 37–48. But see also Fowkes *Building the Constitution* 216–227 for a positive appraisal of the judgment.

20 *Democratic Alliance v Masondo* paras 42, 43. See also the dissenting judgment of O'Regan J at para 72, where she emphasises the need to "undo the separation, exclusion and inequality" that characterised local government in the past, through "shared involvement in deliberation".

21 Paras 43–45.

22 E.g., in *African Christian Democratic Party v Electoral Commission*, the Court preferred an interpretation of a legislative provision which promoted multiparty democracy and citizens' political rights over a more restrictive interpretation.

23 *Oriani-Ambrosini v Speaker* para 46.

24 Para 48.

25 Para 67.

26 *Mazibuko v Sisulu* para 44 (the right of a member of the National Assembly to initiate a motion of no confidence "is central to the deliberative, multiparty democracy envisioned in the Constitution"). See also *Democratic Alliance v Speaker* paras 11–17, 38–45 (a law allowing members of Parliament to be arrested for creating a disturbance while Parliament, a House or a committee is in session,

infringes parliamentary free speech, is inconsistent with the immunity of members from criminal proceedings, arrest, and imprisonment, and detracts from Parliament's nature as a deliberative body characterised by robust debate).

27 *Port Elizabeth Municipality v Various Occupiers* para 41.

28 Paras 39–43.

29 *Occupiers of 51 Olivia Road v City*; *Residents of Joe Slovo Community v Thubelisha Homes*; *Abahlali Basemjondolo Movement v Premier*.

30 *Occupiers of 51 Olivia Road v City* para 19.

31 *Residents of Joe Slovo Community v Thubelisha Homes* para 378.

32 Para 244. See Ray *Engaging with Social Rights* on the capacity of the Court's meaningful engagement jurisprudence to open up spaces for democratic participation.

33 See *Head of Mpumalanga Department of Education v Hoërskool Ermelo*; *Head of Department of Education v Welkom High School*.

34 See *Prince v President* paras 146–149, 155–156, 162, 170; *MEC for Education v Pillay* paras 71–83, 174, 177, 182.

35 Ss 57(1)(b), 70(1)(b) and 116(1)(b) authorise the National Assembly, the National Council of Provinces, and provincial legislatures, respectively, to "make rules and orders concerning [their] business, with due regard to representative and participatory democracy, accountability, transparency and public involvement".

36 Ss 59(1)(a), 72(1)(a) and 118(1)(a) provide that the National Assembly, the National Council of Provinces, and provincial legislatures, respectively, must "facilitate public involvement" in their "legislative and other processes", as well as those of their committees. S 74(5) and (6) requires bills amending the Constitution to be submitted for public comment, and the comments received to be tabled in the National Assembly and, where applicable, the National Council of Provinces. See also s 160(4)(b) in relation to municipal bylaws. S 195(1)(e) stipulates that "the public must be encouraged to participate in policy-making".

37 S 152(1)(e)).

38 S 19(1)(b).

39 *Doctors for Life v Speaker* paras 130–134.

40 Paras 118–129, 145–146.

41 Para 319.

42 Para 292.

43 Böckenförde "Demokratische Willensbildung und Repräsentation" 38.

44 *Doctors for Life v Speaker* para 110.

45 Para 115.

46 See paras 171 and 174 on the importance of adequate consultation with traditional healers, who have been sidelined in the past. See also Sachs J's concurring judgment at para 234 ("Public involvement will also be of particular significance for members of groups that have been the victims of processes of historical silencing. It is constitutive of their dignity as citizens today that they not only have a chance to speak, but also enjoy the assurance they will be listened to. This would be of special relevance for those who may feel politically disadvantaged at present because they lack higher education, access to resources and strong political connections").

47 *Matatiele Municipality v President* para 58.

48 Para 79.

49 *Land Access Movement v Chairperson* para 1.

50 Para 63.

51 Para 58.

52 *Mogale v Speaker* paras 61–81.

53 Not all the judgments refer to deliberative or participatory democracy. However, the Court's willingness in these cases to scrutinise what happens between elections

and to take account of contextual factors, like the ruling party's dominance, party discipline and corruption – in contrast to earlier decisions like *United Democratic Movement v President* – appears to have been enabled by the turn to a richer conception of democracy in *Doctors for Life* and other cases.

54 *Economic Freedom Fighters v Speaker* (2016) para 83.

55 Paras 97–99.

56 *Economic Freedom Fighters v Speaker* (2018). In his dissenting judgment, Mogoeng CJ at para 223 called the majority judgment "a textbook case of judicial overreach – a constitutionally impermissible intrusion into the exclusive domain of Parliament".

57 See Häberle "Die Menschenwürde als Grundlage der staatlichen Gemeinschaft" 351–352.

58 They also tend to engage in more purposive, value-based, and substantive forms of interpretation. The judgment of Ngcobo J in *Doctors for Life v Speaker* discussed above provides a good example. Conversely, the dissenting judgment of Yacoob J relied on grammatical and structural modes of interpretation and insisted that the Court must determine what the Constitution requires and avoid speculating about the ideal balance between democracy's representative and participatory dimensions. Paras 303–319. *New National Party v Government* and *United Democratic Movement v President* (discussed in 2.1 above) provide further examples of judgments that combine textualist interpretation with a formal conception of democracy.

59 In *Ramakatsa v Magashule*, the Court emphasised the role of political parties in helping to realise the right to vote (para 68), linked the legality of a political party's internal proceedings to the fairness of the elections through which voters elect representatives (para 17), and insisted that the constitutions and rules adopted by political parties must be consistent with the provisions in the Constitution (para 72).

60 *United Democratic Movement v Speaker* para 31.

61 Para 47.

62 Paras 81, 88.

63 Para 80.

64 Paras 83, 86.

65 Paras 7, 79, 86.

66 *My Vote Counts v Minister of Justice* para 33. See also paras 35–39.

67 Paras 45–52.

68 *Merafong Demarcation Forum v President*; *Poverty Alleviation Network v President*; *Moutse Demarcation Forum v President*.

69 *Merafong* para 50. See also *Residents of Joe Slovo Community* para 244.

70 See Menga "The Seduction of Radical Democracy" (a representative frame is better able to account for the indeterminacy and plurality that characterise democracy than the idea of direct democracy). See also Lindahl *Authority and the Globalisation of Inclusion and Exclusion* 181–185 (no participation is possible without a prior act of representation).

71 See Bishop "Vampire or Prince" 337–347; Choudhry "He Had a Mandate" 61–67; Botha "Representing the Poor" 529–533 for critical analyses of some of these judgments.

72 Hicks and Buccus "Crafting New Democratic Spaces" 104–106; Liebenberg and Young "Adjudicating Social Rights" 75; Mahomedy "Extra-Judicial Engagement in Socio-Economic Rights Realisation".

73 Tully "The Unfreedom of the Moderns" 223–225.

74 Young *Justice and the Politics of Difference* 100–101.

75 101.

76 106, 118 (referring to Benhabib, who argues that Habermas' thought vacillates between a dialogical understanding of morality, which reasons from the standpoint of the "concrete other", and Kantian universalism, which abstracts from the particularity of individual differences to focus on the "generalized other").
77 112.
78 Mouffe *The Democratic Paradox* 100.
79 Botha "Rethinking the Right to Vote" 502–506.
80 *August v Electoral Commission* para 17.
81 Cf the discussion of *New National Party v Government* and *United Democratic Movement v President* under 2.1 above.
82 *New Nation Movement v President* paras 16–64, 106–120.
83 Paras 163–171.
84 As recognised by Froneman J in his dissenting judgment at paras 96–98.
85 For example, there is a fundamental tension in a democracy between its collective dimension and the capacity of singular individuals to question conventional wisdom and initiate something new. If we highlight only the former, we privilege homogeneity over plurality and stasis over new beginnings. If, however, we focus only on the latter, we lose sight of the common world which provides the horizon for individual thought and action, and the importance in a democracy of dialogue, mobilisation, organisation, and collective action. See Menga "The Seduction of Radical Democracy" 313.
86 It was hoped that the judgment would lead to fundamental changes in the electoral system, particularly since the majority of the ministerial advisory committee appointed by the minister of home affairs favoured combining proportional representation with constituency-based voting. However, a far more limited option was chosen, which accommodates independent candidates whilst leaving the basic premises of the existing system of representation intact. The Electoral Amendment Act 1 of 2023 does not create constituencies, and thus does not make representatives more directly accountable to voters. It forces independent candidates to contest against political parties, which are generally far better resourced. There are also concerns that its provisions relating to the allocation of seats and filling of vacancies will favour big parties. See Mbethe "Electoral Reform in South Africa". In *One Movement South Africa v President*, the majority of the Constitutional Court held that the Act's signature requirements violated independent candidates' right to stand for public office. However, the Court rejected a challenge to the constitutionality of provisions dealing with the recalculation of seats where the surplus votes for an independent candidate are discarded or a seat occupied by an independent candidate becomes vacant.
87 See Mahomedy "Extra-Judicial Engagement in Socio-Economic Rights Realisation" 63–72.
88 Agamben "Introduction" 1.
89 See, on the distinction between the political and politics, Lefort *Democracy and Political Theory* 11.
90 W Brown "We Are All Democrats Now…" 45–46 (emphasis in the original).
91 Lefort *Democracy and Political Theory* 19.
92 17. See also Lefort *The Political Forms of Modern Society* 302–306.
93 Goldman "Beyond the Markers of Certainty" 32.
94 The same goes for the tendency of political scientists to reduce politics to social facts that are to be discovered through the gathering and analysis of social-scientific data (about public opinion, voter behaviour, etc.) Such an approach obscures ontological and epistemological questions from view, which relate to the underlying structures of modern political reality and the theoretical presuppositions that underpin the analyses of political facts. Goldman "Beyond the Markers of Certainty" 30.

95 Mouffe *The Democratic Paradox* 99–100.
96 Mouffe *The Return of the Political* 112–115.
97 Mouffe *The Democratic Paradox* 103.
98 Balibar *Citizenship* 37.
99 See Cachalia "Democratic Constitutionalism in the Time of the Postcolony" 380–381.
100 See Derrida "Declarations of Independence"; Lindahl "Constituent Power and Reflexive Identity".
101 Rancière *Disagreement* 26–27. See chapter 3.4 and 3.5 below; Brown *South Africa's Insurgent Citizens* 20–32.
102 Honig "Another Cosmopolitanism?" 111–115.
103 Mouffe *The Return of the Political* 77.
104 See Mouffe *Agonistics* 127 (a radical politics requires parliamentary and extra-parliamentary struggles to be combined to launch a joint "counter-hegemonic offensive against neo-liberalism"); Van der Westhuizen "Democratising South Africa" 86, 95–101 (in South Africa, protests are connected to attempts to keep elected representatives accountable, and the parliamentary activism of the Economic Freedom Fighters traverses the divide between representative democracy and radical democratic contestation).
105 *New National Party v Government* para 122.
106 Para 120.
107 *Doctors for Life v Speaker* para 110.
108 See *South African Transport and Allied Workers Union v Garvas* paras 12–13 and *Mlungwana v S* para 69 on the link between freedom of assembly and participatory democracy.
109 Conflictual-democratic themes have also been raised in the context of other rights, like freedom of expression and freedom of association. In *Pilane v Pilane* para 69, which involved a dispute about the proposed secession of a village from a traditional community, the Court stated that "there is an inherent value in allowing dissenting voices to be heard and, in doing so, permitting robust discussion which strengthens our democracy and its institutions". In *Economic Freedom Fighters v Minister of Justice* para 1, the Court stated that freedom of expression serves as "the virtual exhaust pipe through which even the most venomous of toxicities within may be let out to help them calm down, heal, focus and move on".
110 *South African Transport and Allied Workers Union v Garvas* para 61.
111 At para 63 note 29, the Court approvingly quotes Woolman's statement that freedom of assembly guarantees a space for political action in which "the will of the people is not always mediated by political parties and the elites that run them".
112 Para 57.
113 See Woolman "You Break It, You Own It" for a critique of the judgment.
114 *Mlungwana v S* paras 46–47. See also paras 87 and 88 on the section's chilling effect.
115 Paras 75–77.
116 Para 72.
117 *Right to Know v City Manager* para 75. See also paras 76–78.
118 Paras 47–49.
119 Para 98.
120 The Court at paras 32–34 rejected the argument that the municipality had the power to levy fees in terms of the Local Government Municipal Systems Act 32 of 2000, since it is not the primary legislation governing assemblies and gatherings and since the provisions of the Regulation of Gatherings Act must prevail in case of a conflict.
121 Duncan "South Africa's Doctrinal Decline on the Right to Protest" 235–242. She notes at 244 that, despite the invalidation of s 12(1)(a) in *Mlungwana v S*, the police often arrest protestors on other grounds that are "nebulous" and "often ill-conceived".

122 245.
123 *Hotz v University of Cape Town* para 72.
124 Miraftab "Feminist Praxis, Citizenship and Informal Politics" 208.
125 195.
126 Mańko "Judicial Decision-Making, Ideology and the Political" 183.
127 191.
128 186–187.
129 186.
130 Greenbaum "Access to Justice for All".
131 Brown *South Africa's Insurgent Citizens* 128.
132 145. See also 137–146.
133 Ballestrin "Coloniality and Democracy" 212. See also the discussion of decolonial critiques of the Constitution in chapter 1.7 above.
134 Mignolo "Geopolitics of Sensing and Knowing" 279.
135 Singh "Decolonising Radical Democracy" 338.
136 Escobar "Beyond the Third World" 213–216; Jooste "Surveillance Capitalism as White World Making".
137 221, 224; Singh "Decolonising Radical Democracy" 331–332.
138 Examples of neoliberal policies adopted in South Africa include the relaxation of exchange controls, lowering of company taxes, deregulation of industries, privatisation of social services, introduction of corporatist union arrangements, and use of cost recovery principles and discontinuation of essential services for non-paying customers. Bond "Constitutionalism as a Barrier to the Resolution of Widespread Community Rebellions in South Africa".
139 Santos "Beyond Neoliberal Governance" 40.
140 35, 37.
141 38–39. See also Madlingozi "Post-Apartheid Social Movements and Legal Mobilisation".
142 Santos *Toward a New Legal Common Sense* 457.
143 458.
144 Mignolo "Geopolitics of Sensing and Knowing" 274–278.
145 Escobar "Beyond the Third World" 218.
146 218–219; Singh "Decolonising Radical Democracy" 335.
147 Singh "Decolonising Radical Democracy" 351. See also Mbembe "Decolonising the University" 36–37.
148 Santos *Toward a New Legal Common Sense* 273–278, 474.
149 Escobar "Beyond the Third World" 225; Conway and Singh "Radical Democracy in Global Perspective" 703.
150 See Gibson "Upright and Free" 704–707; Madlingozi *Mayibuye iAfrika?* 161–197 for a discussion of Abahlali baseMjondolo. See also Santos "Beyond Neoliberal Governance" 46–47 for a discussion of the unique organisational features of the World Economic Forum.
151 Brooks, Ngwane and Runciman "Decolonising and Re-theorising the Meaning of Democracy" 25–29. See also Saul "On Taming a Revolution" 219–223.
152 Singh "Decolonising Radical Democracy" 340.
153 343.
154 Mouffe *Agonistics* 13–15.
155 Wenman "On the Risk and Opportunity in the Mouffean Encounter with Carl Schmitt"; Boonen "At the Outer Limits of Democratic Vision" 532–538.
156 Boonen "At the Outer Limits of Democratic Vision" 538–543.
157 Balibar *Equaliberty* 284–285.

## Bibliography

Agamben G "Introduction: Note on the Concept of Democracy" in G Agamben *Democracy in what State?* (2011) New York: Columbia University Press.

Balibar É *Equaliberty* (2014, translation J Ingram) Durham: Duke University Press.

Ballestrin L "Coloniality and Democracy" (2014) 5 *Revista Estudos Políticos* 210.

Benhabib S "Toward a Deliberative Model of Democratic Legitimacy" in S Benhabib (ed) *Democracy and Difference: Contesting the Boundaries of the Political* (1996) 67 Princeton: Princeton University Press.

Bishop M "Vampire or Prince? The Listening Constitution and Merafong Demarcation Forum & Others v President of the Republic of South Africa & Others" (2009) 2 *Constitutional Court Review* 313.

Böckenförde E "Demokratische Willensbildung und Repräsentation" in J Isensee and P Kirchhof *Handbuch des Staatsrechts der Bundesrepublik Deutschland Bd III* 3rd ed (2004) 31 Heidelberg: CF Müller Juristischer Verlag.

Bond P "Constitutionalism as a Barrier to the Resolution of Widespread Community Rebellions in South Africa" (2014) 41 *Politikon* 461.

Boonen C "At the Outer Limits of Democratic Division: On Citizenship, Conflict and Violence in the Work of Chantal Mouffe and Étienne Balibar" (2020) 33 *International Journal of Politics, Culture and Society* 529.

Botha H "Representing the Poor: Law, Poverty and Democracy" (2011) 22 *Stellenbosch Law Review* 521.

Botha H "Rethinking the Right to Vote" (2015) 26 *Stellenbosch Law Review* 486.

Brooks H, Ngwane T and Runciman C "Decolonising and Re-theorising the Meaning of Democracy: A South African Perspective" (2020) 68 *Sociological Review* 17.

Brown J *South Africa's Insurgent Citizens: On Dissent and the Possibility of Politics* (2015) Auckland Park: Jacana Media.

Brown W "We Are All Democrats Now…" in G Agamben (ed) *Democracy in what State?* (2011) 44 New York: Columbia University Press.

Cachalia F "Democratic Constitutionalism in the Time of the Postcolony: Beyond Triumph and Betrayal" (2018) 34 *South African Journal on Human Rights* 375.

Choudhry S "'He Had a Mandate': The South African Constitutional Court and the African National Congress in a Dominant Party Democracy" (2009) 2 *Constitutional Court Review* 1.

Conway J and Singh J "Radical Democracy in Global Perspective: Notes from the Pluriverse" (2011) 32 *Third World Quarterly* 689.

Derrida J "Declarations of Independence" (1986) 15 *New Political Science* 7.

Duncan J "South Africa's Doctrinal Decline on the Right to Protest: Notification Requirements and the Shift from Fundamental Right to National Security Threat" (2020) 10 *Constitutional Court Review* 227.

Escobar A "Beyond the Third World: Imperial Globality, Global Coloniality and Anti-Globalisation Social Movements" (2004) 25 *Third World Quarterly* 207.

Fowkes J *Building the Constitution: The Practice of Constitutional Interpretation in Post-Apartheid South Africa* (2016) Cambridge: Cambridge University Press.

Gibson NC "Upright and Free: Fanon in South Africa, from Biko to the Shackdwellers' Movement (Abahlali baseMjondolo)" (2008) 14 *Social Identities* 704–707.

Goldman S "Beyond the Markers of Certainty: Thoughts on Claude Lefort and Leo Strauss" (2011) 40 *Perspectives on Political Science* 27.

Greenbaum L "Access to Justice for All: A Reality or Unfulfilled Expectations" (2020) 53 *De Jure*.

Habermas J *Between Facts and Norms: Contributions to a Discourse Theory of Law and Democracy* (1996, translation W Rehg) Cambridge: Polity Press.

Häberle P "Die Menschenwürde als Grundlage der staatlichen Gemeinschaft" in J Isensee and P Kirchhof (eds) *Handbuch des Staatsrechts Band I: Grundlagen von Staat und Verfassung* 3 ed (2004) 317 Heidelberg: CF Müller.
Held D *Models of Democracy* 3rd ed (2006) Stanford: Stanford University Press.
Hicks J and Buccus I "Crafting New Democratic Spaces: Participatory Policy-Making in KwaZulu-Natal, South Africa" (2007) 65 *Transformation* 94.
Honig B "Another Cosmopolitanism? Law and Politics in the New Europe" in S Benhabib (ed) *Another Cosmopolitanism* (2006) 102 Oxford: Oxford University Press.
Jooste Y "Surveillance Capitalism as White World Making" (2021) 53 *Acta Academica* 44.
Laclau E and Mouffe C *Hegemony and Socialist Strategy: Towards a Radical Democratic Politics* (1985) London: Verso.
Lefort C *Democracy and Political Theory* (1988, translation D Macey) Oxford: Polity Press.
Lefort C *The Political Forms of Modern Society: Bureaucracy, Democracy, Totalitarianism* (1986) Massachusetts: MIT Press.
Liebenberg S and Young K "Adjudicating Social Rights: Can Democratic Experimentalism Help?" in H García, K Klare and L Williams (eds) *Social and Economic Rights in Theory and Practice: A Critical Assessment* (2014) 75 Oxon: Routledge.
Lindahl H "Constituent Power and Reflexive Identity: Towards an Ontology of Collective Selfhood" in M Loughlin and N Walker (eds) *The Paradox of Constitutionalism: Constituent Power and Constitutional Form* (2007) 9 Oxford: Oxford University Press.
Lindahl H *Authority and the Globalisation of Inclusion and Exclusion* (2018) Cambridge: Cambridge University Press.
Macpherson C *The Life and Times of Liberal Democracy* (1977) Oxford: Oxford University Press.
Madlingozi T "Post-Apartheid Social Movements and Legal Mobilisation" in M Langford, B Cousins, J Dugard and T Madlingozi (eds) *Socio-economic Rights in South Africa: Symbols or Substance?* (2014) 92 Cambridge: Cambridge University Press.
Madlingozi T *Mayibuye iAfrika? Disjunctive Inclusions and Black Strivings for Constitution and Belonging in "South Africa"*, unpublished thesis, Birkbeck, University of London (2018).
Mahomedy S "Extra-Judicial Engagement in Socio-Economic Rights Realisation: Lessons from #FeesMustFall" (2020) 36 *South African Journal on Human Rights* 49.
Mańko R "Judicial Decision-Making, Ideology and the Political: Towards an Agonistic Theory of Adjudication" (2022) 33 *Law and Critique* 175.
Mbembe A "Decolonising the University: New Directions" (2016) 15 *Arts & Humanities in Higher Education* 29.
Mbethe S "Electoral Reform in South Africa", report prepared for the Organisation Against Tax Abuse (OUTA) & My Vote Counts (MVC) (2022) https://www.outa.co.za/web/content/232269
Menga F "The Seduction of Radical Democracy: Deconstructing Hannah Arendt's Political Discourse" (2014) 21 *Constellations* 313.
Mignolo W "Geopolitics of Sensing and Knowing: On (De)coloniality, Border Thinking and Epistemic Disobedience" (2011) 14 *Postcolonial Studies* 273.
Miraftab F "Feminist Praxis, Citizenship and Informal Politics: Reflections on South Africa's Anti-Eviction Campaign" (2006) 8 *International Feminist Journal of Politics* 194.
Mouffe C *Agonistics: Thinking the World Politically* (2013) London: Verso.
Mouffe C *The Democratic Paradox* (2000) London: Verso.

Mouffe C *The Return of the Political* (1993) London: Verso.
Pateman C *Participation and Democratic Theory* (1970) Cambridge: Cambridge University Press.
Rancière J *Disagreement: Politics and Philosophy* (1999, translation J Rose) Minneapolis: University of Minnesota Press.
Ray B *Engaging with Social Rights: Procedure, Participation, and Democracy in South Africa's Second Wave* (2016) Cambridge: Cambridge University Press.
Roux T *The Politics of Principle: The First South African Constitutional Court, 1995-2005* (2013) Cambridge: Cambridge University Press.
Santos B "Beyond Neoliberal Governance: The World Social Forum as Subaltern Cosmopolitan Politics and Legality" in B Santos and C Rodríguez-Garavito (eds) *Law and Globalization from Below: Towards a Cosmopolitan Legality* (2005) 29 Cambridge: Cambridge University Press.
Santos B *Toward a New Legal Common Sense: Law, Globalization, and Emancipation* 2nd ed (2002) London: Butterworths LexisNexis.
Saul J "On Taming a Revolution" (2013) 49 *Socialist Register* 212.
Singh J "Decolonising Radical Democracy" (2019) 18 *Contemporary Political Theory* 331.
Tully J "The Unfreedom of the Moderns in Comparison to their Ideals of Constitutional Democracy" (2002) 65 *Modern Law Review* 204.
Van der Westhuizen C "Democratising South Africa: Towards a 'Conflictual Consensus'" in H Botha, N Schaks & D Steiger (eds) *The End of the Representative State? Democracy at the Crossroads* (2016) 75 Baden-Baden: Nomos.
Wenman M "On the Risk and Opportunity in the Mouffean Encounter with Carl Schmitt" (2014) 20 *Parallax* 88.
Woolman S "You Break It, You Own It: South African Assembly Jurisprudence after Garvis" (2015) 9 *Vienna Journal on International Constitutional Law* 548.
Young I *Justice and the Politics of Difference* (1990) Princeton: Princeton University Press.

## Case Law

*Abahlali Basemjondolo Movement SA v Premier of the Province of Kwazulu-Natal* 2010 (2) BCLR 99 (CC)
*African Christian Democratic Party v Electoral Commission* 2006 (5) BCLR 579 (CC)
*August v Electoral Commission* 1999 (3) SA 1 (CC)
*Democratic Alliance v Masondo* 2003 (2) SA 413 (CC)
*Democratic Alliance v Speaker of the National Assembly* 2016 (5) BCLR 577 (CC)
*Doctors for Life International v Speaker of the National Assembly* 2006 (6) SA 416 (CC)
*Economic Freedom Fighters v Minister of Justice and Correctional Services* 2021 (2) SA 1 (CC)
*Economic Freedom Fighters v Speaker of the National Assembly* 2016 (5) BCLR 618 (CC)
*Economic Freedom Fighters v Speaker of the National Assembly* 2018 (3) BCLR 259 (CC)
*Ex parte Chairperson of the Constitutional Assembly: In re Certification of the Constitution of the Republic of South Africa 1996* 1996 (4) SA 744 (CC)
*Head of Department, Department of Education, Free State Province v Welkom High School* 2013 (9) BCLR 989 (CC)
*Head of Mpumalanga Department of Education v Hoërskool Ermelo* 2010 (3) BCLR 177 (CC)
*Hotz v University of Cape Town* 2017 (2) SA 485 (SCA)

*Land Access Movement of South Africa v Chairperson of the National Council of Provinces* 2016 (5) SA 635 (CC)
*Matatiele Municipality v President of the Republic of South Africa* 2007 (1) BCLR 47 (CC)
*Mazibuko v Sisulu* 2013 (11) BCLR 1297 (CC)
*MEC for Education: KwaZulu-Natal v Pillay* 2008 (1) SA 474 (CC)
*Merafong Demarcation Forum v President of the Republic of South Africa* 2008 (5) SA 171 (CC)
*Mlungwana v S* 2019 (1) BCLR 88 (CC)
*Mogale v Speaker of the National Assembly* 2023 (6) SA 58 (CC)
*Moutse Demarcation Forum v President of the RSA* 2011 (11) BCLR 1158 (CC)
*My Vote Counts NPC v Minister of Justice and Correctional Services* 2018 (8) BCLR 893 (CC)
*New Nation Movement NPC v President of the Republic of South Africa* 2020 (6) SA 257 (CC)
*New National Party of South Africa v Government of the Republic of South Africa* 1999 (3) SA 191 (CC)
*Occupiers of 51 Olivia Road, Berea Township v City of Johannesburg* 2008 (5) BCLR 475 (CC)
*One Movement South Africa NPC v President of the Republic of South Africa* 2024 (3) BCLR 364 (CC)
*Oriani-Ambrosini v Speaker of the National Assembly* 2012 (6) SA 588 (CC)
*Pilane v Pilane* 2013 (4) BCLR 431 (CC)
*Port Elizabeth Municipality v Various Occupiers* 2005 (1) SA 217 (CC)
*Poverty Alleviation Network v President of the Republic of South Africa* 2010 (6) BCLR 520 (CC)
*Prince v President of the Law Society of the Cape of Good Hope* 2002 (2) SA 794 (CC)
*Ramakatsa v Magashule* 2013 (2) BCLR 202 (CC)
*Residents of Joe Slovo Community, Western Cape v Thubelisha Homes* 2010 (3) SA 454 (CC)
*Right to Know Campaign v City Manager of Johannesburg Metropolitan Municipality* 2022 (5) SA 570 (GJ)
*South African Transport and Allied Workers Union v Garvas* 2013 (1) SA 83 (CC)
*United Democratic Movement v President of the Republic of South Africa* 2003 (1) SA 488 (CC)
*United Democratic Movement v Speaker of the National Assembly* 2017 (8) BCLR 1061 (CC)

# 3 Towards a conflictual democratic reading of dignity, equality, and freedom

Constitutional interpretation is deeply political, as pointed out in the previous two chapters. In the first place, constitutional norms, rights, and values are constitutive of the legal and political order, and their interpretation plays an important part in constructing and redefining the boundaries of the political community. Secondly, constitutional interpretation goes hand in hand with public processes of contestation and dialogue, which go beyond the courtroom. When political antagonism and social struggles spill over into constitutional litigation, courts are asked to interpret, synchronise, and concretise constitutional norms and values. Thirdly, judges who perform that task invariably make contestable value choices – in framing the issues, interpreting the relevant legal materials, and bringing general norms to bear on the specificity of the disputes before them.

In this chapter, I reflect on the capacity of value-based constitutional interpretation to challenge hierarchy, disrupt entrenched power relations, and provide spaces for the articulation of alternative social visions, while remaining alert to its power to induce closure, depoliticise challenges against domination and inequality, and naturalise the status quo. I start by examining and critiquing three assumptions about value-based interpretation that are not conducive to a critical, transformative jurisprudence. The first assumption is that we can neutralise the politics of value-based interpretation if we find the right key to the meaning of constitutional values or the correct method for harmonising them with each other. I argue that neutral principles – or any other method that seeks to provide an objective basis for constitutional adjudication – are incapable of resolving the politics of interpretation. While it is understandable that judges would find the idea of such a method attractive in view of the judiciary's institutional position and need for legitimacy, the language of neutrality is best avoided, as it typically draws on hegemonic beliefs and power relations and shields them from critical scrutiny. The second assumption is that we can defuse the politics of interpretation by subsuming the particularity of conflict and strife under universal categories. I argue that this assumption over-simplifies the relationship between universal principles and particular contexts. A more nuanced understanding of the interplay between them can provide the basis for a better appraisal of the possibilities and limits of attempts to overcome inequality and exclusion in the

DOI: 10.4324/9781003482451-4

name of universal rights and principles. Thirdly, I raise critical questions about the ability of Dworkin's notion of law as integrity to guide the development of a transformative post-apartheid jurisprudence. I argue that this notion, with its twin criteria of justification and fit, is ill-equipped to resist the infiltration of inegalitarian and exclusionary concepts, assumptions, and ideologies into understandings of constitutional rights and values.

The chapter's emphasis on the political nature of constitutional interpretation and interest in its capacity both to politicise and depoliticise social hierarchies invites questions about the meaning of the political. Restrictive understandings of the political serve to shield domination and inequality from democratic contestation and critical inquiry by removing certain issues, spaces, and relationships from what is considered political, and making it difficult for certain subjects to enter the public-political sphere. I first criticise those understandings and argue that the dividing line between the political and nonpolitical and between political subjects and those who have no business participating in democratic politics is unstable and is itself subject to democratic contestation. The ability of constitutional discourse to respond to struggles for dignity, equality, and freedom depends in part on its openness to the disruptive capacity of challenges to current distributions of wealth and configurations of power. Thereafter, I consider the relationship between dignity, equality, and freedom. How must we understand the unity of these values if not in the language of neutral principles, integrity, or oversimplistic understandings of the relation between their universality and the particularity of the contexts on which they are brought to bear? I argue that the tension between the radical promise of these values and the inequality, exclusion, and domination that are produced by the discourses, practices, and representations through which they are institutionalised provides a more promising starting point.

## 3.1 Beyond neutral principles

Laurie Ackermann, the former Constitutional Court judge, has argued that a dignity-based interpretation of equality and freedom provides a common measure of value which can enable judges to mediate constitutional value conflicts in a neutrally principled manner.[1] On this view, dignity provides the foundation for an equality jurisprudence that turns not on the identity of the parties before the court, but on neutral and general principles which extend beyond the confines of a specific case.[2] The idea of neutral principles is derived from an article by Herbert Wechsler. The article was fuelled by the perceived activism of the United States Supreme Court under Chief Justice Warren, which, in Wechsler's view, raised questions about the undemocratic nature of the power of unelected judges to set aside decisions of the legislature and executive. Wechsler sought to place judicial review on a more secure footing by arguing that judicial decision-making should be based on a form of practical reason that rests not on judges' personal preferences, but on a reasoned elaboration of general principles. His critique of the Warren Court rests on a formal understanding of equality and a formalistic conception of judicial review, which do not provide an appropriate starting point for conceptualising equality under the South African Constitution.[3] However, Ackermann seeks to inscribe the idea of neutral principles within a more substantive conception of equality and legal reasoning. He emphasises that neutrality, in the sense he uses it, does not mean that judges can avoid making value judgments.[4] Unlike Wechsler, he does not believe that an inquiry into the impact of potentially discriminatory measures on those affected invariably crosses the line between adjudication and politics. Judges, in his view, can consider the practical, psychological, and material harm caused by discrimination and still act in a principled way – provided that their inquiry is filtered through the neutral principle of dignity.

There are, however, reasons to doubt whether a dignity-based interpretation of the right to equality can truly escape the politics of constitutional adjudication. Equality is a deeply contested concept, and a single theory or interpretation of equality is unlikely to remove it from political contention – particularly in a country where the equality clause bears the imprint of a variety of ideological influences.[5] Judicial disagreement in equality cases is often based not on irreconcilable principles or methodological differences, but on divergent constructions of power, individual choice, social stigma, moral blame, and law's relationship with social attitudes. For instance, in the *Jordan* case, judges of the Constitutional Court disagreed about the question whether a provision which criminalised the conduct of sex workers but not that of clients, discriminated indirectly on the ground of gender.[6] The majority and minority judgments could both be justified in terms of general and neutral principles. The majority judgment could be explained as follows:

> Facially neutral differentiation that affects one sex more than the other does not discriminate indirectly based on sex or gender if it does not impose a significantly greater burden or disadvantage on the former, and if any impairment of the complainants' dignity results not from the differentiation but from their own choice.

On the other hand, the principle governing the minority judgment could be expressed thus:

> Facially neutral differentiation that has a disproportionate impact on either males or females discriminates indirectly based on sex or gender if it has the potential to impair the complainants' dignity, to the extent that it is grounded in and reinforces sexual stereotypes which demean either of the sexes.

Both principles are general and neutral, and both seem unobjectionable when formulated at that level of abstraction. The split between the majority and minority in *Jordan* arose not from disagreement about the principles governing the case but from their application of those principles. They differed about the significance of the fact that most sex workers are women. They disagreed about the causes of the impairment of sex workers' dignity and about whether the legislation reinforced stereotypes that are demeaning to women. Since their disagreement stemmed from divergent social visions and ideological assumptions, it could not be neutralised through recourse to widely shared legal principles.

A second example that casts doubt on the ability of neutral principles to defuse the politics of interpretation derives from Ackermann's discussion of conflicts between freedom of testation and the right not to be unfairly discriminated against. In his view, a dignity-based approach enables constitutional interpreters to make a principled distinction between legitimate exercises of personal and associational freedom and instances of private discrimination that violate somebody's equal moral worth and citizenship. By comparing the impact of private discrimination on the dignity of the plaintiff with the impact of a limitation of the defendant's freedom on her dignity, a court can arrive at a reasoned and principled decision.[7] For him, much depends on whether a testamentary clause that discriminates on the ground of race, gender, or religion causes the complainant to suffer a public indignity. For instance, he claims that where a testator who believes in male primogeniture leaves 1% of his estate to his daughter and 99% to his son, his freedom of testation should outweigh the indignity suffered by his daughter, since that indignity does not occur in the public domain.[8] Ackermann further argues, with reference to the *Syfrets Trust* case, that a will that restricts eligibility for bursaries for tertiary education to male, non-Jewish students of European descent, has little or no impact on the dignity of female, Jewish or non-European students, as they had no pre-existing right to benefit and as the will does not interfere with the free development of their personality.[9] He thus construes the disadvantage and exclusion that can arise from discriminatory testamentary provisions quite narrowly. In his view, it is only where a testamentary provision results in the public humiliation of a person or category of persons, or where a prior right exists to benefit from the will, that there would be an impairment of the dignity of those excluded. Even then, that indignity would sometimes be outweighed by freedom of testation.

Ackermann's proposed mediation of the conflict between freedom of testation and the right against unfair discrimination could be called "neutrally principled" to the extent that it invokes a general principle, which can be applied without reference to the identity of the parties before the court. However, it is possible to think of rival principles that rest on a plausible construction of human dignity that are similarly "neutral". For instance, it could be argued that the public or private nature of a testamentary disposition should be decisive. That was arguably the basis for a range of judgments in which it was held that testamentary provisions that restricted eligibility for bursaries under a charitable trust on the basis of race and/or other prohibited grounds were against public policy.[10] Alternatively, it could be maintained that, regardless of the public or private nature of the disposition, it is impermissible to discriminate on prohibited grounds against someone – like a bursary applicant or a future descendant – that is not known to the testator.[11] Similar to Ackermann's proposed principle, these two principles could be said to distinguish between permissible and impermissible forms of discrimination by attempting to strike a balance between the impact of a discriminatory testamentary clause on the dignity of those excluded, and the impact of a limitation of freedom of testation on the testator's dignity.

In this example, unlike the first, the disagreement extends to the validity of the principles proffered, and the question which of them best gives effect to the constitutional values of human dignity, equality, and freedom. The disagreement cannot be resolved on neutral grounds, as it arises from different articulations of dignity, equality and freedom, and different constructions of the public/private distinction. Importantly, the disagreement also results from different understandings of the types of harm that should be considered. Ackermann conceives harm in individualistic terms, while the rival principles appear to provide more scope for considering the potential of testamentary clauses to perpetuate material and structural disadvantage. They arguably also allow judges to take account of the symbolic effects of judicial findings upholding the validity of bequests that are informed by prejudice and stereotypes. For these reasons, it can hardly be claimed that any of the above constructions of harm and attempts to balance countervailing rights are politically or ideologically neutral.

Thirdly, judicial disagreement over the constitutional requirements for programmes aimed at remedying the inequalities of the past also casts doubt on the capacity of a dignity-based approach to provide neutral principles that can defuse the politics of interpretation. The Constitutional Court held in *Van Heerden* that whether a remedial programme falls within section 9(2) depends on three questions: i) whether it "targets persons or categories of persons who have been disadvantaged by unfair discrimination"; ii) whether it is "designed to protect or advance such persons or categories of persons"; and iii) whether it "promotes the achievement of equality".[12] A programme that complies with these requirements does not trigger the presumption of unfairness under section 9(5), even if it discriminates on listed grounds.[13] It is not clear what role the dignity of the complainants should play under this standard. On the one hand, remedial measures must promote the overall achievement of equality – a goal which, in the view of the Court, is linked closely to respect for human dignity.[14] The dignity of the complainants therefore places limits on the state's power to institute remedial measures. On the other hand, as Mokgoro J indicated in her minority judgment in *Van Heerden*, the primary focus of section 9(2) is not on the impact of the alleged discrimination on the complainants, but on the group of beneficiaries and the mechanisms used to advance them.[15] That places the tension between the dignity of the complainants and the dignity of people disadvantaged by past discrimination at the heart of the constitutional equality clause. Closely related to that is a second tension: between ensuring that remedial measures remain within constitutional bounds and allowing the state sufficient latitude in redressing past discrimination.

These tensions are reflected in judicial pronouncements on the meaning of section 9(2). For instance, in *Barnard*, the judges differed on the judicial standard to be used in testing the implementation of an Employment Equity (EE) plan in a case in which a white female police officer was not promoted to a higher position, despite being recommended by the interviewing panel as the most suitable candidate. In his majority judgment, Moseneke ACJ recognised that remedial measures must not be "punitive" or "retaliatory",[16] and must not infringe the dignity of either the previously advantaged or disadvantaged.[17] He further held that the validity of the implementation of a validly adopted EE plan can be tested and that, as a minimum, there must be a rational connection between the implementation and the terms and objects of the measure.[18] In a separate concurring judgment, Cameron J, Froneman J and Majiedt AJ argued that a mere rationality standard is too deferential, and that fairness is a more appropriate standard. A fairness standard requires decision-makers to give adequate reasons for their decisions. It thus encourages them to justify how they balanced considerations like representativity and service delivery,[19] and to indicate whether and to what extent they factored different categories of disadvantage (like race and gender) into the decision.[20] In their view, this standard is more protective of the dignity of the individual. While it does not rule out reliance on broad social categories like race as a means of redressing past disadvantage, it requires a decision-maker to take account of the "relevant aspects of a candidate's identity",[21] and to explain why it privileged one form of representativity over another. It is therefore more consonant with the idea that every individual deserves to be treated as a unique human being who cannot and should not be reduced to a single identity.[22]

In another concurrence, Van der Westhuizen J noted that Ms Barnard's dignity would be infringed if she were to be treated as a mere means to an end,[23] or if the EE plan were to be implemented in a way that obliterated her chances of advancing in her career.[24] After noting that dignity connotes the value of the individual, the idea that every person should be treated as an end in herself, her sense of self-esteem and her right to develop her talents, he pointed out that dignity also concerns the interdependence of members of the community and the idea that the dignity of all South Africans can be enhanced by measures aimed at remedying the deprivation and disadvantage caused by discriminatory laws and practices.[25] He rejected the idea that the dignity of millions of black people who were discriminated against under apartheid can be weighed up against the dignity of an unsuccessful white female applicant, but held that it should be asked whether her dignity was impacted on disproportionately.[26]

The judicial disagreement in *Barnard* highlights the difficulties inherent in trying to strike an appropriate balance between the dignity of beneficiaries of affirmative action and the dignity of those who feel aggrieved by its implementation. On the one hand, the application of a rationality test appears to load the dice too much in favour of the validity of the remedial measures chosen by the state.[27] On the other hand, more exacting standards also run into problems. For instance, proponents of a proportionality standard disagree about whether a fully fledged or diminished proportionality test is called for. Sachs J in his separate judgment in *Van Heerden* argued for the latter. Such a proportionality standard would be offended by a measure that "is manifestly overbalanced in ignoring or trampling on the interests of members of the advantaged section of the community, and gratuitously and flagrantly imposes disproportionate burdens on them".[28] Rather than tilting the scales too much in favour of the status quo and undermining the rationale behind the inclusion of section 9(2), it recognises that the balance needs to be "heavily weighted in favour of opening up opportunities for the disadvantaged".[29] By contrast, Ackermann proposes a strict proportionality standard, which, in his view, would be better equipped to protect the dignity of complainants and to prevent remedial programmes from imposing undue burdens on the previously advantaged. Such a proportionality test must include the question whether the objective of the measures could be achieved through means that are less restrictive of the rights of those adversely affected by them.[30] In addition, the measures must be restorative in nature and must not be aimed at achieving distributive justice.[31]

The above disagreements are not simply doctrinal in nature, but reflect deeper differences relating to the balance between two constitutional imperatives: the right of every individual to be treated as a unique human being entitled to respect for her inherent dignity and worth; and the need to remedy the lingering effects of past discrimination through measures that must inevitably rely on certain historical generalisations and abstract from the multiple differences between people. That dignity features on both sides of the debate does not make matters any easier, as it is not clear how we are to weigh up the dignity of an individual complainant against the dignity of millions of people who were discriminated against in the past. As with the second example, there are different mediations of these tensions that could qualify as neutrally principled, in the sense proposed by Wechsler and Ackermann. However, the language of neutral principles is likely to impose a heavier burden of justification on judges who uphold the constitutionality of robust remedial measures. That is because what is "neutral" tends to be defined from the baseline of current distributions of wealth and resources and from an individualistic vantage point. Those perspectives overlook the structural nature of inequality, construe historical conquest and dispossession by analogy to private wrongs, and privilege "stability" and "normality" over change.[32] They thus disregard the need for measures that are able not only to redress past patterns of material deprivation, but to destabilise cultural stereotypes and normative expectations that continue to circumscribe the life chances of large parts of the population.[33]

Neutral principles cannot defuse the politics of law. They appear ideologically neutral precisely because they are based on conventional values and assumptions that are taken for granted within the dominant legal and political culture.[34] They reflect hegemonic norms, which, for the most part, remain unarticulated and operate largely in the background, and which, for that very reason, play a powerful role in constraining the legal imagination, and rendering certain forms of disadvantage natural, normal, or invisible.[35] In the words of Patricia Williams:

> Racial discrimination is powerful precisely because of its frequent invisibility, its felt neutrality … Racism inscribes culture with generalized preferences and routinized notions of propriety … It empowers the mere familiarity and comfort of the status quo by labelling that status quo as "natural".[36]

The framing of anti-discrimination law and remedial equality in terms of neutral principles of adjudication must be viewed with suspicion. What seems neutral to South African lawyers will often be the result of their internalisation of a conception of law that is steeped in individualism, privatism, and legal formalism, and precludes alternatives that are more deeply transformative.

### 3.2 Rethinking the universal

The story of South Africa's constitutional transition is typically recounted in terms of a shift away from a divided past in which citizenship and the basic rights associated with it were denied to black people, towards "a future founded on the recognition of human rights, democracy and peaceful co-existence and development opportunities for all South Africans, irrespective of colour, race, class, belief or sex".[37] Several oppositions are at play in this narrative. These include the oppositions between the racial exclusivity on which the apartheid state was premised and an encompassing South African citizenship; between a racial oligarchy and a system of government that is based on the will of the people; between violent conflict and peaceful co-existence; and between the systematic denial of the humanity of black people and the recognition of universal and equal human rights. These oppositions could be reduced to a single conflict: between the violent, reductive particularisms that characterised the legal and political order under colonialism and apartheid, and the commitment to the universality of human rights, citizenship, and the vote that are constitutive of the post-apartheid constitutional order. On this account, the Constitution resorts to universalistic moral and political ideals in its quest to reconstitute and transform the state and political community. Or rather, it articulates these universalistic ideals with a particular vision of the colonial and apartheid past, and of the social and political struggles that led to the demise of the apartheid state.

This articulation of the particular with the apartheid past, and of the universal with the constitutional future resonates with the aspirational statements contained in the preamble and epilogue to the interim Constitution and the preamble to the 1996 Constitution. It also appears to be borne out by constitutional provisions that enunciate foundational values like human dignity, equality, freedom, non-racialism, and non-sexism,[38] and provide for a common citizenship[39] and universal adult suffrage.[40] Moreover, it seems to be supported by judicial pronouncements that link the Constitution's break from a history of inequality, domination, and conflict to its universalistic tendencies. Consider, for example, the following two statements by the Constitutional Court:

> After a long history of "deep conflict between a minority which reserved for itself all control over the political instruments of the state and a majority who sought to resist that domination", the overwhelming majority of South Africans across the political divide realised that the country had to be urgently rescued from imminent disaster by a negotiated commitment to a fundamentally new constitutional order premised upon open and democratic government and the universal enjoyment of fundamental human rights.[41]
>
> [The Constitution] retains from the past only what is defensible and represents a decisive break from, and a ringing rejection of, that part of the past which is disgracefully racist, authoritarian, insular, and repressive and a vigorous identification of and commitment to a democratic, universalistic, caring and aspirationally egalitarian ethos, expressly articulated in the Constitution.[42]

I do not want to diminish the importance of the shift towards universal human rights and citizenship. However, the above juxtaposition of the universal and particular rests on several oversimplifications, which are not helpful in thinking through the emancipatory potential and limits of constitutional interpretation. In the first place, the identification of emancipatory ideals with the universal and inequality and exclusion with the particular does not tell the full story. Exclusionary political ideals and practices often have a universalizing element. For instance, Aletta Norval notes that, even though apartheid originated within and served the interests of a particular racial and ethnic community, it was transformed into a universal prescript: that the protection of that which is particular to a specific *volk* must be the basis for the organisation of all communities.[43] Patriarchy and sexism do not rest exclusively on claims about a particular culture or way of life either, but tend to universalise certain understandings of the differences between men and women and the place of women within the family and society.[44]

Secondly, it is problematic to pretend that the universal could be completely disentangled from its ties with the particular. Étienne Balibar points out, with reference to Hegel, that there is no absolute or privileged position outside discourse from which we can evaluate different articulations of the universal, and that the enunciation of the universal can never be detached from a particular time, place, and conditions. He writes: "By simply stating the universal, or by speaking in the modality of the universal, one immediately, irremediably, finds oneself in extreme particularity".[45] He further notes the paradox that attempts, such as those grounded in Enlightenment thought, to extricate the universal from any particular context, tend to have the opposite effect as they end up relying on "an image of man and the human that suppresses a whole unconscious portion of itself".[46] Ironically, such attempts make it more likely that "anthropological differences", like those based on race, gender, or the distinction between the normal and pathological, will re-enter the very meaning ascribed to the human.[47]

Balibar states that anthropological differences are undeniable, as they have an empirical existence and produce real social effects. At the same time, however, they are undefinable, as their meaning is unstable and the boundaries that they produce are fluid. They thus give rise to exclusion and violence both when we negate them, and when we attempt to fix their meaning or use them to assign exclusive identities to classes or groups of people.[48] Universalist discourse tends to relegate these differences to empirical particularities that are unrelated to the defining characteristics of the human species. In reality, though, anthropological differences are more than simply individual characteristics – because there is something universal about them,

> they inevitably reemerge within moral and legal universality, where they introduce inequality and even exclusion (that is, they introduce places that are withheld, removed, from cosmopolitan humanity even though they are inherent in its construction or progress).[49]

Thirdly, the above juxtaposition of the universal and particular appears to rest on the assumption that the universal exists prior to or stands above antagonism and contestation. On this construction, conflict, like exclusion, always arises from the particularity of a given identity, culture, or polity. That is misleading. The universal is not untouched by conflict. On the contrary, it is a site in which conflicting interpretations of the universal constantly come up against each other.[50] If we recognise, with Balibar, that universality and exclusion are "two faces of the same discourse",[51] the universality of dignity and human rights seems like a double-edged sword. On the one hand, it refers to a radically egalitarian ideal, which is irreconcilable with the exclusion and degradation of any human beings. On the other, it exists alongside, and sometimes normalises, social distinctions that depict some people as lacking in rationality or autonomy (or other characteristics that are seen as central to the meaning of the human) and a wide array of legal, medical, and bureaucratic techniques that are used to criminalise, privatise, and pathologize difference, and subject it to surveillance and control. The universal is thus a site of permanent conflict between the radically emancipatory message of universal human dignity, equality, and freedom, and the inscription of certain distinctions, conditions, and hierarchies into our understanding of the human.

Fourthly, the above juxtaposition of the universal and particular elides important distinctions, like those between abstract statements of universal principles and ideals and their inscription within a particular legal order, and between different spheres of justice (e.g., the international and national spheres). It treats different enunciations of the universal in constitutional discourse, like references to universal human rights[52] and the universality of citizenship and the right to vote, as simply different sides of the same coin, and thus ignores the slippages between them. These slippages derive from the interplay between universals and their institution within specific communities. Balibar notes that, on the one hand, the universal "must be realized within a community, because it becomes effective only when it is part of institutions that are themselves demanded and legitimized by a political community".[53] On the other hand, a political community is not worthy of the name unless it incorporates universality into laws that afford citizens equal treatment. The mutual entwinement of universality and the political community raises fundamental questions about the legal and civic boundaries that separate full members of the political community from those at its margins. For instance, how should a political community respond to the dilemma that those who are affected by their exclusion from membership in the community are at the same time also excluded from the processes through which the norms governing membership are determined?[54] How could it bridge the gap between the universality of human rights and the inscription of the universal within a legal community? Is it possible to mediate the conflicting demands of communitarian closure and cosmopolitan openness in a way that is respectful of the personhood and agency of everyone involved?

In summary: a nuanced understanding of the nature of universal moral and legal categories and ideals must recognise that the universal and particular are mutually entwined, that universal categories and ideals produce conflicting interpretations, that every enunciation of the universal gives rise to exclusions, and that attempts to institute the universal within a particular legal and political order create gaps between the universality of human rights and the bounded nature of the political community. Such an understanding should enable a more realistic assessment of the capacity of universal ideals to challenge inequality and exclusion. Since it recognises that the universal is a site of political and ideological conflict and stands in a complex relationship with the particularity of differences and identities, it must reject the idea that domination and exclusion are but temporary obstacles on the way to the progressive unfolding of universal ideals, like human rights.[55] Rather than viewing persistent inequality as simply a remnant of a past in which the differences between human beings were absolutized and their shared human dignity was denied, it draws our attention to the role played by the universal in normalising inequality and exclusion. It thus recognises that there are limits to the capacity of any legal order to overcome inequality and exclusion in the name of the universal – and that those limits are formidable.

At the same time, this understanding of the relationship between the universal and particular could help open up spaces for contestation and critique by calling for the interrogation of dominant constructions of universal categories and ideals and juxtaposing them to alternative constructions of the universal that are articulated in the course of emancipatory struggles. The challenge is not to resolve, once and for all, the tension between the universal and particular or between different interpretations of the universal. It is rather to keep those tensions alive, and to be open to the capacity of emancipatory struggles to shift the dynamic and terms of their interaction.[56]

### 3.3 Disrupting continuity

Theunis Roux has criticised Karl Klare's politicisation of legal culture and rejection of liberal legal theories – like those of HLA Hart and Ronald Dworkin – that seek to ground adjudication in an objective legal method. Roux argues that it is possible, and would be preferable, to recast Klare's "postliberal" reading of the Constitution in Dworkinian terms as the best interpretation of the Constitution. Judges who ground their decisions in "distinctly legal methods" of reasoning and the best possible interpretation of the Constitution would be less exposed to attacks by politicians who brand them as antidemocratic and counter-revolutionary than judges who candidly admit the political nature of adjudication.[57] I cannot do justice here to Roux's nuanced argument, which accepts that judges sometimes act politically. However, I want to raise questions about the ability of Dworkin's notion of law as integrity to come to terms with the politics of adjudication in South Africa, where the historical record is characterised by fundamental injustice. My aim is not to provide a conclusive answer to questions about the applicability of Dworkin's theory in the South African context, but to draw on the debate to think through the relationship between historical injustice and the politics of value-based interpretation.[58]

For Dworkin, law as integrity requires judges to decide cases with reference to principles that both fit the historical legal record and morally justify it, that is, put it in its best possible light. Emilios Christodoulidis argues, with reference to Etienne Mureinik, that, in the South African context, integrity is vulnerable to the "iniquity thesis". That is because, "according to the logic of law's 'integrity', an iniquity, once it has made a substantial enough incursion into a legal system, continues to proliferate under its own momentum".[59] Put differently, the requirement of fit leads to the further entrenchment of historical injustices that are deeply rooted within a legal system. As Christodoulidis puts it:

> Integrity does not call us to experiment with latent, subordinate and subversive interpretative options, but calls for fidelity to what becomes entrenched as institutional record, in other words with *what carries the interpretative weight of that record.*[60]

It could be objected that, while the iniquity thesis may apply to apartheid South Africa, it has little or no relevance for the post-apartheid legal order, which constitutes a fundamental break with the past and inaugurates a new beginning. The Constitution, so the argument goes, reconstitutes the legal community and fundamentally alters the legal record. It effectively erases the fundamental iniquity that was at the centre of apartheid from the legal record, except in so far as it serves as a reminder never to repeat past injustices.

Viewed in the Constitution's light, fidelity to the historical record cannot and should not mean consistency with the ideas underpinning apartheid laws and practices. Instead, it refers to fidelity to the constitutional vision of an open and democratic society based on respect for the dignity, equality, and freedom of every person. This is an attractive argument; however, it arguably rests on a sanitised version of legal history, which portrays the transition from apartheid to the post-apartheid legal order as a clean break. The reality is far messier. Even though the Constitution radically departs from the apartheid legal order in crucial respects, it also shows continuity with it in others. On the one hand, the Constitution preserves legal and procedural continuity with the past by providing for the continued validity of existing law, subject to amendment, repeal, or constitutional invalidation.[61] Acts of Parliament from before 1994 remain in existence, as do provincial ordinances, legislation of the former Bantustans, subordinate legislation, common law, and customary law. The Constitution thus takes great care to subject the abolition and modification of laws – including ones that are morally reprehensible – to the criteria of legality.[62] On the other hand, despite the Constitution's commitment to democracy, social justice, and human rights, the lives of millions of South Africans continue to be characterised by poverty, hopelessness, violence, and suffering. In many respects, the substantive revolution promised by the Constitution has failed to become part of their lived reality. It is therefore possible to identify a second form of continuity with the apartheid past, which refers to the enduring social reality of inequality, unfreedom, and marginalisation.

Scholars sympathetic to Dworkin's theory of law as integrity are likely to object that neither of these two forms of continuity relates to the Constitution's substantive content. In the first place, the legal-procedural continuity between apartheid and post-apartheid law has nothing to do with reverence for the apartheid past or entrenching the foundations of an unequal society, but derives from the belief that a commitment to the rule of law would place transformation on a more secure footing.[63] Secondly, the endurance of social inequality and exclusion does not prove that the Constitution itself is flawed. This form of continuity is not legal in nature but arises from social and political factors, like corruption, government ineptitude, economic imbalances, and the time needed to translate the Constitution's promise into social reality. On this view, it would be incorrect to state that, given the above two forms of continuity between the old and the new, the idea of law as integrity would allow past injustices to proliferate through the legal record.

However, this response is open to the criticism that it rests on a too rigid distinction between substance and procedure and between the legal and social orders. In the first place, the constitutional transition has left vast bodies of pre-constitutional law in place. These bodies of law comprise not only rules, but also concepts, dichotomies, interpretive practices, and modes of reasoning that developed in a social setting that was undemocratic, exclusionary, racist, and patriarchal. Admittedly, the constitutional injunction to re-interpret and develop existing law in view of constitutional rights and values also extends to those concepts, interpretive practices, and modes of reasoning. However, the problem is that they are often so deeply ingrained in legal discourse that they appear natural and neutral. They may thus become part of the conceptual apparatus and interpretive frames used to construe constitutional provisions. As a result, problematic assumptions and beliefs – e.g., about freedom and consent, individual desert, the distribution of wealth and resources, and the divide between the public and private spheres – may make their way into our understanding of the Constitution itself. The legal-procedural continuity between apartheid and post-apartheid law has made it more likely that the substantive values and assumptions that legitimated injustices in the past would be carried forward into the new legal order.

Secondly, the complex network of assumptions and beliefs that structures South African legal thought stands in a close relationship to the social reality of inequality and exclusion. Critical legal theorists argue that law plays an important role in legitimating social hierarchies. Drawing on Antonio Gramsci's notion of "hegemony", they show how legal discourse makes the existing social order appear inevitable, not only to the dominant but also to the dominated classes. Legal discourse thus serves to foreclose imaginations of alternative, more humane social orders. It accomplishes this through a variety of mechanisms, which include removing social relationships from the contingency of lived experience and reducing them to abstract categories of legal rights and roles.[64] Robert Gordon gives the example of a factory worker who accepts her employer's right to remove her from the premises, based on an analogy with her own ownership rights. In her view, the employer's right to remove employees from the factory floor is similar to her right to tell her brother-in-law to leave her house. Gordon writes that the analogy derives from a belief structure that "abstracts relationships between real people … into relationships between entirely abstract categories of individuals playing the abstract social roles of 'owner', 'employee', etc".[65] It illustrates how legal ideology legitimates coercion, exclusion, and violence and makes them appear natural and inevitable.

Apartheid legal ideology played an important role in legitimating racial and other forms of domination and exploitation. Today it is easy to debunk that ideology to the extent that it relied on openly racist beliefs and stereotypes and served to justify blatant violations of individual rights and freedoms. However, there was another side to apartheid legal ideology, which was far more effective in legitimating inequality and exclusion. It structured legal understandings of social relationships – particularly within the private sphere – in terms of abstract concepts, rules, and rights, and thus "removed" them from the context of state-enforced discrimination and dispossession.[66] The language of subjective rights, ownership, and the sanctity of contract concealed the violence of racial capitalism, and the role played by coercive and discriminatory laws in the allocation of "private" rights and freedoms. It thus normalised relations within the private sphere by treating them as interactions between free and equal individuals that were unaffected by oppressive and discriminatory laws and state policies.[67] Today, legal concepts, assumptions, and ideologies inherited from the colonial and apartheid past can still stifle change and make the status quo appear natural and necessary. They allow legal interpreters to avoid taking responsibility for their interpretive choices and to treat the destitution and dehumanisation that characterise the lives of millions of people as the unfortunate result of poor choices, bad luck, or lack of merit,[68] and instil a sense of helplessness and futility among the dispossessed masses.

A theory of adjudication that highlights the need to decide cases in South Africa in accordance with a legal principle that provides the best possible justification for the historical legal record arguably rests on the assumption that the inegalitarian and exclusionary traces of categories and interpretive practices inherited from the colonial and apartheid past will fall away once they are subsumed under universal constitutional principles. It thus fails to come to terms with the mutual entwinement of the universal and particular and underestimates the risk that past iniquities will infiltrate understandings of constitutional rights and values.[69] What is needed instead is a critical approach that consciously resists the capacity of concepts, methodologies, and dichotomies inherited from the past to normalise domination, inequality, and exclusion. Such an approach must be alive to the fact that supposedly universal rights and values, like dignity, equality, citizenship, and freedom were historically reserved for white, propertied men, and that some of the meanings ascribed to them today still bear traces of that history of exclusion. It must relinquish the idea that the meaning of constitutional values is self-evident or the subject of a broad consensus and must be alert to the conflicting interpretations to which they give rise. It must be prepared to exploit the gaps and contradictions inherent in the legal record, and to explore the transformative potential of concepts, principles, and interpretations that have been relegated to a marginal or exceptional position.[70]

## 3.4 Shifting subjects, variable objects, and remainders of inequality and domination

The previous sections highlighted the tension between the political nature of constitutional interpretation and adjudication and some of the assumptions, distinctions, and techniques that are relied on to detach law from politics. I have argued, firstly, that attempts to ground constitutional interpretation in neutral concepts or principles render certain power relations invisible or lend them an air of inevitability. Secondly, narratives about the constitutional transition that assume that the particularity of conflict, exclusion, and inequality can be gradually overcome by subsuming them under the Constitution's universalistic ethos hides the extent to which universal rights and values are subject to conflicting interpretations and tend to be infiltrated by hierarchical distinctions. Thirdly, reliance on Dworkin's notion of law as integrity could blind us to the capacity of legal concepts, principles, and methodologies derived from the apartheid past to legitimate inequality and unfreedom. In all three cases, a restrictive understanding of the political is at work, which normalises and depoliticises social power and deflects attention away from struggles that challenge hierarchy in the name of alternative social visions. In this section, I critique restrictive understandings of the objects and subjects of democratic politics and argue for a more radical conception that recognises that the meaning of the political cannot be settled in advance but is itself subject to democratic contestation.

Hannah Arendt's political thought provides a helpful backdrop for considering the meaning and bounds of the political. Arendt famously treated plurality as the enabling condition of democratic politics.[71] For her, political action can only occur in an agonistic public sphere in which unique individuals insert themselves into the human world through speech and action. She conceived the public sphere as a space of appearance which allows individuals to leave behind the "shadowy" existence of the private sphere, transcend the necessities of life, establish a common world, and connect their lives with those of previous and future generations. Arendt's theorisation of the agonistic nature of the public sphere and grounding of plurality in the unique distinctness of every citizen[72] hold enormous potential for radical democratic thought. The strict opposition in her thought between a public realm of freedom and a private realm of necessity nevertheless results in an overly narrow conception of the political. This is evident in her negative appraisal of the "rise of the social". Arendt associated the rise of the social with the emancipation of economic processes from the household and the institution of an economic sphere governed by commodity exchange and the pursuit of self-interest.[73] She believed that those developments blurred the distinction between the public and private, and transformed the public-political sphere into a space in which individuals are above all concerned with their narrow self-interest. Arendt's view that economic and social relations are pre-political and that their inclusion in the public agenda distorts politics overlooks the extent to which, in modern societies, "[t]he struggle over what gets included in the public agenda is itself a struggle for justice and freedom".[74] Any attempt to make the boundaries between the public and private realms appear fixed or permanent or ingrained in the "order of things" ignores the fact that conflict and antagonism can erupt in areas of life previously regarded as belonging to a nonpolitical, intimate sphere.[75] Historical examples abound of struggles that have exposed exploitation and oppression in the private sphere, and politicised issues previously considered private, like safety in the workplace, domestic violence, gender roles (e.g., the confinement of women to housework, reproduction, and nurturing), poverty, the environment, sexual orientation, and gender identity.

Arendt's views on who qualify as subjects of democratic politics similarly call for critical engagement. Her famous analysis of the precarious position of refugees and stateless persons, who are no longer part of a political community that can safeguard their rights, suggests that human rights are powerless when the subjects of those rights are not members of a political community. The impotency of the rights proclaimed in international rights declarations is revealed precisely when they are most desperately needed. Arendt argues that, when human rights are uncoupled from citizens' rights, they refer to subjects who have ceased to be part of a common world. Those subjects have "lost the very qualities which make it possible for other people to treat [them] as [fellow human beings]".[76] In her view, inalienable human rights mean nothing if they are not grounded in political membership.

Jacques Rancière shows that Arendt's view of human rights as an abstraction that is powerless to prevent the dehumanisation of refugees and stateless persons derives from the dichotomy in her thought between the public and private spheres. Because she wants to protect politics from contamination by private needs, and because she identifies the ability to act politically with membership in the national community, Arendt cannot conceive of political subjectivity outside the frames of citizenship and the nation-state. She therefore believes that those who are deprived of membership in the nation-state are reduced to a state of bare life that is outside the protective reach of the law.[77] However, Rancière argues that politics cannot be confined to a public sphere reserved for citizens that is sealed off from economic need and struggles for survival. Politics is precisely the activity that brings the border between the public and private realms – and between citizens and non-citizens – into question. Rancière refers to Olympe de Gouges, who stated that if women could be sentenced to death as enemies of the French Revolution, they were by implication entitled to participate in politics. Her statement politicised the borderline that confined women to domestic life and showed that "[i]f they could lose their 'bare life' out of a public judgment based on political reasons, this meant that even their bare life – their life doomed to death – was political".[78]

For Rancière, the gap between the supposed universality of human rights and the rightlessness of certain categories of people opens up "an interval for political subjectivization",[79] in which those who are deprived of rights challenge their subordination in the name of every person's inscription as a free and equal human being. The subject of human rights therefore cannot be settled in advance. Human rights are indeterminate and give rise to disputes about their meaning, scope, and field of application. The subject of those rights thus inheres in the process of subjectivization, which consists not in the progressive eradication of the barriers to freedom, equality, and full citizenship, in accordance with the telos of human rights, but in the disruption of the identity of the political community through the claims of those who have no part in terms of current configurations of membership and power. Rancière writes:

> Political activity is whatever shifts a body from the place assigned to it or changes a place's destination. It makes visible what had no business being seen, and ... makes understood as discourse what was once only heard as noise.[80]

Political subjects arise when a dispute is declared by those who are not recognised as "speaking beings who count".[81] Politics thus takes place when struggles for equality seek to disrupt current distributions of power, places, and bodies by raising disputes and asserting subjectivities that have no place within existing power configurations. Democracy, on this view, refers to that which challenges consensual norms that make the status quo appear natural and inevitable. Dominant understandings of the subjects and objects of democratic politics, as well as the spaces in which democratic politics occurs, are therefore subject to contestation. Rancière's analysis suggests that the idea of a society that has discarded all boundaries and is, therefore, fully inclusive, is not only a pipe dream but is also profoundly antidemocratic. He worries that the quest of contemporary consensus-seeking democracies to chart and fully comprehend the political community through the "science" of public opinion no longer admits of political spaces in which "those who have no part" can declare disputes and disrupt the identity of the people.[82]

Hans Lindahl's work on collective selfhood confirms that boundaries are constitutive of legal and political orders and that democratic struggles can problematise those boundaries, even though there are limits to a political order's ability to respond to claims that are foreign or strange to it. Lindahl argues against the tendency in cosmopolitan legal thought to view global legal orders as having an inside but no outside. He points out that, while a global legal order like the World Trade Organisation (WTO) does not have borders that separate domestic from foreign spaces, it does have limits that separate what it considers its own from what it considers strange. In the sense used here, "own" refers to the spatial unity that is achieved when the legal order joins different markets and spaces together, while "strange" refers to alternative distributions of places that cannot be accommodated within the common space that it has brought into being.[83] These limits include and exclude at the same time. For instance, Lindahl notes that the WTO creates an inclusive global market, which nevertheless excludes understandings of exchange that are inconsistent with its vision of free trade. When the Karnataka State Farmers' Association (KRSS) in India resists trade liberalisation by occupying and destroying fields of genetically modified crops, it draws attention to these limits by invoking "another spatial configuration of the commonality of collective life, and another configuration of the rights and obligations that inure to collective life, which is at loggerheads with the commonality claimed for the WTO's global market".[84] Lindahl's analysis suggests that all legal orders, including those that profess to be global and those that are grounded in universal human rights, join together and separate an inside and outside, and that there are limits to their capacity to be responsive to challenges that invoke an alternative distribution of places.

Lindahl uses the term "a-legality" to refer to behaviour that draws attention to legal boundaries that usually operate in the background. A-legal behaviour resists classification on either side of the dichotomy between legality and illegality and between order and disorder, and therefore gives rise to normative disorientation. It calls legal boundaries into question and gestures towards alternative configurations of norms and spaces that are excluded from the practical possibilities available under the current legal order. Lindahl refers to the example of members of a movement in France that sought to draw attention to the disadvantage and exclusion experienced by impoverished people. They filled supermarket trolleys with food (including luxury items), queued up at a shop's eight check-out points, and then refused to pay, explaining that they sought authorisation to take the food to distribute it among unemployed people. Their actions defied categorisation in terms of the legal/illegal binary, disrupted the ordinary operation of legal norms, rendered legal boundaries (including the spatial boundary of the check-out point) visible, and highlighted the ways in which those boundaries exclude impoverished people from certain spaces and activities.[85] As Lindahl states, they demonstrated that "the needy have no place in the differentiation and interconnection of work-places, shopping-places, taxi-places, home-places, and cinema-places that the legal order makes possible for those who can pay at the check-out point".[86] At the same time, their actions exposed the contingency of the prevailing legal order by pointing towards alternative configurations of spaces and subjectivities.

These reflections do not suggest that egalitarian struggles are bound to result in the progressive overcoming of domination, exclusion, and inequality. In the first place, Lindahl criticises legal universalism for focussing only on misrecognition stemming from exclusion, while overlooking cases in which domination arises from assimilation.[87] That blinds it to struggles waged against misrecognition resulting either from inclusion into a legal order (e.g., the KRSS's resistance to integration into the WTO) or from the terms of inclusion (e.g., where the inclusion of a category or group of subjects is premised on conformity to the mores, worldview, or subjectivity of a dominant group). Secondly, Lindahl points out that every legal and political order has contingent foundations. He quotes Ferdinando Menga, who states that, given its "contingent genealogy", every order "is historically and ontologically bounded".[88] The contingency and boundedness of a legal order limit its capacity to recognise what is strange to it, or that exceeds the range of collective self-understandings available to it. Thirdly, Lindahl insists that every act of collective self-identification or self-recognition is, at the same time, an instance of self-misrecognition, which gives rise to alienation on the part of those who have either been excluded from the collective self or included on terms that do not tally with their own self-understanding.[89]

The contingency of foundations and the misrecognition that it engenders introduce an asymmetry at the heart of the legal order, which cannot be undone through the progressive accommodation of categories of persons or understandings of collective selfhood that have traditionally been excluded. There is often something violent about the translation of demands for recognition into claims that are intelligible to and can be accommodated under the possibilities of inclusion available under a given legal order. As Lindahl states, the response of a legal order to demands for recognition is necessarily asymmetrical, as "it frames the demand of the other in ways that render it amenable to a response in the terms of (transformed) relations of reciprocity available to joint action".[90] Given the contingency of collective identities and, hence, legal orders, there is always a remainder that cannot be accommodated on its own terms. Although that is true of all legal orders, Lindahl insists that it does not absolve decision-makers of responsibility. What is considered outside the bounds of a legal order tends to be identified with what is irrational; hence, there is a danger that the boundaries between the legal and illegal and the own and the strange will be drawn in ways that relegate some to the category of the inhuman.[91] Lindahl therefore calls for an asymmetrical form of recognition, which recognises "the other (in ourselves) as one of us *and* as other than us".[92] "Direct recognition" through acts of "collective self-assertion" should be supplemented by "indirect recognition" through "collective self-restraint".[93] Through the latter, the legal order recognises that

> it has an outside – a domain of the strange – that eludes the collective's self-assertion and that ought to be preserved as its outside … if collective recognition of the other is not to collapse into a project of totalisation and therewith of domination.[94]

These theoretical perspectives resonate with the conflictual democratic frame adopted in this study. They insist that every legal and political order has an outside and that there are, accordingly, limits to its capacity to respond to claims that invoke distributions of norms and places that are considered strange or foreign. At the same time, they emphasise that, despite those limits, democratic struggles have the capacity to unsettle received understandings of the subjects, objects, and places of politics and disrupt current distributions of wealth and power. On this view, politics consists neither in collective self-closure nor in boundless openness to challenges to the status quo. It inheres, rather, in the gaps between freedom and domination, between equality and inequality, and between membership and exclusion, and in the capacity of anti-hegemonic struggles to politicise those gaps and invoke alternative futures.

## 3.5 Articulating dignity, equality, and freedom

Balibar uses the term "equaliberty" to denote the distinctly modern proposition, which was enunciated in the Declaration of the Rights of Man and the Citizen of 1789, that equality and liberty are mutually implicated. In terms of this idea, equality and freedom are both denied when state absolutism results in equal submission to tyrannical power, or when freedom is confined to a privileged few.[95] This proposition resonates with the idea of the unity of constitutional values. However, it also complicates it. That is because the universality of the idea that equality and liberty must be realised together comes up, time and again, against the historical contingency of the concrete legal order in which it is – always imperfectly – embodied.[96] Put differently, the meaning of equal freedom is mediated through social practices, institutions, and cultural and ideological representations that always leave a remainder of inequality, exclusion, and domination. This point is closely related to the one made above that anthropological differences and social hierarchies tend to be reinscribed into understandings of universal categories. The difficulty is compounded by the identification of equality and freedom with universal access to citizenship, which collapses the distinction between man and citizen and introduces a fundamental indeterminacy into fundamental rights, as the subject of those rights moves back and forth between the citizen and the individual.[97]

This account tallies with the conflictual democratic insight that democratic decision-making can challenge and disrupt inequality and domination but can never result in a perfectly symmetrical society which has eradicated exclusion and power.[98] Balibar argues, with reference to the above contradictions, that all states are, to differing degrees, "oligarchic and authoritarian, based on the privileges of class or expertise", and that democracy is "an effort that must be ceaselessly repeated to include within the political space those who have been excluded".[99] Democracy, on this understanding, refers neither to the inexorable march of the universality of citizenship and human rights, nor to the preservation of the democratic system that has been instituted. It is, rather, constituted by the tension between the constitution of citizenship and the insurrectional power of movements which challenge domination and exclusion and assert, in Rancière's formulation, "the part of those who have no part" in terms of current distributions of rights, spaces, and power.[100] Democracy thus derives from the tension between struggles for equal freedom and the institutions, practices, and cultural and ideological presuppositions that provide the horizon for political thought and action.

According to Balibar, the proposition of equaliberty cannot, on its own, resolve the contradictions arising from the tension between "the excess, hyperbolic universality" of the rights of man and the fact that their protection is entirely contingent on certain practices, institutions, struggles, and conflicts.[101] He identifies two – antithetical –principles that are used to mediate this contradiction, namely fraternity (or community) and property (or commerce). Both mediations split into different understandings of the principle in question and thus, in turn, generate conflicting understandings of equal liberty. Fraternity can be associated with either a national community or the proletariat, whereas property can be identified with either capital or labour.[102] Moreover, both these principles give rise to exclusion. As Jacques Derrida points out, dominant understandings of community or fraternity privilege "the masculine authority of the brother (who is also a son, a husband, a father)", as opposed to other figures (like a sister, daughter, wife, or mother), while at the same time connoting "genealogy, family, birth, autochthony, and the nation".[103] They are also associated with the neutralisation of sexual differences, as they assume that assertions of rights that are grounded in differences that straddle the divide between biology and history or between the real and imaginary threaten to introduce singularity and desire into our understanding of citizenship and thus endanger its universality.[104] These conceptions of community are thus closely related to ethnic understandings of the nation and citizenship, as well as patriarchy and heteronormativity. On the other hand, the liberal notion of property in one's own person tends to inscribe hierarchical distinctions based on intellectual ability, self-control, self-ownership, and prosperity into our understanding of equality and freedom.[105]

Jaco Barnard-Naudé states, with reference to Nancy's attempts to rethink fraternity and Derrida's critique of the concept, that it is significant that South Africa's Constitution uses the term "human dignity" rather than "fraternity" alongside equality and freedom. Dignity, unlike fraternity, is not based on the suppression of sexual difference, nor does it carry connotations of the nation, autochthony, citizenship by birth, or nature. He argues that the Constitution thus signals a move away from apartheid's grounding of politics in the preservation of a common substance, and points towards an understanding of freedom – as well as equality – that is founded on respect for others, including those who are radically different. On this understanding, freedom can neither be premised on nor measured in terms of a common metric. It is tied to unconditional respect for human dignity, is immeasurable, and creates spaces for singularity rather than sameness.[106] The Constitution thus espouses an understanding of freedom that is both relational and radical. Freedom, on that view, depends on the presence of others and opens spaces and enables relations that, since they are "exposed to otherness", undercut "any firm, fixed or closed identity".[107] It holds out the possibility of new beginnings, which are made possible by our relationality and exposure to plurality and difference.

Dignity, on this view, is not a neutral principle, nor is it a universal category under which the particular must be subsumed. Far from neutralising the political, unconditional respect for the humanity and uniqueness of every person has a profoundly political effect. It uncovers spaces of contestation, disrupts closure, requires the ongoing revision of normative commitments in response to struggles against oppression and dehumanisation, and is conducive to a radical conception of difference and a pluralistic understanding of democracy. None of this suggests that dignity can resolve the tension between the universality of human rights and the fact that their institutionalisation depends on practices, institutions, discourses, struggles, and conflicts that are culturally and historically contingent and produce certain contradictions and exclusions. In fact, its politicising effect derives precisely from that tension. While the mutual articulation of dignity, equality, freedom, and plurality unlocks emancipatory possibilities, it also draws attention to several ruptures at the heart of democracy: between the universality of citizenship and the exclusions that are constitutive of any political community, between universal human dignity and the insertion of anthropological differences into the definition of the human, between constituent and constituted power, etc. Freedom's articulation with equality also produces contradictions. For instance, Derrida notes, with reference to Nancy, that "equality tends to introduce measure and calculation (and thus conditionality) whereas freedom is by essence unconditional, indivisible, heterogeneous to calculation and to measure".[108] That gives rise to an aporia – the measures and techniques of equality not only provide access to, but also tend to neutralise the singularity and incommensurability at the heart of freedom.[109] The irreconcilability of these tensions and contradictions reveals the impossibility of a legal and political order that is fully based on equal dignity and freedom.

The mutual articulation of dignity, equality, freedom, radical difference, and a pluralistic democracy provides a basis for evaluating and critiquing different attempted mediations between the universality of human rights and the specific contexts, practices, and institutions in which they are embedded. For instance, attempts to use property – in things or in oneself – as a mediating device can be assessed from the perspective of the following questions. Do they rely on a vision of possessive individualism that diminishes the public sphere as the world that we hold in common? Do they conceive freedom as an individual power or exercise of the will, rather than treating it as something relational? Do they articulate freedom with a strong notion of equality, or do they effectively confine it to the privileged strata of society? Similarly, different uses of community as a mediating principle can be subjected to questions like: How inclusive is the community in question? Is membership in the community, and hence equal freedom, premised on a shared characteristic or conformity to certain expectations or norms? Is the mediation predicated on fixed or essential individual and collective identities? Does it allow for the articulation of freedom with respect for radical difference, and the possibility of new beginnings that spring from exposure to the unpredictability of a pluralistic public-political sphere?

Dignity, equality, and freedom not only require but are also constitutive of a robust public sphere in which a plurality of discourses, ideologies, and articulations of the common good coexist, and in which people are free to mobilise and develop new vocabularies in the fight against inequality and oppression. At the same time, they are inscribed into a legal order which, in the very act of giving effect to them, limits their reach and meaning, and in doing so, sometimes reverts to hierarchical distinctions. There are limits to the capacity of even the most progressive laws and judgments to eradicate deeply entrenched forms of exclusion and prejudice. Rafal Manko states, with reference to Chantal Mouffe, that such laws and judgments are best viewed as "steps [in an] on-going struggle, as 'temporary respites in an ongoing confrontation'".[110] The fight for equal dignity and freedom is never finally won. As the above quote from Balibar suggests, it must be repeated constantly.

The key to making sense of the unity of dignity, equality, and freedom thus lies not in a neutral interpretive methodology or the progressive unfolding of their universality but in confronting the tension between their radical promise and the inequality, exclusion, and domination that are produced by the discourses, practices, and representations through which they are institutionalised.

## Notes

1 Ackermann *Human Dignity* 269–288. See also Tsele "'Coercing Virtue' in the Constitutional Court" 193.
2 Cf also Goldstone J's statement in *President v Hugo* para 41 that the ban on unfair discrimination "seeks not only to avoid discrimination against people who are members of disadvantaged groups" but expresses the constitutional vision of "a society in which all human beings will be accorded equal dignity and respect regardless of their membership of particular groups".
3 Wechsler "Toward Neutral Principles of Constitutional Law" 31–34 questioned whether *Brown v Board of Education of Topeka* involved discrimination and argued that it concerned a conflict between black people's freedom of association and the freedom of whites not to associate with them. In his view, the decision in *Brown* was non-neutral, since it preferred the associational interests of blacks who favoured integration over the associational interests of whites who favoured segregation. He further believed that the claim that black children were harmed by school segregation was not sufficiently backed up by evidence and argued that it was impermissible for judges to have regard to how the children experienced the segregation. He even suggested that the Court in *Plessy v Ferguson* 551 may have been right in stating "that if 'enforced separation stamps the colored race with a badge of inferiority' it is simply because its members choose 'to put that construction upon it'".
4 Ackermann *Human Dignity* 284, 287.
5 See Albertyn "Contested Substantive Equality in the South African Constitution" 443–451 for a discussion of the different political traditions (like liberalism, socialism, feminism, Africanism, and Black Consciousness) that have helped shape the discourse about equality in South Africa.
6 *Jordan v S.*
7 Ackermann *Human Dignity* 278–282.
8 281–282.
9 313–314, referring to *Minister of Education v Syfrets.*
10 See the case law discussed in *King v De Jager* paras 29–33.
11 See the judgment of Mhlantla J in *King v De Jager* para 84.
12 *Minister of Finance v Van Heerden* para 37.
13 Paras 33–36.
14 Para 44 (describing this goal as the achievement of "a non-racial, non-sexist society in which each person will be recognised and treated as a human being of equal worth and dignity").
15 Paras 78–80.
16 *South African Police Service v Solidarity obo Barnard* para 30.
17 Paras 30, 31.
18 Para 39.
19 Para 110.
20 Paras 114–116.
21 Para 118.
22 Para 117 ("it is not necessarily an injury to dignity to view a person only through the lens of one ground listed in section 9(3), provided the reason for doing so is to redress historical inequality. But this becomes dissonant if we ascribe only one identity at the cost of seeing the multitudes that make up each individual").
23 Paras 171–172.
24 Para 180.
25 Paras 173–175.
26 Paras 178–179.

27 The dangers of that approach are illustrated by *Solidarity v Department of Correctional Services*, in which the majority upheld the constitutionality of an EE plan that imposes rigid numerical targets and leaves virtually no room for considering individual traits and characteristics in cases where a particular group is already adequately represented.
28 *Minister of Finance* v *Van Heerden* para 152.
29 Para 152. The two criteria listed by Van der Westhuizen J in *Barnard* para 180, namely whether the complainant was treated as a mere means to an end, and whether the implementation of the measure constituted an absolute barrier to the advancement of her career similarly point to a limited form of proportionality analysis.
30 Ackermann *Human Dignity* 363.
31 353.
32 Van der Walt "Un-Doing Things with Words" 264.
33 Cf Sachs J's reminder in *Van Heerden* para 144 of remedial measures' capacity to destabilise the status quo.
34 S Winter *A Clearing in the Forest* 325.
35 As Sachs J observed in *Volks NO v Robinson* para 148, legal issues are sometimes "embedded in an elusive, evolving and resilient matrix made up of varied historical, social, moral and cultural ingredients. At times these emerge and enter explicitly into the legal discourse. More often they exercise a subterranean influence, all the more powerful for being submerged in deep and largely unarticulated philosophical positions".
36 Williams "*Metro Broadcasting, Inc v FCC*" 198. The invisibility and perceived neutrality of racism tends to be strengthened by the organisation of social space and numerous forms of disciplinary power.
37 Epilogue to the Constitution of the Republic of South Africa, Act 200 of 1993 ("the interim Constitution"), titled "National Unity and Reconciliation".
38 S 1(a) and (b), 7(1), 36(1) and 39(1)(a) of the Constitution of the Republic of South Africa, 1996 ("the Constitution").
39 S 3.
40 S 1(d) and 19(3).
41 *Ex parte Chairperson of the Constitutional Assembly* para 10.
42 *S v Makwanyane* para 261. See also *Shabalala v Attorney-General of the Transvaal* para 26 (the Constitution "constitutes a decisive break from a culture of Apartheid and racism to a constitutionally protected culture of openness and democracy and universal human rights for South Africans of all ages, classes and colours").
43 Norval *Deconstructing Apartheid Discourse* 97.
44 Balibar *On Universals* 42 (contemporary critiques of universalism typically rest on a totalisation of difference and are "expressed in the modality of the universal").
45 47 (emphasis in the original omitted). See also Douzinas *Human Rights and Empire* 95.
46 25. See also Honig "Another Cosmopolitanism?" 110–111 (there is something alien and violent about "a universalism that seeks to subsume [the particular] under categories whose fundamental character and validity are unchanged or unaffected" by its encounter with what is strange or new to it).
47 Balibar *On Universals* 97–103.
48 98 100.
49 107 (emphasis in the original omitted).
50 38, 42, 44–54.
51 Balibar *Citizenship* 80.
52 One of the constitutional principles enshrined in the interim Constitution required the new Constitution to guarantee the enjoyment of "all universally accepted

fundamental rights, freedoms and civil liberties". The Constitutional Court interpreted this phrase to refer to "those rights and freedoms recognized in open and democratic societies as being the inalienable entitlements of human beings". *Ex parte Chairperson of the Constitutional Assembly* para 50.

53 Balibar *On Universals* 109.

54 Benhabib *The Rights of Others* 15.

55 Honig "Another Cosmopolitanism?" 114.

56 At the risk of quoting Balibar *On Universals* 18 slightly out of context, the conflicts between different enunciations of the universal and different articulations of the universal and the particular "reflect the very conditions of politics".

57 Roux "Transformative Constitutionalism and the Best Interpretation of the South African Constitution" 281, 284. See also T Roux *The Politics of Principle* (2013).

58 Engagements with Dworkin's work from a South African perspective include Mureinik "Dworkin and Apartheid"; Roederer "Third Path Theorists" 94–113; Davis "Dworkin"; Wesson and Du Plessis "Hart, Dworkin and the Nature of (South African) Legal Theory"; Cornell and Friedman *The Mandate of Dignity*.

59 Christodoulidis "'End of History' Jurisprudence" 64.

60 69 (emphasis in the original).

61 S 229 of the interim Constitution; item 2(1) of Schedule 6 of the Constitution of the Republic of South Africa, 1996.

62 The commitment to the rule of law extended to the constitutional transition, which carefully avoided a rupture in the chain of legality. The new Constitution had to be adopted in accordance with procedural – and substantive – requirements contained in an interim Constitution that, in turn, had been adopted in accordance with the procedures prescribed in the Constitution of the old regime. For this reason, the constitutional transition could be dubbed a "legal" or "Rechtsstaatliche" revolution. See Arato *Civil Society, Constitution, and Legitimacy* xiv, 101–106; Arato "Post-Sovereign Constitution-Making in Hungary".

63 See Ackermann "The Legal Nature of the South African Constitutional Revolution" 645–646 (the constitutional transition does not amount to a procedural revolution in the Kelsenian sense but inaugurates a substantive constitutional revolution).

64 Gabel "The Phenomenology of Rights-Consciousness and the Pact of the Withdrawn Selves"; Gabel and Harris "Building Power and Breaking Images" 373, 377; Tushnet "An Essay on Rights" 1382–1384.

65 Gordon "Some Critical Theories of Law and their Critics" 650.

66 Van der Walt "Tradition on Trial" 172–187.

67 184.

68 See Brand "The 'Politics of Need Interpretation' and the Adjudication of Socio-Economic Rights Claims in South Africa" (discussing various ways in which legal discourse depoliticises poverty and need).

69 Cornell and Friedman *The Mandate of Dignity* 60 recognise that Dworkin's project in *Law's Empire* has limited relevance in the post-colony. They write: "insofar as the bulk of South African law which exists today was developed within and heavily influenced by a comprehensive system of racialised oppression, one cannot meaningfully attribute any shared principles to some idealised community, at least not principles which can be morally defended. In fact, the very attempt to view this bulk of law 'in its best light' is perverse". However, they argue that Dworkin's later work could provide a better basis for a transformative post-apartheid jurisprudence.

70 See Unger *The Critical Legal Studies Movement* 15–22, 88–90.

71 Arendt *The Human Condition* 7.

72 8, 176.

73 38–49.

74 Benhabib *Situating the Self* 94.
75 See Christodoulidis "De-Politicising Poverty" for a critique of Arendt's distinction between the social and political.
76 Arendt *The Origins of Totalitarianism* 300.
77 Rancière "Who is the Subject of the Rights of Man?" 301.
78 303.
79 304.
80 Rancière *Disagreement* 30.
81 27.
82 104–107.
83 Lindahl *Authority and the Globalisation of Inclusion and Exclusion* 24–28.
84 28.
85 Lindahl *Fault Lines of Globalization* 30–38.
86 32–33. Another example of a-legal behaviour was the refusal by an "art collective of queer black and coloured activists from the working and middle class" to vacate a five-bedroom home in Camps Bay that they had rented through a rental website. The group's declared aim was to highlight "the vast economic and moral disparity between those who have no form of formal housing, and those who are rich enough to afford more than one". Kiewit "The Young and the Rentless".
87 Lindahl *Authority and the Globalisation of Inclusion and Exclusion* 326.
88 224.
89 321, 322, 327.
90 327.
91 See 335–336, where Lindahl criticises both particularism and universalism. The former excludes "the other as other than us", whereas the latter includes "the other as one of us"; however, both "turn on the enclosure of plurality into a unity in which everyone and everything would have its proper place".
92 327.
93 342.
94 345.
95 Balibar *Equaliberty* 47.
96 50.
97 44–46; Balibar "Is a Philosophy of Human Civic Rights Possible?" 312–314.
98 See chapter 2.6 above.
99 Balibar *Equaliberty* 187.
100 Rancière "Who Is the Subject of the Rights of Man?" 305.
101 Balibar *Equaliberty* 50.
102 52–56.
103 Derrida *Rogues* 58. See also 61.
104 Balibar *Equaliberty* 57–62. See Young *Justice and the Politics of Difference* 98–111 for a critique of the logic of identity, which is personified by the universal citizen who embraces "a general point of view that leaves behind particular affiliations, feelings, commitments, and desires" (105).
105 62, 108–109.
106 Barnard-Naudé "Beyond the Brother" 289–290.
107 285. See also 281.
108 Derrida *Rogues* 48.
109 52, 53. Cf the discussion under 3.1 above of the tensions characterising judicial efforts to come to grips with the need for measures that remedy the effects of past discrimination.
110 Manko "Judicial Decision-Making, Ideology and the Political" 186.

## Bibliography

Ackermann L "The Legal Nature of the South African Constitutional Revolution" (2004) *New Zealand Law Review* 633.

Ackermann L *Human Dignity: Lodestar for Equality in South Africa* (2012) Cape Town: Juta.

Albertyn C "Contested Substantive Equality in the South African Constitution: Beyond Social Inclusion towards Systemic Justice" (2018) 34 *South African Journal on Human Rights* 441.

Arato A "Post-Sovereign Constitution-Making in Hungary: After Success, Partial Failure, and Now What?" (2010) 26 *South African Journal on Human Rights* 19.

Arato A *Civil Society, Constitution, and Legitimacy* (2000) Lanham: Rowman & Littlefield Publishers.

Arendt H *The Human Condition* (1958) Chicago: University of Chicago Press.

Arendt H *The Origins of Totalitarianism* (1968) San Diego: Harcourt.

Balibar É *Citizenship* (2015, translation T Scott-Railton) Cambridge: Polity Press.

Balibar É *Equaliberty* (2014, translation J Ingram) Durham: Duke University Press.

Balibar É "Is a Philosophy of Human Civic Rights Possible? New Reflections on Equaliberty" (2004) 103 *South Atlantic Quarterly* 311.

Balibar É *On Universals: Constructing and Deconstructing Community* (2020, translation J Jordan) New York: Fordham University Press.

Barnard-Naudé AJ "Beyond the Brother: Radical Freedom" (2008) *Acta Juridica* 273.

Benhabib S *Situating the Self: Gender, Community and Postmodernism in Contemporary Ethics* (1992) Cambridge: Polity Press.

Benhabib S *The Rights of Others: Aliens, Residents and Citizens* (2004) Cambridge: Cambridge University Press.

Brand D "The 'Politics of Need Interpretation' and the Adjudication of Socio-Economic Rights Claims in South Africa" in AJ van der Walt (ed) *Theories of Economic and Social Justice* (2005) 17 Stellenbosch: Sun Press.

Christodoulidis E "De-Politicising Poverty: Arendt in South Africa" (2011) 22 *Stellenbosch Law Review* 501.

Christodoulidis E "'End of History' Jurisprudence: Dworkin in South Africa" (2004) *Acta Juridica* 64.

Cornell D and Friedman N *The Mandate of Dignity: Ronald Dworkin, Revolutionary Constitutionalism, and the Claims of Justice* (2016) New York: Fordham University Press.

Davis D "Dworkin: A Viable Theory of Adjudication for the South African Constitutional Community?" (2004) *Acta Juridica* 96.

Derrida J *Rogues: Two Essays on Reason* (2005, translation P Brault and M Naas) Stanford: Stanford University Press.

Douzinas C *Human Rights and Empire: The Political Philosophy of Cosmopolitanism* (2007) Abingdon: Routledge-Cavendish.

Gabel P "The Phenomenology of Rights-Consciousness and the Pact of the Withdrawn Selves" (1984) 62 *Texas Law Review* 1563.

Gabel P and Harris P "Building Power and Breaking Images: Critical Legal Theory and the Practice of Law" (1982–83) 11 *New York University Review of Law and Social Change* 369.

Gordon R "Some Critical Theories of Law and their Critics" in D Kairys (ed) *The Politics of Law: A Progressive Critique* 3rd ed (1998) 641 New York: Basic Books.

Honig B "Another Cosmopolitanism? Law and Politics in the New Europe" in S Benhabib (ed) *Another Cosmopolitanism* (2006) 102 Oxford: Oxford University Press.

Kiewit L "The Young and the Rentless: Inside Camps Bay's 'Hijacked' Mansion" *Mail & Guardian* (20 Sep 2020). https://mg.co.za/news/2020-09-23-the-young-and-the-rentless-inside-camps-bays-hijacked-mansion/

Lindahl H *Authority and the Globalisation of Inclusion and Exclusion* (2018) Cambridge: Cambridge University Press.
Lindahl H *Fault Lines of Globalization: Legal Order and the Politics of A-Legality* (2013) Oxford: Oxford University Press.
Manko R "Judicial Decision-Making, Ideology and the Political: Towards an Agonistic Theory of Adjudication" (2022) 33 *Law and Critique* 175.
Mureinik E "Dworkin and Apartheid" in H Corder (ed) *Essays on Law and Social Practice in South Africa* (1988) 181 Cape Town: Juta.
Norval AJ *Deconstructing Apartheid Discourse* (1996) London: Verso.
Rancière J "Who is the Subject of the Rights of Man?" (2004) 103 *South Atlantic Quarterly* 297.
Rancière J *Disagreement: Politics and Philosophy* (1999, translation J Rose) Minneapolis: University of Minnesota Press.
Roederer C "Third Path Theorists: Between Positivism and Natural Law, Fuller and Dworkin" in C Roederer and D Moellendorf (eds) *Jurisprudence* (2004) 84 Cape Town: Juta.
Roux T "Transformative Constitutionalism and the Best Interpretation of the South African Constitution: A Distinction without a Difference?" (2009) 20 *Stellenbosch Law Review* 258.
Roux T *The Politics of Principle: The First South African Constitutional Court, 1995-2005* (2013) Cambridge: Cambridge University Press.
Tsele M "'Coercing Virtue' in the Constitutional Court: Neutral Principles, Rationality and the *Nkandla* Problem" (2016) 8 *Constitutional Court Review* 193.
Tushnet M "An Essay on Rights" (1984) 62 *Texas Law Review* 1363.
Unger R The Critical Legal Studies Movement (1983) Cambridge, Massachusetts: Harvard University Press.
Van der Walt AJ "Tradition on Trial: A Critical Analysis of the Civil-Law Tradition in South African Property Law" (1995) 11 *South African Journal on Human Rights* 169.
Van der Walt AJ "Un-Doing Things with Words: The Colonisation of the Public Sphere by Private-Property Discourse" (1998) *Acta Juridica* 235.
Wechsler H "Toward Neutral Principles of Constitutional Law' (1959) 73 *Harvard Law Review* 1.
Wesson M and Du Plessis M "Hart, Dworkin and the Nature of (South African) Legal Theory" (2006) 123 *South African Law Journal* 700.
Williams P "*Metro Broadcasting, Inc v FCC*: Regrouping in Singular Times" in K Crenshaw et al. (eds) *Critical Race Theory: The Key Writings that Formed the Movement* (1995) 191 New York: The New Press.
Winter S. *A Clearing in the Forest: Law, Life, and Mind* (2001) Chicago: University of Chicago Press.
Young I *Justice and the Politics of Difference* (1990) Princeton: Princeton University Press.

## Case law

### *South Africa*

*Ex parte Chairperson of the Constitutional Assembly: In re Certification of the Constitution of the Republic of South Africa, 1996* 1996 (4) SA 744 (CC)
*Jordan v S* 2002 (6) SA 642 (CC)
*King NO v De Jager* 2021 (4) SA 1 (CC)
*Minister of Education v Syfrets Trust Ltd NO* 2006 (4) SA 205 (C)

*Minister of Finance v Van Heerden* 2004 (6) SA 121 (CC)
*President of the Republic of South Africa v Hugo* 1997 (6) BCLR 708 (CC)
*S v Makwanyane* 1995 (3) SA 391 (CC)
*Shabalala v Attorney-General of the Transvaal* 1996 (1) SA 725 (CC)
*Solidarity v Department of Correctional Services* 2016 (10) BCLR 1349 (CC)
*South African Police Service v Solidarity obo Barnard* 2014 (6) SA 123 (CC)
*Volks NO v Robinson* 2005 (5) SA 446 (CC)

### United States

*Brown v Board of Education of Topeka* 347 US 483 (1954)
*Plessy v Ferguson* 163 US 537 (1896)

# 4 Human dignity

## Enunciating universals

Human dignity is at the centre of constitutional interpretation in South Africa. It shapes constitutional interpretation at different levels: as a justiciable right, a value which informs the interpretation of other rights, a factor to be considered in limitation analysis, and a guide to the interpretation of legislation and the development of the common law and customary law.[1] In these different guises, it has done more than any other constitutional right or value to steer the development of fundamental rights jurisprudence. The turn to dignity as a supreme right and value is grounded, firstly, in the conviction that the Constitution is above all a reaction against the systematic denial of the inherent human dignity of black people under colonialism and apartheid. O'Regan J stated in an oft-quoted passage in *Makwanyane*:

> Respect for the dignity of all human beings is particularly important in South Africa. For apartheid was a denial of a common humanity. Black people were refused respect and dignity and thereby the dignity of all South Africans was diminished. The new Constitution rejects this past and affirms the equal worth of all South Africans. Thus recognition and protection of human dignity is the touchstone of the new political order and is fundamental to the new Constitution.[2]

Laurie Ackermann similarly states that the violation of the dignity of black South Africans consisted primarily in a denial of their right to define themselves:

> The state did its best to deny to black South Africans that which is definitional to being human, namely the ability to understand or at least define oneself through one's own powers and to act freely as a moral agent pursuant to this understanding or self-definition. Black people were treated as means to an end and hardly ever as an end in themselves; an almost complete reversal of the categorically imperative concept of priceless inner worth and dignity.[3]

DOI: 10.4324/9781003482451-5

Taken together, these two quotes suggest various ways in which apartheid violated the dignity of black South Africans: by denying their humanity; by failing to respect their inherent and equal human worth; by treating them as mere means in the service of the grand social experiment of apartheid, rather than as ends in themselves; by signalling that they were not capable of moral autonomy; and by systematically depriving them of opportunities for self-definition and self-actualisation. In this view, the multiple and diverse injustices that were visited upon black people – including land dispossession, forced removals, pass laws, denial of economic opportunities, inferior education, political disenfranchisement, incarceration, and police brutality – are best viewed through the lens of their impact on human dignity. However, O'Regan and Ackermann do not only claim that dignity can assist us in identifying and remembering the injustices of the past. They also stress that dignity provides a transformative frame for articulating South Africa's social and historical context with the demand for universal and unconditional respect for every person. Because dignity extends equally to all members of the human family, it is believed to be capable of transforming historical narratives of degradation and oppression into a universalistic imperative to honour the worth of every human person, in a manner that transcends the particularity of local history or any specific group of victims. The warning not to repeat the race-based injustices of the past thus simultaneously serves as an injunction to remember other forms of disadvantage and discrimination and to subject all laws and social practices that impair individuals' equal worth and capacity for self-realisation to the critical light of the Constitution.[4]

Secondly, the turn to a dignity-based jurisprudence is explained with reference to developments in international and comparative constitutional law in the aftermath of the Second World War.[5] Several international treaties declare the international community's resolve to affirm the dignity of the human person, or proclaim that human dignity is foundational to the protection of human rights.[6] Dignity is also central to many of the national constitutions adopted over the past seventy years, particularly in countries trying to come to terms with an authoritarian, oppressive, or colonial past.[7] The Court has not relied heavily on foreign law in defining dignity, but has consulted foreign law – as well as international law – in interpreting rights that are closely associated with dignity, thus enabling it to articulate constitutional rights and standards with evolving international notions of personhood and decency.[8]

Thirdly, it is sometimes claimed that respect for human dignity could provide the basis for an intercultural and interreligious dialogue between different understandings of personhood, freedom, equality, and community. Ackermann notes the centrality of human dignity and worth to the Abrahamic religions, as well as a wide range of secular moral and legal traditions. He argues, with reference to John Rawls, that a shared commitment to dignity could underpin an overlapping consensus, which enables similar political judgments, even if they are based on different conceptions of justice.[9] The Constitutional Court's reliance on the indigenous African concept of ubuntu, which encompasses the values of humanity, solidarity, respect, and interdependence, arguably advances such an intercultural dialogue between different understandings of dignity.[10] What binds these explanations together is a sense that dignity, perhaps more than any other value, can articulate the universalistic premises of the Constitution with the particularity of South Africa's historical and social context. Dignity, on this view, can transform the historical narratives of oppression under colonialism and apartheid into a universal command to honour the worth of every human person. It refers to something absolute and universal, while at the same time providing the basis for resolving disputes in a context-sensitive manner, with reference to the dignity of all concerned.

This account of dignity's emancipatory value raises several questions. Can it be reconciled with the idea, discussed in the previous chapter, that universal ideals are themselves enunciated in a field of conflict and power? Can a dignity-based jurisprudence resist being used to normalise the re-introduction of status-based distinctions into our definition of the human? Conversely, can it face up to the paradoxes that arise from attempts to institute the universal, and create spaces in which alternative articulations of the universal can challenge inequality and exclusion?

The chapter starts with a brief discussion of dignity's role as a constitutional right and value and the various meanings ascribed to it in constitutional discourse. It then examines four questions that can shed light on its capacity to politicise forms of inequality and exclusion that are embedded in social and political structures. The first concerns the difficulty of translating the idea that dignity is inherent in every human person and therefore unconditional and absolute into a legal right and value. The second relates to the contrast between moral-universal understandings of dignity as something that sets limits to democracy and legal and political understandings that view dignity as constitutive of democracy. The third focusses on the tension between the idea that dignity demands respect for individuals' right to self-realisation and the outlawing of occupations or religious or cultural practices that are thought to impair the dignity of those that willingly partake in them. The fourth concerns the relationship between the dignity that is inherent in all human beings and the dignity associated with citizenship.

## 4.1 Dignity as a constitutional right and value

Section 10 of the Constitution provides: "Everyone has inherent dignity and the right to have their dignity respected and protected". By recognising the inherent dignity of every person, the section affirms that dignity vests in all persons, that it is unconditional, and that it cannot be waived through undignified behaviour. In addition, section 10 guarantees an enforceable right which imposes an obligation on others both to refrain from conduct that violates the dignity of any person and to take positive steps to safeguard it from infringement.

Dignity is also referred to in several other constitutional provisions. Section 1(a) declares that South Africa is founded on the values of "human dignity, the achievement of equality and the advancement of human rights and freedoms".[11] Section 7(1) proclaims that the Bill of Rights "affirms the democratic values of human dignity, equality and freedom"; section 36(1) provides that limitations of fundamental rights must be "reasonable and justifiable in an open and democratic society based on human dignity, equality and freedom"; and section 39(1) requires interpreters of the Bill of Rights to "promote the values that underlie an open and democratic society based on human dignity, equality and freedom". Section 35(2)(e) states that every detained person has the right to "conditions of detention that are consistent with human dignity", while section 37(5)(c) shields section 10 from derogation under a state of emergency.

Human dignity is thus firmly entrenched in the constitutional text: as a fundamental right; as a guide to the interpretation of other constitutional rights; as central to the normative vision espoused in the Constitution, which must inform the interpretation of legislation and development of the common law and customary law;[12] and as a key consideration in deciding on the constitutionality of fundamental-rights limitations. The jurisprudence of the Constitutional Court reflects – and in some respects preceded – the prominence given to dignity in the constitutional text. In one of its first judgments under the interim Constitution, which, compared to the 1996 Constitution, provided little textual support for the proposition that dignity enjoyed an elevated status, it described dignity and the right to life as "the most important of all human rights, and the source of all other personal rights".[13] In subsequent cases, it termed dignity the "cornerstone of human rights"[14] and "a value that informs the interpretation of many, possibly all, other rights".[15] The Court has placed the value of dignity at the centre of a wide range of rights. These include the right to privacy,[16] the right not to be subject to cruel, inhuman, or degrading treatment or punishment,[17] and socio-economic rights.[18] Perhaps more surprisingly – given the resonance between these rights and other constitutional values, like equality, freedom, and democracy – they also include the right to equality and non-discrimination,[19] various fundamental freedoms, including freedom of religion[20] and freedom of expression,[21] and political rights.[22]

The Constitutional Court's limitation jurisprudence similarly accords a special place to human dignity. A limitation that affects the core of someone's fundamental human dignity or personhood can only be saved if a compelling justification is advanced in support of it and if there is a tight fit between the limitation and its purpose. Where, on the other hand, dignity (or another foundational constitutional value) is not affected, or is affected only at the margins, the Court is less likely to intervene, as it tends to grant the legislature more leeway in its choice of a particular means to achieve the limitation's purpose.[23]

Dignity is notoriously difficult to define. Rather than trying to provide a comprehensive definition, I will briefly discuss six meanings that are ascribed to it in constitutional discourse. These are the ideas that dignity is inherent in every human being; that human beings are ends in themselves that should not be reduced to mere objects; that they are entitled to a sphere of autonomy or self-actualisation; that every person has equal dignity and worth; that individuals are entitled to membership in a community which recognises their personhood and rights; and that they should have access to the necessities of life.[24] The list is not exhaustive – dignity is a dynamic concept which can acquire new meanings when it is invoked within the context of different struggles. Nor does the discussion pretend to do justice to the richness of the topic. It provides only a cursory overview, which is meant to pave the way for a discussion in subsequent sections of some of the tensions that are relevant to the capacity of a dignity-based jurisprudence to enable different articulations of dignity that can challenge domination, inequality, and exclusion.

First, inherent human dignity refers to the notion that all human beings have inner dignity and worth, irrespective of whether the law treats them as persons who are capable of self-definition and self-actualisation. Used in this sense, dignity refers not to a legal but to an ontological status.[25] It denotes something absolute, whose existence precedes legal recognition. I will discuss this dimension, and the tensions that arise between it and some of dignity's other meanings, more fully in the next section.

Secondly, it is often claimed, in accordance with the Kantian categorical imperative which stipulates that human beings must be treated as ends in themselves, not as means to an end, that dignity proscribes the objectification of the human person. According to Günter Dürig, the German constitutional scholar, human dignity is grounded in the notion that human beings are distinct from the impersonality of nature by virtue of their mind, which enables them to become aware of themselves, to determine their own ends, and to shape their environment.[26] When human beings are treated as objects, their capacity for self-definition and self-realisation is denied. In Dürig's formulation:

> Human dignity as such is affected when a concrete human being is reduced to an object, to a mere means, to a dispensable quantity. [Violations of dignity involve] the degradation of the person to a thing, which can, in its entirety, be grasped, disposed of, registered, brainwashed, replaced, used and expelled.[27]

This formulation has found favour with courts in Germany, South Africa, and other jurisdictions. It has, for instance, been invoked in the context of judicial sentencing.[28] In *Makwanyane*, the Constitutional Court held that the death penalty "instrumentalises the offender for the objectives of State policy",[29] "dehumanises the person and objectifies him or her as a tool for crime control",[30] and places him or her "beyond the pale of humanity".[31] In *Dodo*, the Court similarly held that a disproportionately severe sentence would reduce the offender to a means to an end. The Court declared: "Human beings are not commodities to which a price can be attached; they are creatures with inherent and infinite worth; they ought to be treated as ends in themselves, never merely as means to an end".[32] Respect for individuals as ends in themselves requires judicial officers to pay due regard to the principle of proportionality and the circumstances of the offender and the individual case. They should place particular emphasis on the offender's rehabilitation and treat her not as a mere object of crime prevention or deterrence, but as someone capable of choosing her own ends and developing her personality.

The object formula also implies that individuals should have the opportunity to participate in decision-making procedures affecting them. This has implications for the procedural rights of accused persons and parties involved in litigation, as well as individuals who are affected by administrative action. The Constitutional Court's jurisprudence on meaningful engagement, which requires structured consultation with individuals and communities who are to be evicted from their homes, is informed by the idea that those affected by state decisions should be treated as rights-bearing individuals, rather than objects of state power or obstacles to the implementation of state policies.[33]

Thirdly, the imperative to view all individuals as ends in themselves who have intrinsic human worth gives rise to the idea that they should be treated as capable of self-definition and self-determination. According to the Constitutional Court, dignity requires "respect for the unique set of ends" and moral autonomy of every individual.[34] Everyone should be free to set and pursue their own ends, to forge relationships with others, to find nurture and support in their communities, to search for or find meaning in religious beliefs or other worldviews, and to develop their unique talents.[35] This dimension of dignity is closely bound up with sexual freedom. It encompasses the right to free oneself from restrictive social norms and roles and to define one's own sexual orientation and gender identity. It also includes the right to make reproductive choices, as recognised in section 12(2)(a) of the Constitution. A woman's destiny should not be determined by the state's vision of women's role, but should be shaped, as far as possible, by her own convictions and understanding of her role in society.[36]

Fourthly, the dignity and worth that is inherent in every human person is not subject to distinctions and gradations based on ability, social rank, or any other attribute, but vests equally in every human being. This does not mean that all people should be treated identically, but it does mean that all individuals should be treated with equal respect and concern. The principle of equal dignity is offended when some individuals, based on certain group characteristics that they share, are treated differently from others in a way that degrades them, or denies or impairs their capacity for individual self-determination, autonomy, or the free development of their personalities. That would be the case where, for example, women's contractual capacity is subjected to the control of their husbands or close male relatives, or where women are excluded from certain positions or occupations. As the Constitutional Court stated in a case concerning the exclusion of women from intestate succession in terms of African customary law:

> The principle of primogeniture ... implies that women are not fit or competent to own and administer property. Its effect is also to subject these women to a status of perpetual minority, placing them automatically under the control of male heirs, simply by virtue of their sex and gender. Their dignity is further affronted by the fact that as women, they are also excluded from intestate succession and denied the right, which other members of the population have, to be holders of, and to control property.[37]

The principle of male primogeniture does not treat a woman as a person in her own right. It premises her treatment on a particular groups-based attribute, without reference to her individual abilities, in circumstances where that attribute is not and should not be relevant to her capacity to take care of her own affairs. The Court has employed similar reasoning where laws stigmatise members of certain groups as immoral or irresponsible. In a case dealing with the criminalisation of male same-sex sodomy, Sachs J warned against measures that "stigmatise individuals as members of an inferior caste or view them as not belonging to the community", and thus deny their "full moral citizenship".[38] The prohibition of sodomy signals that gay men are incapable of forming meaningful intimate relationships, and excludes them from the moral community by treating their desire as abnormal and deviant.[39] Laws that brand certain categories of people as immoral or lacking in autonomy typically draw on and reinforce prejudices and stereotypes that deny the individuality and inherent dignity and worth of members of that group, and perpetuate and affirm their exclusion and subordination.[40] Examples of stereotypes which carry connotations of inferiority include the image of mothers as primary caretakers,[41] of women as caring, homely, passive, emotional, and less rational than men,[42] and of poor people as lazy or lacking in initiative.

Violations of equal dignity are usually associated with differentiations in treatment. However, sameness of treatment can also be problematic from an equal dignity perspective, as illustrated by the *Pillay* case, in which the Constitutional Court held that religious and cultural beliefs and practices are important aspects of human dignity and that a public school's failure to make exemptions in its dress code based on religious and cultural grounds amounted to unfair discrimination.[43] The Canadian Supreme Court has also found that a failure to provide sign language interpretation in hospitals violated the equality rights of deaf patients, as it failed to accommodate their special needs and denied them the right to make informed decisions about their own bodies.[44] In both these cases, the actions of the public authorities fell short of the requirements of equal dignity, despite the fact that they were not based on prejudice or rooted in harmful stereotypes. Instead, the findings of unconstitutionality were based on the authorities' failure to take positive steps to safeguard the dignity of those whose needs could not be accommodated through standardised treatment or adherence to general rules.

The references in the Constitutional Court's jurisprudence to belonging, citizenship and moral citizenship allude to a fifth dimension of dignity, namely membership in a moral and political community which recognises individuals' personhood and grounds their capacity to participate in social, economic, and political life. Dignity vests not in atomic individuals, but in embodied human beings who develop their individuality and sense of self through relationships with others and participation in societal structures. Their rights mean little when severed from the concrete contexts and networks of relations that are constitutive of a community based on equal recognition. In cases dealing with discrimination based on sexual orientation, the Court stressed that what was at issue was not simply gays and lesbians' right to be left alone, but their right to public recognition of their identities and relationships[45] and fostering an active citizenship which is rooted in respect for difference.[46] They must be able to express their identities and participate in social life without having to fear that they will be victimised or humiliated based on their beliefs, sexuality, or life style. Laws or conduct that exclude individuals from the moral or political community – for instance, through unfair discrimination, restrictions of political rights,[47] or hate speech[48] – impede their ability to enforce their rights and deprive them of opportunities for personal growth.

A sixth dimension, access to the necessities of life, is closely linked to individual self-realisation, freedom from exploitation, and integration and participation in the community. The Constitutional Court recognises that the constitutional promise of a society based on dignity, equality, and freedom will have "a hollow ring" while millions of South Africans continue to live in poverty and intolerable conditions.[49] It has, however, stopped short of defining and enforcing the minimum core content of socio-economic rights or making them available on demand. Its approach to the interpretation and enforcement of those rights focusses instead on the reasonableness of state measures aimed at giving effect to those rights.[50] This approach seeks to balance concern for the impact of laws and policies on the lives of impoverished people with sensitivity to budgetary constraints, the limits to the judiciary's institutional capacity, and the separation of powers. However, laws and policies that do not have regard to the dignity and equality of the most vulnerable sections of society will not pass the reasonableness test. In *Grootboom*, the Court held that the state's failure to provide for people in urgent need fell short of the requirements of the constitutional right of access to adequate housing.[51] Although the articulation of socio-economic rights with the dignity and equality of all South Africans has transformative potential, the deferential stance taken in some of the Constitutional Court's later judgments raise questions about the limits of its approach.[52]

These dimensions of dignity are closely intertwined. For instance, the notion of non-objectification, the right of every person to self-actualisation, and the principle of equal dignity all express different aspects of the idea that human beings should be considered ends in themselves and not means to an end. However, on closer inspection, certain tensions become apparent. In the first place, the principles of non-objectification and self-actualisation collide when conduct – for instance, sex work – that is willingly engaged in is prohibited because it is seen as objectifying or degrading. Secondly, similar tensions arise when speech impairs the self-worth or reputation of individuals or categories of individuals or when hate speech or defamation laws curtail speech.[53] In these cases, the importance of freedom of expression to personal development and self-realisation comes up against other dimensions of dignity, like membership in a community based on equal recognition. Thirdly, the idea that dignity is inherent in every person, irrespective of nationality or status, comes into conflict with dignity's inscription within a particular legal order, where it is tied to membership in the political community. That raises questions about the position of noncitizens as well as other categories of people who, despite having formal citizenship, are relegated to a position outside the moral and political community. I will examine the first and third tensions in the last two sections of this chapter, which are titled "Dignity and self-realisation" and "The dignity of (non-) citizens", respectively. The second tension will be explored in the discussion of "Freedom of expression in a divided society" in chapter 6.

## 4.2 Lost in translation? Inherent human dignity as a legal and constitutional principle

The most influential statement of the idea that dignity is inherent in every human being can be found in the moral philosophy of Immanuel Kant. Kant distinguished between things with a relative value or price that are replaceable, and those with an inner worth or dignity that is absolute and unconditional.[54] He stated that only "morality, and humanity insofar as it is capable of morality", has dignity.[55] The dignity that inheres in humanity is derived from the capacity to act autonomously in terms of a universal moral law. Autonomy, in the sense used here, involves living in accordance with a moral law that a self-legislating person has given herself. Such a moral law must be universal, i.e., it must be based on a "maxim through which [the individual] can at the same time will that it become a universal law".[56] The moral law requires human beings to be treated as ends in themselves. This is expressed in Kant's second formulation of the categorical imperative: "So act that you use humanity, whether in your own person or in the person of any other, always at the same time as an end, never merely as a means".[57]

Kant's conception of dignity is non-hierarchical, as it recognises the inherent dignity and worth of every human person, without reference to differentiations based on status, role, or intellectual capacity. His moral philosophy thus breaks with a long tradition, which dates to Roman times, in which dignity was conceived in hierarchical, non-egalitarian terms to denote the status, rank, or prestige of certain individuals, as well as state offices and institutions.[58] It also breaks with another tradition, with a long lineage in Catholic thought, in which dignity was tied to "the value something has in virtue of occupying its proper place within a divine order".[59] On that understanding, dignity derives from membership of a particular group (e.g., women or labourers) and conducting oneself in accordance with the role reserved for that group within the social order.[60]

This narrative about the historical shift from hierarchical and groups-based dignity to inherent human dignity follows the dominant historical framings in the jurisprudential and moral-philosophical literature.[61] It also resonates with the constitutional literature (even though, as pointed out below, the idea of unconditional respect for human dignity is not easily translated into a constitutional norm). When a constitution proclaims that dignity is inherent in all human beings, it is not simply stating that it is afforded legal recognition. Inherent human dignity signals that every human being is endowed with dignity and inner worth, even in cases where some people's right to dignity is systematically violated, where the law does not recognise their legal capacity, or where it fails to vest any rights in them.[62] Human dignity is therefore seen to have an existence that is independent of and prior to its recognition through legal and constitutional guarantees.[63]

The claim that dignity expresses something about the essence of what it means to be human is related to the idea that it has an absolute or inviolable core which may not be limited. This idea is stated most emphatically in article 1(1) of the German Basic Law, which declares human dignity to be inviolable. This has been interpreted to mean that dignity can neither be waived nor limited by or in terms of legislation. This interpretation makes sense of the special place that dignity occupies in the German Basic Law: it is not only entrenched in the very first article but is invoked as the foundation of human rights[64] and is shielded from constitutional amendment.[65] The judgment of the German Federal Constitutional Court in the Aviation Security Case epitomises the view that dignity may not be limited. The Court invalidated legislation, adopted in the wake of 9/11, which empowered the security forces to shoot down an aircraft which was to be used to destroy human life. In the Court's view, the legislation impaired the dignity of cabin crew and passengers, who were rendered helpless objects of the state's attempts to protect the public. The Court held that it was not permissible to balance their dignity against the lives of others who may be saved in the process.[66]

The claim that dignity is absolute creates difficulties for law, which is charged with the harmonisation of conflicting rights and freedoms.[67] Given dignity's status as the foundation of human rights and the courts' tendency to rely on it in conjunction with more specific rights, dignity-based claims sometimes come into direct conflict. In those cases, a court may have no choice but to engage in balancing.[68] Some scholars have distinguished between a core of dignity that is absolute and a periphery that is open to balancing.[69] However, the dominant view in the German literature is that dignity cannot be limited. To preserve its absolute character, courts try to prevent its trivialisation by refraining from relying directly on the right to dignity and by interpreting it restrictively.[70]

The South African Constitution, by contrast, appears to treat dignity as a relative right which, like any other right, can be limited. However, not everyone agrees with this interpretation. Francois Venter points out that section 10 consists of two parts: the first declares that everyone has "inherent dignity", while the second confers the right to have one's dignity respected and protected. In his view, the first part has an independent meaning which should not be collapsed onto that of the second, as it recognises dignity as "an inalienable, inborn characteristic of each individual person".[71] Based on this interpretation, it could be argued that the reference in section 10 to the inherent dignity of every person gives absolute protection to an inner and inviolable core of dignity. On this view, section 10, in addition to conferring a right, proclaims that the inherent dignity of the individual exists prior to its recognition in a constitution. Unlike the right to have one's dignity respected and protected, which is subject to limitation, the inherent dignity of the person is absolute, and a restriction of this inner core of dignity cannot be justified with reference to countervailing interests.[72]

The tension between dignity's universal character and the particularity of the contexts in which it is concretised is not only evident from the difficulties arising from attempts to translate dignity as a moral ideal into a legal and constitutional norm. It also manifests in the disconnect between the commitment to the inherent, unconditional dignity and worth of all human beings and continued adherence, in the social and juridical spheres, to status- and groups-based conceptions of dignity.[73] The special dignity that is attributed to the judiciary in many countries, including South Africa, bears testimony to the fact that, even in modern usage, ideas of status or rank are deeply embedded in the concept of dignity.[74] More fundamentally, the persistence in constitutional democracies of hierarchies based inter alia on race, class, gender, sexuality, religion, and nationality raises concerns about the capacity of status- and groups-based hierarchies to exist alongside the commitment to universal human dignity and to infiltrate the meanings ascribed to it. One way of making sense of that tension is by distinguishing between dignity as a moral and a legal category and insisting that, while from a moral perspective, dignity demands absolute and unconditional respect, certain social hierarchies may nevertheless be embedded in legal concepts and principles, even under a legal system that expressly recognises every person's intrinsic dignity. Although the dividing line between law and morality is fluid, particularly under a supreme, value-based constitution, it is important to uphold that distinction. Failing to do so tends to feed into narratives of an ever-closer convergence between moral-universal precepts and positive law, which overlook law's bounded nature and disregard the ubiquity of conflict, exclusion, and inequality.

For such an account to have critical bite, it must be able to explain the capacity of legal categories to inscribe hierarchical distinctions and restrictive conditions into the universal. Étienne Balbar's views, discussed in chapter 3, on the mutual entwinement of the universal and particular and the historical contingency of the legal order in which universal ideals are embodied, provide one such vantage point. Roberto Esposito's work on the legal category of personhood provides another. Esposito notes the centrality of the concept of personhood to the human rights paradigm that developed after the Second World War. In response to Nazism's crude biologism and utter debasement of the person as a locus of will and reason, human rights declarations placed respect for the inherent dignity and worth of the human person at the centre of the emerging international human rights order. However, Esposito shows, with reference to personhood's roots in Roman law and the subsequent transformations of its meaning, that it cannot ground the idea of absolute and unconditional respect for human beings. Since its inception, the concept of personhood has abstracted away from human beings' concrete, embodied existence. The human rights tradition is no exception – it narrowly identifies personhood with individual will, reason, and morality and thus defines it in opposition to human beings' bodily existence, which is identified with "an animal or vegetal dimension".[75] Esposito refers to statements of Jacques Maritain, who played a leading role in drafting the Universal Declaration of Human Rights, in which he grounded human rights in individuals' mastery over their animal nature.[76] These statements suggest that personhood is not only premised on a distinction between human beings' personal (moral and rational) and impersonal (bodily and animal) dimensions but also requires the subjection of the latter. Moreover, it is tied to the body's reification, as the body is depersonalised and acquires a thing-like nature which must be controlled.[77] Personhood, which is supposed to provide the legal grounding for the unconditional and inherent dignity and worth of all human beings, thus reintroduces hierarchies – based most obviously on age and mental capacity, but also race, culture, religion, and other categories – into the definition of the human.

It is tempting to assume, in line with cosmopolitan human rights theories and liberal constitutional discourse, that the gap between inherent, unconditional human dignity and the contingency of the legal order in which it is positivised is the result of factors, like the lingering influence of inegalitarian belief systems, which are external to universal ideals. The above reflections suggest that this understanding is inadequate. We should not assume that the universal is left untouched by the persistence of social hierarchies and exclusion but must be alive to the capacity of legal categories to inscribe gradations into the definition of the human.

## 4.3 Dignity and democracy

The tension between the idea that human dignity refers to an ontological claim about human beings' inherent and absolute worth and its status as a positive legal norm which is inscribed into a bounded legal order raises fundamental questions about the relationship between dignity and democracy. First, is dignity to be understood primarily as a moral-universal concept that sets limits to democracy or as a legal and political concept that is constitutive of democracy? Second, to what extent can dignity provide a basis for democratic dialogue and the contestation of power hierarchies and exploitative social practices? If dignity, like all other concepts, is generated discursively, is there not a danger that its supposed universality could be used to normalise the subordination and degradation of certain segments of the population and insulate social power from democratic debate? Conversely, is its universality indispensable to its capacity to politicise and disrupt extant power relations?

The constitutional literature tends to conceive human dignity as a universal moral concept, which sets limits to the power of democratic institutions. It typically grounds dignity in fundamental truths about human nature, like the idea that human beings are created in God's image, or their capacity for reason, self-determination, and moral autonomy. Whether these understandings can provide the basis for a transformative jurisprudence is, however, controversial. Critics argue that they are based on assumptions about autonomy and free will that are grounded in metaphysical notions which are considered problematic today,[78] and that their appeal to natural law masks disagreement and shields certain social arrangements from critique and contestation.[79] They are also vulnerable to the criticism that they inscribe hierarchical distinctions based, inter alia, on independence and mental competence at the heart of the human.[80]

In view of these problems, some constitutional scholars propose understanding dignity in legal and political rather than abstract moral terms. Dignity, on this view, concerns the rights and duties arising from membership in a concrete human community.[81] It is grounded neither in religious beliefs nor in abstract conceptions of personhood but in social recognition within a community. Hasso Hofmann argues that dignity must be conceived in relational and communicative terms. It is based not on cosmopolitan notions of right or a specific human quality or achievement but on social solidarity and mutual recognition within a concrete community.[82] Christoph Möllers agrees that dignity is best understood as based on a commitment made by a particular political community that is constitutive of its democratic self-understanding.[83] Instead of viewing dignity as an external limit to democracy, he treats these values as complementary and mutually reinforcing. On the one hand, dignity can be protected only within a political community; on the other hand, the commitment to the protection of human dignity is part and parcel of the political community's self-understanding. This understanding resists the idea that dignity is pre-political, or that the determination of its meaning should be left entirely to the judiciary. Instead, it treats dignity as "an argument in an open democratic debate that has to be decided anew, time and time again".[84] Proponents of this theory argue that, unlike understandings of dignity in universal moral terms, it can explain why a state is bound to respect the dignity of everyone within its territory but has no such obligation to foreign nationals outside its borders.[85]

A relational, communicative understanding, which grounds human dignity not in transcendental truth but in a concrete political community, seems well equipped to account for the role played by democratic dialogue and contestation in challenging and revising conventional views on the meaning and implications of dignity. It also highlights dignity's role in constituting the legal and political order. It is therefore arguably better able than a moral-universal conception to shed light on the capacity of dignity-based claims to disrupt institutionalised power and disadvantage and to upset reified understandings of personhood and autonomy. At the same time, its insistence that acts of state-founding involve a demarcation from the outside world could help explain the limits of the state's ability to respond to the dignity claims of foreign nationals – other than asylum-seekers – who are outside the state territory. However, the question arises whether this understanding is not in danger of reducing dignity to the protection afforded to it within a positive legal order.[86] Is it not true that dignity's emancipatory value derives, at least in part, from its capacity to exceed the bounds of a given legal order? According to Paolo Carozza, the reason why legal interpreters can rely on dignity to mediate between "otherwise incommensurable values" and to create new rights or extend the meaning of existing ones is precisely because "it appeals to, draws its authority from, and claims to be the bearer of some extra-legal and supra-positive value".[87] Jürgen Habermas similarly argues that dignity's ability to ground a democratic legal order depends on its status as a moral and universalistic idea. In his view, "human dignity forms the 'portal' through which the egalitarian and universalistic substance of morality is imported into law".[88] When dignity is reduced to the meaning – or range of meanings – ascribed to it by positive law, it loses its ability to challenge sedimented and exclusionary understandings of humanity and personhood.

It would seem, then, that rather than settling for either a moral-universal or democratic conception of dignity, we need to combine them into an understanding which stresses both dignity's role as a positive legal norm and founding constitutional value and its status as a supra-positive value that transcends the bounds of any given legal order. Drucilla Cornell argues along these lines that dignity as a constitutional right and value can never perfectly approximate dignity as a moral ideal, which refers to a normative order or philosophical imagination that is "above and beyond the subjective clash of individual interest".[89] For her, the gap between a legal system that is based on respect for human dignity, and the Kantian ideal of a kingdom of ends that demands the harmonisation of the ends of human beings with infinite worth, is critical to the emancipatory potential of human dignity as a constitutional right and value. Dignity thus not only grounds the democratic order and legal system, but also points beyond positive law "toward a telos of change".[90] On the one hand, every attempt to translate human dignity into legal rights and values invariably falls short of the moral ideal and inscribes it into a legal and constitutional order that developed from a particular constellation of experiences, visions, and power relations. Legal understandings of dignity are inevitably infused with norms and expectations that bear the imprint of specific struggles and interests. It also seems likely that the constitutional ideal of equal and inherent dignity and worth will exist alongside inequality and exclusion; in fact, there is a danger that dignity may be relied on to normalise oppression. On the other hand, the gap between dignity as a moral ideal and its institutionalisation as a legal norm could enable new emancipatory struggles, which push against the boundaries of the legal order to challenge domination and inequality.

We need to tread carefully, though. Just as theories that ground dignity in mutual recognition in a bounded political community risk taking certain limits (e.g., those deriving from the logic of statehood or a nation's constitutional history) for granted, moral-universal conceptions of dignity that are based on transcendental principles have blind spots. Lisa Guenther states, with reference to Denise Ferreira da Silva, that the self-determining subject posited in Kant's transcendental philosophy, that grounds the possibility of an orderly world based on universal knowledge, is constructed in opposition to non-autonomous, racial others that need to be controlled and kept in line.[91] On this view, the coexistence of white supremacy and the figure of the knowing, autonomous subject is no coincidence, as both derive from a belief in the capacity of the latter to categorise and measure all objects, and overcome obstacles in the way of order and progress. According to Guenther,

> Contingent epistemic claims and ontological principles have been grasped and formalized as transcendental conditions for the intelligibility of the world to a self-determining Subject, with the effect of grounding raciality – another contingent, historical concept – in a framework of universal truth.[92]

How, then, could we rely on the principle of universal human dignity to question and disrupt exclusionary legal constructs and oppressive social structures if those concepts and structures are themselves ensconced in understandings of the universal?[93] In the first place, we must recognise, as the previous chapter suggests, that universal ideals do not stand above the fray of disagreement but are deeply embroiled in it. On this understanding, the ideal of inherent and unconditional human dignity and worth does not provide a template that enables domination and inequality to be gradually overcome by subsuming the particular under the universal. Rather, it opens up a permanent dialectic between its radically emancipatory message and its inscription in restrictive and exclusionary legal norms.

Secondly, although progressive laws and judicial decisions can destabilise such norms and provide much needed respite in the struggle against them, more is required. What is needed is an array of different grammars of dignity, which can provide the basis for imaginaries within and beyond the existing national and international legal order. In view of the difficulties inherent in legal constructions of personhood (discussed in the previous section) and transcendental thought (discussed a few paragraphs ago), such alternative imaginaries must include ones that sever dignity from modernist fantasies of order, control, and progress, and link it instead to radical notions of relationality and difference.[94] Conceptions of dignity that are grounded in indigenous African thought seem an obvious starting point. Like Western understandings, they must be subjected to critical scrutiny, particularly in view of the danger that African notions of personhood as something to be achieved through participation in the life of the community could inscribe differences based on gender, sexuality, reproductive capacity, mental ability, and skin colour into the heart of personhood. Reliance on traditional, supposedly timeless African understandings of dignity and personhood is likely to normalise discrimination and violence against women, strangers, and other vulnerable groups. However, the dynamic tension in African thought between being and becoming and between inherent human dignity and the processes through which individuals attain self-realisation could assist us in transforming and critiquing social hierarchies and oppression. The same goes for the struggles of social movements and vulnerable groups that rely on African notions of dignity and ubuntu.[95] I will return to these issues in my discussion of alternative imaginaries of freedom in the final section of chapter 6.

In the next two sections, I consider two manifestations of the tension between human dignity's universality and its inscription in contingent social relations. The first is reliance on dignity to circumscribe the individual's right to choose occupations or lifestyles that are considered undignified or degrading. The second is the link between universal human dignity and the status of membership in a legal and political community.

## 4.4 Dignity and self-realisation

Despite the strong link between human dignity and individual freedom and self-realisation, respect for dignity does not require that some, or all individuals, should have absolute freedom to pursue their own ends. If we value the dignity of all persons, regardless of race, gender, class, or station in life, we must prevent individuals from using their freedom in ways that deprive others of meaningful opportunities for self-realisation. Respect for the inherent dignity and worth of every person demands measures that proscribe unfair private discrimination, provide protection against economic exploitation, and aim to eradicate violence against women, children, and other vulnerable groups. Such measures must ensure that everyone – as opposed to a select few – has the opportunity for self-realisation.[96] However, things get murkier when dignity is relied on to justify or demand serious restrictions on a person's bodily integrity, e.g. where a woman's right to choose to terminate a pregnancy is curtailed to protect the dignity of unborn life. The same goes for reliance on dignity to justify the prohibition of conduct, like sex work or wearing a veil in public, even though the conduct is voluntarily engaged in. That typically happens where the conduct is thought to be objectifying or degrading. In such cases, dignity as self-actualisation comes up against dignity as non-objectification, as noted above.

Rape, sexual trafficking, and forced prostitution involve grave violations of human dignity, personhood, and self-determination, as the victims of these crimes are turned into objects of sexual power through forceful acts aimed at erasing their subjectivity and personhood. The recognition by the International Criminal Tribunal for Rwanda and the International Criminal Tribunal for the former Yugoslavia that the use of rape as a weapon of war constitutes a crime against humanity[97] is viewed by many commentators an important victory in the battle against the objectification of women.[98] But what about cases in which individuals willingly participate in sexual conduct which may be viewed as degrading, demeaning, or unnatural? In a controversial judgment, the German Federal Administrative Court held that "peep shows" objectify the women concerned and thus violate their dignity. The prohibition of such shows was constitutional, even though the women who participated did so voluntarily.[99] The state's duty to protect participants against being reduced to objects of the viewers' lust thus appears to have trumped their freedom.

These and other cases (like the French dwarf-tossing case),[100] in which courts relied on human dignity as non-objectification to uphold laws that outlaw certain occupations, raise difficult questions concerning the relationship between dignity and freedom. Does respect for the self-determination of the persons who willingly engage in these occupations preclude attempts to protect their dignity under the banner of a morality they may not share? Do these judgments risk conflating dignity with dignified behaviour? Are they at odds with the idea that every human person has inherent dignity, which cannot be relinquished through undignified behaviour?[101]

The dangers inherent in such reliance on dignity are also illustrated by a South African High Court judgment, in which it was stated that bestiality is "so repugnant to and in conflict with human dignity as to amount to perversion of the natural order" and that the state is under an obligation to "prevent any individual or group from descending to the level of the beast".[102] There may be valid reasons for criminalising sex between humans and animals; however, the link made in the judgment between dignity and the "natural order" is worrying, as it risks confining the scope of personal and sexual freedom to what is considered normal, natural, and dignified sexual behaviour. The judgment infuses dignity with the hierarchical distinction between individuals who master their animal nature and those who stoop "to the level of the beast".

In *Jordan*, the Constitutional Court rejected the contention that the dignity of sex workers was impaired by a law that criminalises the conduct of sex workers but not that of their clients. It held that, to the extent that there is a diminution of sex workers' dignity, it arises from their own conduct rather than from the operation of the law, since the human body is devalued by its commodification through prostitution.[103] This is deeply problematic. In the first place, the suggestion that individuals can forfeit their dignity through undignified behaviour seems at odds with the idea that dignity is inherent in every human being, and the Court's insistence in other cases that dignity cannot be waived or forfeited through immoral or criminal behaviour.[104] Secondly, as in other cases discussed above, the Court relied on dignity to ground obligations of the individual towards herself. It thus detached dignity from the individual and subsumed it under broader notions of humanity, which can be turned into a standard for measuring individuals' civility and humanity and curtailing their choice of ends.[105] Thirdly, the Court's reasoning validates certain status hierarchies, which can be used to justify intrusions into the lives and beliefs of those who are thought to fall short of the ideals of rationality, self-mastery, and conventional morality. Fourthly, to the extent that it premises sexual freedom on conformity to widely shared sexual mores, it is inconsistent with the link made in the Constitutional Court's jurisprudence between dignity and respect for difference.[106] Finally, the claim that any impairment of sex workers' dignity stems from their own choice seems strangely oblivious to the ways in which poverty, exploitation, prejudice, and violence constrain the range of choices available to many men, women, and non-binary persons who turn to sex work.

Dignity-based arguments have also been used to justify restrictions on the wearing of religious symbols. These justifications rely both on narratives of oppression and norms relating to the kind of behaviour and demeanour that can be expected from free individuals living in a democratic society. In a case concerning a decision not to appoint a Muslim woman to a teaching position on the ground that she would have worn a headscarf in class, the German Federal Constitutional Court held that the decision interfered with her religious freedom and right to equal access to public office.[107] However, a dissenting judgment held that the wearing of a headscarf was inconsistent with the religious neutrality expected of public servants and was bound to create conflicts with the constitutional principle of gender equality. Moreover, it was only one step away from covering the full face, which could be seen as irreconcilable with German constitutional understandings of human dignity, as "free human beings show their faces to others".[108] Similar justifications were advanced for legislation adopted in other European countries that prohibited the wearing of a veil in public. The Belgian Constitutional Court dismissed an application for the invalidation of a law that prohibited appearing in public with one's face hidden or covered. It held that the legislature was entitled to take the view that the formation of human relationships was rendered impossible by the presence of veiled persons in the public sphere, as social life in a democratic society presupposes the ability to see other persons' faces as a mark of their individuality. It was also entitled to the view that the imposition of an obligation on women to wear a veil threatened their dignity and their right to self-determination. The Court further stated that wearing a veil, even where it is done voluntarily, threatens gender equality and deprives women of an important element of their individuality.[109]

The European Court of Human Rights and the Court of Justice of the European Union have decided a wide range of cases dealing with restrictions on the wearing of religious symbols, particularly attire worn by Muslim women. What is perhaps most striking about this case law is the high degree of deference paid to state decisions, which is linked to but not adequately explained by the margin of appreciation shown to member states.[110] In one of its supposedly more progressive judgments in this area, the European Court of Human Rights rejected the contention that a French law that banned the wearing in public of any clothing designed to conceal a person's face was justified based on dignity and gender equality.[111] However, it accepted that the limitation furthered the observance of the minimum requirements of life in society, since the hiding of a person's face is incompatible with French notions of "the ground rules of social communication and more broadly the requirements of 'living together'".[112] In this and several other cases, the Court uncritically accepted that the legislature was entitled to assume that the fostering of social trust and cohesion requires people to show their faces in public. However, its elaboration of the link between face-to-face communication and social cohesion is superficial, and completely disregards the social significance of veiling for the freedom and dignity of the women concerned.[113]

The holding in some judgments that the wearing of a headscarf or veil compromises the dignity and self-actualisation of women seems problematic in view of the evidence that, for many Muslim women, wearing them is both a personal choice and an expression of their cultural and religious identity. Studies suggest that these garments do not have a single, uniform meaning, and that women's reasons for wearing them vary considerably. For instance, some see it as a duty while others see it as a choice; some regard it as an expression of piety or conformity to familial or social values, while others view it as a means of countering objectification or communicating solidarity with an oppressed group. For some Muslim women, wearing a headscarf or veil provides a bridge between their religious and civic identities, and a means of asserting themselves as political subjects.[114] Judgments that uncritically accept the signification of these garments as symbols of women's oppression erase the agency of the women concerned. Moreover, to the extent that they rely on dignity to justify restrictions on wearing them in public or in the workplace, they infuse dignity with dominant constructions of individual autonomy or dignified behaviour. Respect for the unique ends of every individual is reduced to respect for the ends of those who conform to the image of the good citizen. Although the attributes of citizenship are presented in neutral and universal terms, they mirror dominant cultural understandings that are infused with a Protestant view of faith as something which is, for the most part, internal and private.[115] Ironically, these laws, which seek to restore the dignity of Muslim women and prevent their "effacement" from the public sphere, appear to be more likely to have the opposite effect by causing the women in question to withdraw into the domestic sphere.[116]

If dignity is to be a transformative concept, which grounds law in respect for the equal and inherent worth of every human person, it must be delinked from notions of status and dignified behaviour, which define the human capacity for self-definition and self-realisation in contradistinction to the dependence and irrationality of certain categories of people. That does not mean that we must ignore the ways in which cultural prejudice, poverty, economic exploitation, and unequal access to education, jobs, and political influence constrain the life choices of millions of South Africans and impede their capacity for self-realisation.

Nor does it mean that we must be blind to the capacity of constructions of consent and free choice to mask inequality and domination. However, in seeking to eradicate and transform the underlying causes of their disadvantage, we must be careful not to deny their agency. To rely on the dignity of disadvantaged and impoverished individuals to override their freedom to choose an occupation or to participate in religious or cultural practices is to risk falling back onto hierarchical understandings of what it means to be human, and to reserve freedom for some while relegating others to a life characterised by surveillance and control.

### 4.5 The dignity of (non-)citizens

The previous sections examined the tendency of dominant conceptions of personhood, freedom, and sociality to reintroduce hierarchical distinctions into our understanding of the human. In this section, I consider another distinction which has far-reaching implications for the enjoyment of supposedly universal human rights, namely that between citizens and non-citizens. How could we make sense of the divide between the commitment to inherent human dignity, irrespective of nationality, and the degradation experienced by foreign nationals? What could be done to resist the tendency to relegate – certain categories of – foreign nationals to a status that is largely outside the protective ambit of the law, personhood, and human rights? Could legal and political decisions that affirm the dignity of non-citizens destabilise the distinction between citizens and non-citizens, and assist the latter in their struggles to win rights traditionally reserved for citizens?[117]

Even though, today, most rights extend to non-citizens, citizenship underpins the protection of dignity in two ways. First, it serves as a symbol of inclusion within the national community and signifies an "insider" status which is marked out by a set of rights – most notably political rights – that are reserved for citizens.[118] Second, because citizenship denotes an insider status and confers rights of political participation, citizens are generally in a better position than non-citizens to enforce their rights. Non-citizens are not able to hold public representatives to account through the ballot box.[119] Their ability to mobilise politically and to defend their rights is further constrained by their outsider status, their vulnerability to arbitrary arrest, detention and deportation, and fears for their physical safety. The difficulties are compounded when they are desperately poor, undocumented, or unable to call upon their states of origin for diplomatic protection. As Hannah Arendt points out, in those circumstances, non-citizens are not only deprived of membership in an organised political community but are effectively excluded from rights that are presumed to vest in all people by virtue of their humanity.[120]

We can try to make sense of the chasm between intrinsic, unconditional human dignity and the dehumanisation of non-citizens by noting the difficulties inherent in trying to positivise universal rights and ideals within a particular legal order. When dignity is inscribed in a national legal order, its meaning is mediated, at least in part, through the legal category of citizenship, which is constitutive of the state, its identity, and commitments. Citizenship grounds the enjoyment of fundamental rights in membership, belonging, and the right to participate in the political life of the community.[121] However, in a world where growing numbers of refugees, asylum seekers, and stateless persons lack membership in a legal and political community, citizenship's universality is an imprecise approximation of the universality of human dignity. The gap between these universals goes some way towards explaining the precarious position of millions of refugees and stateless people. But the problem is not only that it is difficult to translate universal ideals into a bounded legal order, or that there is a mismatch between universal human rights and the international system of states. We also need to take account of the overlaps between distinctions based on nationality and distinctions based on race, ethnicity, culture, and religion. In South Africa, as in other parts of the world, human rights abuses perpetrated against foreign nationals typically reflect deeply entrenched racial hierarchies, which influence understandings of personhood and humanity.[122]

In trying to come to terms with the capacity of dignity-based constitutional reasoning to destabilise distinctions based on citizenship, it is helpful to distinguish between three broad themes in the constitutional jurisprudence. The first is the link between rights and citizenship; the second the rights vested in all people, regardless of citizenship; and the third the instability between the rights of citizens and those of non-citizens. First, then, the rights associated with – and special dignity attached to – citizenship. Courts often emphasise the historical importance of the move to a common South African citizenship, in view of the severe infringement of black people's dignity and equality that resulted from their exclusion from citizenship under colonialism and apartheid. They describe citizenship as a gateway to the enjoyment of certain rights and stress the close links between equal citizenship and a person's sense of identity, belonging, membership in a community, personal security, private and family life, freedom of movement, and rights of political participation.[123] The Constitutional Court has, accordingly, preferred an interpretation of a legislative amendment which would not strip certain categories of people of their citizenship.[124] Legislation providing for the automatic loss of South African citizenship upon acquisition of citizenship of another country,[125] and the practice of blocking identity documents in cases of suspected identity fraud before an investigation is conducted, have also been declared unconstitutional.[126]

The second theme is the idea that dignity is inherent in all people, irrespective of citizenship. In *Watchenuka*, the Supreme Court of Appeal declared: "Human dignity has no nationality. It is inherent in all people – citizens and non-citizens alike – simply because they are human".[127] In *Lawyers for Human Rights*, the Constitutional Court held that illegal foreigners, i.e., foreign nationals who are present in the national territory without permission, are entitled to freedom and security of the person and the rights of detained persons, given the importance of these rights to the constitutional values of dignity, equality, and freedom.[128] In *Koyabe*, the Court held, with reference to dignity and ubuntu, that the state is obliged to furnish reasons for a decision declaring a person an illegal foreigner.[129] Moreover, a line of cases confirm, with reference to dignity, life, freedom and security of the person, and other rights, that the state may not deport asylum-seekers before a final determination has been made of the validity of their claims for refugee status, including in cases where there was a considerable delay in applying for asylum, or where they failed to renew their asylum-seeker permits within the prescribed period.[130]

There is a tension between these two strands of jurisprudence. The first emphasises citizenship's role in safeguarding basic rights. It can account for some of the difficulties experienced by non-citizens; however, it is not always clear whether and to what extent it can provide the basis for challenging and transforming hierarchical distinctions based on citizenship and immigration status. By contrast, the second highlights unconditional respect for the dignity of every human person. It appears more ready to problematise differentiations between citizens and non-citizens; however, its tendency to play down the significance of citizenship could blind it to the systemic causes of the precarious position of non-citizens.[131] These tensions reflect the gap between formal legal guarantees and the lived reality of foreign nationals. However, they also derive from – and here we get to the third theme – the instability of the distinction between the legal position of citizens and non-citizens. In the remainder of this section, I will discuss the question whether and to what extent such instability can be exploited to challenge the exclusion of non-citizens from rights officially reserved for citizens. I will do so with reference to case law dealing with the right to employment and self-employment, and other social rights.

In *Watchenuka*, asylum-seekers were barred from working or studying. They could not rely directly on section 22 of the Constitution, which reserves the right to choose an occupation to South African citizens. However, the Supreme Court of Appeal relied on their right to human dignity, which vests in all people, regardless of citizenship. It held that a blanket ban on working impairs the dignity of asylum-seekers in cases where they have no other sources of income or support. Asylum-seekers do not have an absolute right to individual self-fulfilment, but they do have the right to live "without positive humiliation and degradation".[132] A general prohibition, that forces asylum-seekers who are destitute to beg or steal, violates their dignity. The judgment thus exploits the instability of the distinction between rights granted to and withheld from asylum-seekers to alleviate their hardship. In *Somali Association*, which dealt with police operations aimed at shutting down businesses run by Somali and Ethiopian nationals, the Court extended the dignity-based reasoning in *Watchenuka* to the context of self-employment. It declared that refugees and asylum-seekers are entitled to apply for and renew business and trading licences in terms of the relevant legislation.[133]

Both judgments are careful not to disrupt the distinctions between citizens and non-citizens and between different categories of non-citizens too much. In *Watchenuka*, the Court confirmed that every sovereign state has the power to distinguish between citizens and non-citizens and to regulate the entry of non-citizens.[134] The judgment does not vest a general right in asylum-seekers to work and study but leaves it to the Standing Committee for Refugee Affairs to determine whether applicants qualify. In *Somali Association*, the Court distinguished the facts from those in *Union of Refugee Women*, in which the Constitutional Court upheld the constitutionality of legislation that restricted employment in the private security industry to citizens and permanent residents, to the exclusion of refugees.[135] It stressed that that case dealt with a narrowly tailored exclusion from employment that applied only to the security industry and that the majority judgment in that case does not provide authority for the proposition that a blanket ban on the employment of refugees is constitutional.[136]

The judgments in *Larbi-Odam* and *Khosa* represent the high-water mark of the Constitutional Court's jurisprudence on the socio-economic rights of non-citizens. In *Larbi-Odam*, the Court stated that differentiations based on citizenship could potentially impair the dignity of non-citizens, and thus constitute discrimination on a ground that is analogous to those listed in the constitutional anti-discrimination clause.[137] It held that a regulation that excluded non-citizens from appointment as teachers in a permanent capacity unfairly discriminated against permanent residents. In *Khosa*, the majority held that the exclusion of permanent residents from benefits under the Social Assistance Act violated their rights to equality and access to social security. Mokgoro J emphasised the devastating consequences of the denial of welfare benefits for the lives and dignity of those affected. It stigmatised permanent residents in need of social security and relegated them to the margins of society.[138] Her reasoning resonates with *Watchenuka* and *Somali Association*; however, there is an important difference. Unlike those judgments, *Khosa* does not rely exclusively on the humanity and dignity inherent in all people, regardless of citizenship or immigration status. It articulates dignity with membership in the community but resists the narrow identification of membership and belonging with the formal status of citizenship. Mokgoro J's judgment stresses the similarities between permanent residents and citizens. Permanent residents, like citizens, have made their homes in South Africa, owe a duty of allegiance to the state, and contribute to the welfare system by paying taxes.[139] The Court thus distinguishes their position from that of temporary residents.[140] That is surprising, in view of the emphasis placed by the majority on the lack of a textual qualification in s 27(1), which confers the right to social security on "everyone".[141] Why should "everyone" be read to refer only to citizens and those in a similar position to citizens? Why did the Court assume, without citing any supporting evidence, that temporary residents lack meaningful ties of allegiance and commitment to their country of residence?[142] Would it not be more sensible to include temporary residents under the beneficiaries of the right, but if necessary, justify their exclusion from specific programmes with reference to the availability of resources[143] or in terms of the general limitation provision in s 36(1)?[144]

Although the universal language employed in s 27 provides more leeway than the reference to citizens in s 22, it cannot fully explain the result in *Khosa*. The majority judgment is shaped less by the belief that "everyone" includes everyone than by the Court's understanding of the community of equals created by the Constitution. On that understanding, non-citizens who have formally assumed the responsibilities attached to permanent residence are entitled to full social citizenship. Their well-being is tied to that of citizens, and they are inextricably part of the network of reciprocal rights and obligations flowing from membership in the community. Importantly, those rights and obligations extend to concern for the well-being of impoverished people. In Mokgoro J's words,

> Sharing responsibility for the problems and consequences of poverty equally as a community represents the extent to which wealthier members of the community view the minimal well-being of the poor as connected with their personal well-being and the well-being of the community as a whole.[145]

What is striking about this statement is not only its egalitarian and relational vision of dignity but also its ambiguity. It makes sense, in view of the Court's emphasis on the similarities between citizens and permanent residents, to read the references to the poor whose well-being is linked to that of the rest of the community to denote only citizens and permanent residents. However, it could also be read more expansively to include poor people generally. In a society where the Constitution enshrines the values of dignity, equality, and freedom and proclaims in its preamble that "South Africa belongs to all who live in it", it seems plausible that the well-being of the entire community is affected negatively not only by the poverty of inhabitants with formalised ties to the legal community but also by the desperation and need of those at the lower rungs of the immigration ladder. Turning a blind eye to the latter's suffering or denying responsibility for it arguably detracts from everyone's dignity.[146]

The extended notion of citizens' dignity articulated in *Khosa* could help pave the way for further challenges to the distribution of social rights. Permanent residence, like citizenship, is not a precise indicator of the web of relationships, rights, and responsibilities that shape membership in a legal community. It could, for example, be argued, with reference to the fluidity of the distinction between permanent residents and refugees, that the failure to extend certain socio-economic rights and entitlements to refugees is arbitrary or unreasonable. Thus far, such arguments have been unsuccessful. In *Union of Refugee Women*, the Constitutional Court held that legislation that restricted employment in the private security industry to citizens and permanent residents did not violate refugees' right to equality and non-discrimination. The majority judgment of Kondile AJ reasoned that the restriction was rationally related to the need to ensure the trustworthiness of people working in the security industry, that refugees do not have a constitutional right to choose a vocation, and that the legislation did not constitute a blanket ban but applied only to one industry.[147] By contrast, the dissenting judgment of Mokgoro and O'Regan JJ highlighted the similarities between refugees and permanent residents and showed how refugees' exclusion perpetuates harmful stereotypes about foreign nationals and deepens their material disadvantage.[148]

In *Rafoneke*, the Court similarly rejected an equality-based challenge to the constitutionality of legislation that restricted access to the legal profession to citizens and permanent residents. Tshiqi J's judgment for a unanimous Court stressed that s 22 excludes non-citizens from the right to choose a profession, that the protection of employment opportunities for South Africans is a legitimate purpose, that the provision is narrowly tailored since it does not prevent non-citizens from taking up other employment, and that it does not consign them to a life of degradation.[149] The judgment places the bar for such restrictions quite low. It effectively holds that, because non-citizens are excluded from the constitutional right to choose a profession, such restrictions will fall afoul of the constitutional equality clause only if they are arbitrary (the Court uses the example of restrictions which apply only to Japanese citizens)[150] or constitute a blanket ban on employment which will leave non-citizens destitute. It is also formalistic – it declines to look beyond formal definitions of citizenship and permanent residence, refuses to question official assumptions about the nature of non-citizens' connection to the country, and fails to consider the administrative burdens involved in trying to secure permanent residence.[151]

The categorical and deferential approach followed in *Union of Refugee Women* and *Rafoneke* provides little scope for challenging legislative constructions of the boundaries separating citizens and permanent residents from those whose residence is considered temporary. These judgments suggest that, at least for now, *Khosa* represents the "outer limits" of the Court's willingness to destabilise those boundaries.[152] Does that mean that we have reached the limits of the capacity of the Court's dignity-based jurisprudence to unsettle the status quo? I would suggest not, but that answer is subject to certain side notes and qualifications. First, the transformative potential of the Court's jurisprudence derives from the instability of the distinction between inherent human dignity and the dignity of members of a concrete legal community, and between a life without degradation and a positive right to self-realisation.[153] It also stems from the tension between a person's formal legal status and residence, and between the hierarchical distinctions existing in a concrete community and the vision of a community (as pictured in *Khosa*) where everyone's dignity is bound up with the dignity of everyone else. These tensions and oppositions cannot be resolved, once and for all, by legislative or jurisprudential innovations. They do not admit of a logical endpoint. It would be misguided to assume that the transformative potential of the Court's jurisprudence cannot be pushed any further.

Second, the transformative potential of the Court's jurisprudence is far from unlimited. It is subject to all kinds of constraints, including the separation of powers and budgetary constraints.[154] Even more fundamentally, courts have little or no power to redress the underlying causes of foreign nationals' dehumanisation, like global inequality, the international system of states, and deeply rooted racial hierarchies. However, that does not mean that their efforts are futile. They must do everything in their power to prevent hierarchical distinctions based on nationality, race, and culture from infiltrating official understandings of humanity. Sometimes, their judgments can also destabilise dominant constructions of membership and rights and help safeguard spaces in which alternative imaginaries can be developed.

Third, courts do not function in isolation. Their ability to effect change depends on the institutional and political environment in which they operate and the traction of different social visions in that society. Jonathan Klaaren argues that the Constitutional Court's judgments on the rights of citizens and non-citizens must be understood in view of the historical tension in South Africa between republican visions of citizenship and more expansive understandings of citizenship in terms of lawful residence.[155] He further suggests that the residence-based concept of citizenship that informs both s 25 of the Immigration Act 13 of 2002 and the Constitutional Court's jurisprudence has roots in principles developed in South African citizenship and migration law between 1897 and 1937.[156] These historical tensions and precedents have arguably helped to facilitate the legal system's responsiveness to the challenges brought by migrants who invoke a residence-based alternative to exclusivist conceptions of citizenship.

Fourth, courts can contribute to the transformation of citizenship and migration law, but their judgments are not a substitute for political mobilisation, consciousness-raising, social struggles, and legislative reform. More could be done to rally around and work out the implications of a residence-based conception of citizenship. The articulation of struggles against the degradation of non-citizens with a broader anti-racist agenda and the development of alternative articulations of the dignity of man and the dignity of the citizen are urgent priorities.

Finally, one of the ways in which the distinction between citizens and non-citizens can be destabilised is through the extension of participatory rights to non-citizens. Although the Constitution reserves political rights like the right to vote or stand for public office for citizens,[157] foreign nationals' participation in other structures (e.g., in school governing bodies) could help facilitate their integration into the community.[158] Moreover, many of the rights that extend to non-citizens (including dignity, equality, socio-economic rights, and administrative justice) require the consultation of individuals affected by public exercises of power. Although the involvement of individuals or communities that stand to be affected by exercises of administrative or executive power differs in several respects from collective decision-making processes, there are significant overlaps. When, as in the *Mamba* case, the government is ordered to engage with non-citizens affected by the imminent closure of the camps that were set up to accommodate victims of xenophobic attacks,[159] respect for their dignity as individuals is transformed into a right to participate actively in conversations about their integration into the community.[160] However, this is subject to an important caveat. When the government is required to consult with non-citizens, there is a substantial danger that their vulnerability and lack of political power will be carried over into the deliberative forum, and that the government will fail to recognise their agency and voice.[161] To be meaningful, consultative processes must be designed to destabilise the power relations among participants.

## Notes

1 *Dawood v Minister of Home Affairs* para 35.
2 *S v Makwanyane* para 329.
3 Ackermann *Human Dignity* 9–10.
4 See *National Coalition v Minister of Justice* para 127 on the disadvantage and prejudice historically suffered by gays. See also Cameron "Dignity and Disgrace" 467 (apartheid laws branded both blackness and homosexuality as inferior and shameful).
5 Chaskalson "The Third Bram Fischer Lecture" 196–198.
6 See the preamble to the Charter of the United Nations (1945); the preamble and article 1 of the Universal Declaration of Human Rights (1948); the preambles to the International Covenant on Civil and Political Rights (1966) and the International Covenant on Economic, Social and Cultural Rights (1966); article 1 of the United Nations Declaration on the Elimination of All Forms of Racial Discrimination (1963); the preface to the Convention on the Elimination of All Forms of Discrimination Against Women (1979); and article 5 of the African Charter on Human and Peoples' Rights (1981).
7 See Barak *Human Dignity*; Daly *Dignity Rights*; Hughes *Human Dignity and Fundamental Rights in South Africa and Ireland.*
8 *S v Williams* paras 39 (noting a "growing consensus in the international community" that judicially imposed whipping "offends society's notions of decency and is a direct invasion of the right which every person has to human dignity") and 50.
9 Ackermann *Human Dignity* 26, 31.
10 See the discussion of ubuntu in chapter 6.6 below.
11 In terms of section 74(1), the amendment of section 1 requires a bigger majority of votes in the National Assembly and National Council of Provinces than the rest of the Constitution.
12 See *Carmichele v Minister of Safety* para 54.
13 *S v Makwanyane* para 144.
14 *Christian Education v Minister of Education* para 36.
15 *Dawood v Minister of Home Affairs* para 35.
16 *Bernstein v Bester* paras 65–67; *NM v Smith* paras 131–132.
17 S v *Makwanyane* para 95; *S v Dodo* para 35.
18 *Government v Grootboom* paras 44, 83.
19 *Prinsloo v Van der Linde* paras 31–33; *President v Hugo* para 41; *Harksen v Lane* paras 46, 50, 51, 53, 91, 92.
20 *Christian Education v Minister of Education* para 36; *Prince v President of the Law Society* paras 48–51; *Minister of Home Affairs v Fourie* para 89.
21 *South African National Defence Union v Minister of Defence* paras 7, 8; *Khumalo v Holomisa* para 21; *South African Broadcasting Corporation v National Director of Public Prosecutions* para 120.
22 *August v Electoral Commission* para 17.
23 *S v Makwanyane* paras 144–146.
24 See also Woolman "Dignity" 36–6 – 36–19; Daly *Dignity Rights* 26–53.
25 McCrudden "Human Dignity and Judicial Interpretation of Human Rights" 658.
26 G Dürig "Der Grundrechtssatz von der Menschenwürde" 125.
27 127 (my translation).
28 In BVerfGE 45, 187 228 (1977), which concerned the constitutionality of life imprisonment, the German Federal Constitutional Court held that the state is not allowed to "turn the offender into an object of crime prevention to the detriment of his or her constitutionally protected right to social worth and respect" (translation by Kommers and Miller *Constitutional Jurisprudence of Germany* 365). See also the judgment of the Namibian Supreme Court in *S v Tcoeib* 1005G-H.
29 *S v Makwanyane* para 313.

30 Para 316.
31 Para 271.
32 *S v Dodo* para 38.
33 See chapter 2.2 above.
34 *MEC for Education v Pillay* para 64. See also *NM v Smit* para 145; *Mayelane v Ngwenyama* para 73; *Teddy Bear Clinic v Minister of Justice* para 52; *AB v Minister of Social Development* paras 50–52.
35 *Ferreira v Levin* para 49.
36 See *Christian Lawyers' Association v National Minister of Health* 1095D ("The fundamental right to individual self-determination lies at the very heart and base of the constitutional right to termination of pregnancy"); and the minority judgment of Khampepe J in *AB v Minister of Social Development* paras 108–110 (discussing the impact of restrictions of reproductive rights on the dignity of infertile persons).
37 *Bhe v Magistrate Khayelitsha* para 92.
38 *National Coalition v Minister of Justice* para 127.
39 See also, in the context of same-sex marriage, *Minister of Home Affairs v Fourie* paras 15, 17, 60, 71.
40 Réaume "Discrimination and Dignity" 679, 681, 684–685.
41 See the debate between Kriegler J and O'Regan J in *President v Hugo* paras 80–86, 110–115.
42 Olsen "The Sex of Law" 691.
43 *MEC for Education v Pillay*.
44 *Eldridge v British Columbia*, as cited by Réaume "Discrimination and Dignity" 687.
45 *National Coalition v Minister of Justice* para 116; *Minister of Home Affairs v Fourie* para 78.
46 *National Coalition v Minister of Justice* paras 132–137; *Minister of Home Affairs v Fourie* para 60. Elsewhere, the Court stated that the equality clause outlaws "legislative distinctions that treat people as second-class citizens, that demean them, that treat them as less capable for no good reason, or that otherwise offend fundamental human dignity". *President v Hugo* para 41, quoting from a judgment of L'Heureux-Dubé J in *Egan v Canada* 104–105.
47 See *August v Electoral Commission* para 17 (noting the historical importance of the right to vote for "the acquisition of the rights of full and effective citizenship by all South Africans").
48 S 16(2)(c) of the Constitution excludes "advocacy of hatred that is based on race, ethnicity, gender or religion, and that constitutes incitement to cause harm" from the scope of constitutionally protected expression. See also s 10(1) of the Promotion of Equality and Prevention of Unfair Discrimination Act 4 of 2000; *Qwelane v South African Human Rights Commission* paras 80–82.
49 *Soobramoney v Minister of Health* para 8; *Government v Grootboom* paras 2, 25.
50 *Government v Grootboom* paras 32–33, 39–44; *Minister of Health v Treatment Action Campaign* paras 26–39; *Mazibuko v City of Johannesburg* paras 52–68.
51 *Government v Grootboom* paras 44, 63–69, 80–83, 95.
52 In *Mazibuko v City of Johannesburg*, the Court held that a municipality's water policy was not in violation of the right of access to water, even though the allocation of 6 kilolitres of free water per stand, coupled with the installation of prepaid water meters, disadvantaged poor, large households. See also *Thubakgale v Ekurhuleni Metropolitan Municipality*, where the Court took a restrictive approach to the granting of relief for the municipality's repeated failure to fulfil its constitutional obligations in relation to the provision of housing.
53 In the context of defamation, see *Khumalo v Holomisa* para 27; and the minority judgment of Cameron J and Froneman J in *Le Roux v Dey* paras 158–194 on the constitutional protection of the dignity (dignitas) and reputation (fama) of individuals, which must be balanced against freedom of expression.

54 Kant "Groundwork of the Metaphysics of Morals" 4:434.
55 4:435.
56 4:421.
57 4:429.
58 Cicero appeared to stray from this understanding when he wrote in a passage in *De Officiis* about the dignity that derives from humans' reason and moral freedom, which distinguishes humans from animals; however, elsewhere in his writings he used dignity in the conventional sense as a status term. Cancik "'Dignity of Man' and '*Persona*' in Stoic Anthropology" 19.
59 Rosen *Dignity* 47–48.
60 49. The shift from a groups-based understanding of human dignity to the idea that dignity is vested in the individual person only occurred in Catholic thought in the twentieth century. See Moyn "The Secret History of Constitutional Dignity" 97–101.
61 Jeremy Waldron offers an alternative reading of that history, which nevertheless shares the assumption that modern understandings of dignity have overcome the hierarchical and inegalitarian features of ancient conceptions of dignity. In his view, modern understandings of human dignity still draw upon the older definitions of dignity in terms of rank, but involve "an upwards equalization of rank, so that we now try to accord to every human being something of the dignity, rank, and expectation of respect that was formerly accorded to nobility". Waldron *Dignity, Rank, and Rights* 33.
62 On the historical relationship between human dignity and legal capacity or personhood, see Eckert "Legal Roots of Human Dignity in German Law".
63 McCrudden "Human Dignity and Judicial Interpretation of Human Rights" 658 (when used in this sense, human dignity refers to human beings' ontological status, as it is based on a claim about the essence of human beings).
64 Article 1(2) declares: "The German people *therefore* uphold human rights as inviolable and inalienable and as the basis of every community, of peace and justice in the world" (emphasis added).
65 Art 79(3).
66 BVerfGE 115, 118 (2006).
67 See Fletcher "Human Dignity as a Constitutional Value" 175–177; Jakl "Human Dignity as a Fundamental Right to Freedom in Law" on the difficulties inherent in attempts to bring Kant's moral philosophy, with its emphasis on the inner moral law, to bear on the concrete, external world of legal relations.
68 See, e.g., BVerfGE 39, 1 (1975); BVerfGE 88, 203 (1993), where the life and dignity of the unborn foetus conflicted with the self-determination and dignity of the mother.
69 Herdegen "Art. 1 Abs. 1" 30–38. See also Alexy *A Theory of Constitutional Rights* 62–64.
70 Dreier *Grundgesetz Kommentar Bd I* 207–209, 226.
71 Venter "Human Dignity as a Constitutional Value" 340.
72 For contrasting views, see Steinmann "The Core Meaning of Human Dignity" 6, 13 (arguing, with reference to the distinction between dignity's ontological dimension and the right to respect for and protection of one's dignity, that dignity has an inviolable core which cannot be limited); and Barak *Human Dignity* 244–248 (arguing that the Constitution protects dignity as a relative right).
73 Meyer "Kant's Concept of Dignity and Modern Political Thought" 319 (in his legal-philosophical writings, Kant recognised the existence of differentiations in dignity in accordance with the social hierarchies of his time).
74 See the reference to the dignity of the courts in s 165(4) of the Constitution. See also Daly *Dignity Rights* 71–100 (long before the United States Supreme Court started referring to human dignity, it ascribed dignity to states and other inanimate objects such as Congress, the Presidency, and the courts).

75 Esposito *Third Person* 91. See also the reference under 2 above to Dürig's claim that dignity is rooted in the idea that humans are distinct from impersonal nature by virtue of their mind.
76 Esposito *Third Person* 72–73, 88–89.
77 91–96.
78 See Woolman *The Selfless Constitution.*
79 McCrudden "Human Dignity and Judicial Interpretation of Human Rights" 697–712.
80 See 2 above. See also Hofmann "Die versprochene Menschenwürde" 361.
81 See Du Bois "Freedom and the Dignity of Citizens" 142–147 (relating that distinction to the differences between Kant's moral and legal philosophy).
82 Hofmann "Die versprochene Menschenwürde" 363–364.
83 Möllers "Democracy and Human Dignity".
84 428.
85 Hofmann "Die versprochene Menschenwürde" 365–375.
86 Isensee "Menschenwürde" 96–197, 215.
87 Carozza "Human Dignity and Judicial Interpretation of Human Rights" 939.
88 Habermas "The Concept of Human Dignity and the Realistic Utopia of Human Rights" 469.
89 Cornell "Bridging the Span toward Justice" 31.
90 31.
91 Guenther "Abolish the World as We Know It" 30 (referring to the latter group as "'no-bodies' or 'affected others' who are represented by dominant power as heteronomously determined by natural laws and therefore properly subjected to social and political laws that expose them to total violence, beyond the scope of ethical concern"), 32.
92 34 (emphasis omitted).
93 For a different formulation of the problem, see Van der Walt "The Future and Futurity of the Public-Private Distinction in the View of the Horizontal Application of Fundamental Rights" 115, who proposes rethinking the public in terms of "a dignity for which we have no normative criterion". Such a non-normative dignity, which gestures towards absolute hospitality, would resist the reduction of the public to private interests. "It signifies a call to respond to the unrepresentable, the non-disposable and the humanly impossible" (133).
94 See Esposito *Third Person* 104–151 for a discussion of different theoretical moments that gesture towards an understanding of rights that detach them from the language of personhood and personal property.
95 Du Toit "African Conceptions of Human Dignity and Violence against Women in South Africa"; Molefe "African Personhood, Metaphysical Capacities and Human Dignity" 65.
96 See *Christian Education v Minister of Education* para 50 (the religious freedom of parents of children in independent schools who consented to the use of corporal punishment is overridden by the importance of "promot[ing] respect for the dignity and physical and emotional integrity of all children"). See also *Freedom of Religion v Minister of Justice.*
97 See the judgment of the Trial Chamber II of the International Criminal Tribunal for the former Yugoslavia in the Kunarac, Kovač and Vuković Case, decided on 22 February 2001. The United Nations Security Council Resolution 1820, adopted on 19 June 2008, declares that "rape and other forms of sexual violence can constitute a war crime, a crime against humanity, or a constitutive act with respect to genocide".
98 See Bergoffen "Exploiting the Dignity of the Vulnerable Body".
99 BVerwGE 64, 274 277–280 (1981).

100 In this case, the Conseil d État held that a mayoral order banning a dwarf-tossing competition was justified in the interests of public order, since treating someone with a physical handicap as a projectile infringes the dignity of the human person. The applicant then approached the European Commission on Human Rights and the Human Rights Committee of the United Nations, both times unsuccessfully. He claimed inter alia that his dignity was infringed by the ban, as it effectively prevented him from pursuing an occupation. See *Manuel Wackenheim v France*, Communication No 854/1999, UN Doc CCPR/C/75/D/854/ 1999 (2002).

101 See Dreier *Grundgesetz Kommentar Bd I* 218–220 for a critique of the peep show case; and Rosen *Dignity* 68–77 for a critique of the conflation of dignity with dignified behaviour in the *Wackenheim* judgments.

102 *S v M* paras 15, 24, quoting approvingly from the High Court judgment in *National Coalition v Minister of Justice* 751B-D.

103 *Jordan v S* paras 16, 74.

104 In *S v Makwanyane* para 57 the Constitutional Court quoted with approval the words of Brennan J in *Furman v Georgia* 273 and *Gregg v Georgia* 230 that "even the vilest criminal remains a human being possessed of common human dignity".

105 Hennette-Vauchez "A Human Dignitas?" 50 argues that dignity here functions in a similar manner to ancient notions of dignitas, as it is placed outside the human person. Whereas ancient dignitas attached to an office or social rank, its modern counterpart is located in humanity. In both cases, the individual is seen as merely the "temporary repository" of a dignity that is never fully her own.

106 See the discussion of equality and difference in chapter 5.6 below.

107 BVerfGE 108, 282 (2003). In its later judgment in BVerfGE 138, 296 (2015), the Court held that an abstract legislative ban on the wearing of headscarves by teachers was disproportionate. The wearing of religious symbols by teachers could only be banned in cases where they posed a concrete danger to the peace at school or the neutrality of the state.

108 333.

109 Belgian Constitutional Court, 6 Dec. 2012, Judgment 145/2012, paras B21-B23.

110 For a discussion and critique of the case law, see Brems, Heri, Chaib and Verdonck "Head-Covering Bans in Belgian Courtrooms and Beyond"; Costello and Ahmed "Citizenship, Identity, and Veiling".

111 *SAS v France* paras 118–120.

112 Para 153.

113 Costello and Ahmed "Citizenship, Identity, and Veiling" 96–98.

114 91–94.

115 97.

116 The judgment in *SAS v France* refers to a resolution of the Parliamentary Assembly of the Council of Europe on Islam, Islamism and Islamophobia in Europe, an opinion of the Commissioner for Human Rights of the Council of Europe, and the submissions of several NGOs which stated that a ban on the wearing of the veil was likely to deepen Muslim women's marginalisation and exclusion. Hopkins "Social Reproduction in France" argues that the French ban on religious headwear in public spaces has led to the exclusion of Muslim female learners from public schools and the exacerbation of class differences among Muslim families. It has rendered more Muslim women unemployed, pushed them into commodified care work in the private sector, and increased hostility and discrimination against them.

117 See Botha "The Rights of Foreigners"; Khan "Does the Right to Dignity Extend Equally to Refugees in South Africa?".

118 The Constitution reserves the following rights for South African citizens: the right to make political choices (s 19(1)), the right to free, fair and regular elections (s 19(2)), the right to vote in elections and to stand for public office (s 19(3)), the right

not to be deprived of citizenship (s 20), the right to enter, remain in and reside anywhere in the Republic (s 21(3)), the right to a passport (s 21(4)) and freedom of trade, occupation and profession (s 22).

119 Even in countries where citizenship is no longer a requirement to be eligible to vote, the right to vote still separates members of the political community from non-members, although membership is now defined in terms of residence and not formal citizenship.

120 Arendt *The Origins of Totalitarianism* 290–302.

121 See the discussion of democratic understandings of human dignity under 4.3 above.

122 Mpofu "Xenophobia as Racism". See also chapter 1.5 above.

123 *Chisuse v Director-General* paras 24–28; *Democratic Alliance v Minister of Home Affairs* paras 9–11. See *August v Electoral Commission* para 17; *Doctors for Life v Speaker* para 115 on the links between dignity, citizenship, and political participation.

124 *Chisuse v Director-General.*

125 *Democratic Alliance v Minister of Home Affairs.*

126 *PPM v Minister of Home Affairs.*

127 *Minister of Home Affairs v Watchenuka* para 25.

128 *Lawyers for Human Rights v Minister of Home Affairs* paras 20, 26.

129 *Koyabe v Minister for Home Affairs* para 62.

130 See, e.g., *Saidi v Minister of Home Affairs* paras 18, 40; *Ruta v Minister of Home Affairs*; *Abore v Minister of Home Affairs*; *Scalabrini Centre v Minister of Home Affairs* paras 36–43.

131 The tension is apparent from *Chisuse v Director-General.* At para 24, the Court warns against overstating the importance of citizenship, since the Constitution does not allow arbitrary distinctions to be made between citizens and non-citizens, vests rights in everyone, except where it expressly states otherwise, and declares in its preamble that "South Africa belongs to all who live in it". However, just a few paragraphs later, it notes that deprivation of citizenship could have far-reaching implications for the enjoyment of basic rights like personal security, particularly "where xenophobia is a lived reality" (para 28).

132 *Minister of Home Affairs v Watchenuka* para 32.

133 *Somali Association v Limpopo Department.*

134 *Minister of Home Affairs v Watchenuka* para 29.

135 *Union of Refugee Women v Director: Private Security Industry.*

136 *Somali Association v Limpopo Department* paras 28, 38.

137 *Larbi-Odam v Member of the Executive Council for Education* para 19.

138 *Khosa v Minister of Social Development* paras 74, 76, 77, 80, 81.

139 Paras 58, 59, 74.

140 Paras 59, 89, 98.

141 Paras 42, 46, 47, 54, 79, 85. At para 54, Mokgoro J counters the argument that most developed countries require citizenship for access to social security, by stating that "those countries do not have constitutions that entitle 'everyone' to have access to social security".

142 Williams "Issues and Challenges in Addressing Poverty and Legal Rights" 468–469.

143 S 27(2) ("The state must take reasonable legislative and other measures, within its available resources, to achieve the progressive realisation of each of these rights").

144 See the dissenting judgment of Ngcobo J at paras 120–121, 132.

145 Para 74.

146 Consider, e.g., the Court's claim in *Lawyers for Human Rights v Minister of Home Affairs* para 20 that "[t]he very fabric of our society and the values embodied in our Constitution could be demeaned if the freedom and dignity of illegal foreigners are violated in the process of preserving our national integrity".

147 *Union of Refugee Women v Director: Private Security Industry* paras 36–42, 54, 57.
148 Paras 99, 104–110, 118.
149 *Rafoneke v Minister of Justice* paras 79, 83, 98–99, 102.
150 Para 78.
151 In response to the contention that people who are ordinarily resident in South Africa have the same fixity of connection to South Africa as citizens and permanent residents, the Court at para 81 states, rather circularly, that "the distinction between foreigners who have been granted permanent residence in this country and those who have not, is exactly the fact that these other groups have not been granted the same status as permanent residents". See also para 82.
152 Liebenberg *Socio-Economic Rights* 161.
153 *Minister of Home Affairs v Watchenuka* paras 27–32.
154 In *Khosa*, the Court held at paras 58–67 that widening the social security net to include permanent residents would not impose a huge additional burden on the state. The state could, in any event, adopt immigration policies that would ensure that only those "who will profit, and not be a burden to, the State" are granted permanent residence status. Para 65.
155 Klaaren "Constitutional Citizenship in South Africa". See also Klaaren "Citizenship, Xenophobic Violence, and Law's Dark Side" 142–145.
156 Klaaren *From Prohibited Immigrants to Citizens*. S 25(1) of the Immigration Act provides: "The holder of a permanent residence permit has all the rights, privileges, duties and obligations of a citizen, save for those rights, privileges, duties and obligations which a law or the Constitution explicitly ascribes to citizenship".
157 See Le Roux "Residence, Representative Democracy and the Voting Rights of Migrant Workers in Post-Apartheid South Africa and Post-Unification Germany (1990 – 2015)".
158 See Kavuro "Impediments to the Democratic Participation of Foreign Nationals in Public School Governance".
159 *Mamba v Minister of Social Development*.
160 See Botha "Democratic Participation and the Separation of Powers" 398–401 on the permeability of the distinction.
161 That is what happened in *Mamba*, where the government started closing the camps without engaging meaningfully with stakeholders on their reintegration.

## Bibliography

Ackermann L *Human Dignity: Lodestar for Equality in South Africa* (2012) Cape Town: Juta.
Alexy R *A Theory of Constitutional Rights* (2002) Oxford: Oxford University Press.
Arendt H *The Origins of Totalitarianism* (1968) San Diego: Harcourt.
Barak A *Human Dignity: The Constitutional Value and the Constitutional Right* (2015) Cambridge: Cambridge University Press.
Bergoffen D "Exploiting the Dignity of the Vulnerable Body: Rape as a Weapon of War" (2009) 38 *Philosophical Papers* 307
Botha H "Democratic Participation and the Separation of Powers" in H Botha, N Schaks and D Steiger (eds) *The End of the Representative State? Democracy at the Crossroads* (2016) 385 Baden-Baden: Nomos.
Botha H "The Rights of Foreigners: Dignity, Citizenship and the Right to Have Rights" (2013) 130 *South African Law Journal* 836.
Brems E, Heri C, Chaib S and Verdonck L "Head-Covering Bans in Belgian Courtrooms and Beyond: Headscarf Persecution and the Complicity of Supranational Courts" (2017) 39 *Human Rights Quarterly* 882.

Cameron E "Dignity and Disgrace: Moral Citizenship and Constitutional Protection" in C McCrudden (ed) *Understanding Human Dignity* (2013) 467 Oxford: Oxford University Press.

Cancik H "'Dignity of Man' and '*Persona*' in Stoic Anthropology: Some Remarks on Cicero, *De Officiis* I, 105–107" in D Kretzmer and E Klein (eds) *The Concept of Human Dignity in Human Rights Discourse* (2002) 19 The Hague: Kluwer Law International.

Carozza P "Human Dignity and Judicial Interpretation of Human Rights: A Reply" (2008) 19 *European Journal of International Law* 931.

Chaskalson A "The Third Bram Fischer Lecture: Human Dignity as a Foundational Value of our Constitutional Order" (2000) 16 *South African Journal on Human Rights* 193.

Cornell D "Bridging the Span toward Justice: Laurie Ackermann and the Ongoing Architectonic of Dignity Jurisprudence" (2008) *Acta Juridica* 18.

Costello R and Ahmed S "Citizenship, Identity, and Veiling: Interrogating the Limits of Article 8 of the European Convention on Human Rights in Cases Involving the Religious Dress of Muslim Women" (2023) 38 *Journal of Law and Religion* 81.

Daly E *Dignity Rights: Courts, Constitutions and the Worth of the Human Person* (2013) Philadelphia: University of Pennsylvania Press.

Dreier H *Grundgesetz Kommentar Bd I* 2 ed (2004) Tübingen: Mohr Siebeck.

Du Bois F "Freedom and the Dignity of Citizens" (2008) *Acta Juridica* 112.

Du Toit L "African Conceptions of Human Dignity and Violence against Women in South Africa" in M Molefe and C Allsobrook (eds) *Human Dignity in an African Context* (2023) 155 London: Palgrave MacMillan.

Dürig G "Der Grundrechtssatz von der Menschenwürde" (1956) 81 *Archiv des öffentlichen Rechts* 117.

Eckert J "Legal Roots of Human Dignity in German Law" in D Kretzmer and E Klein (eds) *The Concept of Human Dignity in Human Rights Discourse* (2002) 41 The Hague: Kluwer Law International.

Esposito R *Third Person: Politics of Life and Philosophy of the Impersonal* (2012) Cambridge: Polity.

Fletcher G "Human Dignity as a Constitutional Value" (1984) 22 *University of Western Ontario Law Review* 171.

Guenther L "Abolish the World as We Know It: Notes for a Praxis of Phenomenology beyond Critique" (2022) 5 *Puncta* 28.

Habermas J "The Concept of Human Dignity and the Realistic Utopia of Human Rights" (2010) 41 *Metaphilosophy* 464.

Hennette-Vauchez S "A Human Dignitas? Remnants of the Ancient Legal Concept in Contemporary Dignity Jurisprudence" (2011) 9 *International Journal of Constitutional Law* 32.

Herdegen M "Art. 1 Abs. 1" in T Maunz and G Dürig (eds) *Grundgesetz Kommentar Bd I* (2009) Munich: CH Beck.

Hofmann H "Die versprochene Menschenwürde" (1993) 118 *Archiv des öffentlichen Rechts* 353.

Hopkins C "Social Reproduction in France: Religious Dress Laws and Laïcité" (2015) 48 *Women's Studies International Forum* 154.

Hughes A *Human Dignity and Fundamental Rights in South Africa and Ireland* (2014) Pretoria: Pretoria University Law Press.

Isensee J "Menschenwürde: die säkulare Gesellschaft auf der Suche nach dem Absoluten" (2006) 131 *Archiv des öffentlichen Rechts* 173.

Jakl B "Human Dignity as a Fundamental Right to Freedom in Law" in W Brugger and S Kirste (eds) *Human Dignity as a Foundation of Law* (2013) 93 Stuttgart: Franz Steiner Verlag.

Kant I "Groundwork of the Metaphysics of Morals" in M Gregor (ed) *Immanuel Kant: Practical Philosophy* (1996) Cambridge: Cambridge University Press.

Kavuro C "Impediments to the Democratic Participation of Foreign Nationals in Public School Governance" (2024) 28 *Law Democracy and Development* 21.

Khan F "Does the Right to Dignity Extend Equally to Refugees in South Africa?" (2020) 20 *African Human Rights Law Journal* 261.

Klaaren J "Citizenship, Xenophobic Violence, and Law's Dark Side" in LB Landau (ed) *Exorcising the Demons Within: Xenophobia, Violence and Statecraft in Contemporary South Africa* (2011) 135 Johannesburg: Wits University Press.

Klaaren J "Constitutional Citizenship in South Africa" (2010) 94 *International Journal of Constitutional Law* 94.

Klaaren J *From Prohibited Immigrants to Citizens: The Origins of Citizenship and Nationality in South Africa* (2017) Cape Town: UCT Press.

Kommers D and Miller R *Constitutional Jurisprudence of Germany* 3rd ed (2012) Durham: Duke University Press.

Le Roux W "Residence, Representative Democracy and the Voting Rights of Migrant Workers in Post-Apartheid South Africa and Post-Unification Germany (1990–2015)" (2015) 48 *Verfassung und Recht in Übersee* 263.

Liebenberg S *Socio-Economic Rights: Adjudication Under a Transformative Constitution* (2010) Cape Town: Juta.

McCrudden C "Human Dignity and Judicial Interpretation of Human Rights" (2008) 19 *European Journal of International Law* 655.

Meyer M "Kant's Concept of Dignity and Modern Political Thought" (1987) 8 *History of European Ideas* 319.

Molefe M "African Personhood, Metaphysical Capacities and Human Dignity" in M Molefe and C Allsobrook (eds) *Human Dignity in an African Context* (2023) 65 London: Palgrave MacMillan.

Möllers C "Democracy and Human Dignity: Limits of a Moralized Conception of Rights in German Constitutional Law" (2009) 42 *Israel Law Review* 416.

Moyn S "The Secret History of Constitutional Dignity" in C McCrudden (ed) *Understanding Human Dignity* (2013) 95 Oxford: Oxford University Press.

Mpofu W "Xenophobia as Racism: The Colonial Underside of Nationalism in South Africa" (2020) 3 *International Journal of Critical Diversity Studies* 33.

Olsen F "The Sex of Law" in D Kairys (ed) *The Politics of Law: A Progressive Critique* 3rd ed (1998) 691 New York: Basic Books.

Réaume D "Discrimination and Dignity" (2003) 63 *Louisiana Law Review* 645.

Rosen M *Dignity: Its History and Meaning* (2012) Cambridge, Massachusetts: Harvard University Press.

Steinmann A "The Core Meaning of Human Dignity" (2016) 19 *Potchefstroom Electronic Law Journal* 1.

Van der Walt J "The Future and Futurity of the Public-Private Distinction in the View of the Horizontal Application of Fundamental Rights" in J van der Walt (ed) *Tangible mais intouchable, la lois du tact, la lois de la lois* (2002) 101 Nijmegen: Wolf Legal Productions.

Venter F "Human Dignity as a Constitutional Value: A South African Perspective" in J Ipsen and E Schmidt-Jortzig (eds) *Recht, Staat, Gemeinwohl: Festschrift für Dietrich Rauschning* (2001) 335 Cologne: Carl Heymanns Verlag.

Waldron J *Dignity, Rank, and Rights* (2012) Oxford: Oxford University Press.

Williams L "Issues and Challenges in Addressing Poverty and Legal Rights: A Comparative United States/ South African Analysis" (2005) 21 *South African Journal on Human Rights* 436.

Woolman S "Dignity" in S Woolman, M Bishop and J Brickhill (eds) *Constitutional Law of South Africa* (2nd ed., OS, December 2005) chapter 36. Cape Town: Juta.

Woolman S *The Selfless Constitution: Experimentalism and Flourishing as Foundations of South Africa's Basic Law* (2013) Cape Town: Juta.

## Case law

### *Belgium*

Belgian Constitutional Court, 6 Dec. 2012, Judgment 145/2012

### *Canada*

*Egan v Canada* (1995) 29 CRR (2d)
*Eldridge v British Columbia (Attorney General)* [1997] 2 SCR 624

### *European Court of Human Rights*

*SAS v France* [2014] ECHR 695

### *Germany*

BVerfGE 39, 1 (1975)
BVerfGE 45, 187 228 (1977)
BVerfGE 88, 203 (1993)
BVerfGE 108, 282 (2003)
BVerfGE 115, 118 (2006)
BVerfGE 138, 296 (2015)
BVerwGE 64, 274 (1981)

### *Human Rights Committee*

Manuel Wackenheim v France, Communication No 854/1999, UN Doc CCPR/C/75/D/854/ 1999 (2002)

### *International Criminal Tribunal for the former Yugoslavia*

Kunarac, Kovač and Vuković Case, Trial Chamber II, decided on 22 February 2001

### *South Africa*

*AB v Minister of Social Development* 2017 (3) BCLR 267 (CC)
*Abore v Minister of Home Affairs* 2022 (2) SA 321 (CC)
*August v Electoral Commission* 1999 (3) SA 1 (CC)
*Bernstein v Bester NO* 1996 (2) SA 751 (CC)
*Bhe v Magistrate Khayelitsha; Shibi v Sithole; SA Human Rights Commission v President of the RSA* 2005 (1) SA 563 (CC)
*Carmichele v Minister of Safety and Security* 2001 (4) SA 938 (CC)
*Chisuse v Director-General, Department of Home Affairs* 2020 (6) SA 14 (CC)
*Christian Education South Africa v Minister of Education* 2000 (4) SA 757 (CC)
*Christian Lawyers' Association v National Minister of Health* 2004 (10) BCLR 1086 (T)
*Dawood; Shalabi; Thomas v Minister of Home Affairs* 2000 (3) SA 936 (CC)
*Democratic Alliance v Minister of Home Affairs* 2023 (6) SA 156 (SCA)
*Doctors for Life International v Speaker of the National Assembly* 2006 (6) SA 416 (CC)
*Ferreira v Levin NO and Vryenhoek v Powell NO* 1996 (1) SA 984 (CC)
*Freedom of Religion South Africa v Minister of Justice and Constitutional Development* 2020 (1) SA 1 (CC)
*Government of the Republic of South Africa v Grootboom* 2001 (1) SA 46 (CC)
*Harksen v Lane NO* 1998 (1) SA 300 (CC)

*Jordan v S* 2002 (6) SA 642 (CC)
*Khosa v Minister of Social Development; Mahlaule v Minister of Social Development* 2004 (6) SA 505 (CC)
*Khumalo v Holomisa* 2002 (5) SA 401 (CC)
*Koyabe v Minister for Home Affairs* 2010 (4) SA 327 (CC)
*Larbi-Odam v Member of the Executive Council for Education (North-West Province)* 1998 (1) SA 745 (CC)
*Lawyers for Human Rights v Minister of Home Affairs* 2004 (4) SA 125 (CC)
*Le Roux v Dey* 2011 (6) BCLR 577 (CC)
*Mamba v Minister of Social Development* (CCT) unreported case no 65/08 of 21 August 2008
*Mayelane v Ngwenyama* 2013 (4) SA 415 (CC)
*Mazibuko v City of Johannesburg* 2010 (4) SA 1 (CC)
*MEC for Education: KwaZulu-Natal v Pillay* 2008 (1) SA 474 (CC)
*Minister of Health v Treatment Action Campaign* 2002 (5) SA 721 (CC)
*Minister of Home Affairs v Fourie; Lesbian and Gay Equality Project v Minister of Home Affairs* 2006 (1) SA 524 (CC)
*Minister of Home Affairs v Fourie; Lesbian and Gay Equality Project v Minister of Home Affairs* 2006 (1) SA 524 (CC)
*Minister of Home Affairs v Watchenuka* 2004 (4) SA 326 (SCA)
*National Coalition for Gay and Lesbian Equality v Minister of Justice* 1999 (1) SA 6 (CC)
*National Coalition for Gay and Lesbian Equality v Minister of Justice* 1998 (6) BCLR 726 (W)
*NM v Smith (Freedom of Expression Institute as Amicus Curiae)* 2007 (5) SA 250 (CC)
*PPM v Minister of Home Affairs* 2024 (3) SA 469 (GP)
*President of the Republic of South Africa v Hugo* 1997 (4) SA 1 (CC)
*Prince v President of the Law Society of the Cape of Good Hope* 2002 (2) SA 794 (CC)
*Prinsloo v Van der Linde* 1997 (3) SA 1012 (CC)
*Qwelane v South African Human Rights Commission* 2021 (6) SA 579 (CC)
*Rafoneke v Minister of Justice and Correctional Services* 2022 (12) BCLR 1489 (CC)
*Ruta v Minister of Home Affairs* 2019 (2) SA 329 (CC)
*S v Dodo* 2001 3 SA 382 (CC)
*S v M* 2004 (1) BCLR 97 (O)
*S v Makwanyane* 1995 (3) SA 391 (CC)
*S v Tcoeib* 1996 (7) BCLR 996 (NmS)
*S v Williams* 1995 (3) SA 632 (CC)
*Saidi v Minister of Home Affairs* 2018 (7) BCLR 856 (CC)
*Scalabrini Centre of Cape Town v Minister of Home Affairs* 2024 (3) SA 330 (CC)
*Somali Association v Limpopo Department of Economic Development* 2015 (1) SA 151 (SCA)
*Soobramoney v Minister of Health, KwaZulu-Natal* 1998 (1) SA 765 (CC)
*South African Broadcasting Corporation v National Director of Public Prosecutions* 2007 (2) BCLR 167 (CC)
*South African National Defence Union v Minister of Defence* 1999 (4) SA 469 (CC)
*Teddy Bear Clinic for Abused Children v Minister of Justice and Constitutional Development* 2014 (2) SA 168 (CC)
*Thubakgale v Ekurhuleni Metropolitan Municipality* 2022 (8) BCLR 985 (CC)
*Union of Refugee Women v Director: Private Security Industry Regulatory Authority* 2007 (4) SA 395 (CC)

### United States

*Furman v Georgia* 408 US 238 273 (1972)
*Gregg v Georgia* 428 US 153 230 (1976)

# 5 Equality

## Contesting hierarchy and discrimination

South Africa's Constitution is often said to go further than most constitutions in seeking to eradicate institutionalised racism, sexism, and other forms of disadvantage and to create an egalitarian society.[1] However, the Constitutional Court sometimes acknowledges that there are formidable obstacles to the achievement of equality and that the Constitution has had limited success in overcoming them. The Court has noted that "colonialism or apartheid is a system so stubborn that its divisive and harmful effects continue to plague us and retard our progress as a nation more than two decades into our hard-earned constitutional democracy".[2] It has recognised that the legacy of the dispossession of black-owned land is still visible in the living conditions of poor black people;[3] that racist attitudes and behaviour are deeply embedded in the workplace and other sectors of society;[4] and that patriarchal attitudes, which are reflected in rules and principles of the common law and customary law, continue to circumscribe the life chances of many women.[5] Its jurisprudence thus wavers between optimism about the capacity of the law to help eradicate inequality and a sense that the challenges are daunting and that there are limits to the capacity of courts-centred processes to undo deeply ingrained inequality and disadvantage.

How could we make sense of the promise of the Constitution's commitment to equality, without falling into the trap of unrealistic expectations about the capacity of rights-based litigation to undo centuries of oppression? The chapter approaches this question from the perspective of a political or conflictual understanding of equality. On that understanding, the meaning of equality, the values underlying the constitutional equality guarantee, the forms of disadvantage it is meant to guard against, and the social and historical frames and factual matrixes within which enquiries into alleged violations of equality are situated, are inscribed in power relations, and are bound to give rise to disagreement. Constitutional adjudication does not provide a neutral vantage point that is elevated above disagreement but is itself immersed in social conflict and power. That could help explain the transformative possibilities as well as the limits of constitutional litigation and adjudication. On the one hand, the legal system is replete with concepts, principles, interpretive sensibilities, and assumptions that bear the imprint of colonialism, apartheid, racial capitalism,

DOI: 10.4324/9781003482451-6

patriarchy, and heteronormativity. Formally, of course, those received meanings and attitudes are now subject to the supremacy of the Constitution, but in practice, they exist side by side with the Constitution and sometimes inform its interpretation. On the other hand, since law itself is immersed in conflict and power, and since equality is open to different interpretations and evokes radically different social visions, equality-based constitutional challenges could help expose the contingency of the status quo and politicise its legal and normative underpinnings.

Drawing on the typology of Nancy Fraser, I examine the meaning and implications of a political understanding of equality through the prism of three types of harm or disadvantage. The first involves misrecognition or status-based inequalities, which occur where some people are denied equal respect based on cultural prejudice or stereotypes. The second concerns distributive or class-based injustices, where the distribution of material resources deprives some people of the opportunity to interact with others as peers. The third refers to political misrepresentation, where the structuring of the political system and the drawing of the boundaries of the political community exclude some people from democratic membership, voice, and participation. These injustices overlap and reinforce each other; however, considering them separately allows me to explore the cultural, economic, and political barriers to equality more systematically, and to reflect on the possibilities and limits of equality law in politicising different forms of institutionalised disadvantage.[6]

The chapter starts with a brief discussion of equality as a constitutional right and value, as understood through the lens of substantive and remedial understandings of equality. Next, it enquires into the possibility of a political understanding of equality, which focusses on the capacity of rights discourse to politicise and challenge dominant understandings of equality, citizenship, and political subjectivity. The following three sections then examine the possibilities and limits of a political understanding of equality within the context of status-based inequality, distributive injustice, and political marginalisation. Finally, the chapter examines different constructions of difference through the prism of a political understanding of equality and conflictual conception of democracy.

## 5.1 Equality as a constitutional right and value

Equality is central to the Constitution's normative system and transformative vision. Section 9, the first substantive rights provision in the Bill of Rights, guarantees the right to equality and non-discrimination. Section 9(1) recognises that everyone is equal before the law and safeguards the right to equal protection and benefit of the law. Section 9(2) states that equality "includes the full and equal enjoyment of all rights and freedoms" and authorises "legislative and other measures designed to protect or advance persons, or categories of persons, disadvantaged by unfair discrimination". Section 9(3) prohibits the state from discriminating unfairly against anyone, directly or indirectly, and provides a non-exhaustive list of prohibited grounds of discrimination. Section 9(4) extends the prohibition of unfair discrimination to the horizontal plane by proscribing unfair discrimination by natural persons and juristic persons other than the state. It also mandates the enactment of national legislation that prevents unfair discrimination. Finally, section 9(5) provides that discrimination on any of the grounds listed in section 9(3) is presumed to be unfair.

Equality is also a founding constitutional value. Section 1(a) declares that South Africa is founded on the values of "human dignity, the achievement of equality and the advancement of human rights and freedoms". Section 7(1) states that the Bill of Rights "affirms the democratic values of human dignity, equality and freedom", while sections 36(1) and 39(1) place human dignity, equality, and freedom at the heart of limitation analysis and the interpretation of the Bill of Rights, respectively. The importance of equality as a constitutional right and value is reflected in judicial statements that equality "permeates and defines the very ethos upon which the Constitution is premised",[7] that it "goes to the bedrock of our constitutional architecture" and is a "standard which must inform all law",[8] and that it is "the lodestar of our transformative constitutional project".[9] It is also evident from judgments that stress the role of the value of equality in guiding the interpretation of rights, including socio-economic rights.[10]

The constitutional commitment to equality must be seen against the background of South Africa's history of institutionalised and pervasive discrimination against black people, women, persons with disabilities, religious minorities, sexual minorities, and other vulnerable groups.[11] The reference in section 1(a) to "the achievement of equality" and the statement in section 9(2) that "equality includes the full and equal enjoyment of all rights and freedoms" indicate that the Constitution does not simply require formal equality or identical treatment. The Constitutional Court has held that the Constitution endorses a substantive vision of equality, which recognises that the mere abolition of discriminatory laws will not eradicate deeply entrenched forms of disadvantage,[12] and that the identical treatment of differently situated categories of people may aggravate inequality.[13] On this view, the achievement of equality sometimes requires treating different categories of people differently. In deciding whether such differential treatment is unfairly discriminatory, a court must carefully consider the historical and social context, as well as the impact of the differentiation on the complainants.[14] The commitment to a substantive and transformative vision of equality is also evident from other features of section 9. For instance, sections 9(3) and 9(4) refer to direct and indirect discrimination, thus placing the emphasis on the impact of discrimination, rather than its form or the intention behind it. That allows constitutional interpreters to invalidate seemingly neutral laws that disproportionately affect certain groups.[15] In addition, these sections refer to discrimination on "one or more grounds", which opens the door to the consideration of intersectional forms of disadvantage.[16]

The Constitutional Court has further stated that the Constitution demands a remedial or restitutionary understanding of equality,[17] which acknowledges the need, as stated in section 9(2), for "measures designed to protect or advance persons, or categories of persons, disadvantaged by unfair discrimination". This understanding has important implications for the construction of section 9. In the first place, it confirms that, in addition to imposing a negative duty to refrain from discriminating unfairly, section 9 places a positive obligation on the state to create conditions in which everyone can fully and equally enjoy all rights and freedoms.[18] As Ngcobo J stated in *Bato Star*:

> Our Constitution differs from other constitutions which assume that all are equal and in so doing simply entrench existing inequalities. Our Constitution recognises that decades of systematic racial discrimination entrenched by the apartheid legal order cannot be eliminated without positive action being taken to achieve that result. We are required to do more than that. The effects of discrimination may continue indefinitely unless there is a commitment to end it.[19]

Secondly, a remedial understanding of equality requires a holistic reading of section 9, which recognises that remedial measures do not deviate from the constitutional right to equality but are integral to it. Sections 9(1) and 9(2) should thus be seen as complementary.[20] Thirdly, this reading does not exempt remedial measures from constitutional scrutiny but eases the justificatory burden. Measures that discriminate on listed grounds but fall within the scope of section 9(2) are not deemed to be presumptively unfair.[21] Moreover, even though the presumption of unfairness applies to measures that do not fall squarely within the ambit of section 9(2), the discrimination in question will not necessarily fall foul of section 9(3) if it serves an important purpose, such as furthering equality for all.[22]

The Promotion of Equality and Prevention of Unfair Discrimination Act 4 of 2000 ("PEPUDA"), which was enacted in terms of section 9(4) of the Constitution, also evinces a substantive and remedial vision of equality. Its preamble notes that "systemic inequalities and unfair discrimination remain deeply embedded in social structures, practices and attitudes", and recognises the need to eradicate "social and economic inequalities, especially those that are systemic in nature, which were generated in our history by colonialism, apartheid and patriarchy". Although it is not always a model of clarity, PEPUDA helps to flesh out the meaning of the constitutional commitment to the eradication of unfair discrimination. For instance, section 1 defines prohibited grounds;[23] section 34 contains a directive principle stating that the inclusion of HIV/AIDS status, socio-economic status, nationality, family responsibility, and family status in the definition of prohibited grounds must be considered; sections 7–9 provide illustrative examples of practices that constitute unfair discrimination on the grounds of race, gender, and disability; and section 14 spells out the factors to be taken into account in determining unfairness.

Despite the prominence of equality in the constitutional text and the references in case law to its importance as a right and value, it is dignity, rather than equality, that appears to do the bulk of the work in the Court's section 9 analysis. The Constitutional Court has placed the idea that all human beings should be treated with equal dignity and respect at the centre of its analysis of the constitutional right to equality and the right not to be unfairly discriminated against. In the first place, dignity plays an important role in determining whether laws or conduct that differentiate between people on grounds that are not listed in section 9(3) constitute discrimination. In deciding whether a law or conduct differentiates on the basis of an analogous ground, it is asked whether "it is based on attributes or characteristics which have the potential to impair the fundamental dignity of persons as human beings, or to affect them adversely in a comparably serious manner".[24] Secondly, in determining whether discrimination on listed or unlisted grounds is unfair, one of the most important factors to be considered is the extent to which it has resulted in an impairment of the complainants' fundamental human dignity or constitutes an impairment of a comparably serious nature.[25] Despite the reference to an impairment of a comparably serious nature, dignity remains the benchmark against which unfairness is tested.[26] Thirdly, dignity has an important role to play in determining whether a limitation of the right to equality or non-discrimination is nevertheless reasonable and justifiable in an open and democratic society based on human dignity, equality, and freedom. Finally, dignity is relied on to distinguish legitimate remedial measures under section 9(2) from measures that go too far in impairing the dignity of previously advantaged sections of the community.[27]

In the Court's view, a dignity-based understanding of the right to equality places the commitment to substantive and remedial equality on a firm foundation. Laurie Ackermann argues in his extra-curial writings that dignity provides an answer to a problem that plagues attempts to conceptualise and adjudicate equality, namely the question of "equality of what". He claims that the statement that all persons are equal is counterintuitive, as human beings differ in almost all respects, including their natural abilities, physical and intellectual attributes, and wealth. To make sense of equality, we must first specify in relation to what human beings are equal. According to Ackermann, it is only in respect of their dignity and worth that all persons could be said to be equal.[28]

The political understanding of equality advocated in this chapter acknowledges the emancipatory possibilities inherent in the idea that all human beings have equal dignity. However, it demands close attention to the mechanisms through which hierarchies that are embedded in the political and social order become inscribed in official understandings of dignity. The previous chapter examined the tendency of exclusionary conceptions of personhood, autonomy, citizenship, rationality, and normality – which are closely linked to hierarchies based inter alia on race, culture, religion, nationality, disability, and sexuality – to infiltrate the meaning of dignity. It further asked whether the slippages between the universality of inherent human dignity and dignity's inscription in a bounded legal order could help open up spaces for emancipatory social struggles. This chapter builds on that analysis by exploring whether and to what extent South Africa's equality jurisprudence has enabled or closed down challenges to hierarchies based on social status, wealth, and political voice. It also raises questions about the capacity of the courts' jurisprudence to help redress the underlying structural causes of inequality.[29] Given the complexity of equality, the chapter supports a multidimensional approach, which grounds the right to equality in different overlapping values and seeks to come to terms with the shifting determinants of disadvantage.[30]

## 5.2 Towards a political understanding of equality

In chapter 3 above, I criticised the idea that judges can avoid becoming embroiled in political questions about the meaning of equality by appealing to neutral and objective legal rules and principles. Such rules and principles are based on contestable social and political views that appear neutral because they rest on assumptions that are deeply embedded in legal culture. Those assumptions entrench conventional constructions of individual choice and responsibility, the types of harm that the legal system should guard against, and the demarcation of the public and private spheres, and constrict our ability to imagine alternatives. Against that background, this section proposes a conception of equality that is expressly political. Such a political understanding of equality views the politics of law as ineradicable and is interested in the capacity of egalitarian struggles to expose the hidden biases and premises inherent in established legal doctrine and modes of reasoning, and to suggest alternative visions of the social world that may be more deeply transformative.

The political understanding of equality that is proposed here does not only take issue with concepts and principles that derive from South Africa's predemocratic past. It is also distrustful of constitutional narratives that present the historical development of the right to equality in linear terms as the progressive overcoming of inequality and exclusion. These narratives instrumentalise past suffering, rely on sweeping generalisations about colonialism, apartheid, the liberation struggle, and the constitutional transition, monumentalise the Constitution, and are overly confident of the capacity of constitutional litigation and adjudication to undo historical injustices and prevent them from recurring.[31] They present the expansion of rights to groups that were formerly excluded from citizenship as instances of a historical process through which the gap between the ideals of human dignity, equality, and freedom, on the one hand, and remaining traces of inequality, exclusion, and domination, on the other, is gradually and systematically reduced in accordance with a logic intrinsic to constitutionalism and human rights.[32] The narratives in question overlook the persistence of existing patterns of disadvantage, or explain them away as temporary obstacles on the way to a rational and inclusive legal order. Moreover, they understate the extent to which current developments – like the widening gap between rich and poor and between the global North and South, the dispossession and disempowerment of poor and marginalised populations, the upsurge in right-wing and nationalist populism, the inhumane treatment of refugees and migrants, and rising conflict between racial, ethnic, and religious groups – threaten to undo the advances made in the past.[33]

A political understanding of equality is also critical of the tendency of those narratives to underplay the role of political mobilisation, organisation, contestation, and struggle in gaining recognition for the rights of those previously excluded.[34] It worries that, to the extent that they recognise the role of past struggles in establishing new rights or extending existing ones to new beneficiaries, they reify their outcomes and narrow the scope for future resistance.[35] Unlike accounts that treat conflict and struggle as instantiations of the particular that, for the most part, stand in the way of the universal realisation of human rights, a political understanding of equality insists that conflict is ineradicable and plays a vital role in keeping alive the tension between contending enunciations of the universal.[36]

An essay by Kendall Thomas on racial justice in the United States provides important glimpses of what a political – or conflictual – understanding of equality may look like. Thomas is critical of the dominant discourse of what he terms racial moralism, which centres on moral consensus, neutral principles, and the reputation of different race groups. According to him, this model of racial justice

> fails to capture the distinctive and constitutive role of the political in racial claims-making.... The moral concept of racial justice tries to capture and control the explosive, agonistic conflicts that characterize American racial politics. If it cannot altogether remove questions of racial power from its agenda, the racial moralism model can aspire to confine them within the dispassionate discursive boundaries of juridical settlement, bureaucratic administration, and deliberative legislation. If contemporary history teaches us anything about our racial dilemma, it is that conflicts over the forms and substance of racial injustice have been primarily contests about access to the means of political power, about social relations of domination, subordination, and resistance. These distinctively political dimensions of race in America resist the normative logic of the moral view that continues to predominate in public debates about racial justice.[37]

Thomas argues that moral conceptions of racial justice deflect attention away from the capacity of facially neutral measures to weaken black people's political power.[38] In his view, a better strategy is to acknowledge and confront the political dimension of racial justice. The right to racial equality must be grounded not in moral consensus, neutral principles, or individual or group reputation but in democratic citizenship and a radical understanding of democracy, which views conflict as constitutive of social life and seeks to prevent any consensus on the meaning of political values from congealing into something permanent and incontrovertible. For Thomas, a political understanding of racial equality not only concerns vulnerable racial publics' access to democratic processes, as guaranteed through the right to vote and the right to stand for public office, but also requires their voices to be heard and their interests to be considered. Decision-making processes that entrench racial hierarchies and diminish vulnerable racial publics' democratic power lack political legitimacy. In addition, a political understanding of equality demands spaces in which "subaltern counterpublics" can develop "oppositional ideas about racial justice".[39] His political understanding of equality thus goes beyond representation in official decision-making processes and includes the right to resist racial domination and hierarchy through the advancement of alternative democratic discourses.

Thomas' articulation of racial equality with racial democratic citizenship raises important questions. For example, what does it mean to refer to "racial citizenship", or for that matter, "gendered citizenship" or "sexual citizenship"? Is the point about citizenship not that it affords an equal status to a diverse range of people and binds them together, irrespective of racial, gender, sexual, and other differences? Can citizenship carry the weight of a radical understanding of equality? Is citizenship itself not too torn between different dimensions and conflicting interpretations? I cannot analyse these questions in depth, but I will make a few cursory observations that could shed light on the capacity of an analysis that centres on democratic citizenship to politicise inequality and domination.

To start with, there is a tension between citizenship's emancipatory and regulatory functions.[40] On the one hand, citizenship is at the heart of many struggles for emancipation, in which members of marginalised groups politicise the gap between their formal status as citizens and their exclusion from the full rights and opportunities associated with citizenship.[41] On the other hand, citizenship is always inscribed within a particular legal order. To that extent, it bears the imprint of social hierarchies and subjugation, and plays an important role in normalising certain social roles, subjectivities, and ways of being in the world, while consigning others to the realm of the strange or perverse. The language of citizenship typically incorporates certain assumptions about race, class, gender, sexuality, family, and marriage, and privileges certain cultural values over others.[42] Those hegemonic assumptions and values tend to reassert themselves during the course and in the wake of emancipatory struggles. The extension of rights associated with citizenship is often achieved through the assimilation of previously excluded identities into the mainstream. At such moments, exclusionary laws are problematised and seemingly dismantled; however, in many respects, the hierarchies underpinning them remain in place, and the recognition of previously excluded groups is conditioned on conformity to mainstream norms. That could take the sting out of anti-hegemonic struggles, as differences that were once viewed as subversive of citizenship are depoliticised, and activists come under pressure to work from within established institutions.[43]

The privatisation of sexual citizenship illustrates the tendency to contain the disruptive effects of emancipatory struggles within "acceptable" bounds. Such privatisation may arise from either an exclusive emphasis on the cultural, as opposed to material, conditions of citizenship, or a focus on sexual minorities' consumption and lifestyle, rather than their political voice and participation. This results in a weakening of their capacity to develop oppositional ideas that challenge mainstream conceptions of gender, sexuality, family, and citizenship, and a failure to defend the rights of LGBTQI individuals whose life chances are severely restricted by poverty or who do not have access to private spaces in which they can safely express their identities.[44]

The moralisation of the citizenship of vulnerable groups is a second mechanism through which inequality is depoliticised. It refers to the conditioning of the citizenship of members of previously excluded groups on conformity to the ideal of the "good" or "morally respectable" citizen. Thomas refers in this regard to justifications of the crack cocaine/ powder cocaine sentencing differential in the United States, which has had a vastly disproportionate impact on African American men. Some commentators argue that the disparate prison sentences for crack-related offences enhanced the racial reputation of law-abiding black people and were therefore not discriminatory. Their arguments condition the citizenship of African Americans on good moral behaviour, and draw attention away from the severe impact of the sentencing provision on their political power.[45] It has similarly been argued that sexual citizenship tends to be premised on preconceived ideas about morality and normality, and that gays and lesbians are able to enjoy equal rights only to the extent that they do not disrupt the privileged position accorded to idealised notions of the heterosexual citizen.[46]

Thirdly, the extension of citizenship rights to women and sexual minorities is sometimes instrumentalised for political purposes, like projecting the unity of a nation-state – or a transnational political entity like the European Union – or juxtaposing the liberal values underpinning one's own political culture against the backwardness of others.[47] For instance, Francesca Ammaturo argues that the promotion of the rights of sexual minorities in the European Union has gone hand in hand with the creation of "lines of fracture between presumably queer-friendly and homo-transphobic countries both within and outside the European borders".[48] These fault-lines not only allow the EU and the nation-states comprising it to exhibit their commitment to the universality of human rights. Under the guise of distinctions between "good" and "bad" citizens and between the "normal" and "abnormal", they also facilitate the reintroduction of distinctions based on race, class, nationality, religion, and culture into the definition of sexual citizenship. Paradoxically, the commitment to eliminate discrimination based on sexual orientation and to "rescue" persecuted sexual minorities exists side by side with the fortification of internal and external borders, which allows the political community to co-opt "acceptable racialised segments" of the LGBTQI population, whilst excluding those that are viewed as a potential threat to hegemonic values.[49]

The political understanding of equality that is proposed in this chapter does not treat citizenship as a stable or unitary concept. It is alive to the contradictions arising from the tension between its regulatory and emancipatory aspects.

It is also sensitive to the tensions between dimensions like "residency, administrative subjection, democratic participation, and cultural membership",[50] and the various processes – locally, nationally, and globally – through which their supposed unity is fractured, and citizenship is disaggregated into its constituent components. It recognises that those developments could help open up spaces in which the bounds of citizenship can be contested and redrawn. That could result in the deepening of democratic practices and the extension of the rights associated with citizenship.[51] However, because it views conflict and power as central to democracy, it is attentive to the ways in which deep-seated prejudices and inequalities reinsert themselves into the law and social relations, despite human rights victories that point in the direction of universal citizenship and acceptance.

Citizenship must thus be understood as a conflictual category, which refers simultaneously to membership in an established political community and the capacity to challenge existing distributions of rights through political speech and action. In the words of Étienne Balibar, the rights of citizenship are established through conflicts between the "constitution" of citizenship and "the 'insurrectional' power of universalist political movements that aim to conquer rights that do not yet exist, or to widen the scope of existing rights".[52] Or, as Balibar notes elsewhere, there is a permanent tension between the "excessive, hyperbolic universality" of the idea that all citizens are entitled to equal freedom and the fact that the institutionalisation of this idea is left "entirely up to practice, to struggle, to social conflict".[53] This indeterminacy explains both the resilience of privilege, domination, and exclusion, and the possibility to unmask and challenge inequality and subjugation through social struggles which politicise what may at first appear to be neutral and apolitical.[54]

The work of Jacques Rancière similarly provides the basis for a conflictual understanding of equality, which shuns a too easy identification of political subjectivity with formal conceptions of citizenship. Rancière argues, against Hannah Arendt, that politics should not be confined to the nation-state, that political subjectivity should not be reduced to permanent membership in a national community, and that the public-political sphere cannot be neatly demarcated from a private sphere of necessity. In his view, it is precisely through politics that the boundaries between the public and private and between members and non-members of the political community are called into question. Rancière conceives rights as open predicates whose meaning and scope of application are subject to contestation. The gap between universal human rights and the rights of citizenship opens up "an interval for political subjectivization",[55] in which those who effectively have no rights can stage scenes of dissensus which politicise established distributions of membership and rights.

Drawing on the theoretical perspectives discussed above, I will conclude this section with brief observations on the meaning and import of the political understanding of equality that is proposed in this chapter. In the first place, the harm caused by discrimination is often conceived in overly individualistic terms, and the political dimension of inequality is overlooked in the process.

Against that background, a political understanding of equality demands closer attention to the impact of discriminatory measures on the democratic participation and voice of marginalised groups. However, that is not to say that the discourse on equality must focus narrowly on political marginalisation, to the exclusion of other forms of disadvantage. That would detract from the multiple forms and manifestations of inequality and discrimination and overlook the extent to which our understanding of the distinctions between citizenship and personhood, or between "political" and other forms of harm is shaped by assumptions that are themselves politically contestable. Following Rancière, the understanding of equality advanced here resists confining politics to a particular sphere of human interaction and is open to the idea that the political – and the politics of law – can manifest itself in disputes that are typically characterised as "private" or "economic". Rather than reducing the right to equality to protection against a single form of harm, it is interested in the ways in which different types of harm intersect to produce and normalise disadvantage, and in the capacity of anti-hegemonic struggles to politicise forms of harm that appear natural and inevitable.

Secondly, a political understanding of equality is alive to the contradictions inherent in attempts to view citizenship through the lens of race, class, gender, or sexual orientation. On the one hand, it acknowledges that those types of analysis could provide a vantage point from which to critique and challenge the inscription of racial and other hierarchies into official understandings of citizenship. On the other, it is concerned about the tendency of those perspectives to de-emphasise other grounds of disadvantage, and to blind us to the widely divergent needs and experiences of people categorised as "black", "female", "poor", or "homosexual".

## 5.3 Recognition and status

The previous section suggested that a conflictual or political understanding of equality can help us make sense of both the persistence of inequality and exclusion under a "post-apartheid" constitution and the capacity of equality-based claims to politicise inequality and open up spaces for the articulation of conflicting social visions. In this section, I use a conflictual lens to try to come to terms with the tension between the Constitution's promise of equal dignity and the tenacity of social hierarchies derived from South Africa's colonial, apartheid, and patriarchal past. The section focusses on what Fraser refers to as misrecognition or status-based inequalities, which occur where institutionalised cultural values deprive members of certain groups of the ability to participate fully and equally in social interaction. On the one hand, it is interested in the capacity of the equality jurisprudence developed by the courts to challenge and transform hierarchical social relations. (How) can that jurisprudence create openings for challenges to hegemonic constructions of personhood, citizenship, and the distinction between the public and private spheres? On the other hand, it enquires into the ways in which – even ostensibly progressive – judicial decisions normalise social hierarchies. Is the Constitutional Court's dignity-based equality jurisprudence in danger of moralising and privatising conflicts over access to power? Does it risk premising equality on conformity to the image of the good citizen?

In *National Coalition I*, the Constitutional Court invalidated the criminalisation of sex between men under the common law and legislation. In his main judgment, Ackermann J focussed on how these prohibitions reinforce societal prejudices against gay men. He highlighted both their symbolic and psychological effect, on the one hand, and their real-world, social effects on the other. The former refers to the laws' message that gay men are criminals who are not worthy of the equal protection of the law, and the feelings of guilt, anxiety, fear, and a lowering of personal self-esteem that they give rise to. The latter refers to the ways in which the criminalisation of same-sex desire "builds insecurity and vulnerability into the daily lives of gay men".[56] The prohibitions in question not only place gay men at constant risk of arrest and prosecution, but also increase their exposure to "blackmail, police entrapment, violence ('queer-bashing') and peripheral discrimination, such as refusal of facilities, accommodation and opportunities".[57] In his concurring judgment, Sachs J further unpacked the impact of the ban on gay men's dignity. Focussing on the unique nature of the harm suffered by gays and lesbians resulting from prejudice and stigmatisation, he wrote:

> In the case of gays, history and experience teach us that the scarring comes not from poverty or powerlessness, but from invisibility. It is the tainting of desire, it is the attribution of perversity and shame to spontaneous bodily affection, it is the prohibition of the expression of love, it is the denial of full moral citizenship in society because you are what you are, that impinges on the dignity and self-worth of a group.[58]

Violations of the equal dignity and worth to which every person is entitled can thus arise from laws or conduct that entrench prejudice against a particular group or class of persons, further their stigmatisation, perpetuate harmful stereotypes about them, increase their vulnerability, or signal that they are not worthy of full citizenship or equal respect and concern. Such a denial of equal membership and worth is likely to have a negative psychological impact, which may manifest in feelings of humiliation, internalisation of the idea of their own inferiority, and withdrawal from social life. However, the sting of social stigmatisation lies not only in the subjective feelings of those affected, but also in its objective social meaning. As the Canadian author Denise Réaume argues, the wholesale classification of a particular group or class of persons as unworthy of equal moral respect and concern "operates to subordinate members of the group in ways that stand to affect every corner of their lives, infect every attitude and predisposition toward them".[59] Legislative distinctions that exclude them from rights and benefits enjoyed by other members of the community reinforce the idea that they are inferior, and thus increase their vulnerability to existing and new forms of exclusion. The symbolic meaning and social impact of discrimination against vulnerable groups thus combine to thwart the capacity of those concerned to develop their personalities and participate in societal structures as full, equal members of society.

The factors identified in *National Coalition I* were applied in several other cases dealing with discrimination based on sexual orientation. It was held in these cases that laws that excluded same-sex partners in a permanent relationship from benefits accruing to spouses, impaired the former's dignity and thus constituted unfair discrimination.[60] The judgments emphasised that the laws in question perpetuated prejudices and stereotypes about gays and lesbians and signalled that they were incapable of forming meaningful, committed, and enduring relationships and providing care and support to partners or children. In *National Coalition II*, the Constitutional Court held that immigration legislation that conferred rights relating to the granting of immigration permits on the spouses or dependent children of permanent residents, but not on partners in a permanent same-sex relationship, rested on and perpetuated harmful stereotypes. These stereotypes reduced the identity of gays and lesbians to a single dimension, namely their sexuality, and viewed them as incapable of assuming familial responsibilities simply because same-sex couples are not able to procreate in the same manner as heterosexual couples. The legislation thus denied the capacity of gays and lesbians to love, and to care for and support loved ones.[61] In *Fourie*, the Constitutional Court found that same-sex couples' exclusion from the definition of marriage not only denied them socio-economic benefits accruing to spouses but also placed them outside the detailed regulatory framework that institutionalises mutual rights and responsibilities, protects vulnerable partners, and deals with the consequences of the dissolution of their relationship.[62] It further deprived same-sex partners of the choice to formalise their relationship through marriage and impaired their right to self-definition.[63] Moreover, it "signifies that their capacity for love, commitment and accepting responsibility is by definition less worthy of regard than that of heterosexual couples".[64]

A similar frame of analysis was used in relation to other forms of discrimination. For instance, in a case concerning South African Airways' refusal to employ an applicant because of his HIV status, the Constitutional Court noted that persons who are HIV positive are a vulnerable minority who are subjected to systemic disadvantage and extreme prejudice. A decision not to employ applicants living with HIV, without having regard to their ability to perform the duties of the job, perpetuates the stigmatisation of and stereotypes associated with people who are HIV positive and aggravates their disadvantage and exclusion.[65] The Court rejected the argument that the airline's decision was justified in view of commercial considerations, and held that differentiations based on HIV status can only be justified on the basis of "reasoned and medically sound judgments", not fear or ignorance.[66]

The transformative potential of *National Coalition I* derives not only from its attention to the social and historical context and the overlaps between social and symbolic harm but also from its insistence that the right to be treated equally is not limited to those who conform to dominant social norms. In the Court's view, the Constitution affirms the variability of human experience and behaviour, spurns the idea that what is considered normal or acceptable should be based on majoritarian norms and prejudices, disallows the subordination, exclusion, or silencing of groups and categories of people who are considered different, and views difference as a strength rather than a burden.[67] This theme is echoed in subsequent judgments.[68] However, despite the emphatic rejection of the idea that equality is premised on sameness, some of the normative distinctions that sustained inequality in the past have seeped back into the Constitutional Court's jurisprudence.

In *National Coalition II*, it was held that the term "spouse" could not reasonably be interpreted to include a partner in a permanent same-sex relationship, as its ordinary meaning is that of a husband or wife in an opposite-sex marriage.[69] The Court invalidated the section and cured the constitutional defect by reading the words "or partner, in a permanent same-sex life relationship" into the provision. Although its use of the remedy of reading-in has the same practical effect as a finding that the term "spouse" should be read to include same-sex life partners, the latter option would have gone much further in destabilising the idea that marriage is essentially a heterosexual institution.[70] The judgment has been criticised for premising the legal recognition of same-sex partnerships on conformity to an idealised model of heterosexual marriage and for privatising and depoliticising same-sex relationships. It is also said to have laid the foundation for a "separate but equal" regime, which reserves marriage for opposite-sex couples whilst creating a separate category for same-sex life partnerships.[71] The establishment of a separate category was further enabled by the decision in *Fourie* to suspend the declaration of invalidity to give Parliament time to decide how to cure the constitutional defect. Referring the matter back to Parliament to decide how to recognise same-sex marriage could, in principle, enhance the law's democratic pedigree and public acceptance. However, the decision cleared the way for a two-tiered system, which allows same-sex couples to get married in terms of the newly enacted Civil Union Act 17 of 2006, but not in terms of the Marriage Act 25 of 1961, which is still reserved for marriages between a man and a woman.[72]

Hegemonic conceptions of normal behaviour and the good sexual citizen also featured prominently in *Jordan*. The majority of the Court held that section 20(1)(aA) of the Sexual Offences Act, which criminalised the conduct of sex workers but not that of clients, constituted neither direct nor indirect gender-based discrimination. The Court reasoned that the prohibition applied both to male and female sex workers and was thus gender neutral.[73] It further pointed out that clients could be prosecuted as accomplices to the offence under common law and were liable to the same punishment as sex workers under the Riotous Assemblies Act. The majority viewed the argument that the conviction of sex workers carries a greater stigma than that of clients as legally irrelevant, since the stigma arises from social attitudes rather than the law and attaches to them "not by virtue of their gender, but by virtue of the conduct they engage in".[74] It also dismissed the argument that, in practice, only sex workers are prosecuted and not clients. In its view, the selective application of the law has no bearing on its constitutionality.[75] The formalism of the judgment is striking. It divorces the law from social attitudes and questions about its enforcement, disregards law's role in sustaining deeply ingrained prejudice, and fails to situate the inquiry into the impact of the differentiation within a broader context of poverty and systemic gender discrimination.[76] The formal understanding of equality that is at work here masks the extent to which the judgment draws on and normalises conventional moral views about sex, which are offended by a profession which straddles the divide between sexual intimacy and business and between the private and public spheres.[77] The judgment fails to entertain the possibility that those views may themselves be complicit in deepening and legitimising the stigmatisation and violence faced by many women. Moreover, its uncritical acceptance of the legitimacy of a law that entrenches sexual double standards and drives sex work underground, legitimises the suppression of oppositional discourses on sex and sexuality.

The Court in *Robinson* similarly attributed the disadvantage suffered by vulnerable people to the choices they made. The majority held that the exclusion of permanent life partners from benefits under the Maintenance of Surviving Spouses Act did not amount to unfair discrimination. It conceded that many women in permanent heterosexual partnerships "are left destitute and suffer hardships on the death of their male partners",[78] but argued that extending the protection afforded under the Act to unmarried partners would interfere with their freedom to choose whether to get married. The judgment thus failed to come to terms with the vulnerability and material need of those partners and relied uncritically on abstract notions of individual choice. It overlooked the differences among unmarried partners, ignored the capacity of stereotypical views of marriage to perpetuate gender inequality, and did little to resist hegemonic conceptions of the good sexual citizen. However, sixteen years later, the Court in *Bwanya* held that the exclusion of surviving partners in a permanent heterosexual life partnership from maintenance and intestate succession was unfairly discriminatory. Writing for the majority, Madlanga J was critical of the way in which the majority in *Robinson* privileged marriage, employed definitional reasoning, construed choice, and ignored the vulnerability of women in permanent heterosexual life partnerships.[79]

## 5.4 Distribution and class

The previous section centred on the capacity of the right to equality and non-discrimination to challenge and transform status-based social hierarchies (although distributive inequalities also entered the picture when discussing cases in which status- and class-based inequalities intersect). In this section, the focus shifts to the ability of the right to equality to challenge and respond to inequalities based on economic distribution, class, and poverty (although here, too, class- and status-based inequalities are bound to overlap). The gap between the Constitution's commitment to substantive and remedial equality and the persistence, three decades after the constitutional transition, of severe deprivation and economic inequality suggests that it is not sufficient to adjust the economic status quo through legislation, policies, and adjudication aimed at expanding access to basic goods and services. More comprehensive changes, which redress the structural causes of poverty and material inequality, are needed. Such changes likely require a rethink of the foundations of the political economy rather than simply tinkering at its edges. They further presuppose the involvement of a wide range of social movements, which raise awareness, mobilise, and organise around initiatives that are aimed at the eradication of domination, inequality, and exploitation. Can constitutional litigation and adjudication help to create conditions that are favourable to such changes? In thinking through this question, I will examine judicial decisions that invalidated the exclusion of certain groups from material benefits, addressed inequalities in the delivery of basic services, and outlawed private conduct that furthers material inequality.

In the first place, there are several cases in which courts invalidated statutory provisions that exclude certain categories of people from material benefits.[80] In *Khosa*, the exclusion of permanent residents from social grants was held to violate the rights to equality and access to social security. The Court noted the impact of permanent residents' exclusion from social grants on their material position, as they are forced into relations of dependence and denied the full capacity to exercise their constitutional rights.[81] Even more emphatically, it underscored the stigmatising effect of the measures, which signalled that "permanent residents are in some way inferior to citizens, and less worthy of social assistance".[82] The Court's analysis of the impact of the law on permanent residents' status (i.e., the recognition aspect) enabled it to focus on their rootedness in the community and is central to its holding that it violated the rights of permanent residents, but not those of temporary residents.[83]

In *Mahlangu*, the Court held that the exclusion of domestic workers from protection under the Compensation for Occupational Injuries and Diseases Act 130 of 1993 ("COIDA") unjustifiably limited domestic workers' rights to equal protection of the law, non-discrimination, human dignity, and access to social security. In her majority judgment, Victor AJ found that the law discriminated indirectly on the grounds of race, sex, and gender, as it disproportionately affected black women.[84] She emphasised the need to view the discrimination through an intersectional lens, which is better able to identify the multiple axes of disadvantage faced by poor black women, and to capture the systemic nature of the discrimination to which they are subject.[85] Her judgment accordingly situated the discrimination against domestic workers within the context of "the lingering gendered implications of apartheid's racist system".[86] She pointed out that influx control and migrant labour had restricted black women's access to employment opportunities, and rendered them financially dependent on absent male family members. Moreover, they were typically given the "least skilled, lowest paid and most insecure jobs",[87] like domestic work, which exposed them to poor living and working conditions and kept them away from their own families. She emphasised that material deprivation still drives many black women to domestic work, and that their lives as domestic workers continue to be characterised by poverty and vulnerability.[88]

Victor AJ's judgment also stresses the role played by sexist and patriarchal attitudes that brand domestic work as "women's work", which warrants low compensation and little regulation. It states that the undervaluing of domestic work leads to the treatment of domestic workers as mere objects, which amounts to a denial of their dignity and worth.[89] The judgment is thus sensitive to the overlaps between the status and class harms affecting domestic workers. However, unlike many other judgments, which either pay scant attention to material disadvantage or filter it through moral harm, the majority judgment in *Mahlangu* places poverty and systemic disadvantage at the centre of its unfair discrimination analysis.[90] It treats the perpetuation of domestic workers' material disadvantage and economic vulnerability through their exclusion from protection under COIDA as an independent ground for its finding of unfair discrimination. The finding is bolstered by – but is not contingent on – the Court's observations on how it furthers the stigmatisation of domestic work.[91]

Secondly, in a country in which the rich generally have access to better services than the poor, the equality guarantee could be used to challenge inequalities in service delivery and the resources that the state makes available to different communities. In *Social Justice Coalition*, the Equality Court held that the allocation of police human resources in the Western Cape amounted to indirect unfair discrimination on the grounds of race and poverty. Poverty is not expressly listed as a prohibited ground in the Promotion of Equality and Prevention of Unfair Discrimination Act 4 of 2000. However, section 34(1) mandates the Minister to consider the inclusion of socio-economic status as one of the listed grounds, and section 34(2) provides that nothing in the section prevents a court from determining that socio-economic status is a prohibited ground of discrimination. Despite the Minister's inaction, the Court held that poverty qualifies as a prohibited ground of discrimination under paragraph (b) of the definition, which refers to discrimination that causes or perpetuates systemic disadvantage, undermines human dignity, or adversely affects the equal enjoyment of rights and freedoms in a serious manner that is comparable to discrimination on one of the listed grounds.[92] In support of its finding of unfair discrimination, the Court relied on the report of the Khayelitsha Commission of Inquiry, which found that the system of human resources allocation used by the South African Police Service was detrimental to poor black areas. The skewed allocation was not caused by intentional bias but resulted from the system's emphasis on reported crime. The Court noted that crime in poor black areas is typically under-reported. As a result, "[police] stations that serve poor, Black areas", which tend to have the highest rates of violent and contact crimes, also "have the lowest police to population ratios, relatively speaking, as compared to wealthier, rich areas which are predominantly White".[93] It linked the skewed allocation of police resources to larger patterns of poor or minimal service delivery in townships and informal settlements.[94] The judgment's transformative impact has been weakened by the Equality Court's unreasonable delay in providing a remedy;[95] however, its reasoning raises the possibility that challenges based on PEPUDA could be brought in other instances in which affluent communities are afforded better public goods and services than impoverished communities.[96]

Thirdly, judgments in which the Bill of Rights is applied to horizontal relations could have redistributive effects. Although the decision in *Daniels v Scribante* was not based on the right to equality, it sheds light on the capacity of horizontal application to challenge material deprivation. The case concerned the question whether section 6(1) of the Extension of Security of Tenure Act 62 of 1997 (ESTA), which guarantees the right to reside on land, affords an occupier the right to make improvements to her dwelling without the consent of the owner. The Constitutional Court read section 6(1) with section 5(a) of ESTA, which provides that an occupier has the right to human dignity. It noted that dignified living conditions are indispensable to security of tenure, as intolerable conditions could effectively amount to an eviction. Depriving occupiers of the right to make improvements would impair their dignity by forcing them either to live in inhabitable conditions or to give up their home. Forcing them to relocate could have a negative effect on their way of life, sense of place, and ability to participate in social and political life.[97] Since the occupier in this case was planning to pay for the improvements herself, the Court's finding that she was entitled to make improvements did not place a direct obligation on the owner to finance the improvements. However, the respondents contended that a finding in favour of the occupier could have indirect redistributive effects, as ESTA provides that, upon an occupier's eviction, a court may order the owner to compensate the occupier for improvements made. In their view, that would go beyond section 8(2) of the Constitution, which does not place an obligation on natural and juristic persons to take positive steps to ensure that an occupier is afforded dignified living conditions. The Court rejected this argument. Madlanga J held that the Court's previous judgments on horizontal application did not establish that private persons should never bear a positive obligation under the Bill of Rights. The right of security of tenure necessarily imposes negative and positive obligations on private persons, and the mere possibility that a court may order compensation in certain cases cannot exempt owners from their constitutional obligations.[98]

*King NO v De Jager* further illustrates the redistributive possibilities arising from the horizontal application of the Bill of Rights. The case concerned the validity of a clause in a will containing a fideicommissum substitution that discriminated against female descendants. The judges of the Constitutional Court agreed that the clause was invalid but arrived at the conclusion through different routes. In a minority judgment, Mhlantla J held that the case called for the indirect horizontal application of constitutional values. She found that the common law principle of freedom of testation, which gives effect to constitutional rights like property, dignity, and privacy,[99] needs to be qualified to prevent it from being used to reinforce gender inequality. The common law accordingly had to be developed to prevent testators from discriminating against lineal descendants based solely on their gender, in circumstances where the descendants are not even known to them.[100] Importantly, Mhlantla J recognises "that the facially neutral principle of freedom of testation as it currently stands reinforces patriarchal and outdated ideas concerning sex, gender, property, ownership, family structures and norms",[101] and she attempts to recalibrate the relationship between equality and freedom of testation. It could nevertheless be asked, in view of the role played by common law concepts and principles in perpetuating and legitimising unequal access to wealth and resources, whether direct horizontal application would not have more transformative potential. Indirect horizontal application involves the incremental development of the common law to give effect to constitutional values; it seeks to harmonise the common law with the Constitution without upsetting the scheme of the common law too much. Direct horizontal application, on the other hand, allows private conduct to be tested directly against constitutional rights. Since it starts from the Constitution, it is less constrained by the inner logic and coherence of the common law.[102]

The majority measured the testamentary clause directly against section 9 of the Constitution and PEPUDA. In his majority judgment, Jafta J held that the testamentary clause was unfairly discriminatory and was hence against public policy and unenforceable. His insistence that freedom of testation is always already qualified by public policy considerations breaks with the tendency to treat freedom of testation as something that is near absolute, or that exists prior to legal regulation, and sends out a powerful signal that unfair discrimination will not be tolerated in the private sphere.[103] However, Jafta J's judgment is surprisingly sterile, and at times seems more interested in abstract logic than in transforming deeply entrenched patterns of inequality. His claim that freedom of testation is a "neutral principle" which is not in need of development,[104] obscures the role played by supposedly neutral legal concepts and principles in normalising the perpetuation of inequality through intergenerational wealth transfers. Moreover, his cursory analysis of the right to equality and the thinness of his reasoning suggest that his judgment will offer little guidance to courts in subsequent cases in which the discrimination may be less blatant, and the distributive impact may appear neutral.

By contrast, Victor AJ in a concurring judgment placed the dispute squarely within the context of the need to overcome systemic disadvantage and deeply unequal distributive patterns and power relations. She found that the Court was bound to apply the Bill of Rights directly in view of the intensity, nature, and purpose of the right to equality, the presence of inequality and disadvantage in the private sphere, and the overall goal of achieving substantive equality.[105] She further held that the principle of subsidiarity required the Court to adjudicate the matter within the framework provided by PEPUDA, rather than relying directly on section 9 of the Constitution.[106] This approach is to be welcomed. PEPUDA provides a better vantage point than the common law from which to identify and respond to structural inequality and disadvantage and a more encompassing framework for the adjudication of discrimination in the private sphere than section 9.

Victor AJ preceded her analysis of PEPUDA with observations on the need to revisit public policy in view of a substantive understanding of equality. She rejected the idea that law consists of "a set of neutral principles that has no bearing on power dynamics in society".[107] Instead, she emphasised that law shapes power relations, and that a transformative reading of the Constitution requires us to be alive to its ideological and distributive consequences. Moreover, we need to remove freedom of testation from an "individualist, libertarian and neo-liberal" framework, and reconsider it in view of the values of ubuntu and gender equality.[108] She also highlighted the need for "a contextual analysis" that underscores "how inheritance laws sustain and legitimise the unequal distribution of wealth" along class and gender lines.[109] These observations enabled her to situate her analysis of the relationship between freedom of testation and gender equality within a broader historical and social context, which takes account of the racial, class, and gender hierarchies that continue to keep many women trapped in poverty. She warned, with reference to Joel Modiri, that a failure to come to terms with the reinforcement of these hierarchies through supposedly neutral legal principles, like freedom of testation, would amount to an erasure of the memories of colonialism and the normalisation of its continued legacy.[110] She also noted, with reference to Cathi Albertyn, that a transformative equality jurisprudence must move beyond a concern with the accommodation of those hitherto excluded within existing social and economic structures, and work towards the eradication of the systemic barriers that impede their equal enjoyment of rights and freedoms. Such an approach must focus not only on the impact of discriminatory measures on human dignity, but also on their implications for the distribution of wealth and resources. That means that the Court's enquiry should "extend beyond the failure to treat women with equal concern and respect", and focus on "the way freedom of testation sustains iniquitous gender-based hierarchies which the Constitution seeks to uproot or abolish".[111] Against that background, Victor AJ held that the impugned clause was unfairly discriminatory, as it discriminated against a vulnerable group, which faces systemic material disadvantage and patterns of discrimination based on sex and gender. Freedom of testation therefore had to give way to the Constitution's determination to abolish patriarchy and sexism.[112]

These judgments arguably show that the right to equality can be used to challenge and respond to poverty and material need. But how far can the right be pushed and how do we explain the chasm between the Constitution's egalitarian aspirations and the persistence of severe poverty and inequality? One way of making sense of these questions is by invoking the distinctions between status-based and distributive harm and between sufficiency and economic equality.

Samuel Moyn points out that the era of human rights coincides with the era of neoliberalism and unprecedented economic inequality. Although he does not claim that human rights promote material inequality, he argues that they seek to eradicate status inequality and safeguard material sufficiency but offer no theoretical or practical resources that can be used to resist rampant economic inequality under market fundamentalism. As far as distributive issues are concerned, human rights focus on sufficiency or the minimum conditions of dignified living, as opposed to material equality. They thus seek to provide a floor of protection against poverty, without placing a ceiling on inequality.[113]

The equality cases discussed above appear to fit into that mould, as they mostly concern access to material benefits and services that are meant to safeguard the basic conditions of a dignified life. In some of the judgments (e.g., in *Khosa*, where it was stressed that the exclusion of permanent residents from socio-economic entitlements signalled that they are morally inferior, or less worthy of membership in the community), the references to a sufficient material threshold are bolstered by analyses of symbolic and psychological harm. Does that mean that we must resign ourselves to accepting that, while the equality clause and the socio-economic rights provisions in the Constitution could be used to soften some of capitalism's excesses, they are unable to challenge material inequality? Are they powerless to transform its underlying structures of exploitation and expropriation?

I would argue that constitutional litigation and adjudication can play a limited, yet meaningful, role in challenging material inequality. The first reason is that capitalism depends on law to protect property, regulate, and enforce contracts, structure markets, and enable the flow of capital, goods, and services across national boundaries. Law thus facilitates and regularises economic interaction. Capitalism's pervasiveness (i.e., its transnational character and tendency to extend its logic to all spheres of society) makes it more difficult for national and judge-made law to challenge it; however, it does not exclude the possibility that equality-based strategies can politicise and challenge laws and policies that deepen poverty and material inequality. Cases involving the horizontal application of the Bill of Rights, in particular, present opportunities for scrutinising some of the background rules and conditions that structure dominant legal understandings of concepts like property and contract and questioning their distributive and ideological implications. For example, the decision in *King* to test the validity of a will directly against the constitutional equality clause and PEPUDA constitutes a major departure from the common law's individualistic and libertarian premises. Victor AJ's judgment, through its careful contextualisation of the racial, class, and gender hierarchies that are encoded in legal concepts and emphasis on the need to dismantle structural barriers to the equal enjoyment of fundamental rights, politicises the perpetuation of economic inequality through intergenerational wealth transfers and invites further challenges to the legal infrastructure that enables it.

Secondly, capitalist societies are riddled with conflict and contradictions. Fraser notes, for example, that capitalist economies rely on and are sustained by non-commodified spheres of life, like nature, social reproduction, and politics. At the same time, the logic of commodification and accumulation invades and erodes (or, to use Fraser's term, "cannibalizes") these spheres, for example, through the commodification of essential needs, harm to the environment, and impairment of the rights of future generations. These developments spark ecological, social, and political crises that imperil the very conditions that make capitalism possible. That gives rise to struggles over the boundaries that separate the economy from the natural, social, and political spheres, in which participants draw on the "distinctive ontologies of social practice and normative ideals" that derive from those spheres.[114] Although boundary struggles take place among a variety of actors and within diverse settings, law plays an important role in shaping participants' strategies and expectations and deciding disputes. In such cases, judicial reliance on values like equality, democracy, social solidarity, and intergenerational equity can help set limits to capitalist expansion and the cannibalisation of other spheres.

Thirdly, status-based harms often shade into material disadvantage. In fact, some theorists claim that distributive injustices in capitalist societies arise from status hierarchies that signal that some categories of persons are unworthy of full membership in the community, or less capable of participating in the social, economic, or political spheres. Axel Honneth argues, for example, that the devaluation of domestic and reproductive labour stems from the use of "the economic activity of the independent, middle-class, male bourgeois" as the "normative reference point" for measuring individual achievement.[115] Unlike Honneth, I do not believe that all distributive injustices can be traced back to status harms. As Fraser notes, there are aspects of maldistribution that are "rooted not in ideologies about achievement, but in the system imperatives and governance structures of globalizing capitalism".[116] Viewed through a recognition lens, those injustices may look like inevitable consequences of impersonal market forces. However, the language of recognition can be used to challenge certain forms of material inequality, such as the devaluation of domestic labour and underpayment for jobs that are traditionally done by women or poor black women.

Fourthly, social grants and other measures aimed at ensuring that every person can satisfy their basic material needs are typically viewed as mechanisms for including those in need rather than transforming the underlying structural causes of inequality.[117] However, the distinction between these two categories is contextual, not absolute. Depending on the context and overall strategy, policies that at first appear "reformist" could have effects that are more deeply transformative. Such strategies, which are referred to as "non-reformist reform", accept that it is not possible to undo the underlying causes of domination, inequality, and dispossession at once. They are, however, not content to reassert and reform a fundamentally unjust system but aim to destabilise the status quo by gesturing at alternative configurations of economic, social, and political power, and seek to build democratic capacity through the mobilisation and organisation of ordinary people. For example, the provisioning of social welfare ordinarily qualifies as reformist reform but becomes non-reformist when it forms part of a broader strategy to empower citizens to participate in economic decision-making, and to wrest control over the economy from capitalist and technocratic elites.[118]

The transformative potential of judicial decisions that outlaw discrimination based on poverty (and other intersecting grounds) or challenge private law rules and concepts that normalise material inequality thus derives from the societal conflicts from which they arise. These conflicts can open up spaces in which material inequality can be politicised and the Constitution's commitment to equality and social justice can be linked to alternative visions in which capitalist dispossession and exploitation are dismantled and economic decision-making is democratised. Constitutional adjudication thus depends on other sites of democratic struggle – including state institutions, trade unions, social movements, and civic associations – and should not be elevated above them.

## 5.5 Political voice and participation

Discrimination not only consists in the message that members of a particular class of persons are unworthy of equal respect, or an impairment of their capacity to participate in economic life and access the material goods needed for a dignified existence. It sometimes also involves an impairment of their capacity for political participation and democratic citizenship. That would be the case where a law or conduct makes it difficult or impossible for certain groups, or a disproportionate number of the members of those groups, to air their views, participate in the activities of a political party or social movement, campaign for a political party or cause, vote in elections, make submissions to legislatures or government departments, assemble and demonstrate, or institute legal claims to vindicate their own rights or those of the general public.[119] Admittedly these rights are guaranteed expressly by more specific provisions, which will in many cases give more adequate protection to the activities in question.[120] However, equality as a constitutional right and value could complement and enhance these provisions, as there is a close affinity between equality and rights of democratic participation. The equality of the vote is not only a fundamental principle of democracy, but universal adult suffrage and other rights of democratic participation are important correctives to inequality in the private sphere and the capacity of private power and influence to shape political outcomes.[121] The value of equality should therefore play a vital role in the interpretation of rights of political participation.

The right to equality and non-discrimination could supplement and strengthen constitutional guarantees of rights and freedoms in cases where restrictions arise from measures that impact differently on different groups. The facts of the *Rajbala* case in India provide an example, even though the Indian Supreme Court failed to uphold the rights of democratic participation of vulnerable classes of citizens. The case concerned a challenge to provisions governing eligibility to contest elections for the village panchayats at the local government level. The provisions disqualified persons who did not meet the minimum educational qualification or did not have a functional toilet at their place of residence. Despite evidence that the educational criterion disqualified a high percentage of voters and had a disproportionate impact on vulnerable groups, like women from the scheduled castes, the Court held that it was rationally connected to the legislative purpose of ensuring better administration of the panchayats.[122] It also rejected the contention that the toilet requirement violated the right to equality, as the state provided financial assistance to families who wished to build a toilet at their place of residence.[123] The judgment failed not only to come to terms with the ways in which the criteria perpetuated prejudice based on the intersecting grounds of caste, class, and gender, but also to respond to an assault on the democratic voice and participation of vulnerable sections of the community.

The political marginalisation of certain groups does not occur in isolation but takes place within a larger context of structural inequality. In some cases, the primary – or at least the more visible – breach is status- or class-based, for instance where same-sex intimacy is criminalised or where economically vulnerable people are deprived of their means of subsistence. Although these are clear instances of moral harm and material disadvantage, respectively, it is important not to lose track of the impact of the treatment on the citizenship or political voice and participation of those concerned. In those cases, the isolation and fear that result from the deprivation of private freedom and the destruction of intimacy, and the desperation and dependence that arise from economic deprivation make serious inroads into their political freedom.[124] Focussing on the impact of discrimination on the political voice and power of marginalised groups is in line with the idea, advocated in chapter 1 above, that judicial review can enhance democracy when it is used to protect citizens against laws and decisions that threaten their capacity to participate as equals in the public-political sphere, even where the rights relied on are not traditionally viewed as "political" rights.

Recognising the impact of discrimination on the democratic participation of vulnerable groups could provide a corrective to the tendency to view discrimination claims through a restrictive, individualistic lens, which conceals systemic discrimination and ascribes disadvantage to individuals' choices, lack of talent or hard work, or the impersonal workings of the market. The realisation that democratic representation and citizenship may be at stake when laws or conduct discriminate against vulnerable populations draws attention to the interrelatedness of our "private" freedom as individuals and "public" freedom as citizens.[125] On the one hand, incursions into the civil and social rights of certain sections of the population may have a negative impact on their citizenship and capacity to participate in political life. On the other hand, the devaluation of their citizenship and restrictions on their political rights could severely impede their ability to enforce civil and socio-economic rights.[126] Attention to the intersections between political disempowerment and status- and class-based harms is bound to give rise to more nuanced assessments of the impact of discrimination, which are more likely to come to grips with the capacity of seemingly neutral distinctions to deepen the disadvantage experienced by vulnerable classes of persons.[127]

The right to equality could be used to politicise ostensibly neutral measures that deny the citizenship and impede the political participation of certain classes of people. Kendall Thomas' analysis of the sentencing differential between crack and powder cocaine violations in the United States is a case in point. Although the differentiation is facially neutral, it has a vastly disproportionate impact on African Americans and intersects with state legislation providing for criminal disenfranchisement in ways that are devastating for African Americans' political power.[128] Coming to terms with the impact of the sentencing differential on African Americans' citizenship requires careful attention to several interlocking structural issues: institutionalised racism, the carceral state, its connection to racial capitalism and the exploitation of black labour, the history of the disenfranchisement of black people, and neoliberal policies which treat impoverished populations as disposable.

A political understanding of equality presupposes a variety of discourses and critical social theories that can assist us in identifying, contextualising, connecting, and critiquing inequality's material, ideological, and political underpinnings. It is committed to safeguarding spaces in which such discourses can flourish and champions the right of "subaltern counterpublics" to politicise hegemonic social understandings and to develop "oppositional ideas" of personhood, citizenship, race, gender, family, community, nature, the economy, development, intergenerational equity, etc.[129] Such a political understanding could provide the basis for an alternative reading of *Jordan*, which focusses not only on the majority's failure to come to terms with the material disadvantage, prejudice, and stigma faced by sex workers, but also its reliance on a conventional discourse of gender, sexuality, and citizenship. That discourse situates "normal" sexual relations within a sphere of intimacy that is untouched by money and power, and brands those who flout such norms as sexual deviants who chose to forfeit their dignity and privacy. By endorsing these conventional views and upholding the constitutionality of discriminatory legislation, the Court prevented oppositional understandings of sexual difference, autonomy, choice,[130] and the relation between sex, power, and poverty, from entering mainstream public discourse.

## 5.6 Reconceiving difference

The political understanding of equality advocated in this chapter demands a critical and transformative approach to the construction of difference. In the first place, such an approach requires us not only to eschew the fallacy that we should disregard – or be "blind" to – race, sex, and other markers of disadvantage, but also to avoid uncritical reliance on reified understandings that treat these categories as natural, self-evident, or unchanging. We need to work with these categories, since they produce powerful real-world effects; however, we must remain critical of how they abstract away from the complexity of individual and collective identities and resist their capacity to foreclose alternative social imaginaries. Secondly, a transformative understanding of difference calls for attention to the complex interplay between status hierarchies, distributive injustices, and political marginalisation. Thirdly, it requires a critical awareness of the tendency to premise respect for difference on conformity to dominant social norms and the capacity of hierarchical distinctions to infiltrate seemingly progressive laws and judgments.

The Constitutional Court's jurisprudence acknowledges and seeks to redress the effects of South Africa's history of institutionalised racism, sexism, and other forms of prejudice, which are deeply embedded in social structures and continue to circumscribe the life chances of certain categories of people.[131] At the same time, however, it cautions that these categories should not be treated as rigid identities which define more or less homogenous social groups, as that would perpetuate the legacy of apartheid, where legally imposed categories stifled individuals' capacity for self-definition and determined their destinies and opportunities.[132] In navigating these difficulties, the Court has relied on the idea that the right to be treated the same and the right to be treated differently are both grounded in respect for every person's equal dignity.[133] In the Court's view, equality refers not to identical treatment, but to the idea that all persons should be treated with equal respect and concern, regardless of the differences between them.[134] Conversely, treating all persons as individuals who are capable of choosing their own ends demands having regard to the differences that are constitutive of their identities, or have a bearing on their status, political representation, or access to basic resources and capabilities.[135] In many cases, a failure to take account of those differences would be tantamount to ignoring deep-seated inequalities and overlooking section 9(2)'s injunction to overcome past discrimination and promote the full and equal enjoyment of all rights and freedoms.

The Court's equality jurisprudence thus provides the basis for a seemingly nuanced approach, which construes sameness and difference with reference to contextual factors such as the position of the complainants in society, whether they have been subjected to past discrimination, and the impact of identical or differential treatment on their dignity and worth.[136] This approach rejects the idea that sameness and difference refer to conformity to or divergence from the objective properties that define a particular social category, and is consonant with the view that social identities are fluid, dynamic, and overlapping. There are nevertheless cases, discussed above under the heading "Recognition and status", in which uncritical reliance on broad categories and identities resulted in the reification of difference and perpetuation of hierarchy and inequality. For instance, the majority judgment in *Jordan* overlooked the differences among women by taking middle-class norms and expectations for granted and by ignoring the lived reality of women who cannot or do not wish to conform to its idealised construction of femininity. Some of the decisions that extend rights to sexual minorities similarly impose a false unity on those labelled "different" and condition acceptance on conformity to idealised notions of the heterosexual citizen. These judgments reflect the difficulties inherent in attempts to balance reliance on general categories like race, gender, and sexual orientation with the need to resist reified and hierarchical understandings of difference.[137] They are also a reminder that whiteness, patriarchy, and heteronormativity still exert a powerful hold on the legal and political imagination.

A conflictual conception of difference resists the pull of hierarchical and reified constructions of groups-based identities and differences in several ways. In the first place, it insists that difference does not refer to objective properties of a group or individual, but derives its meaning from the discourses, institutions, and social practices in which our lives are embedded. Martha Minow argues that difference is not something inherent in individuals but derives from the relationship between individuals and institutions that have been designed around the needs of some people (e.g., men or the able-bodied) to the exclusion of others.[138] Judith Butler's theorisation of the performativity of gender provides a different lens. For her, the idea that gender refers to an inherent substance or core is a fabrication that is created through discourses and regulatory practices that postulate the coherence of sex, gender, and (hetero)sexuality.[139] Gender is not an essence, but something that is reproduced performatively, that is, through its enactment by subjects who are "prompted by obligatory norms to be one gender or the other (usually within a strictly binary frame)".[140] Gender's performativity suggests both the possibility of resistance and its limits. On the one hand, gendered subjects always act within the constraints of norms that act upon them. They are never free to step outside those norms. On the other hand, because gender is brought into existence through its performance, it could be re-enacted in ways that disrupt the apparent stability of the norms governing it, thereby opening up new possibilities.

Secondly, conflictual understandings reject the idea that difference can have a singular or unitary meaning. Difference is not the same as identity. As Iris Marion Young points out, the logic of identity that underpins Western philosophical thought preserves unity and eliminates the uncertainty and unpredictability associated with difference by identifying certain attributes – like reason, impartiality, and autonomy – with universality, while expelling others – like feeling, needs, and dependency – to the realm of the particular. It posits a form of moral subjectivity that transcends the particularity of different subject positions. It accordingly treats difference as deviance from the dominant norm, and conditions the recognition of those constructed as other on their assimilation into the mainstream. Young rejects this dichotomous and hierarchical conception of difference, which denies heterogeneity by measuring everyone against an "impartial" and "universal" standard.[141] Her insistence that group differences result from intersubjective experiences and are ambiguous, shifting, and cross-cutting puts uncertainty, dialogue, disagreement, and multiplicity back into difference.[142]

Translated into the language of discrimination law, we should be distrustful of laws that treat the experiences of certain groups as universal or tolerate difference only to the extent that it does not displace the silent norm. From this perspective, the reasoning in *Pillay* is to be welcomed. The Constitutional Court held that a public school's code of conduct, which banned the wearing of jewellery other than earrings and watches, unfairly discriminated against a learner who wore a nose stud as an expression of her South Indian Tamil Hindu culture. It recognised that, far from being neutral, the code "enforces mainstream and historically privileged forms of adornment, such as ear studs which also involve the piercing of a body part, at the expense of minority and historically excluded forms".[143]

Thirdly, an understanding of difference as ineradicable, rather than something that can be contained within the strictures of identity categories, is political to the core. Young's dialogical conception of difference presupposes a form of participatory democracy that is committed to the public discussion of divergent social experiences and perspectives. It does not condition participation in political life on the adoption of a universal or impartial standpoint, and does not exclude feelings, needs, or affiliations from public discourse.[144] Honig argues that there is no social category or entity – whether the nation, the community, the family, the self, or "immutable" or "chosen" group characteristics – that can escape the relentless play of difference or the conflict that it engenders. Social categories, like coalitions, involve the constant negotiation and renegotiation of differences, identities, and loyalties through dialogue and struggle.[145]

Fourthly, if we view difference as inextricably bound up with democracy and respect for dignity, equality, and freedom, we need a multiplicity of discourses, practices, institutions, and subject positions that enable different understandings of social categories to be articulated publicly and to challenge hegemonic constructions of difference.[146] Constitutional guarantees of fundamental rights and the democratic process can play an important role in safeguarding spaces in which different understandings of those categories can be articulated. However, although it is not directly involved in party politics or wrangling for control over the levers of state power, constitutional adjudication does not offer a neutral Archimedean point that stands outside power and conflict but is itself caught up in the tension between emancipatory and regulatory citizenship. Sometimes constitutional judgments help to secure spaces in which different subjectivities and discourses can take hold; sometimes they validate laws and practices that restrict how people can live and assert their difference; and sometimes they do both.[147] Constitutional judgments form part of a larger configuration of discourses, institutions, and power relations, which could have a significant bearing on their actual effect. Judgments that appear to close down spaces for oppositional constructions of difference could give rise to intensified social struggles,[148] while court victories could end up diverting attention away from the underlying causes of disadvantage. The point is not that judicial decisions do not matter, but that their impact is often unpredictable.

Fifthly, courts, legislatures, the state administration, and non-state actors face difficult choices when confronted with the dilemma that, to eradicate and redress discrimination, they need to acknowledge groups-based difference, but that they must also guard against the capacity of reified understandings of those categories to perpetuate the disadvantage of vulnerable and marginalised groups. Fraser's distinction between the affirmation and transformation of difference is helpful in that regard. She points out that strategies that affirm difference run the risk of simplifying and reifying collective self-understandings, blinding us to internal differences within groups, and inducing conformity to communitarian norms. She argues instead for a more radical strategy centred on the deconstruction or transformation of difference. This entails destabilising hierarchical oppositions between subjectivities and modes of being in the world that are considered normal and those branded as deviant. In her view, this strategy could empower individuals to come to terms with the complexity of cross-cutting group identifications and to form alliances across differences.[149]

Finally, intersectionality analysis could help legal interpreters to respond to the shifting and dynamic nature of difference. The idea of intersectionality originated from attempts to come to terms with the complexity of the disadvantage suffered by black women. Authors like Kimberle Crenshaw argued that black women experience forms of disadvantage that cannot be reduced to a single axis of discrimination, and that some of their experiences are lost from view when looked at from either a feminist or anti-racist perspective. Conventional understandings of gender- and race-based discrimination cannot account for the interlocking patterns of disadvantage, subordination, and privilege that produce different experiences of inequality within groups. Those understandings have given rise to judicial decisions in the United States that reject the claims of black women either because the laws in question do not discriminate against all women or because they do not have an adverse impact on black people in general.[150] They conceal the internal divisions and hierarchies within social categories like "women" and "black people", misconstrue the nature and severity of the disadvantage suffered by black women, and normalise their social and cultural devaluation.[151]

Victor AJ's majority judgment in *Mahlangu* contains the most elaborate judicial statement to date of the meaning and implications of intersectionality.[152] She stated that attention to the intersectional nature of discrimination "enables courts to consider the social structures that shape the experience of marginalised people", and "reveals how individual experiences vary according to multiple combinations of privilege, power, and vulnerability".[153] She used that frame to situate her analysis of the disadvantage experienced by domestic workers, who are predominantly black women, within the context of multiple intersecting forms of discrimination based on race, gender and class.[154] She highlighted how poverty and social subordination confined black women largely to insecure, low-paid and exploitative jobs, and showed that their exclusion under COIDA perpetuated harmful stereotypes and reinforced their material disadvantage.[155]

Atrey argues that intersectionality inhabits a "middle ground", as it "both [works] with and [is] critical of identity categories and identity politics".[156] It allows us to treat "identities as 'ideologically powerful, experientially salient (but not essentialist), and … fluid'".[157] Intersectionality thus recognises that social categories are dynamic, unstable, and immersed in power relations, yet insists that dispensing with those categories would deprive us of important analytical tools for uncovering and remedying institutionalised inequality. Moving back and forth between generalisations about the disadvantage experienced by social groups and the specific experiences of individuals within those groups, it resists both reified understandings of identity categories and a universalist position that ends up assimilating vulnerable groups into a pre-existing social order that reflects the values, identities, and expectations of dominant groups.[158]

One of the most important challenges for equality and discrimination analysis is coming to terms with the intersections between poverty or class and categories like race, sex, gender, marital status, age, and disability. Incorporating poverty into intersectionality analysis could have several advantages. It could help us make sense of the interrelatedness of material disadvantage and cultural misrecognition, or the ways in which distributive injustices and social prejudice, stereotypes, and violence feed off each other. It could alert us to the harsh and disproportionate impact of seemingly neutral laws and policies on people who are unemployed, homeless, illiterate, or suffering from malnutrition.[159] It could help us avoid the pitfalls of race and gender essentialism by drawing attention to the class divisions within groups, and serve as a reminder of the complexity of the "structural adjustments" that need to be made "across multiple categorical axes" to remedy inequality.[160]

An intersectional understanding of difference is also conducive to the consideration of the impact of discriminatory measures on the political voice and participation of groups that experience intersectional disadvantage. Crenshaw's discussion of "political intersectionality" is instructive in that regard. She refers to the difficulties faced by black women who assert their rights in the face of interlocking forms of discrimination. Their own voices tend to be drowned out as their causes are appropriated by (white) feminist and (male) anti-racist activists, and as they become embroiled in cultural conflicts in which they are accused of anti-feminism when they show solidarity with the men in their communities, and reproached for being disloyal to their husbands, partners, male relatives, and communities when they stand up against patriarchy.[161] An intersectional frame of analysis not only requires attention to the impact of interlocking forms of oppression on the political rights of marginalised groups, but also demands remedies that are aimed at eradicating barriers to their participation in social and political life.

## Notes

1 *Du Plessis v De Klerk* para 126 (the interim Constitution is "unabashedly egalitarian and libertarian", and the fundamental rights enshrined in it "have a poignancy and depth of meaning not echoed in any other national constitution I have seen"); *Bato Star Fishing v Minister of Environmental Affairs* para 74; *Minister of Finance v Van Heerden* paras 26, 136.
2 *City of Tshwane Metropolitan Municipality v Afriforum* para 4.
3 *Daniels v Scribante* paras 116-132.
4 *Duncanmec v Gaylard* para 7 (while courts have a critical role to play in combating racial discrimination, "the Constitution has had a limited impact in eliminating racism in our country. Its shortcomings flow from the fact that it does not have the capacity to change human behaviour").
5 *Gumede v President* paras 1, 17, 35.
6 Fraser treats the three categories as distinct, yet overlapping, impediments to the realisation of the ideal of participatory parity, which requires social arrangements to permit everyone to participate as peers in social life. Fraser "Social Justice in the Age of Identity Politics" 35–37; Fraser *Scales of Justice* 16–18. See also Mc Manus "A Fraserian Theory of Anti-Discrimination Law"; Basson "Poverty Discrimination under the Promotion of Equality and Prevention of Unfair Discrimination Act" on the relevance of Fraser's thought to discrimination law.
7 *Fraser v Children's Court* para 20.
8 *Minister of Finance v Van Heerden* para 22.
9 *King v De Jager* para 77.
10 *Khosa v Minister of Social Development* para 42; *Mahlangu v Minister of Labour* para 54.
11 *Brink v Kitshoff* para 40 (the constitutional equality guarantee is a product of South Africa's history of systematic discrimination and must be interpreted "in the light of that history and the enduring legacy that it bequeathed").
12 *National Coalition v Minister of Justice* para 60.
13 *President v Hugo* para 112.
14 Para 41.
15 *City Council of Pretoria v Walker* paras 31–32; *Mahlangu* paras 73, 92–94, 105.
16 See the discussion of intersectionality under chapter 5.6 below.
17 *National Coalition v Minister of Justice* paras 61–62.
18 That is in line with s 7(2), which provides: "The state must respect, protect, promote and fulfil the rights in the Bill of Rights".
19 *Bato Star Fishing v Minister of Environmental Affairs* para 74. See also *Minister of Finance v Van Heerden* paras 26, 29, 147–148.
20 *Minister of Finance v Van Heerden* para 30. The Court stated at para 31: "Absent a positive commitment progressively to eradicate socially constructed barriers to equality and to root out systematic or institutionalised under-privilege, the constitutional promise of equality before the law and its equal protection and benefit must, in the context of our country, ring hollow".
21 Paras 32–35.
22 *National Coalition v Minister of Justice* paras 61–62.
23 Para (a) of the definition refers to the same grounds as those listed in s 9(3) the Constitution, while para (b) refers to discrimination on any other ground that "(i) causes or perpetuates systemic disadvantage; (ii) undermines human dignity; or (iii) adversely affects the equal enjoyment of a person's rights and freedoms in a serious manner that is comparable to discrimination on a ground in paragraph (a)". The definition section also contains definitions of "age", "pregnancy", and "sex".
24 *Harksen v Lane* para 46; *Larbi-Odam v Member of Executive Council* paras 19–20.
25 *Harksen v Lane* para 51.

26 Ackermann *Human Dignity* 186 argues that it may have been unwise to add the reference to an impairment of a comparably serious nature and that dignity should be the sole criterion. He writes: "It was certainly not the Court's intention, in formulating the qualification, to expand without limit the criterion of attribution provided by human dignity"). PEPUDA does not include the reference to an impairment of a comparably serious nature under the factors listed in s 14(2) and (3) but separates the impairment of human dignity (s 14(3)(a)) from the impact of the discrimination (s 14(3)(b)). It thus keeps open the possibility that different types of harm can be considered. It also adds the question whether the discrimination is systemic in nature (s 14(3)(e)).

27 *Minister of Finance v Van Heerden* paras 54, 101, 131, 145, 146; *South African Police Service v Solidarity obo Barnard* paras 32, 93, 168–183.

28 Ackermann *Human Dignity* 21–26. See also Cowen "Can 'Dignity' Guide South Africa's Equality Jurisprudence?" 40.

29 See Albertyn and Goldblatt "Facing the Challenge of Transformation" 252, 258.

30 See Fredman "Redistribution and Recognition" 226–227; Botha "Equality, Plurality and Structural Power" 6–17; Albertyn "Contested Substantive Equality in the South African Constitution" 465–468 for different attempts to develop such a multidimensional approach.

31 Some scholars have called for a "memorial" rather than "monumental" understanding of the Constitution. Memorial constitutionalism worries about the selectivity of our memory, refuses to assume that the violations of the past have been, or are about to be overcome, and proposes a careful, contextual approach to constitutional interpretation, which eschews the idea of a single, authoritative method of interpretation that absolves constitutional interpreters of responsibility for their choices. See Snyman "Interpretation and the Politics of Memory"; Du Plessis "Affirmation and Celebration of the 'Religious Other' in South Africa's Constitutional Jurisprudence on Religious and Related Rights"; Le Roux and Van Marle (eds) *Law, Memory and the Legacy of Apartheid*; De Ville (ed) *Memory and Meaning*.

32 See Honig "Another Cosmopolitanism?" 111, 113–114 for a critique of cosmopolitan theories of human rights which rest upon a "progressive" and "linear" "temporal register" in which limits to the universal unfolding of cosmopolitan law are "always already about to be overcome".

33 109.

34 116–117.

35 Van Marle "Lives of Action, Thinking and Revolt".

36 See chapter 3.2 above.

37 Thomas "Racial Justice" 84.

38 91–98.

39 87.

40 Manicom "Constituting 'Women' as Citizens" 24 (citizenship is both "a productive and disciplinary category", and "political subjects, as citizens, are both *subject of* the powers and potential that attach to [citizenship], but at the same time, *subject to* its regulatory aspects") (emphasis in the original).

41 See Marshall *Class, Citizenship, and Social Development* for a classical study of citizenship's capacity to resist inequalities, including those inherent in the capitalist system of production.

42 Richardson "Rethinking Sexual Citizenship" 211, 213.

43 Manicom "Constituting 'Women' as Citizens" 23 (while citizenship may enable women to engage in anti-hegemonic struggles, it may also "work as a modality of subjection, potentially channelling opposition into containable, governable forms"). See also 34 (the elaborate "gender [policies], mainstreaming strategies, women's empowerment strategies", etc. that were established after 1994 "enhance women's capacity to engage in citizenly activities, but at the same time delimit and regulate the forms of that engagement").

44 Richardson "Rethinking Sexual Citizenship" 217–219. See also Wilson "The 'Neat Concept' of Sexual Citizenship" 79–80.
45 Thomas "Racial Justice" 94–98.
46 See De Vos "The 'Inevitability' of Same-Sex Marriage in South Africa's Post-Apartheid State" 457; Robson "Sexual Democracy" 420; Barnard-Naudé "Spectres to Come" 45–47. See also Richardson "Claiming Citizenship?" 268–269.
47 See Manicom "Constituting 'Women' as Citizens" 30, 43 on the relationship between the regulation of women's bodies and behaviour and the construction of citizenship and the boundaries of the nation-state.
48 Ammaturo "The 'Pink Agenda'" 1152 (emphasis in the original omitted).
49 1154.
50 Benhabib *The Rights of Others* 144 (emphasis in the original omitted). See also Preuß "Citizenship and Identity".
51 Benhabib *The Rights of Others* 146-163.
52 Balibar *Citizenship* 37.
53 Balibar *Equaliberty* 50.
54 287–293.
55 Rancière "Who Is the Subject of the Rights of Man?" 304.
56 *National Coalition v Minister of Justice* para 28.
57 Para 24.
58 Para 127.
59 Réaume "Discrimination and Dignity" 684–685.
60 In addition to the cases discussed below, legislation that conferred rights and benefits on spouses, to the exclusion of partners in a permanent same-sex relationship, was held to be unconstitutional in *Satchwell v President of the RSA* (pension benefits accruing to the surviving spouses of judges); *Du Toit v Minister for Welfare* (right to adopt children); *J v Director-General* (rights of spouses in relation to children conceived by artificial insemination); *Gory v Kolver* (intestate succession).
61 *National Coalition v Minister of Home Affairs* paras 49–54.
62 *Minister of Home Affairs v Fourie* paras 63–74.
63 Para 72.
64 Para 71.
65 *Hoffmann v South African Airways* para 28.
66 Para 35.
67 *National Coalition v Minister of Justice* paras 22, 130–138. De Vos "From Heteronormativity to Full Sexual Citizenship?" 261–265 argues that the judgment rejects the idea of unified sexual categories and undermines heteronormativity.
68 See, e.g., *Minister of Home Affairs v Fourie* para 60.
69 *National Coalition v Minister of Home Affairs* paras 25–26.
70 See Le Roux "Undoing the Past through Statutory Interpretation" 533–536, 539 for a critique of the Court's textualist approach, in contrast to the somewhat more purposive and functionalist approach followed in *Daniels v Campbell*, in which it was held that the term "spouse" could reasonably be interpreted to include a person married according to Muslim rites.
71 De Vos "From Heteronormativity to Full Sexual Citizenship?" 266–271; Barnard-Naudé "Spectres to Come" 49–51.
72 In her dissenting judgment in *Minister of Home Affairs v Fourie*, O'Regan J argued at paras 165–173 that the declaration of invalidity should have immediate prospective effect. Such an order would facilitate the recognition of same-sex marriages under the Marriage Act through the development of the common law and the reading of words into s 30(1) of the Marriage Act.
73 *Jordan v S* para 9.
74 Para 16.

75 Para 19.
76 By contrast, the dissenting judgment of O'Regan and Sachs JJ notes the "markedly differential impact" of the provision on men and women and argues that it "directly reinforces a pattern of sexual stereotyping which is itself in conflict with the principle of gender equality". Para 60. It points out that the greater social stigma associated with the principal offender "tracks and reinforces in a profound way double standards regarding the expression of male and female sexuality". Para 67.
77 See para 29.
78 *Volks v Robinson* para 63.
79 *Bwanya v Master of the High Court* paras 60–70.
80 See, e.g., *Hassam v Jacobs* (invalidating the exclusion of spouses in polygynous Muslim marriages from the Intestate Succession Act and reading in words to cure the defect); *Gory v Kolver* (invalidating the exclusion of partners in a permanent same-sex life partnership who have undertaken reciprocal duties of support from the Intestate Succession Act and reading in words to cure the defect). In *Daniels v Campbell*, the Court avoided a declaration of invalidity by reading the word "spouse" in the Intestate Succession Act 81 of 1987 and Maintenance of Surviving Spouses Act 27 of 1990 to include partners in a monogamous Muslim marriage.
81 *Khosa v Minister of Social Development* paras 76–77.
82 Para 74.
83 See the discussion under chapter 4.5 above.
84 *Mahlangu v Minister of Labour* paras 92–94.
85 Paras 75–91, 95–96, 98.
86 Para 98.
87 Para 99.
88 Para 104.
89 Paras 108–115.
90 Victor AJ's critical engagement with the multilayered and systemic nature of the disadvantage faced by domestic workers stands in stark contrast to the narrow approach adopted by Jafta J in his minority judgment. He held that the impugned provision violated s 9(1) of the Constitution and that it was unnecessary to decide whether it infringed s 9(3) (paras 158–160). He argued that the status of a domestic worker is not among the grounds listed in s 9(3), that it does not trigger the presumption of unfairness in s 9(5), and that other classes of workers, like members of the National Defence Force and Police Service, were also excluded from COIDA's definition (paras 161–163). He denied that the exclusion of domestic workers impaired their dignity, since their dignity "is not bound up with the type of work they do" (para 164).
91 The "systemic disadvantage" experienced by domestic workers and "the cycle of poverty they suffer" were also central to the decision to declare the provision invalid with retrospective effect. Para 128.
92 *Social Justice Coalition v Minister of Police* (WCC) paras 61–65. See G Basson *Poverty as a Ground of Unfair Discrimination in Post-Apartheid South Africa* for an analysis of poverty as a ground of discrimination under the Constitution and PEPUDA.
93 Para 87.
94 Paras 53, 90.
95 In *Social Justice Coalition v Minister of Police* (CC), it was held that the Constitutional Court did not have the jurisdiction to intervene in the case before the Equality Court provided a remedy. See Basson "Procedural Justice as a Feature of Transformative Substantive Equality" for a critique of the Constitutional Court's judgment.
96 See Budlender "20 Years of Democracy" 443–444.

97 *Daniels v Scribante* paras 33–35.
98 Paras 37–55.
99 *King v De Jager* paras 64–69.
100 Paras 83–85.
101 Para 79.
102 Direct horizontal application, which involves testing private conduct directly against constitutional rights, is provided for in s 8(2) of the Constitution, which states that constitutional rights bind natural and juristic persons, depending on the nature of the right and the nature of the duty imposed by the right. S 8(3) further provides that, if a right is unjustifiably limited, the common law must be developed to give effect to it. While some judgments have used s 8(2) to progressive effect, the insistence of the majority in *Barkhuizen v Napier* and *AB v Pridwin* that s 8(2) is not applicable to contractual relationships has limited its transformative reach. See Ally and Linde "*Pridwin*".
103 Para 94.
104 Paras 93, 95, 96.
105 Para 178.
106 Paras 182–194.
107 Para 198.
108 Para 203.
109 Paras 205, 206.
110 Para 209.
111 Para 216.
112 Paras 234–236.
113 Moyn *Not Enough*.
114 See Fraser *Cannibal Capitalism*.
115 Honneth "Redistribution as Recognition" 141.
116 Fraser "Distorted Beyond All Recognition" 215.
117 See Albertyn "Substantive Equality and Transformation in South Africa" 256 (arguing for a transformative approach to difference which goes beyond the mere inclusion of those formerly excluded).
118 Fraser "Social Justice in the Age of Identity Politics" 78–80; Evans "Land and the Limits of Liberal Legalism"; Akbar "Non-Reformist Reforms and Struggles over Life, Death, and Democracy" 2527–2531; "Perolini "Limited Tools for Emancipation?".
119 See Fraser *Scales of Justice* 17–18.
120 See ss 16, 17, 19, 34, and 59 of the Constitution.
121 *August v Electoral Commission* para 17; *Doctors for Life v Speaker* para 115.
122 *Rajbala v State of Haryana* paras 73–87.
123 Paras 93–95.
124 See *National Coalition v Minister of Justice* para 127 (criminalisation of male same-sex sodomy "stigmatise[s] individuals as members of an inferior caste or view them as not belonging to the community", and thus denies their "full moral citizenship").
125 Habermas "Struggles for Recognition in the Democratic Constitutional State" 110–116.
126 To use Hannah Arendt's term, it could effectively deprive them of the right to have rights. Arendt *The Origins of Totalitarianism* 296. See also Balibar *Citizenship* 68, who describes the right to have rights as "the active ability to assert rights in a public space" or "the possibility of not being excluded from the right to fight for one's rights" (emphasis in the original omitted).
127 That is not to suggest that political oppression should be privileged over other forms of harm, or that the plaintiffs in non-discrimination cases should always be required to show that the impugned discrimination adversely affects their political rights.
128 Thomas "Racial Justice" 91–98.

129 87.
130 See Cornell *At the Heart of Freedom* 58 (sex workers have not renounced their right to a "psychic, political, and ethical space" in which they can "represent themselves").
131 *Brink v Kitshoff* paras 40–44; *Minister of Finance v Van Heerden* paras 26–27.
132 *National Coalition v Minister of Justice* para 126 ("One of the great gains achieved by following a situation-sensitive human rights approach is that analysis focuses not on abstract categories, but on the lives as lived and the injuries as experienced by different groups in our society. The manner in which discrimination is experienced on grounds of race or sex or religion or disability varies considerably – there is difference in difference").
133 The Court stated in *President v Hugo* para 41 that the constitutional goal of equality cannot be achieved "by insisting upon identical treatment in all circumstances" and noted that "[it] is the logical corollary of the principle that 'like should be treated like', that treating unlike alike may be as unequal as treating like unlike" (footnote 63).
134 *National Coalition v Minister of Justice* paras 22, 134.
135 Sachs J stated in *Minister of Home Affairs v Fourie* para 60: "The acknowledgment and acceptance of difference is particularly important in our country where for centuries group membership based on supposed biological characteristics such as skin colour has been the express basis of advantage and disadvantage. South Africans come in all shapes and sizes. The development of an active rather than a purely formal sense of enjoying a common citizenship depends on recognising and accepting people with all their differences, as they are. The Constitution thus acknowledges the variability of human beings (genetic and socio-cultural), affirms the right to be different, and celebrates the diversity of the nation".
136 *Harksen v Lane* para 51.
137 *President v Hugo*, in which it was held that the exclusion of imprisoned fathers from a presidential pardon did not discriminate unfairly on the grounds of sex and gender, illustrates the dilemma. On the one hand, the pardon perpetuated root causes of gender inequality like the gendered division of labour and the stereotype of mothers as caregivers. On the other hand, it would be unfair to ignore the reality that in South Africa, mothers generally bear far greater child-rearing burdens than fathers. See the debate between Kriegler and O'Regan JJ at paras 80–86, 109–115.
138 Minow *Making all the Difference* 87–94.
139 Butler *Gender Trouble* 185–186.
140 Butler "Performativity, Precarity and Sexual Politics".
141 Young *Justice and the Politics of Difference* 98–107.
142 See also Honig "Difference, Dilemmas, and the Politics of Home" 258 (difference is not what distinguishes the unitary self from other selves, but what disrupts it from within).
143 *MEC for Education v Pillay* para 44. Both the majority and minority judgments held open the possibility, without deciding the issue, that it is not always necessary for a party alleging unfair discrimination to identify a comparator or dominant group. Paras 44, 164. Not requiring a comparator could help avert the danger of affirming dominant cultural norms. See Basson "Poverty Discrimination under the Promotion of Equality and Prevention of Unfair Discrimination Act" 41–42.
144 Young *Justice and the Politics of Difference* 116–121.
145 Honig "Difference, Dilemmas, and the Politics of Home" 271.
146 Mouffe *The Democratic Paradox* 103–104.
147 Cf Robert Cover's discussion of the tension between law's jurisgenerative and jurispathic functions. The former refers to the processes through which multiple interpretive communities generate diverse legal meanings, whereas the latter denotes the role of the law in containing the free play of meaning. Cover "The Supreme Court 1982 Term" 12–19.

148 The continued mobilisation for the decriminalisation of sex work after *Jordan* is a case in point. After decades of strategising, advocacy, and organising by movements like the Sex Workers Education and Advocacy Taskforce (SWEAT) and Sisonke, the cabinet announced that the Criminal Law (Sexual Offences and Related Matters) Amendment Bill of 2022, which decriminalises sex work, would be published for public comment. The process has however been paused. See Spies "Better Late than Never"; Lakhani "You Can't Break a Sweat".

149 Fraser "Social Justice in the Age of Identity Politics" 72–78. Individuals' right to self-determination arguably also militates against state decisions that affirm dominant conceptions of difference. Cornell *At the Heart of Freedom* 23 claims that the state should refrain from relying on a substantive definition of sexual difference, as that would curtail individuals' right to forge their own identities. The individual, rather than the state, should be "the source of the representation of her sexuate being". She further argues at 61 that conflicts about cultural identity are best resolved not by the state but through the politics of the street.

150 Crenshaw "Demarginalizing the Intersection of Race and Sex".

151 Crenshaw "Mapping the Margins" 1268, 1270, 1272, 1280, 1282.

152 But see also *Harksen v Lane* para 49 (the "temptation to force [the listed grounds of discrimination] into neatly self-contained categories should be resisted"); *National Coalition v Minister of Justice* para 113 (certain groups of people, e.g., black foreigners, unmarried mothers, homosexual parents, and African widows are subject to compounded forms of disadvantage); *Hassam v Jacobs* para 33 (exclusion of spouses in a polygamous Muslim marriage from statutory benefits discriminates unfairly on the overlapping grounds of gender, religion, and marital status); *Social Justice Coalition v Minister of Police* (WCC) paras 87–88, 87, 90 (unequal allocation of police resources discriminates unfairly on the intersecting grounds of race and poverty).

153 *Mahlangu v Minister of Labour* para 79.

154 Paras 90, 96, 98.

155 Paras 98–107.

156 Atrey *Intersectional Discrimination* 55.

157 59.

158 58, 61, 71.

159 Atrey "The Intersectional Case of Poverty in Discrimination Law" 436.

160 Dugard and Sánchez "Bringing Gender and Class into the Frame" 29.

161 See Crenshaw "Mapping the Margins" 1251–1282.

## Bibliography

Ackermann L *Human Dignity: Lodestar for Equality in South Africa* (2012) Cape Town: Juta.

Akbar A "Non-Reformist Reforms and Struggles over Life, Death, and Democracy" (2023) 132 *Yale Law Journal* 2497.

Albertyn C "Contested Substantive Equality in the South African Constitution: Beyond Social Inclusion towards Systemic Justice" (2018) 34 *South African Journal on Human Rights* 441.

Albertyn C "Substantive Equality and Transformation in South Africa" (2007) 23 *South African Journal on Human Rights* 253.

Albertyn C and Goldblatt B "Facing the Challenge of Transformation: Difficulties in the Development of an Indigenous Jurisprudence of Equality" (1998) 14 *South African Journal on Human Rights* 248.

Ally N and Linde D "*Pridwin*: Private School Contracts, the Bill of Rights and a Missed Opportunity" (2021) 11 *Constitutional Court Review* 275.

Ammaturo F "The 'Pink Agenda': Questioning and Challenging European Homonationalist Sexual Citizenship" (2015) 49 *Sociology* 1151.

Arendt H *The Origins of Totalitarianism* (1968) San Diego: Harcourt.

Atrey S "The Intersectional Case of Poverty in Discrimination Law" (2018) 18 *Human Rights Law Review* 411.

Atrey S *Intersectional Discrimination* (2019) Oxford: Oxford University Press.

Balibar É *Citizenship* (2015, translation T Scott-Railton) Cambridge: Polity Press.

Balibar É *Equaliberty* (2014, translation J Ingram) Durham: Duke University Press.

Barnard-Naudé J "Spectres to Come: Reproductive Futurism, Queer Africa, Die-ins and Drag". In T Morison, I Lynch and V Reddy (eds) *Queer Kinship: South African Perspectives on the Sexual Politics of Family-Making and Belonging* (2018) 43 Pretoria: Unisa Press.

Basson G *Poverty as a Ground of Unfair Discrimination in Post-Apartheid South Africa*, unpublished LLM thesis, Stellenbosch University (2022).

Basson G "Poverty Discrimination under the Promotion of Equality and Prevention of Unfair Discrimination Act: A Transformative Substantive Equality Approach" (2023) 39 *South African Journal on Human Rights* 26.

Basson G "Procedural Justice as a Feature of Transformative Substantive Equality: Critical Notes on *Social Justice Coalition v Minister of Police* (CC)" (2024) 141 *South African Law Journal* 349.

Benhabib S *The Rights of Others: Aliens, Residents and Citizens* (2004) Cambridge: Cambridge University Press.

Botha H "Equality, Plurality and Structural Power" (2009) 25 *South African Journal on Human Rights* 1.

Budlender G "20 Years of Democracy: The State of Human Rights in South Africa" (2014) 25 *Stellenbosch Law Review* 439.

Butler J "Performativity, Precarity and Sexual Politics" (2009) 4 *Revista de Antropologia Iberoamericana* i.

Butler J *Gender Trouble: Feminism and the Subversion of Identity* (2006) New York: Routledge.

Cornell D *At the Heart of Freedom: Feminism, Sex, and Equality* (1998) Princeton: Princeton University Press.

Cover R "The Supreme Court 1982 Term – Foreword: Nomos and Narrative" (1983) 97 *Harvard Law Review* 4.

Cowen S "Can 'Dignity' Guide South Africa's Equality Jurisprudence?" (2001) 17 *South African Journal on Human Rights* 34.

Crenshaw K "Demarginalizing the Intersection of Race and Sex: A Black Feminist Critique of Antidiscrimination Doctrine, Feminist Theory and Antiracist Politics" (1989) *University of Chicago Legal Forum* 139.

Crenshaw K "Mapping the Margins: Intersectionality, Identity Politics, and Violence Against Women of Color" (1991) 43 *Stanford Law Review* 1241.

De Ville J (ed) *Memory and Meaning: Lourens du Plessis and the Haunting of Justice* (2015) Durban: LexisNexis.

De Vos P "From Heteronormativity to Full Sexual Citizenship? Equality and Sexual Freedom in Laurie Ackermann's Constitutional Jurisprudence" (2008) *Acta Juridica* 254.

De Vos P "The 'Inevitability' of Same-Sex Marriage in South Africa's Post-Apartheid State" (2007) 23 *South African Journal on Human Rights* 432.

Du Plessis L "Affirmation and Celebration of the 'Religious Other' in South Africa's Constitutional Jurisprudence on Religious and Related Rights: Memorial Constitutionalism in Action?" (2008) 8 *African Human Rights Law Journal* 376.

Dugard J and Sánchez A "Bringing Gender and Class into the Frame: An Intersectional Analysis of the Decoloniality-as-Race Critique of the Use of Law for Social Change" (2021) 32 *Stellenbosch Law Review* 24.

Evans M "Land and the Limits of Liberal Legalism: Property, Transitional Justice and Non-Reformist Reforms in Post-Apartheid South Africa" (2021) 48 *Review of African Political Economy* 646.

Fraser F *Cannibal Capitalism: How Our System Is Devouring Democracy, Care, and the Planet – and What We Can Do about It* (2022) London: Verso.

Fraser N "Distorted Beyond All Recognition: A Rejoinder to Axel Honneth". In N Fraser and A Honneth (eds) *Redistribution or Recognition? A Political-Philosophical Exchange* (2003a) 198 London: Verso.

Fraser N *Scales of Justice: Reimagining Political Space in a Globalizing World* (2009) New York: Columbia University Press.

Fraser N "Social Justice in the Age of Identity Politics: Redistribution, Recognition, and Participation". In N Fraser and A Honneth (eds) *Redistribution or Recognition? A Political-Philosophical Exchange* (2003b) 7 London: Verso.

Fredman S "Redistribution and Recognition: Reconciling Inequalities" (2007) 23 *South African Journal on Human Rights* 214.

Habermas J "Struggles for Recognition in the Democratic Constitutional State". In C Taylor (ed) *Multiculturalism: Examining the Politics of Recognition* (1994) 107 Princeton: Princeton University Press.

Honig B "Another Cosmopolitanism? Law and Politics in the New Europe". In S Benhabib (ed) *Another Cosmopolitanism* (2006) 102 Oxford: Oxford University Press.

Honig B "Difference, Dilemmas, and the Politics of Home". In S Benhabib (ed) *Democracy and Difference: Contesting the Boundaries of the Political* (1996) 257 Princeton: Princeton University Press.

Honneth A "Redistribution as Recognition: A Response to Nancy Fraser". In N Fraser and A Honneth (eds) *Redistribution or Recognition? A Political-Philosophical Exchange* (2003) 110 London: Verso.

Lakhani I "You Can't Break a Sweat – Creatively Fighting for the Rights of Sex Workers in South Africa" (2022) 17 *Global Public Health* 2342.

Le Roux W "Undoing the Past through Statutory Interpretation: The Constitutional Court and Marriage Laws of Apartheid" (2005) 26 *Obiter* 526.

Le Roux W and Van Marle K (eds) *Law, Memory and the Legacy of Apartheid: Ten Years after AZAPO v President of South Africa* (2007) Pretoria: Pretoria University Law Press.

Manicom L "Constituting 'Women' as Citizens: Ambiguities in the Making of Gendered Political Subjects in Post-Apartheid South Africa". In A Gouws (ed) *(Un) thinking Citizenship: Feminist Debates in Contemporary South Africa* (2005) 21 Aldershot: Ashgate.

Marshall T *Class, Citizenship, and Social Development: Essays by TH Marshall* (1977) Chicago: University of Chicago Press.

Mc Manus A "A Fraserian Theory of Anti-Discrimination Law" (2020) 20 *International Journal of Discrimination and the Law* 88.

Minow M *Making all the Difference: Inclusion, Exclusion, and American Law* (1990) Ithaca: Cornell University Press.

Mouffe C *The Democratic Paradox* (2000) London: Verso.

Moyn S *Not Enough: Human Rights in an Unequal World* (2018) Cambridge, Massachusetts: Belknap.

Perolini M "Limited Tools for Emancipation? Human Rights and Border Abolition?" (2023) 58 *Sociology* 1.

Preuß U "Citizenship and Identity: Aspects of a Political Theory of Citizenship". In R Bellamy, V Bufacchi & D Castiglione *Democracy and Constitutional Culture in the Union of Europe* (1995) 107 London: Lothian Foundation Press.

Rancière J "Who is the Subject of the Rights of Man?" (2004) 103 *South Atlantic Quarterly* 297.
Réaume D "Discrimination and Dignity" (2003) 63 *Louisiana Law Review* 645.
Richardson D "Claiming Citizenship? Sexuality, Citizenship and Lesbian/Feminist Theory" (2000) 3 *Sexualities* 255.
Richardson D "Rethinking Sexual Citizenship" (2017) 5 *Sociology* 208.
Robson R "Sexual Democracy" (2007) 23 *South African Journal on Human Rights* 409.
Snyman J "Interpretation and the Politics of Memory" (1998) *Acta Juridica* 312.
Spies A "Better Late than Never: Lessons from *S v Jordan* in Strengthening Women's Participation in Litigation" (2015) 30 *SA Public Law* 505.
Thomas K "Racial Justice". In A Sarat, B Garth and R Kagan (eds) *Looking Back at Law's Century* (2002) 78 Ithaca: Cornell University Press.
Van Marle K "Lives of Action, Thinking and Revolt – A Feminist Call for Politics and Becoming in Post-Apartheid South Africa" (2004) 19 *SA Public Law* 605.
Wilson A "The 'Neat Concept' of Sexual Citizenship: A Cautionary Tale for Human Rights Discourse" (2009) 15 *Contemporary Politics* 73.
Young I *Justice and the Politics of Difference* (1990) Princeton: Princeton University Press.

## Case law

### *India*

*Rajbala v State of Haryana* (2016) 1 SCC 643

### *South Africa*

*AB v Pridwin Preparatory School* 2020 (5) SA 327 (CC)
*August v Electoral Commission* 1999 (3) SA 1 (CC)
*Barkhuizen v Napier* 2007 (5) SA 323 (CC)
*Bato Star Fishing (Pty) Ltd v Minister of Environmental Affairs and Tourism* 2004 (4) SA 490 (CC)
*Brink v Kitshoff* 1996 (6) BCLR 752 (CC)
*Bwanya v Master of the High Court, Cape Town* 2022 (4) BCLR 410 (CC)
*City Council of Pretoria v Walker* 1998 (3) BCLR 257 (CC)
*City of Tshwane Metropolitan Municipality v Afriforum* 2016 (6) SA 279 (CC)
*Daniels v Campbell NO* 2004 (7) BCLR 735 (CC)
*Daniels v Scribante* 2017 (4) SA 341 (CC)
*Doctors for Life International v Speaker of the National Assembly* 2006 (6) SA 416 (CC)
*Du Plessis v De Klerk* 1996 (3) SA 850 (CC)
*Du Toit v Minister for Welfare and Population Development* 2002 (10) BCLR 1006 (CC)
*Duncanmec (Pty) Ltd v Gaylard NO* 2018 (11) BCLR 1335 (CC)
*Fraser v Children's Court, Pretoria North* 1997 (2) SA 261 (CC)
*Gory v Kolver NO* 2007 (4) SA 97 (CC)
*Gumede (born Shange) v President of the Republic of South Africa* 2009 (3) SA 152 (CC)
*Harksen v Lane NO* 1997 (11) BCLR 1489 (CC)
*Hassam v Jacobs NO* 2009 (5) SA 572 (CC)
*Hoffmann v South African Airways* 2001 (1) SA 1 (CC)
*J v Director-General, Department of Home Affairs* 2003 (5) BCLR 463 (CC)
*Jordan v S* 2002 (6) SA 642 (CC)

*Khosa v Minister of Social Development; Mahlaule v Minister of Social Development* 2004 (6) SA 505 (CC)
*King NO v De Jager* 2021 (4) SA 1 (CC)
*Larbi-Odam v Member of Executive Council for Education* 1998 (1) SA 745 (CC)
*Mahlangu v Minister of Labour* 2021 (2) SA 54 (CC)
*MEC for Education: KwaZulu-Natal v Pillay* 2008 (1) SA 474 (CC)
*Minister of Finance v Van Heerden* 2004 (6) SA 121 (CC)
*Minister of Home Affairs v Fourie* 2006 (1) SA 524 (CC)
*National Coalition for Gay and Lesbian Equality v Minister of Home Affairs* 2000 (2) SA 1 (CC)
*National Coalition for Gay and Lesbian Equality v Minister of Justice* 1999 (1) SA 6 (CC)
*President of the Republic of South Africa v Hugo* 1997 (4) SA 1 (CC)
*Satchwell v President of the RSA* 2002 (6) SA 1 (CC)
*Social Justice Coalition v Minister of Police* 2019 (4) SA 82 (WCC)
*Social Justice Coalition v Minister of Police* 2022 (10) BCLR 1267 (CC)
*South African Police Service v Solidarity obo Barnard* 2014 (6) SA 123 (CC)
*Volks NO v Robinson* 2005 (5) BCLR 446 (CC)

# 6 Towards new imaginaries of freedom

Freedom is a contested political ideal and constitutional right and value. The wide range of meanings to which it is susceptible is typically described in oppositional terms, like negative and positive freedom, freedom as an attribute of the will and as a capacity, metaphysical and relational understandings of freedom, personal and political freedom, and different articulations of freedom with dignity, equality, and democratic citizenship. In recent years, contestations about the meaning of freedom have often been acrimonious, as there is a growing sense that freedom is under threat, and as it is weaponised in clashes between different identities and ideologies. The perception that freedom is in danger derives from a variety of factors, including the weakening of state power in the wake of economic globalisation, the erosion of the public-political sphere under pressure from a neoliberal order that reduces everything to economics, the disconnect between neoliberal conceptions of individual autonomy and a social world characterised by increasing (inter)dependence, and the rise of populism and authoritarianism. In South Africa, those developments are closely bound up with the failure of the post-apartheid legal and political order to deliver on the promise to emancipate poor black people and other vulnerable groups from oppression and the continuing hold of liberal conceptions of freedom that are based on exclusionary notions of autonomy, rationality, and property.

In this chapter, I argue that freedom is best conceived in relational and political terms. Freedom is relational, since social attachments, practices, relations, and institutions play an indispensable role in developing individuals' capacity for self-realisation. Freedom is, moreover, political, not only because it is partly constitutive of a democratic society, or because a political community must create conditions in which its members have meaningful opportunities for self-actualisation, but also since the meaning of freedom and the mutual articulation of different freedoms are determined through ongoing processes of democratic dialogue and contestation. Relational and political conceptions of freedom are closely linked, since the need for laws and policies that create conditions in which freedom can thrive follows from humans' vulnerability as relational beings. However, different relational and political concepts of freedom are informed by different understandings of relationality,

DOI: 10.4324/9781003482451-7

the public sphere, the political, and the types of intervention needed to enable freedom. For example, they may differ about whether freedom is compatible with a market economy, whether it demands the accommodation of radical difference, and whether it requires reformist reform, non-reformist reform, or a revolutionary break with the past.[1] In this chapter, like in previous ones, I conceive the political through a conflictual democratic lens that highlights the central role played by power, conflict, and disagreement in safeguarding spaces in which freedom can thrive, and insists that freedom demands a radical transformation of the status quo.

Freedom is multifaceted. It encompasses aspects of human existence that range from the personal to the political and from the observance of life forms and practices that are given rather than freely chosen to the capacity to reinterpret and depart from convention. On a political understanding, these dimensions of freedom are interrelated and the boundaries between them are constantly renegotiated. The causes of unfreedom are similarly multilayered and include institutionalised racism, sexism, heteronormativity, neoliberalism, spatial apartheid, and the denigration of certain belief systems and forms of knowledge. In view of these complexities, the chapter is not divided into separate discussions of the different freedoms guaranteed in the Constitution but is structured around themes that could shed light on freedom's contested nature and the possibility of alternative imaginaries that articulate freedom with human dignity, equality, democracy, and radical difference. The only exception is freedom of expression, which is discussed separately in view of its importance to democratic dialogue and contestation. Freedom of assembly and the freedom to make political choices, which are similarly crucial to a political understanding of freedom, were discussed in chapter 2 above.

The chapter starts with a brief discussion of freedom as a constitutional right – or range of rights – and value. It then examines different reasons for the growing ideological polarisation about freedom's meaning and the sense that it is under threat. Next, it sketches the outlines of a relational and political understanding of freedom against the background of debates about the relationship between negative and positive liberty, between metaphysical and relational understandings of freedom, and between personal and political freedom. That leads into an analysis of the ways in which legal discourse obscures and privatises vulnerability or associates it with classes of people that are seen to lack the capacity for self-realisation, and an exploration of the possibility of an alternative conception of freedom, which enables radical critiques of the unequal distribution of the burdens of vulnerability and stresses the responsibility of the political community to create conditions in which everyone can be free. The chapter then turns to consider freedom of expression in view of the tension between speech's capacity to interrogate social, economic, and political power and the replication of inequality in the discursive sphere. It argues for a relational and conflictual understanding which, while being mindful of structural discursive violence, would not give up on the power of speech to disrupt inequality and to articulate more humane alternatives. Finally, the chapter asks whether alternative imaginaries of freedom that are grounded in anti-hegemonic struggles and the philosophy of ubuntu could help us articulate freedom with equality and respect for radical difference.

## 6.1 Freedom as a constitutional right and value

Freedom, together with human dignity and equality, is central to the Constitution's normative vision. Section 1(a) lists them as foundational constitutional values; section 7(1) affirms the importance of these "democratic values" to the Bill of Rights; and sections 36(1) and 39(1) place them at the heart of constitutional limitation and rights analysis, respectively. Section 12(1) safeguards the right to freedom and security of the person, which includes the right "not to be deprived of freedom arbitrarily or without just cause" and "to be free from all forms of violence from either public or private sources", while section 12(2) protects the right to bodily and psychological integrity, which includes the right "to make decisions concerning reproduction". Moreover, sections 15 to 19 and 21 to 22 guarantee freedom of religion, belief, and opinion; freedom of expression; the freedom to assemble, demonstrate, picket, and present petitions; freedom of association; freedom to make political choices, including forming a political party, participating in its activities, and campaigning for a political party or cause; freedom of movement and residence; and freedom to choose a trade, occupation, or profession.

The reference in the preamble to the need to "improve the quality of life of all citizens and free the potential of each person" could be taken to suggest that freedom does not simply entail the absence of undue outside interference but requires the creation of conditions that enable meaningful choices between different alternatives. This impression is confirmed by several constitutional provisions. Section 7(2) requires the state to respect, protect, promote, and fulfil the rights in the Bill of Rights. The state is thus under both a negative duty to abstain from conduct that interferes with the enjoyment of fundamental rights and freedoms, and a positive duty to protect them from encroachment by third parties and to create conditions in which they can thrive.[2] The inclusion of enforceable socio-economic rights in the Constitution and the link made by the courts between these rights and individuals' dignity and self-actualisation further indicate that freedom is understood to have a positive dimension.[3] The articulation of freedom with dignity and equality in sections 1(a), 7(1), 36(1), and 39(1) and the declaration in section 9(2) that "[e]quality includes the full and equal enjoyment of all rights and freedoms" confirm the constitutional commitment to the creation of an environment in which all people have an equal right to self-realisation. Moreover, the provision made in sections 8(2) and 8(3) for direct horizontal application signals that society, and not only the state, bears a responsibility for defending and promoting freedom. Based on these provisions, it could be argued that the Constitution is best interpreted as enshrining an understanding of freedom as social, political, and egalitarian, and encompassing both negative and positive protection.

Despite freedom's centrality to the Constitution's normative vision, its meaning as a constitutional value remains underdeveloped. There are several reasons for that. Freedom is not only a deeply contested concept, but it covers such diverse aspects of individuals' existence, ranging from making intensely personal decisions to participating in economic, social, and political life, that it is difficult, and arguably ill-advised, to try to distil it to a single essence. It is therefore not surprising that the Constitutional Court, in its own words, "has repeatedly expressed a reluctance to examine the 'philosophical foundation or the precise content' of freedom".[4] Moreover, in most contexts, the Court relies primarily on the value of dignity to express the idea that the Constitution demands respect for individuals' agency and self-determination, even though it sometimes acknowledges the interconnectedness of dignity and freedom.[5]

There are nevertheless cases in which courts expressly relied on the value of freedom. The *Pillay* case concerned the question whether a public school was obliged under the Promotion of Equality and Prevention of Unfair Discrimination Act 4 of 2000 (PEPUDA) to allow a learner to wear a nose stud as an expression of her South Indian Tamil Hindu culture. The values of dignity and freedom played a prominent role in the Court's interpretation of the right to equality. Langa CJ stated that dignity and freedom demand "respect for the unique ends" pursued by different individuals.[6] Respect for freedom requires the acknowledgement and celebration of difference. In his view, the protective reach of cultural and religious freedom – and of the right not to be unfairly discriminated against on the grounds of culture and religion – is not limited to practices that are obligatory under a given tradition but extends to practices that are assumed voluntarily. Section 9(3) and PEPUDA can therefore be offended by the failure to accommodate the practices of subsets of cultural or religious groups. The judgment recognises that, far from being monolithic, cultures are based on a range of "practices, ideas or ways of being" that allow considerable variations in how they are practised.[7] In *AB*, Khampepe J wrote in a minority judgment that the value of freedom is animated by "the recognition of each person's distinctive aptitude to understand and act on their own desires and beliefs".[8] She held that legislation restricting surrogacy agreements to instances where one or both of the commissioning parents provided a gamete violated the bodily and psychological integrity and equality of parents who were unable to do so. In *Bwanya*, the Court identified the value of freedom with respect for individuals' autonomy and agency. Relying on Sachs J's dissent in *Robinson*, Madlanga J held that freedom demands respect for alternative lifestyle choices, and that the exclusion of surviving partners in permanent heterosexual life partnerships from maintenance benefits was unfairly discriminatory.[9] All three these judgments link the value of freedom to respect for difference and suggest that it can help ground an equality jurisprudence that accepts and celebrates diversity.

Questions about the nature and scope of freedom featured prominently in the *Ferreira* case, which was decided under the interim Constitution. In a minority judgment, Ackermann J read section 11(1) of the interim Constitution, which guaranteed freedom and security of the person, to confer a general constitutional right to freedoms that are not expressly mentioned in the Constitution. Ackermann J gave freedom and security of the person a broad interpretation, to encompass every person's right "not to have 'obstacles to possible choices and activities' placed in their way by ... the State".[10] His expansive reading of freedom was backed up by references to the systematic violation of black people's freedom under apartheid.[11] He grounded this interpretation not only in freedom's "intrinsic constitutional value", but also in its relation with the founding value of human dignity. He stated:

> An individual's human dignity cannot be fully respected or valued unless the individual is permitted to develop his or her unique talents optimally. Human dignity has little value without freedom; for without freedom personal development and fulfilment are not possible. Without freedom, human dignity is little more than an abstraction. Freedom and dignity are inseparably linked. To deny people their freedom is to deny them their dignity.[12]

The majority decided the case on the right against self-incrimination. Chaskalson P cautioned that the broad interpretation of freedom and security of the person favoured by Ackermann J would result in judicial overreach and the disruption of the state's regulatory functions. He held that the primary purpose of section 11(1) was to protect individuals' physical integrity and not to provide a residual freedom right.[13] Although he left open the possibility that unenumerated fundamental freedoms could be protected under s 11(1), this category of freedoms is far narrower than that envisaged in Ackermann J's judgment.[14] The Constitutional Court has since used other rights, like dignity and privacy, to protect areas of decisional freedom that are not expressly guaranteed in the Bill of Rights.[15] These judgments extend to personal choices – for example, choices concerning the nurturing of relationships and expression of sexuality – that are of central significance to individuals' identity and personal fulfilment. This approach, like that of Ackermann J in *Ferreira*, offers flexibility and open-endedness, and recognises that freedom cannot be reduced to "any enumerated set of liberties".[16] However, the scope of protection that it offers is considerably narrower than that afforded by Ackermann's judgment in *Ferreira*.[17]

More recently, contestations over the nature and scope of the right to freedom and security of the person resurfaced in *AB*. Khampepe J held in her minority judgment that the holding of the majority in *Ferreira* that section 11(1) of the interim Constitution does not create a broad residual right to unenumerated freedoms also applies to section 12 of the 1996 Constitution. However, she pointed to important textual differences between the two constitutions. Most notably, section 12(2) creates a new, freestanding right to bodily and psychological integrity that expressly includes the right to reproductive freedom. Based on the textual differences between the two constitutions and the reference to both bodily and psychological integrity, Khampepe J gave section 12(2)(a) a generous interpretation to include decisions relating to surrogacy, even if those decisions do not physically affect the right-holder's body.[18] Her judgment perceptively analyses the effects of infertility on psychological integrity,[19] and is attentive to the role of the law in enabling and constraining personal choices.[20] On the other hand, Nkabinde J in her majority judgment interpreted section 12(2) more narrowly to refer only to women's control over their own bodies. In her view, reading the section to include the psychological integrity of a commissioning parent in the context of surrogacy would unduly strain the ordinary meaning of the words.[21]

## 6.2 Freedom under threat

Discussions about the meaning of freedom have become particularly polarised in recent years, and there is a growing sense that freedom is under threat. Several factors have contributed to this situation. In the first place, the postmodern dissolution of the belief in truth that is grounded in absolute foundations has led to the proliferation of subject positions and the intensification of identity politics, as every attempt to base rights on universal principles or to ground emancipatory politics in a universal class such as women or the working class gives rise to the charge that it is exclusionary or privileges the identities, worldviews, and experiences of some social groups over others.[22] Wendy Brown suggests that the demise of the belief in absolute foundations could help to give rise to the development of democratic practices that are characterised by the recognition of plurality and difference and a commitment to the public articulation of and dialogue among different conceptions of the public good.[23] However, she points out that it could also, and often does, lead to a fixation on group identities and the moral harm inflicted on members of particular groups. That tends to have a depoliticising effect, not only because it risks reducing politics to a question of identity, but also because it juridifies and moralises social justice by concentrating on individual injury and culpability, rather than focussing on systemic injustices and seeking to address underlying power relations.[24]

Secondly, the ideal of autonomous, self-sufficient individuals who can pursue freely chosen ends has been questioned. Communitarian theorists claim that the liberal notion of the unencumbered, unitary subject denies the constitutive role of communal ties, affective relations, social practices, and conversations with others in forging the identities of subjects who think of themselves as free.[25] Feminists argue that liberal constructions of individual autonomy, which view it in abstraction from the specific needs of and contexts in which real people find themselves, affirm the perspectives of certain groups and elevate them into a universal position.[26] Conversely, they normalise the subordination of women and other groups whose identity is forged by the bonds of solidarity, and whose needs and desires are not easily rendered in the neutral language of rights.[27] Studies in neuroscience, cognitive psychology, and social theory confirm that traditional notions of the self and free will radically underestimate the extent to which the self is conditioned by cultural givens and social practices.[28]

Thirdly, conventional assumptions about freedom's protection and its relation to citizenship have been problematised by the impact of economic globalisation and mass migration on the power and legitimacy of nation-states. Traditionally, the nation-state is viewed not only as the primary protector of fundamental rights and freedoms, but also as the site of political freedom and collective self-government. On the one hand, claims for the protection of civil, political, and socio-economic rights are addressed to the nation-state; on the other hand, membership in the political community grants citizens a say in the democratic processes through which rights are delineated and enforced. The state's capacity to safeguard fundamental rights and freedoms and serve as the locus of democratic self-government has, however, been weakened by economic globalisation. The flow of goods, services, capital, and technologies across national borders, the economic power wielded by multinational corporations, and the proliferation of international trade policies have constrained the economic policy options available to nation-states. Moreover, the transnational mobility of people and increases in the numbers of refugees and stateless persons have resulted in a disconnect between residence and citizenship.[29] These developments raise questions about the capacity of the Westphalian system of states to provide adequate protection to basic rights and freedoms. The problem is twofold. First, non-citizens are generally excluded from participation in the political processes through which laws are created, even though they are subject to those laws. Second, there are limits to the capacity of nation-states to address rights infringements that derive from decisions taken at the supranational level. Treating such issues purely as national matters amounts to a misrepresentation, as Nancy Fraser points out. It hides the power of supranational decision-making bodies and multinational conglomerates, and exempts decisions taken beyond the nation-state from democratic dialogue and contestation. For example, Fraser notes how "the claims of the global poor are shunted into the domestic political arenas of weak or failed states", and how they are "blocked from confronting the offshore sources of dispossession".[30]

Fourthly, freedom's association with democratic citizenship has been weakened by the erosion of the public-political sphere. The ascendancy of neoliberal reason, with its emphasis on market competition and the pursuit of private preferences has resulted in the hollowing out of democracy and citizenship and the recasting of freedom in economic terms. As Wendy Brown shows, the citizen makes way for economic man, the public sphere is displaced by the market, and public services are supplanted by services that are individually purchased. Freedom not only becomes detached from liberal notions of individual self-realisation but is dissociated from the ideals of democratic deliberation and the pursuit of the common good.[31] It is delinked from equality and a common citizenship and is reduced to the investment choices made by economic actors wishing to maximise their human capital.[32] The idea that society or the state is under an obligation to promote citizens' right to self-actualisation makes way for a universe in which it is every person for him- or herself, and in which obstacles to freedom are viewed as the product of individuals' poor investment choices. Human beings are thus viewed as disposable, and inequality is explained away as the result of individuals' failure to optimise their market value.

The fact that the political transition in South Africa coincided with the global ascendance of neoliberalism had a profound impact on the new government's perception of the range of available economic policy options. The adoption in 1996 of the Growth, Employment and Redistribution (GEAR) strategy marked the government's conversion to neoliberal economic policy, characterised by "tight fiscal austerity, monetary discipline, wage restraints, reducing corporate taxes, trade liberalization, and phasing out exchange controls".[33] It effectively replaced the Reconstruction and Development Plan (RDP) with policies that are premised on the idea that a free market will attract international investors, and that the resulting economic growth will have a "trickle-down" redistributive effect. These policies have enabled the growth of the black middle class but have left vast portions of the black population, who are unemployed and on the fringes of the consumption economy, in a permanently precarious state.[34]

Fifthly, neoliberalism's radical privileging of the private realm and assault on democracy and social justice have given rise to a growing sense of disorientation, misrecognition, and disenfranchisement, which, in turn, have led to the revival of nationalist and ethnic forms of belonging, which provide symbolic compensation for the exclusion of substantial sections of the population from meaningful social and political citizenship.[35] As Margaret Somers shows, freedom not only becomes associated with "a radical free-market ideology", but is also identified with "a militant security-driven nationalism".[36] Brown similarly argues that the recasting of freedom in economic terms has facilitated freedom's identification with authoritarianism, social exclusion, and violence. The nation is no longer comprehended in terms of notions like social cooperation, equality, and citizenship but is conceived as "a competitive business needing to make good deals and attract investors, on the one hand, and as an inadequately secured home, besieged by ill-willed or non-belonging outsiders, on the other".[37] The second analogy explains why right-wing political parties and movements that advocate minimal state interference in the economy favour an expansion of the state's security apparatus and condone police violence against immigrants and racial minorities. If the nation or neighbourhood is viewed as the equivalent of a household that is vulnerable to attacks from outside, the remedy cannot lie in democratic deliberation, social inclusion, or the accommodation of difference. What is needed is the fortification of the boundaries that separate the nation from the outside world and its protection from threats to its security and ability to provide support to "family" members. The rhetoric used legitimises authoritarianism (as Brown points out, authority within the household rests not on "negotiation, deliberation, or even the rule of law but [on] diktat"),[38] and responds to the neoliberal dismantling of jobs and social provisioning by blaming immigrants, black people, and globalisation.

Brown writes that the reconceptualization of the social and political in economic and familial terms enables the fantasy of unbridled freedom, which must offset the psychological pain caused by the end of "the age of the secure white male provider and nation-state sovereignty".[39] In this imaginary, freedom is detached from its association with democratic self-government, citizenship, and equality, and is seen as unfettered by the common good, the rights of others, or even the future of the planet. It becomes a right to unlimited accumulation and protection of one's own against immigrant jobseekers and the threats posed by anti-racist, feminist, queer and other struggles to the perceived unity of the nation. Freedom, so conceived, is wielded as a weapon used to resist mask mandates and other measures aimed at curbing the spread of COVID-19, to oppose universal healthcare, and to ban the teaching of critical race theory.[40] Moreover, it is relied on to cement the power and political influence of wealthy individuals and corporations.[41]

It is tempting, in view of the libertarian, authoritarian, racist, sexist, and xenophobic overtones of these discourses to place less reliance on freedom and to focus more on other ideals like equality. However, that strategy cedes too much ground to right-wing understandings of freedom. It fails to challenge the narrow identification of freedom with economic liberty, ignores the range of meanings that have historically been attached to freedom, and declines to develop more emancipatory interpretations of freedom and its relation to equality, citizenship, and democracy.[42] Against that background, the rest of the chapter examines whether and to what extent relational and political understandings of freedom can respond adequately to the developments outlined above and provide viable alternatives to the economic and familial conceptions of freedom that have become so pronounced in contemporary discourse.

## 6.3 Towards a relational and political understanding of freedom

In this section, I explore relational and political understandings of freedom in view of three tensions or fault lines, which deal with the relationship between the negative and positive dimensions of freedom, the tension between metaphysical and relational understandings of freedom, and the connections between personal and political freedom.

First, the tension between negative and positive freedom. While acknowledging that there is a need for state intervention in social and economic life, Ackermann J reasoned in *Ferreira* that the state's role in helping to provide for people's material and educational needs should not be conflated with freedom. He held, with reference to Isaiah Berlin, that section 11(1) of the interim Constitution is concerned with negative freedom, i.e., non-interference with a person's liberty, and not positive freedom, i.e., securing the conditions of freedom's exercise.[43] Berlin's insistence that the term *freedom* should be reserved for the absence of external restraints is tied up with his view that breaches of freedom involve coercion, which he defines as "the deliberate interference of other human beings within the area in which I wish to act".[44] The narrowness of this formulation is striking. First, it excludes restrictions of freedom arising from poverty, disability, or individuals' lack of knowledge about their rights, since these conditions are not caused by direct, deliberate acts of interference. This seems arbitrary, since there are many restrictions of freedom that are not caused by discrete acts of interference. They are produced, wholly or in part, by legal, social, and economic structures, and they could be prevented by human intervention.[45] Second, in confining negative freedom to non-interference, Berlin overlooks a long tradition in Western political thought that identifies freedom with non-domination. On that understanding, (negative) freedom is not only breached by direct interference, but also by political domination, which occurs in a system of arbitrary political rule where citizens, who depend on the ruler's goodwill, censor their own speech and action.[46]

Berlin's concept of negative freedom seems ill-equipped to capture the meaning, scope, and depth of freedom under the Constitution. In the first place, it overlooks the interrelatedness of the negative and positive dimensions of freedom,[47] and is unhelpful in a country in which unfreedom stems from centuries of institutionalised racism, sexism, and capitalism. Secondly, Berlin's understanding seems at odds with the constitutional provisions referred to above that express an understanding of freedom as social, democratic, inclusive, egalitarian, and affording negative as well as positive protection. Locating the creation of conditions in which freedom can thrive outside the scope of freedom could undermine the emancipatory potential of the idea, captured in Ackermann J's elaboration of the relationship between dignity and freedom, that all people, regardless of class or status, have the right to self-definition and self-actualisation. Thirdly, Berlin's insistence that the term *freedom* should be reserved for the absence of external restraints derived from his concern, against the background of rising totalitarianism, that freedom is sometimes defined in terms of the achievement of a definition of what it means to be human.[48] His fear that state-enforced conceptions of freedom that are based on essentialised notions of human nature constitute a serious threat to freedom is undeniably valid. However, a positive conception of freedom is not necessarily inconsistent with value pluralism. There is no reason why an understanding of freedom that recognises its negative and positive dimensions cannot accommodate both individuals' substantive freedom to choose the kind of life that they value and the creation of social conditions in which they are able to do so.[49] Fourthly, the distinction between negative and positive freedom is unstable. Jeremy Waldron argues, for example, that property rules that prevent homeless people from accessing spaces in which they are allowed to sleep, undress, urinate, and defecate severely curtail their negative, and not only their positive freedom.[50] The instability of the distinction could be exploited to show that private law rules deny people's negative freedom, or that the state's failure to adopt and implement reasonable laws and policies aimed at the reduction of climate change violate the negative freedom of future generations.[51] However, privileging negative over positive freedom could strengthen the hold of libertarian and privatist ideology on the legal imagination, making it less likely that judges will subscribe to that line of argument.

The second fault line concerns the tension between metaphysical and relational understandings of freedom. Metaphysical understandings conceive freedom in abstract terms as the property of rational, self-sufficient individuals who freely determine their own ends. These understandings overstate individuals' rationality and capacity to control their world and understate the extent to which their identities are forged through, and their choices are influenced by attachments, beliefs, practices, networks, and institutions that precede them. They legitimise domination and inequality by construing freedom in abstraction from the power relations in which individuals' lives are enmeshed. Moreover, they establish certain worldviews, subjectivities, and lifestyles, which are associated with rationality and autonomy, as the norm, while relegating others to the realm of the strange, the irrational, and the dependent.[52] By contrast, relational understandings stress the importance of rules, institutions, practices, and networks of interdependence in developing individuals' capacity for self-realisation. As Drucilla Cornell argues, freedom is not premised on individuals' ability to extricate themselves from their cultural background or history; it only requires the chance to create a life they can call their own from their past experiences and struggles. Freedom, so conceived, is concerned with the potential of persons who are always already immersed in a social world to forge their individuality through "a lifelong process of engagement with the constitutive relationships upon which [they] base [their] identities".[53] Rather than blaming poverty and dependence on individuals' poor choices or lack of merit, relational theories recognise that vulnerability is a shared human condition and highlight the need for rules, institutions, and practices that foster conditions in which all people can be free.

This distinction is related to Hannah Arendt's critique of understandings of freedom in terms of the sovereignty of the individual will and her claim that freedom must be understood in political terms. Arendt notes that, in the Christian and philosophical traditions, freedom is identified with the inner personal realm. It is thus divorced from its ancient connection to politics and is grounded, instead, in freedom from politics. In her view, this understanding of freedom is untenable. The will tends to get divided and turn against itself; it is the seat of impotence, not freedom; and far from being able to ground democratic politics, it gives rise to the will to oppression. For Arendt, freedom is essentially a political term. It should be conceived not as the will to be independent from and prevail against others, but as the human capacity for public action, and thus for beginning something new.[54] The capacity for action and new beginnings does not inhere in individuals who fence themselves off from others but derives from their appearance within a common public space, in which they are exposed to a plurality of viewpoints and the uncertainty and unpredictability that characterise human action.[55] Relational understandings of freedom do not necessarily commit us to Arendt's privileging of political over personal freedom and adherence to a strict division between the public and private spheres, but they share her view that freedom is fostered through our interactions with other.

There are several themes in the Constitutional Court's jurisprudence that resonate with a relational understanding of freedom. The Court has tied dignity and freedom to human interdependence and mutual recognition within a community,[56] stressed the centrality of religion and culture to the identity and dignity of the person,[57] linked the well-being of wealthier members of the community to the well-being of those in desperate need,[58] and tied dignity to the indigenous African concept of ubuntu, which encompasses human solidarity, respect, and interdependence.[59] It has rejected the notion that privacy is premised on the idea of isolated, disembodied individuals, and held instead that it enables the fostering of relations and forging of public identities. Like freedom, privacy does not simply denote a right to be left alone, but places "at least some responsibility on the state to promote conditions in which personal self-realisation can take place".[60]

There are nevertheless judgments that reflect a metaphysical understanding of freedom. For instance, the majority judgment in *Jordan*, discussed in chapters 4 and 5 above, rests upon an overblown ideal of autonomy, which ignores the vulnerability and material need that induce many women to do sex work and denies their freedom by assimilating their claims to middle-class social norms and expectations.[61] Some of the judgments dealing with contracts similarly rest on abstract conceptions of freedom. Those judgments focus predominantly on the logical coherence of seemingly neutral private law concepts and principles, like pacta sunt servanda, and obscure their capacity to perpetuate poverty and inequality. Contractual freedom – conceived as the absence of external interference, rather than something that needs to be fostered through legal rules and social policies – is understood in near absolute terms. The constitutional values of dignity and freedom are interpreted to bolster contractual autonomy;[62] however, the possibility that dignity, equality, and freedom sometimes require limiting contractual freedom, e.g., in cases of unequal bargaining power, remains underdeveloped.[63] The principles of public policy and good faith, which could play a significant role in trimming the excesses of contractual freedom, are relegated to such a marginal position that they are unlikely to play a significant role in combating inequality and protecting consumers.[64]

In *New Nation Movement*, the Constitutional Court relied on an abstract, reified understanding of freedom in interpreting political rights. It held that the requirement in the Electoral Act that only candidates standing for political parties were allowed to contest national or provincial elections violated the section 19(3)(b) right to stand for, and, if elected, to hold public office. Madlanga J reasoned that, if section 19(3)(b) were to be read to permit the exclusion of independent candidates, it would come into conflict with freedom of association (section 18), understood negatively as the right not to be coerced into associating with others. It would also pit section 19(3)(b) against section 19(1), since it would diminish the political choices available to citizens who want to stand for public office. The three sections could only be harmonised by reading section 19(3)(b) to include the right of independent candidates to contest elections.[65] Madlanga J rejected the contention that that reading is inconsistent with the Constitution's emphasis on the role of political parties in the legislative process, and its requirement that the electoral system must result, in general, in proportional representation.[66] His finding that the Constitution requires a role for independent candidates is surprising in view of the centrality of proportional representation and multiparty democracy to the design of the representative system. Unlike Froneman J's dissent, with its careful contextualisation of the constitutional scheme and analysis of the relationship between different forms of democracy,[67] the majority relied almost exclusively on the abstract freedom of prospective candidates who do not wish to join or establish a political party. It grounded the freedom to make political choices in the sovereignty of individuals' will and severed it from the – parliamentary and extra-parliamentary – structures and practices that sustain it.[68]

The third fault line concerns the relationship between personal and political freedom. When freedom is construed as the absence of external interference or as an abstract property inherent in sovereign individuals, it is thought to exist prior to and outside of politics. Conversely, when freedom is understood to be threatened not only by overt restrictions on individual liberty but also by material need and systemic power, and to require social relations, practices, and institutions that allow it to thrive, personal freedom is seen as inextricably linked to political freedom. Freedom, on this view, requires political dialogue and social struggles; it is "built upon a 'we' instead of an 'I'".[69] On the one hand, the protection of personal freedom is enabled through the formulation of complaints and the expression, in public, of the claims to equal recognition that accompany them. It is contingent on the development of a vocabulary through which claims are made and violations are articulated, and through the communication of those claims to a larger public. Freedom of expression, together with freedom of conscience, religion, thought, belief, and opinion, freedom of association, freedom of assembly, and political rights, is vital to the articulation and dissemination of those challenges.[70] On the other hand, claims for the recognition of individual freedom have direct implications for the collective self-understanding of the legal and political community. The recognition of new freedoms, or extension of existing freedoms to new scenarios, or shifts in the mutual articulation of different freedoms must, inevitably, have an impact on understandings of the identity and boundaries of the legal and political community.[71]

The interconnectedness of our private freedom as individuals and public freedom as citizens is expressed eloquently by Sachs J in his dissenting judgment in *Prince*. The case concerned a challenge to a law that prohibited the possession and use of cannabis, without providing a religiously based exemption for Rastafari. The majority held that the creation of an exemption would weaken the state's ability to enforce restrictions on the use of controlled substances.[72] In his dissenting judgment, Sachs J highlighted the stigmatisation and political marginalisation of Rastafari, and showed how their vulnerability is deepened through laws that condition their right to equal recognition on conformity to mainstream norms.[73] He also emphasised the centrality of freedom of religion to an open and democratic society. He wrote:

> [F]aith and public interest overlap and intertwine in the need to protect tolerance as a constitutional virtue and respect for diversity and openness as a constitutional principle. Religious tolerance is accordingly not only important to those individuals who are saved from having to make excruciating choices between their beliefs and the law. It is deeply meaningful to all of us because religion and belief matter, and because living in an open society matters.[74]

On this view, freedom of belief is fundamental to the diversity and openness that characterise democratic societies. A political community can only be free if it respects difference and allows marginalised groups to disrupt hegemonic norms.[75] The democratic ideals of plurality, contestation, dialogue, and individual and collective self-renewal presuppose the freedom of members of marginal groups to hold beliefs and engage in practices that are, from a majoritarian perspective, "unusual, bizarre or even threatening".[76]

The judgment in *Pillay* similarly reveals an appreciation of the interconnectedness of public and private freedom and of freedom as something evolving, relational, and dialogical. The Court's finding that the Constitution protects voluntary as well as mandatory cultural and religious practices rests on a nuanced understanding of the interplay between the givenness of the networks of relationships and belonging that constitute individuals' social world and the contestation and difference at the heart of cultural and religious traditions. Those networks precede the formation of the individual and are not simply a matter of individual choice.[77] At the same time, however, cultures are "living and contested formations", and the Constitution protects "all those for whom culture gives meaning, not only … those who happen to speak with the most powerful voice in the present cultural conversation".[78] Freedom, on this view, is not secured through a single act of liberation or the gradual unfolding of the logic of universal human rights. It depends, rather, on the practices and institutions that sustain different traditions and ways of being, and the discourses and participatory processes through which shared norms and beliefs are contested and remoulded. It thus refers both to our embeddedness in life forms that are not of our choosing and the relentless play of difference that enables contestation and creates spaces for individual choice.

In conclusion, there is an affinity between understandings of freedom in exclusively negative terms, i.e., as the absence of external interference, and metaphysical conceptions, which construe freedom as an abstract property inherent in individuals. These understandings overlook the role played by structural power and material disadvantage, underestimate the need for social practices and institutions that create conditions in which freedom can thrive, and regard personal freedom as external to politics. Conversely, the idea that freedom must be understood both in negative and positive terms overlaps with relational notions of freedom, which recognise the role played by laws, institutions, practices, attachments, and commitments in enabling individuals to forge their own, unique identities. These understandings are better able to account for the interconnectedness of personal freedom and the dialogical and conflictual processes through which a political community reconstitutes itself.

## 6.4 Freedom and vulnerability

On a relational understanding, respect for freedom requires us to acknowledge that all individuals depend on institutions and relationships to develop their capabilities. If there are certain individuals or classes of individuals who appear unencumbered by ties of dependence and commitment, that is a function of legal and social norms which distribute social roles and goods in a way that facilitates their autonomy. Conversely, those whose lives are characterised by a greater degree of dependence and vulnerability should not be treated as if they lack the capacity for freedom. They should, rather, be enabled to develop that capacity, through laws and institutional arrangements that allow them to come to terms with their vulnerability and to access a wider range of choices and opportunities.

References to the vulnerability of various classes of persons, and the need to take account of their vulnerability in the enactment and interpretation of laws and in exercises of the courts' review power abound in South African legal discourse.[79] These references contain traces of an approach that promises to overcome the dichotomy between vulnerability and autonomy by viewing freedom not as the property of self-sufficient individuals, but as a capacity that depends on legal and moral structures of recognition and support. For instance, in *Daniels*, the Court referred to the violations of human dignity that resulted from the precarious residence of black people during apartheid and emphasised the importance of security of tenure for a tenant's self-determination, self-expression, and full participation in social and political life.[80]

However, legal and political discourse continues to find ways to deny vulnerability, to hide it away in the deepest recesses of the private sphere, or to project it onto certain sections of society. First, the tendency to deny the vulnerability of poor and marginalised members of the community is exemplified by the primacy accorded to the principles of contractual autonomy and pacta sunt servanda in the law of contract. These principles have been situated within a classical liberal paradigm, which treats individuals in terms of a strictly formal equality of opportunity and views the law as a neutral mechanism for the optimisation of individual choice. What is obscured from view is the coercive nature of the market, and the capacity of legal rules to structure relationships in a way which privileges some while disfavouring others.[81] As Deeksha Bhana points out, even in cases in which the courts grapple with the unequal bargaining power of contractual parties, they do so with reference to notions like public policy that are viewed as external to contractual autonomy. They thus continue to ground contractual autonomy in classical liberal notions of freedom, instead of reconceptualising it in terms of the triad of constitutional values of dignity, equality, and freedom. As a result, contractual autonomy is understood solely in terms of a negative conception of freedom. What is needed, in her view, is a more fluid understanding of contractual autonomy, in which the relationship between the constitutive values of dignity, equality, and freedom is constantly shifting, depending on the context.[82] Such an understanding could enable a more constructive approach to the enhancement of the capabilities of poor and vulnerable members of the community through the development of the common law of contract.

A second mechanism for the evasion of collective responsibility for the vulnerability of certain categories of individuals is the privatisation of dependence and need. The spread of neoliberalism has extended the logic of capital and the market to all spheres of social and political life. As a result, the responsibility for social problems is displaced onto individuals who must carry the blame for their failure to optimise their human "capital".[83] The state itself becomes "marketized", which diminishes its capacity to resist the inequalities that allow some individuals to enjoy autonomy, while others are labelled as "dependent".[84] The privatisation of public services, electricity and water cut-offs, outsourcing, and growing socio-economic inequality are indicative of the spread of neoliberal policies in South Africa.[85] These policies construe poverty as a choice rather than something that is embedded in social and economic structures. They accordingly punish the poor for their inability to pay for services and hold "consumers" of those services to account even when non-payment results from government failures.[86] Traditional legal rules and concepts further facilitate the privatisation of vulnerability. For instance, the responsibility for vulnerability and dependence is, as a rule, placed squarely within the family. As Martha Fineman shows, this results in the privatisation of caregiving work. Despite the fundamental importance of caregiving to society, it is done without compensation – except in cases where a family can afford to pay someone else to do the work, typically against low wages. This increases the vulnerability of many women, who perform the bulk of the caregiving work. Moreover, because vulnerability is hidden away in the intimate sphere, it is seen as something exceptional, rather than as something universal which affects all human beings. It thus becomes possible to stigmatise those in need of public assistance as lacking the independence and self-sufficiency associated with the idea of the autonomous individual.[87]

A third way, in which the dichotomy between autonomy and vulnerability is affirmed in legal and political discourse, is through the projection of vulnerability onto certain groups. Here, vulnerability is recognised, but in a way which carves up the social world into autonomous selves and vulnerable others. The projection of our own vulnerability onto others is closely bound up with the distinction between mind and body and with the associated distinctions between the ideal and material, between reason and feeling, between universality and particularity, and between autonomy and dependence. In Western thought, these terms stand in a hierarchical relationship, as the first term of each pairing is privileged over the second. The first term of each binary is associated with white, able-bodied, middle-class men, who are thought to exemplify the ideals of freedom, independence, and citizenship, while the second is linked to women, persons with disabilities, colonised peoples, and impoverished populations, who are seen to lack these attributes. Since they are defined in terms of the materiality of their bodies and their attachment to others, those who belong to the second category are identified with the vulnerability that is in fact a universal human condition.[88] Referring to the identification in the Western symbolic order of masculinity with autonomy and femininity with vulnerability, Debra Bergoffen writes that "women are required to carry the vulnerability of the human condition as a burden so that men can imagine that they can escape the vulnerabilities of being human".[89]

The splitting of the world into autonomous selves and dependent others obscures the extent to which the former's freedom is enabled by networks of privilege and support that attend to their needs and alleviate their vulnerability, whilst normalising the latter's subordination. That creates a conundrum for members of vulnerable groups who wish to draw on the ideal of individual autonomy in their struggles against inequality. For instance, feminists are confronted with the question whether the ideal of autonomy is so deeply immersed in fantasies of male independence and control that it remains unattainable for most women. If that is the case, do they risk legitimating the status quo when relying on the language of individual autonomy to carve out a sphere of private freedom and bodily integrity for women? Are their struggles likely to result in a mere redrawing of the line that divides individuals that are considered autonomous from those viewed as needy and vulnerable, without affecting the disadvantage suffered by most women, who remain relegated to the category of dependent others? Are they in danger of becoming complicit in interventions on vulnerable people's behalf that are designed to overcome otherness, by imposing Western conceptions of individual autonomy – and gender equality – on the rest of humanity?[90]

Vulnerability is not just a function of our bodily existence – our need for food, water, and shelter, and the vulnerability of our bodies to disease, force, or violence. It also arises from the social nature of our embodiment.[91] Contrary to the fantasy of the sovereign individual who is always already autonomous, all human beings are "born into a condition of radical dependency".[92] It is only because of the care provided by others that we can achieve a measure of autonomy. Even once we appear to have outgrown our profound bodily and emotional dependence on others, our ability to live "independent" and fulfilled lives is still contingent on the existence of social and material structures that allow us to come to terms with our vulnerability as embodied beings. However, the point is not only that no one is ever completely autonomous. It is also that laws and social relations, institutions, and practices have a sharply differential impact on people's mobility, access to food, shelter, healthcare, and clothing, and capacity to articulate and challenge injustice. The unequal distribution of the resources required to attain a degree of autonomy tracks social hierarchies based on categories like race, citizenship, class, and gender, and reinforces the identification of certain classes of people as abnormal, irrational, deviant, emotional, dependent, or passive. Our bodies thus not only depend for survival and support on other bodies and social and material structures. How we experience our bodies and the tendency of those experiences to facilitate or impede our freedom are also mediated through norms and representations that are socially produced and immersed in power relations.[93]

Butler grounds the ideal of equal freedom not in self-sufficiency but in interdependence. She starts from the premise that our survival and welfare as embodied beings depend on certain material conditions and social structures, and that our existence is entangled with the lives of others (including non-human animals, ecosystems, and people who find themselves outside our national borders).[94] She further notes that – physical and systemic – violence against vulnerable groups derives from distinctions that treat some lives as more valuable and grievable than others. Against those manifestations of bio-power, she posits the ideal of the "radical equality of the grievable",[95] which holds that all people's lives matter equally, that they should all be allowed to flourish, and that their equal grievability should be the basis for the distribution and organisation of social goods like healthcare, food, and shelter and the enjoyment of personal and civic rights and freedoms. She thus combines the insight that vulnerability is a universal human condition with an egalitarian commitment to the creation of social and material conditions that honour the equal value of all lives. Life is precarious, but that does not absolve laws and social structures of responsibility for the ways in which the burden of that precariousness is distributed.[96]

This understanding of freedom and selfhood is not only relational but also political. In the first place, it rejects freedom's uncoupling from the distribution of the burdens of vulnerability and opportunities for self-realisation, and articulates freedom with a radical ideal of equality, which insists that the equal value of all lives should underpin the organisation of political life and the distribution of social and material resources. Secondly, equal freedom, so conceived, does not denote an abstract right but provides a basis for the exposure of "the racial phantasms that inform public ideas about what kind of life deserves an open-ended future, and whose lives are grievable",[97] and an ongoing political struggle against the devaluation and instrumentalization of certain lives. Thirdly, this articulation of freedom with equality and vulnerability has implications for understandings of collective selfhood and self-determination. To show why that is the case, it is helpful to refer to the role of historical narratives in the formation of understandings of collective self-determination. Ethnic or nationalist understandings of collective selfhood often rest on narratives about a nation or group's historical struggles against oppression. These narratives serve to transform vulnerability into autonomy through the heroic tales of historical figures who resisted the powers that sought to reduce them to a life of dependence or a mere bodily existence. For example, Johan Snyman shows how the memorialisation of the trauma suffered by women and children during the Anglo-Boer War was transformed under the weight of Afrikaner nationalism. The victims of the war were turned into heroines and their suffering and despair were converted into bravery and love of the fatherland. At the same time, the suffering of black people during the war was effaced from the historical record, so that the meaning of the trauma of the war could be monopolised for whites only.[98]

The instrumentalisation of vulnerability and suffering in the service of ethnic or nationalist conceptions of selfhood is at odds with the above articulation of individual freedom with vulnerability and the equal value of all lives. This understanding of freedom takes issue with the way in which narratives about heroic individuals or groups who are said to have overcome their vulnerability are used to carve the world into autonomous selves and vulnerable others. It interrogates the accompanying distinctions between civilised and uncivilised populations, rational and irrational human beings, and disciplined and deviant bodies, and politicises their reproduction within dominant conceptions of personhood and citizenship. It resists the idea that interdependence stops at the border of the nation state or that the responsibility to assist vulnerable people can or should be confined to people from the same national or ethnic group. Its conceptualisation of equal freedom thus lends itself to the disruption of exclusivist notions of membership and belonging and requires the creation of spaces in which all people can come to terms with their vulnerability and develop their personalities through engagement with the attachments, relationships, and contradictions that helped forge them. In the words of Lorraine Code, it requires "climates of recognition, mutual responsibility, and trust" which will enable all human beings to "live their vulnerabilities well".[99]

## 6.5 Freedom of expression in a divided society

Freedom of expression is a vital resource in struggles against inequality and oppression. It facilitates the free circulation of information and ideas, the development of alternative social and political visions, the formulation and public dissemination of complaints of rights violations and social injustice, and the exposure and critique of concentrations of wealth, opportunities, and power in the hands of certain groups.[100] However, freedom of expression cannot escape the contradiction between the radical promise of equal freedom for all and the inscription of that ideal within representations, institutions, and practices that bear the imprint of an unequal society. In a society characterised by spatial apartheid and vastly unequal access to education, employment, and social capital, poor black people and other marginalised groups often lack the opportunities or resources to make themselves heard.[101] Other systemic barriers – including the power relations that shape deliberative processes and the discursive conventions that favour modes and tones of expression that are associated with the ruling and intellectual classes – further impede their participation in the public sphere and could result in a denial of their normative capacity to speak and to represent their own interests.[102]

Not surprisingly, those barriers track the racialised, class-based, and gendered hierarchical distinctions – between civilised and uncivilised people, between reason and superstition, between autonomy and dependence, between law and custom, between the public and private spheres, etc. – that are embedded in our colonial, apartheid, and patriarchal past. Decolonial studies note that, during the European Enlightenment, freedom of expression was conceived in terms of notions of autonomy, rationality, and a belief in societal progress that were developed in direct opposition to the "savagery" of colonised peoples. These notions served to rationalise the exclusion of indigenous populations, slaves, impoverished people, and women from the "marketplace of ideas". They were also used in settler-colonial states to justify assimilationist policies that were aimed at "civilising" indigenous peoples, inter alia through the provision of Western education and the forcible separation of children from their families.[103] Freedom of expression thus came to be identified with "an ontology of social life" that erased the agency and voice of indigenous people and ruled out the possibility of politics beyond the liberal state.[104] When indigenous people were granted citizenship, their ability to participate in public life was subject to their assimilation into mainstream – white – culture. Today, many of the above hierarchies exist side-by-side with and qualify the meaning of universal citizenship, as the rights associated with active citizenship continue to be restricted to those conforming to the image of the idealised Western, male subject.

The silencing of those who challenge or fail to conform to the image of the self-owning subject is aggravated by understandings of freedom of expression as a subjective right that is analogous to private property. The casting of subjects as owners of their speech fits with liberal understandings of freedom as the property that individuals have in their body and person.[105] These understandings are exclusionary and lend themselves to the commodification of expression. Moreover, they overlook freedom of expression's relational and dialogical nature and assume that opinions exist prior to the public dialogical processes through which they are articulated.[106]

By contrast, relational understandings articulate freedom of expression with equality, are alive to the danger that powerful individuals or groups may monopolise speech or silence others, and account for the need for positive measures to ensure that everyone is able to speak out and that a diversity of voices can be heard. The Constitutional Court tends to construe freedom of expression in relational terms. It frequently points out that the Constitution does not treat freedom of expression as absolute, or as a supreme right that automatically trumps other rights or values. Unlike the Constitution of the United States, which proclaims freedom of speech in bold, unqualified terms, section 16 of the Constitution is carefully worded, and its meaning, scope, and range of permissible limitations must be determined with reference to the – mutually reinforcing and sometimes conflicting – values of dignity, equality, democracy, and freedom.[107] The Court has also been careful not to conflate freedom of expression with, or subordinate it to, intellectual property rights. In *Laugh It Off*, it warned against giving statutory provisions protecting trademarks an overly extensive interpretation, which converts them into "a monopoly adverse to other claims of expressive conduct of at least equal cogency and worth in our broader society".[108] In *Blind SA*, the Court invalidated provisions in the Copyright Act that required the consent of a copyright owner to convert literary works into formats that would make them accessible to people with visual disabilities. It cautioned that incorporeal property rights should not be turned into a mechanism for depriving people with disabilities of the freedom to receive or impart information or ideas or deny them access to educational resources or the ability to participate in cultural life.[109]

The Constitutional Court's jurisprudence also contains traces of a conflictual understanding of freedom of expression, which recognises the need for open, robust, and vigorous debate. The Court noted in *McBride* that, under the law of defamation, "extreme, unjust, unbalanced, exaggerated and prejudiced" criticism is protected in the interests of untrammelled public debate and truth-finding.[110] In *Democratic Alliance*, it acknowledged that political life in South Africa tends to be "loud, rowdy and fractious",[111] and held that a provision in the Electoral Act 73 of 1998 that prohibits the publication of false information with the intention of influencing the outcome of an election and provides for severe penalties for breaches, should be interpreted restrictively. In *Laugh It Off*, Sachs J, in a concurring judgment, noted that it was relevant that the applicant's use of parody, which allegedly tarnished a well-known trademark, used laughter "as a means of challenging economic power, resisting ideological hegemony and advancing human dignity".[112] And in *Economic Freedom Fighters*, Mogoeng CJ stated:

> It is no exaggeration to characterise the right to freedom of expression as the lifeblood of a genuine constitutional democracy that keeps it fairly vibrant, stable and peaceful. When citizens are very angry or frustrated, it serves as the virtual exhaust pipe through which even the most venomous of toxicities within may be let out to help them calm down, heal, focus and move on. More importantly, free expression is an indispensable facilitator of a vigorous and necessary exchange of ideas and accountability.[113]

In that case, Julius Malema was charged with inciting the EFF's followers to occupy land illegally and thus to commit the offence of trespass. The Court declared section 18(2)(b) of the Riotous Assemblies Act 17 of 1956 unconstitutional. Mogoeng CJ reasoned that the section, which criminalises inciting another person to commit "any offence" is too sweeping, since the purpose of the limitation could be achieved through a more narrowly tailored provision which applies only to the incitement of serious offences.[114] Mogoeng CJ further stated that citizens must be able to express themselves fully and fearlessly on matters of public concern, that the protection of that freedom must extend to views that "offend, shock or disturb",[115] and that a sweeping prohibition would have a chilling effect on robust debate and contestation.[116]

A conflictual conception of freedom of expression not only demands the freedom to engage in robust debate but also requires attention to structural discursive violence. Balibar notes that structural discursive violence deprives many citizens of active citizenship and the opportunity to participate in public deliberation; moreover, it relies on "universalistic" discourses to hide its own operation behind a "veil of ignorance".[117] According to him, a conflictual understanding of freedom of expression is not grounded in the "'regulating idea' of perfect communication or 'ideal speech situation'", as postulated by Habermas, but takes its cue from the need for "the radical transformation of the always already existing situation of 'imperfect communication' that is saturated with violence" and the possibility of terror.[118] The critical challenge is to enable "suppressed or distorted voices" to be heard, to "lift the veil of ignorance", and to "cross and displace every boundary that limited the reciprocity of interpellations".[119] Challenging structural discursive violence through discourse is a daunting task, which is not made any easier by the globalisation of communication, digitalisation, the erosion of the public sphere, the rise of identity politics and populist and authoritarian tendencies, and the multiplication of internal and external borders. What complicates matters even more is that we lack the linguistic resources to conceptualise and communicate certain injustices.[120] A conflictual understanding of freedom of expression thus challenges us to be mindful of the absences, exclusions, and silences produced by social and institutional power, and highlights the need for the invention of new vocabularies that will allow us to verbalise wrongs that are presently unnamed and to articulate democratic possibilities that are currently unavailable.

Put differently, a conflictual understanding calls for a critical awareness of the links between speech, structural racism, and other forms of institutionalised power. It is interested in the ways in which discourse normalises social and economic oppression and renders it invisible.[121] It also draws attention to the operation of those hierarchies within the discursive field, which relegates certain speakers and viewpoints to a place outside rational discourse. These exclusions rest inter alia on the colonial belief that freedom of expression is essentially "a Western value" and that certain people are "incapable of cultivating freedom of speech".[122] And yet, a conflictual understanding refuses to give up on speech's emancipatory potential. It is suspicious of theories that present the boundaries of the political community as fixed or the range of what can plausibly be asserted as immutable.[123] It does not subscribe to an understanding of social power as something absolute, even if its distribution is unequal. It insists that speakers that are critical of the status quo have power and that their speech could help draw attention to structural violence, disrupt the unequal distribution of discursive freedom and power, and gesture towards more humane alternatives.[124]

The regulation of hate speech is one of the areas in which the tension between freedom of expression and structural violence comes to the fore. Section 16(2)(c) of the Constitution expressly excludes "advocacy of hatred that is based on race, ethnicity, gender, or religion, and that constitutes incitement to cause harm" from the scope of constitutionally protected expression. Section 10(1) of PEPUDA seeks to give effect to section 16(2)(c) by providing that

> no person may publish, propagate, advocate or communicate words that are based on one or more of the prohibited grounds, against any person, that could reasonably be construed to demonstrate a clear intention to be harmful or to incite harm; and to promote or propagate hatred.

These provisions are based on the need to prevent racial and other forms of hate speech from violating human dignity and equality, endangering national unity and reconciliation, and undermining democratic pluralism.[125] In *Qwelane*, the Constitutional Court referred to "the presence of deeply rooted structural subordination in relation to race" and other markers of disadvantage like sexual orientation and gender identity.[126] In a country in which the enduring legacy of historical divisions and patterns of oppression remains starkly visible in daily life and in which certain social identities still carry strong connotations of inferiority, hate speech is likely to impede the ability of vulnerable categories of people to participate freely in social, political, and economic life.[127] To the extent that hate speech exposes already vulnerable individuals and groups to "extreme detestation and vilification" and the risk of further discrimination and harassment,[128] it inhibits their ability to express and challenge the injustices that they experience. In *Qwelane*, the Court referred to evidence "that hate speech results in its victims internalising the notions of inferiority engendered by hate speech, suffering from self-doubt and self-loathing and often experiencing suicidal ideation", and "prevents them from becoming fully functioning members of society".[129] Seen from that perspective, the regulation of hate speech can strengthen freedom of expression and contribute to a pluralistic public sphere by seeking to remove structural barriers to vulnerable people's freedom to speak out.[130]

The categorical exclusion of hate speech from constitutional protection nevertheless raises concerns. In the first place, even though a conflictual understanding of freedom of expression does not subscribe to free speech absolutism,[131] it nevertheless worries that hate speech prohibitions, which are typically formulated in broad terms, could place too much power in the hands of state officials and judges to decide the bounds of acceptable discourse.[132] The Constitutional Court's judgment in *Qwelane* has gone some way towards addressing concerns about the overbreadth and lack of clarity of section 10(1) of PEPUDA. The Court invalidated the section to the extent that it prohibited speech that is merely "hurtful",[133] and provided interpretive guidance which narrows the ambit of the provision.[134] However, questions remain. In a country in which reasonableness has for centuries been defined in terms of hegemonic European norms, the reasonable person test that is used to determine whether speech "could reasonably be construed to demonstrate a clear intention to be harmful or to incite harm; and to promote or propagate hatred" can be expected to perpetuate the historical privileging of certain forms and registers of speech over others.[135] Even more worryingly, the Prevention and Combating of Hate Crimes and Hate Speech Act 16 of 2023 has recently been signed by the President. Unlike PEPUDA, the Act criminalises hate speech. It is vague, overbroad, and can be expected to have a chilling effect on freedom of expression.

Secondly, hate speech legislation risks reducing discursive injustice to acts of individual transgression. Treating hate speech as deviant individual behaviour could normalise deep-seated, systemic inequality, and substitute abstract and reified rights discourse for nuanced analyses of the structural power relations that enable discursive injustice. PEPUDA appears to guard against these dangers: it emphasises the need to eliminate systemic discrimination and creates equality courts with flexible remedial powers whose proceedings are informal and designed to facilitate access and participation. But equality courts are courts, nonetheless, staffed by judges whose education and training are likely to have instilled in them mental habits and reflexes that are conducive to formalistic, acontextual, and uncritical modes of legal reasoning, and whose ideology and background colour their interpretation of the terms used in section 10(1). The holding in *Afriforum v Malema* is a case in point. The Court held that the singing of a struggle song containing words that have been translated as "Kill the Boer" constitutes hate speech.[136] Joel Modiri rightly argues that the judgment fails to come to terms with the power and socio-economic privilege enjoyed by white people, favours reified understandings of rights over the lived experience of poor black people, uncritically assumes that the advent of constitutionalism has eradicated inequality and oppression, and unduly narrows the range of expression available to black people struggling for a dignified existence.[137] In a more recent case, in which the same words were sung, the Court rejected the literal interpretation advanced by the applicants and found that the lyrics had to be interpreted within the context of the struggle against the dispossession of black people.[138] However, the worry remains that the focus on individual manifestations of alleged racist, sexist, and homophobic prejudice will draw attention away from the underlying structural causes of disadvantage. The danger will be aggravated through the criminalisation of hate speech, since the framing of the inquiry into the guilt of the individual accused can be expected to deflect attention away from the complex social processes through which speech becomes injurious.[139]

Thirdly, communities and movements that are looking to disrupt structural discursive and other forms of violence and to enunciate new emancipatory possibilities face formidable obstacles. Not surprisingly, their articulation of grievances and imagination of alternative futures often involve unconventional and non-discursive means of communication that traverse the distinctions between speech and action and between reason and affect,[140] and test the boundaries between legality and illegality.[141] That places them outside the classical liberal paradigm of rational, disembodied discourse and makes them more vulnerable to state restrictions, including restrictions under the rubric of hate speech.

Fourthly, although proscribing speech that perpetuates the subjugation of poor black people and other vulnerable groups could have important symbolic and practical effects, we should not underestimate the power of the dominant culture to recast harmful speech in "neutral" terms. The point is not that we should widen the net to include a more extensive range of expression under hate speech but rather that there are limits to the capacity of hate speech legislation to address discursive injustices.

Finally, despite the need to understand the meaning and effects of words in relation to the discourses and structural power relations in which they are embedded and to be alive to the ways in which hate speech re-enacts the exclusion of those targeted from recognition as equals, we must be careful not to treat them as hapless victims who can only be protected by policing the boundaries of acceptable speech and are incapable of fending for themselves. Butler argues that those wronged by hate speech are not wholly determined by language but are sometimes able to resist linguistic violence through counter-speech. For example, the "counter-appropriation" of offensive terms (like "queer") through "a ritual chain of resignifications" can sometimes help to subvert and defuse the original threat.[142] Admittedly, the future effects of such efforts at resignification are uncertain, as they invariably become part of larger discourses in which the meanings assigned to terms are prone to variation. However, the effects of judicial decisions declaring certain utterances impermissible are similarly unpredictable. Like counter-speech, they are best viewed as "temporary respites" in an "on-going struggle" against structural discursive violence.[143] Legal protections against hate speech can help bolster the agency of subjects engaged in those struggles but are no substitute for the invention of vocabularies that facilitate the naming of previously unnamed wrongs and the articulation of new democratic possibilities.

## 6.6 Towards new imaginaries of freedom

Throughout this chapter, I have referred to the tension between the radical promise of equal freedom for all and the continued hold on the legal imagination of categories that split the world into autonomous selves and dependent others and condition freedom on conformity to the image of the white, heterosexual, able-bodied, middle-class male. I have also alluded to the need for new vocabularies and imaginaries of freedom that could enable us to move beyond the dichotomies between autonomy and dependence, modernity and premodernity, reason and superstition, Enlightenment and tradition, rationality and feeling, and individuality and mindless conformity. In the previous sections,

I suggested that the work of Butler and others who stress the interrelatedness of vulnerability and autonomy and articulate freedom with radical equality could contribute to the development of alternative vocabularies of freedom.[144] In this section, I ask whether traces of such imaginaries can be found in the philosophy of ubuntu and the struggles of social movements in South Africa.

The indigenous Southern African notion of ubuntu was introduced into constitutional discourse through the epilogue to the Interim Constitution, which referred to the "need for understanding but not for vengeance, a need for reparation but not for retaliation, a need for ubuntu but not for victimisation". The aim of the epilogue was to advance national unity and reconciliation and, to that end, to mandate legislation providing for amnesty in respect of politically motivated acts and omissions committed in the past. However, ubuntu came to be relied on in several other contexts, besides the constitutionality of amnesty.[145] In the first case heard by the Constitutional Court, several judges referred in their judgments to ubuntu to bolster the Court's finding that the death penalty was unconstitutional. They stated that ubuntu encompasses broad notions of humaneness, solidarity, dignity, respect, compassion, fairness, social justice, interdependence, and sharing.[146] Although ubuntu is not expressly mentioned in the text of the 1996 Constitution, it is treated as a value that animates several of its provisions. It is relied on, inter alia, to emphasise the cultural and relational dimensions of freedom,[147] to require individuals and communities affected by exercises of public power to be consulted and to be treated with respect,[148] to infuse aspects of restorative justice into civil and criminal law,[149] and to balance contractual freedom with considerations of fairness.[150]

Could ubuntu assist us in developing more radically inclusive imaginaries of freedom? Two objections immediately come to mind. First, it may be objected that, while ubuntu could help trim away the excesses of liberal conceptions of freedom and thus enable a better balance between individual and communal interests, it is best seen as external to, rather than inherent in freedom. This view informs some of the discourse on ubuntu's potential to soften the harsh implications of classical liberal understandings of contractual autonomy. For example, in *Beadica*, in which the Constitutional Court recognised that ubuntu must inform understandings of public policy, the majority judgment of Theron J nevertheless treated classical liberal notions of contractual autonomy as the norm, which may be deviated from only in exceptional cases.[151] This approach is problematic. It assumes that freedom can be disconnected from the life forms in which it is embedded and privileges an outdated, distinctly Western, conception of freedom that is rooted in instrumental rationality and metaphysical notions of autonomy. If we want to extend equal liberty to all people who live in South Africa, we must transform the dominant liberal understanding of freedom, rather than making it somewhat more palatable by removing some of its worst excesses.[152]

A second, more fundamental objection is that ubuntu is at odds with the equal freedom of all human beings. On this view, attempted articulations of individual rights with African notions of human solidarity, respect, and interdependence underestimate the extent to which ubuntu is steeped in patriarchy[153] or is based on collectivist views that obscure disagreement and difference and induce conformity to dominant mindsets.[154]

This objection must be taken seriously; however, it has less force when ubuntu is referred to not as a "cultural praxis" but as a "philosophical practice".[155] Leonhard Praeg describes the latter as a contemporary version of ubuntu, which transcends the cultural praxis of local, kinship-based communities and informs understandings of "larger, imagined communities of political practice".[156] He notes that ubuntu's transformation into a philosophical concept was enabled by, inter alia, colonialism, resistance against colonialism, urbanisation, and the anti-apartheid struggle. Ubuntu as a philosophical practice arose from confrontations between local praxis and the "discourses through which Western modernity articulated its imposition on Africa, namely Christianity and a liberal discourse on individual human rights".[157] These confrontations gave rise to a dialectic between Western views of Africans as communal beings who lack individuality, and the reaffirmation of communalism and solidarity as positive values that are distinctly African. They also resulted in a tension between ubuntu's ontic orientation (the notion of becoming a person through other people) and the idea that our personhood derives from our status as rights-bearing individuals. Ubuntu as a philosophical practice and constitutional value is thus balanced precariously between the local and the global, between an ethic of obligation and rights-based constitutionalism, and between a discourse of cultural authenticity and the realisation that a politics that affirms the communal nature of African societies – and African selves – fails to challenge the binary logic that informs colonial constructions of black people.[158] As Praeg states,

> The meaning of Ubuntu reproduced in and through the interface with constitutionalism is neither one in which Ubuntu is simply reducible to human rights discourse nor one that can simply be dismissed as a traditional form of communitarianism at odds with the constitutional regime of rights. Instead, Ubuntu must be considered a glocal phenomenon that must be understood both as a product of and a critical response to Western modernity.[159]

Drucilla Cornell similarly argues that the constitutional principle of ubuntu is not a static concept that is stuck in an imaginary past but serves as a "conversion principle" that allows us to recollect it as an ideal and reimagine it in view of a constitution that is committed to the democratic values of human dignity, equality, and freedom.[160] Understood thus, ubuntu transcends the dichotomy between individualistic and communitarian understandings of the self and society. Through its emphasis on interdependence and becoming, it holds out the possibility of an alternative to reified understandings of both abstract individual rights and customary law.

Ubuntu, on this view, does not provide a mere gloss to liberal understandings of individual rights. Mogobe Ramose notes that the tendency in Western legal thought to treat individuals as abstract legal subjects who are at the centre of the legal universe is foreign to ubuntu's concept of law. The latter is interested in the concrete contexts in which law arises, rather than law as an abstract system. It does not believe that the legal subject can ground law's stability and finality; the legal subject is rather "an active and transient participant" in a process which is continually becoming, and which has no centre.[161] To view the legal subject as a fixed point of reference is to hold on to the idea that the world can be fragmented into distinct, separate entities. That is inconsistent with the belief, which is central to ubuntu, that being and becoming are mutually entwined and interdependent, and that it is impossible to arrest "the incessant flow of simultaneously multi-directional motion".[162] It is also at odds with ubuntu's recognition of three levels of human existence, namely the living, the living dead, and the yet to be born, which introduces something unknowable and unstable at the heart of social relations, and gives rise to the quest for harmony.[163] The emphasis on interdependence and becoming is clear from the maxim *umuntu ngumuntu nga bantu (motho ke motho ka batho)*, which means that "to be a human be-ing is to affirm one's humanity by recognising the humanity of others and, on that basis, establish humane relations with them".[164]

The philosophy of ubuntu can challenge colonial constructions of the selfhood of subjects and their relegation to a time and space outside modernity by rejecting the racist assumption that all philosophy must be based on categories and distinctions that are taken for granted in Western thought,[165] by exposing the contradictions inherent in Western modernity's constructions of selfhood, and by unmasking the falsity of its claims to universality.[166] Its elaboration of alternative conceptions of personhood and justice can help to enable the recognition of the dignity and freedom of subjects who are seen to be on the wrong side of the dividing line between modernity and premodernity and between autonomous selves and dependent others. While ubuntu shares Western modernity's insistence on the need to respect the dignity of every human person, it rejects the fragmentation of human life into distinct spheres of existence, like reason and emotion, or the rational and the spiritual. Ramose points out that, in African philosophy, rationality and feeling are viewed as indivisible and mutually dependent.[167] The philosophy of ubuntu can thus help us move beyond the idea that the world is split into rational, enlightened human beings and those who are controlled by tradition, superstition, and emotion.

On the other hand, the philosophy of ubuntu does not mirror colonial understandings of Africans as communal beings who lack individuality. Ubuntu, on this view, neither privileges the community over the individual nor fosters a form of collectivism which stifles freedom or suppresses disagreement. The community is not seen as static but stands in a dynamic relationship with its members. Just like individuals are shaped through their interaction with each other, communal relations are constantly transformed through the agency of individuals who participate in the life of the community.[168] Ubuntu is a dynamic concept whose meaning is updated and transformed through everyday practices of solidarity and care and struggles for equal recognition, including the struggles of women who are subject to and participate in customary law structures and practices.[169] It enables us to rethink freedom in relational and egalitarian terms by insisting that it is only through our joint participation in a shared world that we can flourish, and that a social and economic order that reduces some populations to lives of destitution and oppression denies our shared humanity and fails to live up to the responsibility to create conditions that give everyone a fair chance of coming to terms with their vulnerability.[170] Cornell states that ubuntu can facilitate a radical critique of racial capitalism, the exploitation of black workers, and neoliberal policies that relegate large sections of humanity to a state of indentured servitude. She adds that ubuntu points to a revolutionary vision of freedom, which requires the emancipation of black workers and an extensive transformation of economic relations.[171]

Anti-racist, feminist, queer, and class-based struggles provide further examples of relational understandings and practices of freedom that politicise the dichotomy between autonomous selves and dependent others and evoke alternative visions of freedom. I will refer to only two examples. The first is Abahlali baseMjondolo, a shack dwellers movement that demands land and housing for the urban poor, as well as water, electricity, healthcare, education, and participatory, bottom-up democracy. The movement is known, inter alia, for refusing assimilation into hegemonic society, resisting the tendency of elites – both in government and the NGO sector – to speak on behalf of impoverished people, and structuring collective action in ways that are democratic and participatory. The second is the student protests of 2015–2016, which occurred under banners like #RhodesMustFall and #FeesMustFall. The students' demands included eradicating white supremacy and other oppressive systems on campuses, decolonising syllabi and spaces (e.g., by removing symbols of colonial oppression, like the statue of Cecil John Rhodes at the University of Cape Town), ending financial exclusion and student debt, and stopping the outsourcing of labour on campuses. I will touch briefly on some aspects of these struggles that are relevant to the quest for new imaginaries of freedom.

First, both these movements resist narratives that suggest that South Africa has been liberated from the yoke of colonialism and apartheid. Every year, on 27 April, which is officially designated Freedom Day, Abahlali, in collaboration with other organisations, stages an UnFreedom Day celebration. On that day, communities get together to share music, dance, and theatre and mourn the various causes of their continued unfreedom, such as a capitalist system that entrenches poverty and inequality, the commodification of essential services, the denial of the right of poor black people to think for themselves, and the repression by the state and governing party of their efforts to build democratic communities.[172] Participants in the student protests similarly rejected the label of "born frees", which is used to refer to young people born after 1994,

The term overlooks the extent to which freedom is enabled through social, economic, and political relations and practices, ignores the fact that the lives of millions of South Africans are still characterised by inequality and dehumanisation, and fails to account for intergenerational trauma and violence.[173]

Second, the movements' demands and modes of organisation challenge existing distributions of roles and places. For example, Abahlali rejects the assumption that it should be left to political and technocratic elites to address the needs of poor and marginalised communities. It calls upon the poor and downtrodden "to become 'professors of their own suffering'" and to build "political and economical consciousness through constant discussion and reflection on [their] situation".[174] What is required of them is not to learn to think like elites but to develop their own perspectives that are rooted in local knowledge, epistemologies, and values.[175] In Rancièrean terms, Abahlali invokes a radical understanding of intellectual equality and politicises the gap between the capacity of poor black people for political speech and action and a socio-political order that relegates them to the level of the subhuman. Students involved in FMF similarly subverted the distribution of roles and responsibilities in the university by demanding the decolonisation of education. In doing so, they challenged the supposed neutrality of syllabi and universality of dominant epistemologies, questioned the assumption that the power to determine curricula should reside exclusively with faculties and professional bodies, and claimed a more prominent role for students in the production of knowledge.

A third feature is that these movements are aware of and consciously resist the danger – or rather likelihood – that master concepts and dichotomies that framed colonial constructions of poor black people would be reinscribed into understandings of liberation, and thus suppress difference and limit the range of choices and subjectivities available to them. Abahlali has distanced itself from racialism, tribalism, and discourses of autochthony. During the 2008 xenophobic attacks, it defended foreign nationals, disavowed the idea that people can be illegal, and declared that those who live in settlements are neighbours and comrades, regardless of their nationality. According to Madlingozi, Abahlali is committed to "a vision of cities as multi-class, multi-racial, multicultural, inter-cultural and perhaps plurinational spaces where multiple forms of belonging and ways of living are embraced and celebrated".[176]

Fourth, these movements insist that the causes of unfreedom are varied and overlapping and include several systemic – social, economic, sexual, spatial, political, and epistemic – barriers to the citizenship, agency, and belonging of marginalised people. The fight against oppression must therefore not be fought along a single axis but requires multiple, intersecting struggles. For example, during the student protests, feminist and LGBTIQ+ activists challenged patriarchy and heteronormativity both within the student movement and in society at large, called attention to rape and sexual violence, and objected against the erasure of certain bodies from official narratives of the students' movement.[177]

Constitutional interpretations of freedom could help secure spaces in which counter-hegemonic movements could debate, develop, and advance radical, alternative visions of freedom. However, there are several dangers that need to be guarded against. In the first place, even progressive understandings of law sometimes fall into the legalistic trap of believing that all people are free since the law proclaims them to be so. This belief not only allows widespread poverty, systemic inequality, and structural violence to be explained away as temporary obstacles to the realisation of the Constitution's progressive vision, but also places a substantial burden on activists and disadvantaged communities to act civilly in an abnormal society.[178] A relational and conflictual understanding of constitutional freedom must avoid normalising the status quo through recourse to legalistic fallacies and complacent narratives of reconciliation and progress. Secondly, when alternative visions of freedom, such as those derived from ubuntu, are uncritically inscribed into an oppressive social, economic, and political order, they can be used to suppress difference and detract from the freedom of those at the margins of society. The reliance on ubuntu in *Afriforum v Malema* to limit the expression of those protesting against the continued subjugation of poor black people illustrates this danger.[179] The likelihood that ubuntu could be used to deny difference and stifle dissent increases when it is equated with Christian morality or liberal understandings of rights,[180] or when it is treated as a communitarian concept that premises freedom on conformity to a particular ethos.[181] Thirdly, although a relational and political interpretation of constitutional freedoms resonates with the imaginaries of freedom discussed in this section, care should be taken not to conflate the two. The divide between intra- and extra-institutional politics is fluid and shifting, but it is nevertheless important to uphold the distinction between them and to recognise the extent to which anti-hegemonic imaginaries point beyond the current constitutional order.

## Notes

1 See the discussion of non-reformist reform in chapter 5.4 above. See also Dean "Critiquing Capabilities".
2 See e.g., *Glenister v President* para 198 (the state's failure to safeguard the independence of the Directorate for Priority Crime Investigation unjustifiably limited several constitutional rights, including equality, human dignity, freedom, and security of the person).
3 See Liebenberg "The Value of Freedom in Interpreting Socio-Economic Rights".
4 *AB v Minister of Social Development* para 55.
5 See *Ferreira v Levin* para 49 on the interconnectedness of dignity and freedom.
6 *MEC for Education v Pillay* para 64.
7 Para 66.
8 *AB v Minister of Social Development* para 52. See also para 67 (s 12(2) "acknowledges the multifaceted lives people may choose to live by providing for [an] expansive range of bodily and psychological protections").
9 *Bwanya v Master of the High Court* para 69.
10 *Ferreira v Levin* para 54.

11 Para 51.
12 Para 49.
13 Paras 170, 173–174, 180–183.
14 Para 174.
15 *Dawood v Minister of Home Affairs* paras 36–37 (relying on dignity to protect the decision to marry and to sustain the marriage relationship); *National Coalition v Minister of Justice* para 32 (the criminalisation of same-sex sodomy infringes the right to privacy).
16 Cornell "Bridging the Span toward Justice" 23 states that Ackermann J's judgment in *Ferreira* recognises that no set of legal guarantees can ever capture freedom's radical promise, and that freedom "underscores the ethical and moral incompleteness of any legal system ever fully to actualise justice, equality and dignity".
17 Michelman "Freedom by Any Other Name?" 99–107.
18 *AB v Minister of Social Development* paras 75–81. One of the textual differences that support this interpretation is that, unlike s 33 of the interim Constitution, which subjected limitations of s 11 to stricter scrutiny, s 36 of the Constitution prescribes the same limitation standard for all constitutional rights, thus mitigating the danger that a generous interpretation of s 12(2) would hamper the state's regulatory powers. Para 62.
19 Paras 83–89.
20 Paras 93–96.
21 Paras 313–315.
22 See Brown *States of Injury* 30–51 on feminism's varied attempts to come to terms with the loss of absolute foundations.
23 51.
24 27.
25 Taylor "Atomism" 56, 60.
26 Young *Justice and the Politics of Difference* 112, 115.
27 109.
28 See Woolman *The Selfless Constitution* 79–125.
29 Benhabib *The Rights of Others* 144.
30 Fraser *Scales of Justice* 6.
31 Brown *Undoing the Demos* 39–45.
32 33.
33 Hart *Disabling Globalization* 18.
34 20.
35 Somers *Genealogies of Citizenship* 134 refers to this nationalist patriotism as "a symbolic garb that compensates for the loss of rights by cultural and symbolic identification".
36 133.
37 Brown "Neoliberalism's Frankenstein" 68.
38 68.
39 69.
40 Anker "The Exploitation of 'Freedom' in America".
41 See, e.g., *Citizens United v Federal Election Commission* (United States Supreme Court ruling that the free speech clause of the first amendment prohibits the government from placing restrictions on corporations' right to make independent electioneering expenditures).
42 See Brown *States of Injury* 10–11, who criticises late-twentieth century theorists on the left for their failure to develop an alternative account of freedom. She claims that their endorsement of "state-administered 'economic justice' combined with a panoply of private liberties" fails to provide an alternative to "the sovereign subject of liberalism".

43 Para 52.
44 Berlin *Two Concepts of Liberty* 7.
45 Edge "A Theory of Freedom" 379–381.
46 Pettit *Republicanism*; Skinner "A Third Concept of Liberty".
47 See Forst "Politische Freiheit" 400–403.
48 Skinner "A Third Concept of Liberty" 242–243.
49 See Sen *Development as Freedom*.
50 Waldron "Homelessness and the Issue of Freedom".
51 In BVerfGE 157, 30 (2021), the German Constitutional Court held that the legislature, when taking climate action in accordance with article 20a of the Basic Law, is obliged to respect the freedom of future generations. If sufficient action is not taken in the present to reduce greenhouse gas emissions, it will have a disproportionate impact on freedom in future.
52 See Woolman *The Selfless Constitution* 117–120.
53 Cornell *At the Heart of Freedom* 62. See also Michelman *Brennan and Democracy* 66–67, 133.
54 Arendt *Between Past and Future* 162–164.
55 147, 167.
56 *Bernstein v Bester* para 67.
57 *Christian Education v Minister of Education* para 36; *Bhe v Magistrate Khayelitsha*; *MEC for Education v Pillay*.
58 *Khosa v Minister of Social Development* para 74.
59 See the discussion under 6.6 below.
60 *National Coalition v Minister of Justice* para 116.
61 *Jordan v S*.
62 *Brisley v Drotsky* para 94; *Afrox Healthcare v Strydom* para 23.
63 See Bhana "The Substance of Contractual Autonomy in the Twenty-First Century".
64 Some Constitutional Court judgments have shown a greater willingness to use notions of good faith and ubuntu to balance contractual freedom against equity and fairness. See, e.g., *Barkhuizen v Napier*; *Everfresh Market v Shoprite Checkers*; and the dissenting judgments of Froneman J and Victor AJ in *Beadica v Trustees*.
65 *New Nation Movement v President* paras 16–64. See also the discussion of the case in chapter 2.4 above.
66 Paras 65–100.
67 Paras 196–232.
68 This is evident not only from the majority's interpretation of s 19(3)(b), but also from its approach to the justifiability of the limitation under s 36(1). It found at paras 113–120 that no valid reason had been advanced for the exclusion of independent candidates. However, the majority neither considered whether the contentions made by the respondents relating to the structural design of the representative system could shed light on the limitation's purpose, nor inquired into the policy choices underlying the Electoral Act.
69 Nelson *On Freedom* 10.
70 The interrelatedness of personal and political freedom is confirmed by the idea that freedom of expression is underpinned both by the value of individual self-determination and self-fulfilment, and by its contribution to collective processes of truth-seeking, debate and democratic will-formation. See *South African National Defence Union v Minister of Defence* para 7.
71 The phrase "an open and democratic society based on human dignity, equality and freedom" in sections 36(1) and 39(1) of the Constitution suggests that freedom is part and parcel of the definition of that society.
72 *Prince v President of the Law Society* paras 129–142.

73 Paras 146, 150, 157.
74 Para 170.
75 Para 147.
76 Para 172. See also Michelman *Brennan and Democracy* 70–71.
77 *MEC for Education v Pillay* para 53 ("Cultural identity is one of the most important parts of a person's identity precisely because it flows from belonging to a community and not from personal choice or achievement. And belonging involves more than simple association; it includes participation and expression of the community's practices and traditions".).
78 Para 54.
79 See, e.g., *University of Stellenbosch Legal Aid Clinic v Minister of Justice* para 132 (low-income earners); *De Vos v Minister of Justice* para 46 (persons with mental illnesses or intellectual disabilities); *Daniels v Scribante* para 22 (occupiers, particularly women); *Lawyers for Human Rights v Minister of Home Affairs* (2004) paras 21–22; *Minister of Home Affairs v Rahim* para 23 (undocumented migrants).
80 *Daniels v Scribante* paras 21, 33.
81 Davis and Klare "Transformative Constitutionalism and the Common and Customary Law" 446–448.
82 Bhana "The Substance of Contractual Autonomy in the Twenty-First Century" 492.
83 See the discussion of neoliberalism under 6.2 above.
84 *Brown Undoing the Demos* 24–27; *Somers Genealogies of Citizenship* 81–82.
85 See Desai "Neoliberalism and Resistance in South Africa". The Life Esidimeni tragedy provides a shocking example of neoliberal policies' disregard for the dignity and lives of vulnerable people. Mentally disabled patients in Gauteng were transferred from an outsourced healthcare provider to families, hospitals, and NGOs, many of which were not able to provide the specialised care that the patients required. The transfers resulted in the death of 141 patients. See Ornellas and Engelbrecht "The Life Esidimeni Tragedy".
86 In *Eskom Holdings v Vaal River Development*, Eskom reduced the electricity supply to two municipalities, due to their failure to pay for the electricity supplied to them, even though the residents had paid the municipalities for services. The Constitutional Court dismissed an appeal against the granting of an interim interdict against Eskom.
87 Fineman *The Autonomy Myth* 31–54. See also Clark and Goldblatt "Gender and Family Law" 202–204.
88 See Young *Justice and the Politics of Difference* 54–55.
89 Bergoffen "Exploiting the Dignity of the Vulnerable Body" 318.
90 See Butler *Precarious Life* 41–42 for a critique of the way in which the liberation of women was used by the Bush administration to justify military intervention in Afghanistan.
91 See Bergoffen "Exploiting the Dignity of the Vulnerable Body" 312 on the interrelatedness of our existence as "conscious beings, subjects who bring meaning and value to the world, and bodied beings, material objects in the world".
92 Butler *The Force of Non-Violence* 41.
93 Butler *Bodies that Matter* 9. For instance, we learn from a young age to discipline our bodies in accordance with social mores, sexual roles, and images of masculinity or femininity. Our vulnerability arises in part from the conflict that we experience when our bodies and desires resist or exceed those norms and representations.
94 Butler *The Force of Non-Violence* 40–51.
95 56.
96 Butler *Frames of War* 25 distinguishes between precariousness, which is a feature of all life, and precarity, which "designates that politically induced condition in which certain populations suffer from failing social and economic networks of support and become differentially exposed to injury, violence, and death".

97 Butler *The Force of Non-Violence* 147.
98 Snyman "Interpretation and the Politics of Memory" 335.
99 Code "A New Epistemology of Rape?" 328.
100 See *National Defence Union v Minister of Defence* paras 7–8; *Democratic Alliance v African National Congress* paras 122–123; *Qwelane v South African Human Rights Commission* paras 68–74. In *Print Media v Minister of Home Affairs* para 93, Van der Westhuizen J stated: "Being able to speak out, to educate, to sing and to protest, be it through waving posters or dancing, is an important tool to challenge discrimination, poverty and oppression".
101 See *Print Media v Minister of Home Affairs* para 97.
102 See Bonotti and Seglow "Freedom of Speech" 522 for a discussion of "speech-related injustice[s]".
103 Leigh "The Settler Coloniality of Free Speech" 7–11.
104 6.
105 Balibar *Secularism and Cosmopolitanism* 149 notes that John Stuart Mill stated that "an opinion only carries intrinsic value to the owner of that opinion, thus silencing the expression of that opinion is an injustice to a basic human right". See Asad "Free Speech, Blasphemy, and Secular Criticism" 27–33 on the relation between free speech and the ontology of the self-owning subject.
106 Balibar *Secularism and Cosmopolitanism* 149–150.
107 *S v Mamabolo* paras 40–41; *Khumalo v Holomisa* para 25. In *Case v Minister of Safety and Security* para 27, Mokgoro J described freedom of expression as "part of a web of mutually supporting rights enumerated in the Constitution". See also *South African National Defence Union v Minister of Defence* para 8.
108 *Laugh It Off v South African Breweries* para 48.
109 *Blind SA v Minister of Trade* para 66.
110 *The Citizen v McBride* para 83. Such criticism must, however, express "an honestly-held opinion, without malice, on a matter of public interest on facts that are true". See also paras 82, 99–100.
111 *Democratic Alliance v African National Congress* para 133. See also paras 134, 194.
112 *Laugh It Off v South African Breweries* para 108.
113 *Economic Freedom Fighters v Minister of Justice* para 1.
114 Paras 52–65.
115 Para 45.
116 Para 61.
117 Balibar *Secularism and Cosmopolitanism* 151.
118 150.
119 152.
120 This is what Jean-Francois Lyotard defined as the differend. See Cartlidge "Lyotard, the *Differend* and the Philosophy of Deep Disagreement" 362.
121 See Ndelu "We Refuse to be Silenced".
122 Balibar *Secularism and Cosmopolitanism* 154.
123 See chapter 3.4 above.
124 Robbins "Power Talking".
125 *Islamic Unity Convention v Independent Broadcasting Authority* paras 27–28.
126 *Qwelane v South African Human Rights Commission* para 86. See also *Afriforum NPC v Nelson Mandela Foundation Trust* para 49 on how public displays of the old South African flag recall and celebrate a system in which "only white people were treated as first-class citizens while black people were denigrated and demeaned".
127 Butler *Excitable Speech* 5 notes that our social constitution depends on being addressed by others. It is for that reason that we are so vulnerable to the address by the other: language has the power to confer or withhold recognition; it "can sustain the body [but] it can also threaten its existence". Moreover, utterances that violate the other re-enact a pre-existing discursive (or "interpellating") operation (27).

It is for that reason that the meaning and effects of such words must always be understood in relation to the discourses and structural power in which they are embedded. On this understanding, neither the speaking subject nor the addressee of her words is ever fully autonomous in the sense of being in control of or mastering the meanings of the words that they speak or that are used to define them.

128 *Qwelane v South African Human Rights Commission* para 81.

129 Para 180.

130 Para 168 ("ensuring the LGBT+ community has equal social standing and public assurance against exclusion, hostility, discrimination and violence is part of the greater transformative constitutional project").

131 See Delgado "First Amendment Formalism Is Giving Way to First Amendment Realism".

132 See Dworkin "Foreword" vii–ix (hate speech laws could diminish political legitimacy by excluding certain viewpoints from the outset from participating in democratic processes of opinion- and will-formation). But see also Waldron *The Harm in Hate Speech* 173–203.

133 *Qwelane v South African Human Rights Commission* paras 139–144.

134 For instance, it held that the terms "(b) be harmful or … incite harm; (c) promote or propagate hatred" should be read conjunctively (para 104) and that the term "communicate" should be interpreted restrictively to exclude private communications (paras 115–120).

135 Jeewa and Bhima "Discriminatory Language" 13–16. See the elaboration of the reasonable person test in *Qwelane v South African Human Rights Commission* paras 96–101. The Court has cautioned against using "the dominant, racist view of the past – of what is neutral, normal and acceptable – … as the starting point" in determining how a reasonable person would interpret the words. *Rustenburg Platinum Mine v SAEWA obo Bester* para 48; *South African Human Rights Commission v Masuku* para 144.

136 *Afriforum v Malema*.

137 Modiri "Race, Realism and Critique".

138 *Afriforum v Economic Freedom Fighters*.

139 Butler *Excitable Speech* 39.

140 Botha "Fundamental Rights and Democratic Contestation" 234–236.

141 See the discussion of Hans Lindahl's work on a-legality in chapter 3.4 above.

142 Butler *Excitable Speech* 14.

143 Manko "Judicial Decision-Making, Ideology and the Political" 186.

144 See also De Ville *Deconstructive Constitutionalism* 61–82 for a deconstructive reading of freedom and democracy.

145 *Azanian Peoples Organisation v President* paras 19, 48.

146 *S v Makwanyane* paras 224 (Langa J), 237 (Madala J), 263 (Mahomed J), 308 (Mokgoro J).

147 *MEC for Education v Pillay* para 53; *AB v Minister of Social Development* para 51.

148 *Port Elizabeth Municipality v Various Occupiers* para 37.

149 *Dikoko v Mokhatla* paras 68–69, 112–120; *Van Vuren v Minister of Correctional Services* para 51.

150 *Barkhuizen v Napier* para 51; *Everfresh Market v Shoprite Checkers* paras 23–24, 71–72; *Beadica v Trustees* paras 72, 206–228.

151 Consider, e.g., the assertion in *Beadica v Trustees* paras 82, 88 that a "court will use the power to invalidate a contract or not to enforce it, sparingly, and only in the clearest of cases".

152 As Froneman J recognised in his dissenting judgment in *Beadica v Trustees* para 177, what is needed is the "transformation of the rigid classical notion of freedom of contract into a more socially situated or communally understood conception of personal autonomy".

153 Keevey "Ubuntu versus the Core Values of the South African Constitution" 70–75.
154 English "*Ubuntu*"; Van der Walt *Law and Sacrifice* 109–115.
155 Praeg "From ubuntu to Ubuntu" 100.
156 106.
157 106.
158 Praeg states, with reference to WEB du Bois' notion of double consciousness and Frantz Fanon's statement that blackness is "a white construction" (110), that "to accept the idea that the most significant fact about the African self is its communal (as opposed to its individualist) nature, is to affirm the very violence of Western thought through the act of contesting it *on its own terms*" (111).
159 114.
160 Cornell "A Call for a Nuanced Constitutional Jurisprudence" 671.
161 Ramose *African Philosophy through Ubuntu* 84.
162 40. See also 36.
163 46.
164 37.
165 5–34; Cornell and Van Marle "Ubuntu Feminism" 3–4.
166 Gordon "Ubuntu Otherwise" 15.
167 Ramose *African Philosophy through Ubuntu* 42. See also Cornell "A Call for a Nuanced Constitutional Jurisprudence" 670, 673.
168 Cornell and Van Marle "Exploring Ubuntu" 206; Ramose *African Philosophy through Ubuntu* 82.
169 Cornell "A Call for a Nuanced Constitutional Jurisprudence" 671.
170 Cornell and Van Marle "Ubuntu Feminism" 6 argue that ubuntu rests on the understanding that "[w]e are all equal before the contingencies, fragility, and finitude of our human being, and therefore we all need care and support if we are to flourish".
171 Cornell *Law and Revolution in South Africa* 180–181.
172 Abahlali baseMjondolo "UnFreedom Day to be Marked in Three Provinces"; Madlingozi *Mayibuye iAfrika?* 168–169.
173 Kenyon and Madlingozi "Rainbow is not the New Black" 499–500; Rose "The Legacy" 33–34.
174 Madlingozi *Mayibuye iAfrika?* 185.
175 190–192.
176 184.
177 Gouws "#EndRapeCulture Campaign in South Africa"; Kenyon and Madlingozi "Rainbow is not the New Black" 500.
178 Rose *The Legacy* 34–35.
179 *Afriforum v Malema* paras 18, 108, 111.
180 See, e.g., *Bophuthatswana Broadcasting Corporation v Ramosa*; Mogoeng CJ's dissent in *The Citizen v McBride* paras 216–218, 243.
181 In their minority judgment in *City of Tshwane Metropolitan Municipality v Afriforum*, Froneman and Cameron JJ argued that the majority's reliance on ubuntu imposes the ubuntu worldview on citizens and conditions constitutional protection on conformity to that ethos. They argued at para 159 that the Constitution demands recognition of difference even if we find someone's beliefs and aspirations deeply problematic.

## Bibliography

Abahlali baseMjondolo "UnFreedom Day to be Marked in Three Provinces" (25 April 2023) https://abahlali.org/node/17632/

Anker E "The Exploitation of 'Freedom' in America" *New York Times* (4 Feb 2022) https://www.nytimes.com/2022/02/04/opinion/ugly-freedom-discrimination-racism-sexism.html

Arendt H *Between Past and Future: Eight Exercises in Political Thought* (2006) New York: Penguin Books.
Asad T "Free Speech, Blasphemy, and Secular Criticism" in T Asad, W Brown, J Butler and S Mahmood *Is Critique Secular? Blasphemy, Injury, and Free Speech* (2009) 20 Berkeley: Townsend Center for the Humanities.
Balibar É *Secularism and Cosmopolitanism: Critical Hypotheses on Religion and Politics* (2018) New York: Columbia University Press.
Benhabib S *The Rights of Others: Aliens, Residents and Citizens* (2004) Cambridge: Cambridge University Press.
Bergoffen D "Exploiting the Dignity of the Vulnerable Body: Rape as a Weapon of War" (2009) 38 *Philosophical Papers* 307.
Berlin I *Two Concepts of Liberty* (1958) London: Oxford University Press.
Bhana D "The Substance of Contractual Autonomy in the Twenty-First Century: The South African Experience" (2015) 48 *Verfassung und Recht in Übersee* 492.
Bonotti M and Seglow J "Freedom of Speech: A Relational Defence" (2022) 48 *Philosophy and Social Criticism* 515.
Botha H "Fundamental Rights and Democratic Contestation: Reflections on Freedom of Assembly in an Unequal Society" (2017) 21 *Law, Democracy & Development* 221.
Brown W "Neoliberalism's Frankenstein: Authoritarian Freedom in Twenty-First Century 'Democracies'" (2018) 1 *Critical Times* 60.
Brown W *States of Injury: Power and Freedom in Late Modernity* (1995) Princeton: Princeton University Press.
Brown W *Undoing the Demos: Neoliberalism's Stealth Revolution* (2015) New York: Zone Books.
Butler J *Bodies that Matter: On the Discursive Limits of Sex* (1993) New York: Routledge.
Butler J *Excitable Speech: A Politics of the Performative* (1997) London: Routledge.
Butler J *Frames of War: When Is Life Grievable?* (2010) London: Verso.
Butler J *Precarious Life: The Powers of Mourning and Violence* (2004) London: Verso.
Butler J *The Force of Non-Violence: An Ethico-Political Bind* (2020) London: Verso.
Cartlidge J "Lyotard, the *Differend* and the Philosophy of Deep Disagreement" (2022) 200 *Synthese* 359.
Clark B and Goldblatt B "Gender and Family Law" in E Bonthuys and C Albertyn (eds) *Gender, Law and Justice* (2007) Cape Town: Juta 195.
Code L "A New Epistemology of Rape?" (2009) 38 *Philosophical Papers* 327.
Cornell D *At the Heart of Freedom: Feminism, Sex, and Equality* (1998) Princeton: Princeton University Press.
Cornell D "Bridging the Span toward Justice: Laurie Ackermann and the Ongoing Architectonic of Dignity Jurisprudence" (2008) *Acta Juridica* 18.
Cornell D "A Call for a Nuanced Constitutional Jurisprudence: Ubuntu, Dignity, and Reconciliation" (2004) 19 *SA Public Law* 666.
Cornell D *Law and Revolution in South Africa: Ubuntu, Dignity, and the Struggle for Constitutional Transformation* (2014) New York: Fordham University Press.
Cornell D and Van Marle K "Exploring Ubuntu: Tentative Reflections" (2005) 5 *African Human Rights Law Journal* 195.
Cornell D and Van Marle K "Ubuntu Feminism: Tentative Reflections" (2015) 36 *Verbum et Ecclesia* 1.
Davis D and Klare K "Transformative Constitutionalism and the Common and Customary Law" (2010) 26 *South African Journal on Human Rights* 403.
Dean H "Critiquing Capabilities: The Distractions of a Beguiling Concept" (2009) 29 *Critical Social Policy* 261.
Delgado R "First Amendment Formalism is Giving Way to First Amendment Realism" (1994) 29 *Harvard Civil Rights-Civil Liberties Law Review* 169.
Desai A "Neoliberalism and Resistance in South Africa" (2003) 54 *Monthly Review* 16.

De Ville J *Deconstructive Constitutionalism: Derrida Reading Kant* (2023) Albany: SUNY Press.
Dworkin R "Foreword" in I Hare and J Weinstein (eds) *Extreme Speech and Democracy* (2009) v Oxford: Oxford University Press.
Edge M "A Theory of Freedom" (2013) 12 *European Journal of Political Theory* 368.
English R "*Ubuntu*: The Quest for an Indigenous Jurisprudence" (1996) 12 *South African Journal on Human Rights* 641.
Fineman M *The Autonomy Myth: A Theory of Dependency* (2004) New York: New Press.
Forst R "Politische Freiheit" in P Schink (ed) *Freiheit: Zeitgenössische Texte zu einer philosophischen Kontroverse* (2017) 397 Berlin: Suhrkamp.
Fraser N *Scales of Justice: Reimagining Political Space in a Globalizing World* (2009) New York: Columbia University Press.
Gordon L "Ubuntu Otherwise: Thoughts on Ubuntu" in L Praeg and S Magadla (eds) *Curating the Archive* (2014) 10 Pietermaritzburg: University of KwaZulu-Natal Press.
Gouws A "#EndRapeCulture Campaign in South Africa: Resisting Sexual Violence Through Protest and the Politics of Experience" (2018) 45 *Politikon* 3.
Hart G *Disabling Globalization: Places of Power in Post-Apartheid South Africa* (2002) Berkeley: University of California Press.
Jeewa T and Bhima J "Discriminatory Language: A Remnant of Colonial Oppression" (2021) 11 *Constitutional Court Review* 1.
Keevey I "Ubuntu versus the Core Values of the South African Constitution" in L Praeg and S Magadla (eds) *Curating the Archive* (2014) 54 Pietermaritzburg: University of KwaZulu-Natal Press.
Kenyon K and Madlingozi T "'Rainbow is not the New Black': #FeesMustFall and the Demythication of South Africa's Liberation Narrative" (2022) 42 *Third World Quarterly* 494.
Leigh D "The Settler Coloniality of Free Speech" (2022) 16 *International Political Sociology* 1.
Liebenberg S "The Value of Freedom in Interpreting Socio-Economic Rights" (2008) *Acta Juridica* 149.
Madlingozi T *Mayibuye iAfrika? Disjunctive Inclusions and Black Strivings for Constitution and Belonging in "South Africa"*, unpublished thesis, Birkbeck, University of London (2018).
Manko R "Judicial Decision-Making, Ideology and the Political: Towards an Agonistic Theory of Adjudication" (2022) 33 *Law and Critique* 175.
Michelman F *Brennan and Democracy* (1999) Princeton: Princeton University Press.
Michelman F "Freedom by Any Other Name? A Comparative Note on Losing Battles While Winning Wars" (2008) *Acta Juridica* 91.
Modiri J "Race, Realism and Critique: The Politics of Race and *Afriforum v Malema* in the (In)Equality Court" (2013) 130 *South African Law Journal* 274.
Ndelu S "'We Refuse to be Silenced': Writing a Fallist Politics into the Criminalization of Racist Hate Speech in South Africa" (2020) 3 *International Journal of Critical Diversity Studies* 8.
Nelson M *On Freedom: Four Songs of Care and Constraint* (2021) Minneapolis: Graywolf Press
Ornellas A and Engelbrecht L "The Life Esidimeni Tragedy: Why a Neoliberal Agenda Leaves no Room for the Mentally Ill" (2018) 54 *Social Work* 296
Pettit P *Republicanism: A Theory of Freedom and Government* (1997) Oxford: Oxford University Press.
Praeg L "From ubuntu to Ubuntu: Four Historical a Prioris" in L Praeg and S Magadla (eds) *Curating the Archive* (2014) 96 Pietermaritzburg: University of KwaZulu-Natal Press.
Ramose M *African Philosophy through Ubuntu* (2002) Harare: Mond Books.

Robbins B "Power Talking: A Commentary on Balibar" *Politics/Letters* (14 April 2016) http://quarterly.politicsslashletters.org/power-talking-a-commentary-on-balibar/
Rose J "The Legacy" in J Barnard-Naudé (ed) *Decolonising the Neoliberal University: Law, Psychoanalysis and the Politics of Student Protest* (2022) 27 London: Routledge.
Sen A *Development as Freedom* (1999) Oxford: Oxford University Press.
Skinner Q "A Third Concept of Liberty" (2002) 117 *Proceedings of the British Academy* 237.
Snyman J "Interpretation and the Politics of Memory" (1998) *Acta Juridica* 312.
Somers M *Genealogies of Citizenship: Markets, Statelessness, and the Right to Have Rights* (2008) Cambridge: Cambridge University Press.
Taylor C "Atomism" in A Kontos (ed) *Powers, Possessions and Freedom: Essays in Honour of CB Macpherson* (1979) 39 Toronto: University of Toronto Press.
Van der Walt J *Law and Sacrifice: Towards a Post-Apartheid Theory of Law* (2005) London: Birkbeck Law Press.
Waldron J "Homelessness and the Issue of Freedom" (1991) 39 *UCLA Law Review* 295.
Waldron J *The Harm in Hate Speech* (2012) Cambridge, Massachusetts: Harvard University Press.
Woolman S *The Selfless Constitution: Experimentalism and Flourishing as Foundations of South Africa's Basic Law* (2013) Cape Town: Juta.
Young I *Justice and the Politics of Difference* (1990) Princeton: Princeton University Press.

## Case law

*Germany*

BVerfGE 157, 30 (2021)

*South Africa*

*AB v Minister of Social Development* 2017 (3) BCLR 267 (CC)
*Afriforum v Economic Freedom Fighters* 2022 (6) SA 357 (GJ)
*Afriforum v Malema* 2011 (6) SA 240 (EqC)
*Afriforum NPC v Nelson Mandela Foundation Trust* [2023] ZASCA 58
*Afrox Healthcare Bpk v Strydom* 2002 (6) SA 21 (SCA)
*Azanian Peoples Organisation (AZAPO) v President of the Republic of South Africa* 1996 (4) SA 671 (CC)
*Afrox Healthcare Bpk v Strydom* 2002 (6) SA 21 (SCA)
*Barkhuizen v Napier* 2007 (5) SA 323 (CC)
*Beadica 231 CC v Trustees for the Time Being of the Oregon Trust* 2020 (5) SA 247 (CC)
*Bernstein v Bester NO* 1996 (2) SA 751 (CC)
*Bhe v Magistrate Khayelitsha; Shibi v Sithole; SA Human Rights Commission v President of the RSA* 2005 (1) SA 563 (CC)
*Blind SA v Minister of Trade, Industry and Competition* 2023 (1) SA 353 (CC)
*Bophuthatswana Broadcasting Corporation v Ramosa* 1997 HOL 283 (B)
*Brisley v Drotsky* 2002 (4) SA 1 (SCA)
*Bwanya v Master of the High Court, Cape Town* 2022 (4) BCLR 410 (CC)
*Case v Minister of Safety and Security; Curtis v Minister of Safety and Security* 1996 (3) SA 617 (CC)
*Christian Education South Africa v Minister of Education* 2000 (4) SA 757 (CC)
*City of Tshwane Metropolitan Municipality v Afriforum* 2016 (6) SA 279 (CC)
*Daniels v Scribante* 2017 (4) SA 341 (CC)
*Dawood; Shalabi; Thomas v Minister of Home Affairs* 2000 (3) SA 936 (CC)

*Democratic Alliance v African National Congress* 2015 (2) SA 232 (CC)
*De Vos v Minister of Justice and Constitutional Development* 2015 (9) BCLR 1026 (CC)
*Dikoko v Mokhatla* 2006 (6) SA 235 (CC)
*Economic Freedom Fighters v Minister of Justice and Correctional Services* 2021 (2) SA 1 (CC)
*Eskom Holdings SOC Ltd v Vaal River Development Association (Pty) Ltd* 2023 (4) SA 325 (CC)
*Everfresh Market Virginia (Pty) Ltd v Shoprite Checkers (Pty) Ltd* 2012 (1) SA 256 (CC)
*Ferreira v Levin NO and Vryenhoek v Powell NO* 1996 (1) SA 984 (CC)
*Glenister v President of the Republic of South Africa* 2011 (3) SA 347 (CC)
*Islamic Unity Convention v Independent Broadcasting Authority and Others* 2002 (4) SA 294 (CC)
*Jordan v S* 2002 (6) SA 642 (CC)
*Khosa v Minister of Social Development; Mahlaule v Minster of Social Development* 2004 (6) SA 505 (CC)
*Khumalo v Holomisa* 2002 (5) SA 401 (CC)
*Laugh It Off Promotions CC v South African Breweries International (Finance) BV t/a Sabmark International* 2006 (1) SA 144 (CC)
*Lawyers for Human Rights v Minister of Home Affairs* 2004 (4) SA 125 (CC)
*MEC* for *Education: KwaZulu-Natal v Pillay* 2008 (1) SA 474 (CC)
*Minister of Home Affairs v Rahim* 2016 (3) SA 218 (CC)
*National Coalition for Gay and Lesbian Equality v Minister of Justice* 1999 (1) SA 6 (CC)
*New Nation Movement NPC v President of the Republic of South Africa* 2020 (6) SA 257 (CC)
*Port Elizabeth Municipality v Various Occupiers* 2005 (1) SA 217 (CC)
*Prince v President of the Law Society of the Cape of Good Hope* 2002 (2) SA 794 (CC)
*Print Media SA v Minister of Home Affairs* 2012 (6) SA 443 (CC)
*Qwelane v South African Human Rights Commission* 2021 (6) SA 579 (CC)
*Rustenburg Platinum Mine v SAEWA obo Bester* 2018 (5) SA 78 (CC)
*S v Makwanyane* 1995 (3) SA 391 (CC)
*S v Mamabolo* 2001 (3) SA 409 (CC)
*South African Human Rights Commission v Masuku* 2022 (7) BCLR 850 (CC)
*South African National Defence Union v Minister of Defence* 1999 (4) SA 469 (CC)
*The Citizen 1978 (Pty) Ltd v McBride* 2011 (4) SA 191 (CC)
*University of Stellenbosch Legal Aid Clinic v Minister of Justice and Correctional Services* 2016 (6) SA 596 (CC)
*Van Vuren v Minister of Correctional Services* 2010 (12) BCLR 1233 (CC)

*United States*

*Citizens United v Federal Election Commission* 558 US 310 (2010)

# Conclusion

The disjuncture between the constitutional promise of an open and democratic society based on human dignity, equality, and freedom and the dehumanisation, inequality, and unfreedom experienced by millions of South Africans raises fundamental questions about the capacity of value-based adjudication to normalise injustice or disrupt systemic patterns of disadvantage and power. The conflictual democratic reading of constitutional values developed in this book provides different frames for understanding these questions. In the first place, it emphasises the fundamental indeterminacy that characterises democracy, and its institutionalisation of uncertainty, conflict, and social division. Rather than seeking to eliminate conflict and power, it aims to enable a diverse range of discourses, institutions, and practices, which can keep conflicting articulations of a society's founding commitments in play. It conceives democratic citizenship neither as a status nor as a symmetrical relationship between perfectly equal members of the political community; instead, it situates it at the interface of what is instituted and the capacity of emancipatory movements to unsettle, disrupt, and transform the status quo. Those movements may win important rights and create spaces in which alternative discourses, subjectivities, and imaginaries can flourish, but they can never fill the void at the heart of the people. Rights victories – including those won through the courts – can help disrupt the status quo; however, they are themselves vulnerable to contestation, backlash, and the ability of the legal order to contain the disruptive effects of democratic struggles.

Secondly, the conflictual conception of democracy that is favoured here enables a radical understanding of the political, which recognises that politics can neither be confined to citizens nor restricted to affairs that are traditionally considered public. The subjects, places, and objects of politics cannot be defined with reference to pre-existing boundaries but are themselves subject to democratic contestation. The ability of democratic challenges to disrupt existing distributions of powers, places, and bodies derives from the tension between the universal ideals of dignity, equality, and freedom and the contingent foundations of the legal order in which these ideals are – imperfectly – embodied. Such challenges evoke alternative articulations of those ideals and different configurations of norms, spaces, and subjectivities. On this understanding,

DOI: 10.4324/9781003482451-8

democratic politics can challenge and disrupt, but can never completely eradicate inequality, domination, and exclusion. A conflictual democratic reading of dignity, equality, and freedom must be open to the capacity of democratic struggles to disrupt closure and uncover spaces of contestation; however, it must also be attentive to the legal order's limited ability to respond to challenges that evoke configurations of norms and spaces that are outside the range of collective self-understandings available to it.

Thirdly, from a conflictual democratic perspective, law is an important site of contestation and struggle. Law's structuring and regulatory power extends to all spheres of society. It plays a significant role in defining people's status, structuring markets, distributing wealth, determining access to public resources, configuring space, shaping the electoral system, facilitating public participation, and regulating protests. It is important to recognise law's role as a determinant of power and to be alive to the transformative possibilities inherent in challenges to oppressive laws and reinterpretations of legal constructs. However, it does not follow that law is the primary agent of social change. On a conflictual democratic view, laws and judicial decisions are enabled by, and in turn feed into and become part of larger configurations of discourses, conflicts, and power relations. Their transformative capacity cannot be judged in isolation from the dynamic interplay between these forces. Moreover, litigation strategies carry certain risks, like obscuring the systemic nature of inequality and violence and diverting energy and resources away from other sites of contestation. Whether these risks outweigh the possibility that rights-based strategies could destabilise unequal distributions of power and enhance the agency and voice of marginalised people can only be decided in view of the relevant contexts.

Fourthly, the conflictual democratic frame developed in the book rejects the assumption that the particularity of domination, inequality, and conflict can be overcome through its subsumption under universal rights and principles. Universal ideals are not untouched by conflict and power. The hierarchical divisions that are at the heart of structural domination and inequality are not necessarily extrinsic to universalistic ideals but are sometimes inscribed in them. This helps to explain the persistence of the normative distinctions between autonomy and vulnerability, self-sufficiency and dependence, reason and superstition, normality and deviance, and active citizens and passive objects of administrative power. These distinctions are central to the justification of neoliberal policies, which deepen disadvantage based on traditional fault lines like race, class, gender, and disability. Because conflictual democratic theories view the universal and particular as mutually entwined and recognise that conflict is engendered by different enunciations of the universal, they cannot claim to have access to a neutral Archimedean point. Instead, they place their trust in the development of conflicting enunciations of the universal that are grounded in critical theory and concrete struggles against deprivation, dehumanisation, inequality, and unfreedom. Exposing the falsity of enunciations of the universal that uphold hierarchical distinctions, disrupting existing patterns of disadvantage and power, and laying bare more humane alternatives are tasks that must be constantly repeated.

The central role played by human dignity in the Constitutional Court's jurisprudence is best explained in terms of its perceived ability to transform historical narratives of oppression under colonialism and apartheid into a universal command to honour the worth of every human person. Dignity, on the Court's view, appeals to something absolute, which nevertheless enables disputes to be adjudicated in a context-sensitive manner, with reference to every person's inherent worth. In trying to make sense of this understanding, it is better not to define dignity exclusively as either a moral or a legal and political term. It is both, and its emancipatory potential derives in part from the interplay between these dimensions. On the one hand, moral understandings of dignity exceed the bounds of positive legal norms and can spark new emancipatory struggles. On the other hand, democratic dialogue and contestation can help expose the limits of and exclusions produced by moral-universal understandings. A conflictual reading emphasises the need for different discourses, grammars, and imaginaries of dignity, and asks whether and to what extent they enable or resist the inscription of status-based distinctions into constructions of the human.

The tension between dignity's emancipatory promise and the persistence of hierarchical and exclusionary understandings of dignity and freedom is evident from – South African and foreign – case law in which dignity is relied on to proscribe voluntary sexual conduct that is deemed objectifying or degrading or to prevent Muslim women from wearing a veil or headscarf in the workplace or in public. When that happens, dignity is turned into a standard for measuring conformity to mainstream notions of civility, rationality, autonomy, and self-control and a pretext for intervening in the lives of individuals who are thought to fall short of those norms. These tendencies need to be countered through struggles that articulate dignity with radical difference.

The gap between the commitment to inherent human dignity, irrespective of nationality, and the dehumanisation experienced by certain foreign nationals raises further questions about dignity's mediation through the legal concept of citizenship. Was Arendt right that universal human rights amount to little when they are delinked from citizenship, or can dignity be used to destabilise the distinction between citizens and non-citizens? An overview of case law suggests that the instability of the distinction between universal human dignity and the dignity of citizens could assist certain categories of non-citizens in their struggles to win rights traditionally reserved for citizens. However, there are limits to the ability of courts-centred strategies to unsettle the hierarchies embedded in citizenship and immigration law. Litigation and adjudication can supplement other strategies but are no substitute for political mobilisation, consciousness-raising, social struggles, and legislative reform.

A political understanding of equality recognises that conflict and antagonism are an indispensable part of struggles about the meaning of equality, and that democratic contestation and dialogue play an important role in mediating those conflicts. It is concerned with the impact of inequality and discrimination on marginalised groups' ability to participate in public life, challenge inequality and domination, and advance alternative understandings of racial, gender, class, and other forms of equality. A conflictual understanding does not seek to reduce the right to equality to a single metric or value but is attentive to distinct forms of disadvantage and the intersections and overlaps between them. Democracy, in this view, is not only at stake where discriminatory measures have a clear and direct impact on certain groups' political voice and participation. It is also at issue in cases where misrecognition or a skewed distribution of resources diminishes those groups' capacity for political participation, or where their claims politicise matters that were previously thought to fall outside the public realm.

A political understanding of equality recognises that there is a tension at the heart of citizenship between its regulatory and emancipatory dimensions. The former refers to its inscription within an already constituted legal and political order and the tendency to condition the full citizenship of members of marginalised communities on their assimilation within the dominant culture, while the latter denotes respect for radical difference and the possibility of new beginnings. The tension is ineradicable and is a condition of the possibility of democratic politics. Citizenship's meaning and bounds – and relationship to other key concepts like personhood and subjectivity – are negotiated and renegotiated through dialogue and struggle. Its regulatory dimension is evident from cases in which the stigmatising effects of discriminatory laws are explained away as the result of individual choices or societal attitudes and in which conventional understandings of family, marriage, personal choice, merit, and the public/private distinction normalise the status quo. The emancipatory dimension is displayed in cases in which courts confront the prejudice and stigma experienced by gays and lesbians, HIV positive people, and other marginalised groups and emphasise the Constitution's commitment to respect for difference. But even in the latter category of cases, the conflict between these two dimensions sometimes manifests in the tension between perceptive analyses of the harm caused by discriminatory measures and impassioned pleas for the recognition of difference, on the one hand, and the normative pull of idealised models of citizenship, on the other.

Similar tensions are at play in case law involving challenges to the exclusion of certain groups from material rights and benefits, inequalities in the delivery of basic services, and discriminatory private conduct. Several judgments suggest that the right to equality can be used to contest and respond to poverty and material need. However, such challenges are more likely to succeed where the targeted groups are deprived of material benefits or services that are meant to safeguard the basic conditions of a dignified life or where their exclusion signals that they are not worthy of equal respect and concern. Conversely, they are less likely to succeed in placing a ceiling on economic inequality. It seems, therefore, that equality-based adjudication can play a limited, yet meaningful role in politicising laws and policies that deepen poverty and material inequality and commodify essential social needs. Its transformative potential is perhaps most evident in cases involving the horizontal application of the Bill of Rights, which present opportunities to interrogate the distributive implications of some of the background rules and conditions that structure dominant legal understandings of concepts like property, succession, and contract.

The Constitutional Court generally adopts a nuanced, context-sensitive approach to the construction of sameness and difference. However, there are cases in which it relies uncritically on broad social categories and identities, treats social groups as homogeneous, and overlooks the differential impact of discriminatory laws on different members. Viewed through a relational and political lens, difference is embedded in social relations, discourses, institutions, and regulatory practices. It does not have a unitary meaning, nor does it signify deviation from a universal standard. Differences are ambiguous, unstable, and cross-cutting, and result from intersubjective and dialogical experiences and processes. They are internal to individual and collective selves and threaten to destabilise their perceived unity. Even though the categories through which we view difference have a powerful hold on our social imagination and constrain our ability to rethink identities, individuals and social movements can re-enact difference in ways that rupture the supposed stability of group identities and politicise reified understandings. This conception of difference shuns the idea of a universal standpoint from which different rights claims are to be assessed and insists that we need a multiplicity of discourses, practices, and institutions which allow contending understandings of social categories to be articulated and debated. It recognises the need to deconstruct the symbolic oppositions and hierarchies that underpin dominant constructions of difference and emphasises interlocking patterns of disadvantage, subordination, and privilege that fail to be detected under single-axis forms of analysis.

Relational and political understandings of freedom recognise the role played by social relations, practices, and institutions in creating conditions in which freedom can thrive. They further stress that personal and political freedom are inextricably linked: on the one hand, personal freedom can only be safeguarded through public processes of dialogue and contestation, while on the other, struggles for the recognition of personal freedoms that are at odds with dominant norms can inject contestation and plurality into public life. These understandings reject the view that freedom is a property inherent in self-owning individuals. They insist that vulnerability is inherent in all life; however, some people lack access to adequate networks of support and are hence far more susceptible to injury and violence. Respect for equal freedom requires the distribution of freedoms, social goods, and the burdens of vulnerability to be based on the principle that all people's lives matter equally. Freedom therefore demands ongoing political struggles against the devaluation and instrumentalization of the lives of those that continue to be unfree. Freedom, thus conceived, is closely interlinked with equality, human dignity, radical difference, active citizenship, and pluralistic and conflictual understandings of democracy. Some judicial decisions demonstrate such a relational and political understanding of freedom, while others revert to metaphysical conceptions that ground freedom in the individual will and fail to come to terms with systemic barriers to individuals' capacity for self-realisation.

Conflictual understandings of freedom of expression situate democratic dialogue in a context of conflict, power, and disagreement, and are interested in the mechanisms through which the speech of the subaltern is suppressed or distorted. They view freedom of expression as a vital resource in democratic and counter-hegemonic struggles but recognise that the ability to be heard when speaking out against injustice and articulating alternative social and political visions is itself affected by systemic power relations that are embedded in a deeply unequal past. From a conflictual democratic perspective, it is important to resist the effects of discursive injustices on the agency and voice of disadvantaged groups; however, the capacity of hate speech prohibitions to inhibit speech and deflect attention away from the structural nature of discursive violence is a cause for concern.

In a society characterised by massive poverty, inequality, and unfreedom, visions that are based on the principle that all people's lives matter equally gesture beyond the status quo towards alternative imaginaries of freedom. The philosophy of ubuntu, with its emphasis on the mutual entwinement of being and becoming and the dynamic relationship between the individual and community could offer a bridge that allows us to move back and forth between the Constitution and alternative imaginaries. If we resist its uncritical conflation with either African custom or Western understandings of rights, it could enable challenges to false universals and assist us in overcoming the modernist/colonial splitting of the world into rational, enlightened human beings and those controlled by tradition, superstition, and emotion. Anti-hegemonic struggles that question mainstream narratives of liberation, whilst asserting the capacity of poor black people and other vulnerable groups for political speech and action, provide further examples of alternative imaginaries, which challenge the political community's self-closure and point towards more radically emancipatory visions of dignity, equality, and freedom.

The conflictual reading of constitutional values that is proposed in this book suggests that questions about the capacity of value-based constitutional interpretation to help safeguard spaces in which anti-racist, anti-sexist, anti-capitalist, and other emancipatory imaginaries can flourish cannot be answered in the abstract. They require careful attention not only to the dialectic between democracy's capacity to make new beginnings and its inscription in what is already instituted, but also to the dynamic interplay between legal decisions and larger configurations of discourses, conflicts, and power relations.

# Index

For Product Safety Concerns and Information please contact our EU representative GPSR@taylorandfrancis.com
Taylor & Francis Verlag GmbH, Kaufingerstraße 24, 80331 München, Germany

www.ingramcontent.com/pod-product-compliance
Lightning Source LLC
LaVergne TN
LVHW011125300926
849160LV00008B/514
* 9 7 8 1 0 3 2 7 7 3 2 2 3 *